W9-CKD-295

NCPEA
2000

MARCHING INTO A NEW MILLENNIUM

Challenges to Educational Leadership

THE EIGHTH YEARBOOK OF THE NATIONAL COUNCIL
OF PROFESSORS OF EDUCATIONAL ADMINISTRATION

Editor

PATRICK M. JENLINK, ED.D.

Stephen F. Austin State University

Associate Editor

THEODORE J. KOWALSKI, PH.D.

University of Dayton

The Scarecrow Press, Inc.
Scarecrow Education
Lanham, Maryland, and London
2000

0017296

SCARECROW PRESS, INC.

Published in the United States of America
by Scarecrow Press, Inc.
4720 Boston Way, Lanham, Maryland 20706
http://www.scarecrowpress.com

4 Pleydell Gardens, Folkestone
Kent CT20 2DN, England

British Cataloging in Publication Information Available

Library of Congress Cataloging-in-Publication Data

Marching into a new millennium : challenges to educational leadership / edited by
Patrick Jenlink
    p. cm.
    "NCPEA 2000 yearbook."
    Includes bibliographical references and index.
    ISBN 0-8108-3839-7
    1. Educational leadership—United States. 2. School administrators—Training of—United
States. I. Jenlink, Patrick M. II. National Council of Professors of Educational
Administration.

LB1738.5 .M38 2000
371.2'011—dc21

        00-044050

NCPEA HONOR ROLL OF PRESIDENTS, 1947–2000

1947   Julian E. Butterworth, *Cornell University*
1948   William E. Arnold, *University of Pennsylvania*
1949   Russell T. Gregg, *University of Wisconsin*
1950   Clyde M. Campbell, *Michigan State University*
1951   Dan H. Cooper, *Purdue University*
1952   Walter K. Beggs, *University of Nebraska*
1953   Robert S. Fisk, *University of Buffalo*
1954   Van Miller, *University of Illinois*
1955   Harold E. Moore, *University of Denver*
1956   Walter A. Anderson, *New York University*
1957   A.D. Albright, *University of Kentucky*
1958   Jack Childress, *Northwestern University*
1959   Richard C. Lonsdale, *Syracuse University*
1960   William H. Roe, *Michigan State University*
1961   Howard Eckel, *University of Kentucky*
1962   Daniel E. Griffiths, *New York University*
1963   Kenneth McIntyre, *University of Texas*
1964   Luvern Cunningham, *University of Chicago*
1965   William H. Roe, *Michigan State University*
1966   Willard Lane, *University of Iowa*
1967   Harold Hall, *California State University, Los Angeles*
1968   Kenneth Frasure, *SUNY, Albany*
1969   Samuel Goldman, *Syracuse University*
1970   Malcolm Rogers, *University of Connecticut*
1971   Paul C. Fawley, *University of Utah*
1972   Gale W. Rose, *New York University*
1973   Anthony N. Baratta, *Fordham University*
1974   John T. Greer, *Georgia State University*
1975   C. Cale Hudson, *University of Nebraska*
1976   John R. Hoyle, *Texas A&M University*
1977   J. Donald Herring, *SUNY Oswego*
1978   Charles Manley, *California State University, Northridge*
1979   Jasper Valenti, *Loyola University of Chicago*
1980   Max E. Evans, *Ohio University*
1981   Lesley H. Browder, Jr., *Hofstra University*
1982   John W. Kohl, *Montana State University*

NCPEA HONOR ROLL OF PRESIDENTS, 1947–2000 *(continued)*

1983 Bob Thompson, *SUNY, Oswego*
1984 Donald L. Piper, *University of North Dakota*
1985 Robert Stalcup, *Texas A&M University*
1986 Robert O'Reilly, *University of Nebraska, Omaha*
1987 Donald Coleman, *San Diego State University*
1988 Charles E. Kline, *Purdue University*
1989 Larry L. Smiley, *Central Michigan University*
1990 Frank Barham, *University of Virginia*
1991 Paul V. Bredeson, *Pennsylvania State University*
1992 Rosemary Papalewis, *California State University, Fresno*
1993 Donald Orlosky, *University of South Florida*
1994 Paula M. Short, *University of Missouri, Columbia*
1995 Maria Shelton, *NOVA Southeastern University*
1996 Clarence Fitch, *Chicago State University*
1997 Clarence M. Achilles, *Eastern Michigan University*
1998 Robert S. Estabrook, Stephen F. Austin State University
1999 Cheryl Fischer, *California State University, San Bernadino*
2000 Michael Martin, *University of Colorado, Denver*

CONTENTS

CONTRIBUTING AUTHORS

Judith Adkison, *University of North Texas*
James E. Berry, *Eastern Michigan University*
Lynn K. Bradshaw, *East Carolina University*
Genevieve Brown, *Sam Houston State University*
Kermit G. Buckner, *East Carolina University*
Edward W. Chance, *University of Nevada Las Vegas*
Patti L. Chance, *University of Nevada Las Vegas*
Laura Chew, *Willow Run Community Schools*
Clark Ealy, *Texas A&M University*
Lance D. Fusarelli, *Fordham University*
Rita E. Guare, *Fordham University*
Kristine A. Hipp, *Cardinal Stritch University*
Dawn Hogan, *Texas A&M University*
John R. Hoyle, *Texas A&M University*
Martha B. Hudson, *University of North Carolina at Greensboro*
Jane B. Huffman, *University of North Texas*
Beverly J. Irby, *Sam Houston State University*
Judy A. Johnson, *Murray State University*
Michael Martin, *University of Colorado at Denver*
Rodney Muth, *University of Colorado at Denver*
Joseph Murphy, *Vanderbilt University*
Arnold Oates, *Texas A&M University*
Martha N. Ovando, *The University of Texas at Austin*
Rosemary Papalewis, *California State University*
Marvin Pasch, *Eastern Michigan University*
Lucretia D. Peebles, *University of Denver*
Elizabeth Saavedra, *The University of New Mexico*
Linda Skrla, *Texas A&M University*
Jenny D. Thomas, *Leesburg, Virginia*
Ronald D. Williamson, *University of North Carolina at Greensboro*

REVIEW BOARD

PREFACE

The NCPEA 53rd Annual Conference was held in Jackson Hole, hosted by Idaho State University. In keeping with the Jackson Hole conference theme, the title of the yearbook is *Marching into a New Millennium: Challenges to Educational Leadership*. This theme speaks to the uncertainty of what awaits both professors and practitioners of educational leadership in the year 2000 and beyond.

Crossing the threshold of a new millennium sets apart past efforts in the professional preparation and practice of educational leaders, giving time for pause and reflection on accomplishments as well as what lies before professors and practitioners in the field of educational leadership. The field must acknowledge past accomplishments, building on this foundation while simultaneously seeking to address dialectical dualisms that have given way to the divisiveness and fragmentation that we have experienced in past decades. As a profession responsible for preparing leaders for our nation's schools, we must seek an intellectual and moral center from which to guide our actions in the new millennium.

Joseph Murphy (1999), in his Corwin Lecture at the NCPEA Conference in Jackson Hole, addressed the need to develop a coherent center of values as we enter the new millennium. This center would act as a guidance system for professors, students, and practitioners as we face the continued challenges for rethinking both preparation and practice of educational leaders as we journey toward our future. The challenges we face as we journey forward will require us to reexamine not only the nature of such values as social justice, democratic community, caring, diversity, moral consciousness, scholarly practice and ethical praxis, but also the critical place that these values have in the preparation and practice of educational leaders. Likewise, as we cross the threshold we are necessarily challenged to reconsider the divisive boundaries set by such ongoing dialectics as modernist versus postmodernist perspectives of knowledge, unity versus diversity, formal versus practical knowledge, social criticism versus social creativity, traditional versus alternative paradigms of research, and scholars versus practitioners.

Rosemary Papalewis (1999), in her Cocking Lecture, focused our attention on the need for asynchronous partners as universities move forward into the next century. Surveying the future landscape and the new reality for educational leaders of tomorrow, she centered on three forces, including technology, globalization, and adaptation, that will dictate this reality. Leadership, both for the university preparation program and for the K–12 educational system, will need to forge new models to stay ahead of what Papalewis posits as detrimental "disintermediating" influences.

As a profession responsible for the future of educational leadership, we must cross boundaries and transform past dialectics into present and future dialogues that seek to create coherence and centeredness. As professors of educational administration and leadership, we must embrace the intellectual and moral responsibilities required to create more authentic preparation programs while acknowledging the changing dynamics of education and schools. This requires of us the recognition and acknowledgment that the practical day-to-day world of educational leadership is facing an increasing complexity generated by a changing society. Many of the demands of a new millennium are greatly different from those that we leave behind.

The theme, *Marching into a New Millennium: Challenges to Educational Leadership*, is one which directs our attention to the future, a future which will be shaped in large part by decisions we make that influence the preparation and practice of educational leaders. The challenges before us will engage us in many responsibilities including a continued examination of professionalism, reducing dialectical dualisms, crossing boundaries, and revisiting the critical role of scholarship in preparation and practice.

This volume is organized into six sections: vision quest for leadership, professional learning in leadership preparation, connecting preparation and practice, meeting challenges of gender and diversity, issues of performance and quality in leadership practice, and creating learning communities and cultures of change. The purpose of the narrative shared within the sections, chapters, and pages of this yearbook is to generate critically important conversations that focus our minds and our work on the challenges that await us across the threshold as we journey into a new millennium.

PATRICK M. JENLINK
April 2000

ACKNOWLEDGMENTS

Only in looking back at the path taken and the help provided along the way is one able to fully realize the true measure of contributions that others have made to the realization of a goal. It is with the greatest of appreciation and respect that I extend my heartfelt thanks and gratitude to my friends and colleagues, particularly those individuals who found value in the work put forth in this yearbook and gave equally of their time, encouragement, and spirit. Likewise, I would recognize Debbie Clausen and Linda Mack, administrative assistants in the Department of Secondary Education and Educational Leadership. Finally, I wish to acknowledge the contribution of Ted Creighton and his committee, who set the theme for the NCPEA 53rd Annual Conference in Jackson Hole, Wyoming, therefore setting the theme for this yearbook. Truly, the efforts and support of many have contributed invaluably to the completion of this work.

Marching to the New Millennium: Making Changes in the Way We Do Our Work in Preparing Future School Leaders

MICHAEL MARTIN

This yearbook will be the first of the new century, and it seems appropriate to reflect upon our past efforts to improve preparation programs and identify some future directions for our field if we are to remain viable in the next millennium.

OVERVIEW

Churchill once wrote that "a pessimist sees the difficulty in every opportunity; an optimist sees the opportunity in every difficulty." As an observer who regularly scans the terrain of administrator preparation programs it is easy to see that both difficulties and opportunities abound for this coming century.

I took the opportunity recently to review the recent conference programs of the three leading organizations for educational administration in the United States: NCPEA, UCEA, and the Conference within a Conference at AASA, along with the two most recent yearbooks by NCPEA, published in 1998 and 1999. All five venues are refereed by appropriate peer processes that give them immeasurably more credibility than mere opinion or intuition. I was looking for issues, difficulties and opportunities, and found plenty of each! I then categorized them into five main suggestions for improving administrator preparation programs.

1. Continue to Design Quality Preparation Programs. It has only been since 1947 that the spotlight on educational administration began through the support of the Kellogg Foundation and AASA, and the creation of NCPEA, followed shortly thereafter by the formation of UCEA. During this past half century or so, we have developed an extensive knowledge and experience base upon which to draw for the continuous improvement of our programs, chided appropriately by the landmark book, Leaders for

---

Michael Martin, President, National Council of Professors of Educational Administration, University of Colorado at Denver

America's Schools, among others. While there is no "one size fits all" model, we are beginning to identify some "best practices" on how to strengthen the recruitment and selection of diverse administrator candidates, integrate knowledge and practice, form partnerships with educational agencies, employ varied instructional strategies, develop creative curricula, design multiple forms of assessment, and demonstrate that our graduates are having an impact on the field. Solid information and research which supports these new designs is emerging in the above 5 professional outlets, which include: increased attention to the recruitment of people of color to the profession, standards-based programs, integrated curricula, problem-based learning, portfolios to assess performance, and increased use of technology via the Net and distance learning. While always "works in progress," preparation programs are responding to the calls for greater excellence, as evidenced by the hundreds of institutions and individuals presenting or writing in these five refereed outlets. Obviously we will need increased scholarship about our programs which can reflect this success and help us achieve even greater excellence in our field.

2. Form Partnerships with Educational and Related Agencies. Ward & Pascarelli (1987) argue that bringing together a diverse set of agencies for the improvement of education is both "timely and necessary" (p. 193). Block suggests that "partnership is the willingness to give more choice to the people we choose to serve. Not total control, just something more equal..."(1993). There are, however, many "contradictions" between preparation programs and the practice of school administration which must be resolved if we are to achieve the equality, rigor, credibility and impact necessary for success. These "contradictions" often result in stereotypical attitudes: Professors and university officials often feel that the "ivory tower" knows what's best for students, particularly in the realm of theory and research; Practitioners often prefer clinical or apprentice-like programs to help administrators acquire the skills requisite to successful school leadership (Muth & Martin, 1998).

Partnerships, when carefully crafted from the outset, can build a better bridge to quality, by diminishing the barriers to successful program reform, as perceived by professors, practitioners and policymakers. In a parallel movement, Schools of Education in America are finding this to be true with the movement toward partner schools in preparing future teachers. With the explosion of knowledge and advance preparation levels attained by school administrators, greater expertise can thus be shared between professors and practitioners to advance the quality of preparation programs. In our field, newly emerging partnerships under the leadership of the National Policy Board for Educational Administration (NPBEA) are beginning to examine national certification, accreditation and performance assessments, all linked to high-quality standards. NCPEA is working with the "big ten" national educational leadership groups under the leadership of the NPBEA, for superintendents, principals, school board members, curriculum and supervision leaders, teacher and administrator educators, chief state school officers and professors of educational administration (AASA, NASSP, NAESP, NSBA, ASCD, NCATE, AACTE, CSSSO (ISSLC),

UCEA and NCPEA), among others, to collaboratively design programs to take our profession to the next level of quality.

3. Demonstrate the Efficacy of Preparation Programs. Critics abound in every aspect of American education, and debates about a real or "manufactured crisis" should nevertheless stimulate educators at every level to examine the efficacy of their programs. We must address this issue in our preparation programs by more clearly identifying the "value-added" dimensions to our work with administrator candidates. This must include more intensive data collection around: (1) improved knowledge and skills of graduates; (2) increases in positive attitudes and dispositions toward the role of leadership in school improvement; (3) improved problem solving, decision making, and "ways of thinking" critically about the difficult problems of practice; (4) better abilities to communicate orally and in writing; (5) more effective resolution of difference and conflicts in democratic environments with greater diversity among stakeholders than ever before in history; and (6) using the knowledge gained from theory, research and exemplary practice to improve educational programs for all clients, regardless of age or economic setting. We need to demonstrate to accrediting and state agencies, employers, university skeptics and colleagues, and the scholarly community, that our programs can and do make a difference with both our students, and in their place of employment.

4. Foster Multiple Forms of Appraisal in Relation to High Standards. Upon attaining my first positions in higher education in California, Ohio and Colorado, I lectured a lot, assigned term papers, case studies and book reviews to my students, and followed all that up by "cleverly" designed true-false, multiple-guess, short-answer and essay tests, designed to sort out the best and brightest from the rest of the class. My syllabus was power and I decided what students should know in my classes. That was what I was taught, and thus was the same model of teaching perpetuated throughout the nation, at all levels of education.

During the past decade or so, however, this has all changed. My colleagues and I at the University of Colorado at Denver (UCD) read the criticisms of preparations programs, visited innovative delivery models, scoured the literature, and listened to practitioners and students regarding their ideas on how to improve our programs. As soon as we started focusing upon learning, rather than teaching, things began to improve in our program. We have tried to effect "whole" change in all our programs during the past decade, from the PhD to the MA and administrator licensing programs. At UCD, we are now standards-based, cohort organized, portfolio assessed, problem-based, partnership built, action researched, clinically oriented, curricular integrated rather than course based, technologically bold, and instructionally diverse. We use mentors, expect rfp's for project-based learning, integrated our internships and dissertation credits with academic coursework, and developed criteria-based supervision of student work in the field. The result has been better candidates for leadership positions, as measured by a state developed and validated standards-based exam, fewer dropouts, intact cohorts, improved program and faculty evaluations, 25 nationally refereed papers and publications about the program, and national, state and university recognition, among other accomplishments. Other programs throughout the country are experiencing equal success with similar innovations in program design, stimulated by the calls for reform over a decade ago.

How then can we all demonstrate that our programs are working and convince our critics about the efficacy of our programs? By designing multi-faceted appraisals which provide diverse and precise feedback and critiques on our programs, students and faculty, as follows: (1) What do employers say about our graduates? Their accomplishments? Our program? (2) What do the clinical supervisors and site coordinators/mentors say about the candidates? Their accomplishments? Our program? (3) What do the peers say about their colleagues? Our program? (4) What do the clinical, academic and related faculty have to say about the students? Their accomplishments? Our program? (5) What do the students say about themselves, their growth, their accomplishments, and our program, from start to finish, in all their learning experiences.(6) What do reliable and valid examinations have to say about our graduates in contrast to other programs and students? (7) What do accrediting agencies say about our students? Our programs?

High standards whether from national or state organizations now provide us with clearer, although somewhat controversial, guidance about the most appropriate frameworks for our programs, and what we should expect students (and professors) to "know and do" in order to be successful school leaders. While quizzes and tests are still important, they must be part of a comprehensive appraisal process for both administrator candidates and programs.

5. Strengthen the Professorial Reward System in Universities. Accountability seems to be the mantra of the 1990s as policymakers, trustees, citizens and clients are increasingly challenging conventional practices in higher education. These targets include tenure, academic freedom, action learning, the value of research, community service and outreach, conventional classrooms, and the professorial role, as differentiated from public school teachers. Our tendency is to debate these issues, write editorials, and strengthen post-tenure review and promotion criteria, among other responses.

What seems to be needed is a fresh look at the reward system, particularly for professors of educational administration, which emphasizes and recognizes the myriad roles we perform in support of the university or college mission. I propose 6 broad categories: (1) Knowledge Transmission, including advising, preparation, teaching, guiding internships and clinical activities, testing and grading, among others. (2) Shared Discovery, such as thesis supervision, mentoring, conducting lab research, critiquing student work, attending professional seminars, etc. (3) Knowledge Generation, such as library or internet research, manuscript or grant preparation, data analysis, reflection, etc. (4) Community Service, such as collaboration with schools, building partnerships, data collection, field research with practitioner's application of research to problems of practice, etc. (5) Service Learning, such as internship supervision, workshops, hosting conferences, public school consultation/service, media interviews, etc. and (6) Knowledge Application such as developing web pages, reviewing manuscripts, reviewing manuscripts, involvement in university governance, expert testimony, speaking at clinics, book reviews, peer evaluation of instruction, service on boards and councils, etc.

Browder (1998), Boyer (1990) and Krahenbuhl (1998), among others, have written extensively on this topic, with the recognition that professional schools such as education and medicine have differing roles than the traditional arts and sciences professors in higher education.

In addition to broadening the definition of scholarship as earlier identified, Educational Administration programs can enhance their contributions to the university by four other methods: (1) adding a differentiated work load policy to encourage diversity of work effort within department beyond the traditional split of 40/40/20, in research, teaching and service (scholarship); (2) Develop both departmental and individual criteria for promotion, merit and tenure, based on the appropriate definitions of scholarship as identified above; (3) Link individual and departmental criteria to school and university mission and goals; and, (4) Design a "professional plan" whereby all the above are agreed to in advance by the professor and the institution to thus lock the agreements into the "organizational memory" so that administrative and faculty turnover do not cause unnecessary disruptions in the plan. There is no "one size fits all" model of professor, and we must recognize the unique contributions each faculty member makes to the value of the department in educating students and advancing the field.

In short, we now have the knowledge and wisdom to strengthen our administrator preparation programs and thereby demonstrate their efficacy to our clients in this new century. "Ready, Fire Aim," to quote the management guru, Tom Peters.

REFERENCES

Achilles, C.M. (1999). Are training programs in educational administration efficient and effective? Paper presented to the 1999 Conference within a Conference. New Orleans, LA.

Block, P. (1993). Stewardship: Choosing service over self-interest. San Francisco: Berrett-Koehler.

Boyer, E. (1990). Scholarship reconsidered: Priorities of the professoriate. Menlo Park, CA: Carnegie Foundations for the Advancement of Teaching.

Browder, L. H. (1998). Tomorrow's service ideal: A vocational calling or token obligation? In Muth, R & Martin, M., (Eds.), Toward the year 2000: Leadership for quality schools (pp. 16-28). Lancaster, PA: Technomic.

Fenwick, L. (Ed.)(1999). School leadership: Expanding horizons of the mind and spirit. Lancaster, PA: Technomic.

Glassick, C.E., Huber, M.T., & Maeroff, G.I. (1997). Scholarship assessed: Evaluation of the professoriate. San Francisco: Jossey-Bass.

Griffiths, D.E. (1964). Behavioral science and educational administration. Chicago, IL: University of Chicago Press.

Griffiths, D.E., Stout, R.T., & Forsyth, P.B. (1988). Leaders for America's schools: The report and papers of the National Commission on Excellence in Educational Administration. Berkeley, CA: McCutchan.

Krahenbuhl, G. (1998, November/December). Faculty work: Integrating responsibilities and institutional needs. Change. 18-25.

Martin, W.M., Ford, S.M., Murphy, M.J., & Muth, R. (1998). Partnerships for preparing school leaders: Possibilities and practicalities. In, Muth, R. and Martin, M., (Eds.), Toward the year 2000: Leadership for quality schools (pp. 238-246). Lancaster, PA: Technomic.

Ward, B. A. & Pascarelli, J.T. (1987). Networking for educational improvement. In J.I. Goodlad (Ed.), The ecology of school renewal. Chicago: University of Chicago Press.

Muth, R. & Martin, M. (Eds.)(1998). Toward the year 2000: Leadership for quality schools. Technomic: Lancaster, PA.

UCEA; AASA, Conference within a Conference; and, NCPEA, National Conference Programs (1999).

April 7, 2000

VISION QUEST FOR LEADERSHIP

Asynchronous Partners: Leadership for the Millennium*

ROSEMARY PAPALEWIS

Good morning. I cannot tell you of a greater honor for a professor of Educational Administration than the opportunity to deliver the Walter Cocking Lecture. Mark Twain once said "It's Dangerous to Make Predictions, Especially About the Future," (Bracey, 1999) . . . yet I will attempt to prognosticate the future for those that lead the leaders. However I promise you that you will not hear about Y2K, millennial fervor, or a bridge to the twenty-first century.

Let me begin with some of the thoughts of those that preceded us. "Everything that can be invented has been invented."

Charles H. Duell (Commissioner of U.S. Office of Patents), urging President William McKinley to abolish his office, 1899. (Cerf & Navasky, 1998, p226).

"The horse is here to stay, but the automobile is only a novelty—a fad."

President of the Michigan Savings Bank, advising Horace Rackham (Henry Ford's lawyer) not to invest in the Ford Motor Company, 1903. (Cerf & Navasky, 1998, p248).

"With over fifty foreign cars already on sale here, the Japanese auto industry isn't likely to carve out a big share of the market for itself." Business Week, 1968. (Cerf & Navasky, 1998, backcover).

"There is no reason for any individual to have a computer in their home."

President of Digital Equipment Corporation, 1977. (Cerf & Navasky, 1998, backcover).

"640k ought to be enough for anybody."

Bill Gates, Microsoft, 1981. (Cerf & Navasky, 1998, p231).

Universities have long served as repositories of culture. Born from religious orders that passed down oral and written rules and stories, universities have evolved into

---

*This is the text of the Walter D. Cocking Invited Lecture given at the annual conference of the National Council for Professors of Educational Administration (NCPEA) in Jackson Hole, Wyoming, on August 12, 1999. Walter D. Cocking (1891–1963) was a pioneer in the field of educational administration and founded NCPEA to advance the knowledge base for educational leaders.

Rosemary Papalewis, California State University

modern, generally secular institutions, still invested with that historic mission to disseminate cultural information. As the needs of society began to dictate a broadened view of study, the universities adapted by becoming the primary storehouses of general knowledge. This, primarily, is how today's universities honor their point of origin and enhance the society around them.

What then of today's university leaders, those that catalyze educational experience, preserve tradition, and shape culture? The key element today, as in the case of the cleric or scribe in the past, is the person labeled professor. The role of the professor is changing dramatically as the university adapts to differing cultural expectations. How was the religious scribe's role changed when the printing press was introduced at the beginning of the Renaissance? The greater availability of books allowed the public easier access to information, and knowledge no longer was limited to clerics. Prior to Gutenburg's press, societies held tight to the culture of religiously focused schools. Ultimately, the mass production of books helped led us to modern, more egalitarian universities. Now, the professorate faces the transition into the Information Age, as great a change in the means of conveying and preserving knowledge as that of the printing press. What can we, as professors, expect during this remarkable time?

Dag Hammarskjold, former Secretary General of the United Nations, once said, "Never look down to test the ground before taking your next step: Only he who keeps his eyes focused on the far horizon will find the right road." Here is what I see on the horizon, what I think is the right road. This address focuses on five trends I see emerging:

- *The first trend* is the rapid expansion and infusion of technology into all aspects of society.
- *The second trend* is the technological transformation of higher education.
- *The third trend* is the changing professorate.
- *The fourth trend* is public-private partnering.
- *The final trend* is leadership in the global education arena.

TREND ONE: THE RAPID EXPANSION AND INFUSION OF TECHNOLOGY INTO ALL ASPECTS OF SOCIETY

Information technology has become ubiquitous in modern society. For instance, NASA's everyday use of computer-mediated exploration has lead to the development of contract cybernauts (Friel, August 1997). While NASA's space shuttles and probes explore outer space, the agency has set up an office in cyberspace for its Small Business Innovation Research (SBIR) contracts programs. Dr. Barry Jacobs of Goddard National Space Science Data Center in Greenbelt, Maryland., working with REI Systems Inc., has created a World Wide Web–based system called "Electronic Handbooks," through which companies can learn online about NASA contract opportunities and submit forms electronically. NASA employees at 10 field centers then conduct the entire contract review and selection process across the Internet. The paperless system will be, according to Shyam Salona, Vice President of REI Systems, "the largest, end-to-end, completely electronic Internet use in the federal government. . . . The Electronic Handbooks make it easy for paper-centric employees to get comfortable doing their jobs online. . . . The beauty of the Handbooks is that they are guides which not only talk about the system, but that are the system." As with the Gutenburg press, the wonder of technology has progressed with a cascade effect startling in its rapidity. Electricity was the twentieth century's foundation, moving us from an agrarian society to the factories and homes of the industrial city. The technological revolution now underway will, without question, lay the foundation of tomorrow.

Today, cyber-government, as underwritten by IBM, is now on display in an office building in downtown Washington. A mock town square has been set up in 15,000 square feet of the building, featuring a police station, courtroom, library, classroom and other offices, as well as the family room of a typical house. In every setting, visitors can use a computer connected to various types of agencies operating at the city, county, state, and federal levels. The Government of the Future Studio is a project of IBM's recently formed Institute for Electronic Government. "Technology is changing the lives of police officers and judges; teachers and schoolchildren; public servants and citizens," says Institute director Janet Caldow. "[This studio] demonstrates how governments can put all the pieces together on the information highway using advanced network computing strategies" (The Cyberscape, July 1996). The demonstration includes public access kiosks for government information about tax forms, unemployment benefits, jobs applications, and automobile registration. The studio includes a "collaboratory" of networked computers where cross-governmental teams can work on problems such as local, state, and federal response to natural disasters.

We, in the everyday business of life, often overlook the pervasive presence of new technologies. How many times do we, for example, use a computer to communicate information that in the past would have been conveyed via a phone or letter? How many times a week do we use an ATM? Do we carry mechanical car keys or the increasingly common electronic key? Does your health plan include a smart card with encoded information about your medical history? All of these examples are small but significant illustrations of the growing role of technology in our lives. And next up on the agenda for change is education. Are we, as educators, ready?

TREND TWO: TECHNOLOGICAL TRANSFORMATION OF HIGHER EDUCATION

Asynchronous learning has become a catchphrase of late in many of the journals. Simply put, the term defines a learning exchange that does not take place concurrently. Instruction and reception do not occur, that is, at the same time. Most commonly, the term relates to computer mediated learning, when the teacher and student are separated spatially and meet only by exchange of information over an electronic medium. The advent of the term asynchronous learning is much more than our discipline's peculiar love for difficult language. Asynchronous learning defines a breathtaking change in the possibilities for education. Technology is moving learning out of the constraints of the classroom. No longer are student and teacher bound by geography or even time. Now, they can meet in a new manner, at their own pace, and from the location of their choice.

I cannot express what a dramatic development this is for our profession. In the past, we all worked as teachers out of the same general setting: the classroom. Early classrooms had a chalk board, seats, and textbooks. Soon we added technology like overhead projectors, a television screen, and perhaps a telephone. With the 1980s came the entrance of the computer. Even then, though, the setting was the same. True, the computer allowed us to teach in different ways, but the general scheme of the teaching and learning experience was very familiar. The advent of a new means of communicating independent of the classroom is a watershed event that will reverberate through higher education long into the future.

Why is this technology so significant? Let's take a tour of the prospective college student's environment. Most college students are still electing to go to traditional postsecondary institutions; that has not changed. However, new options are emerging quickly. We are all familiar with schools like the University of Phoenix that have catered to nontraditional students that, we must admit, were not so well served by the conventional university setting. At these alternative schools, nontraditional students found classes at night, an academic calendar that made sense for people working full time, and a focused vocational program. In this way, a population of students formerly inhibited by the rigid structure of higher education has been able to pursue an academic program with much greater ease. A similar event is now occurring with the traditional college population, though the change is in this case mediated by information technology.

Even now, college students do not have to rely on traditional university education to acquire a degree. There are a handful of programs emerging that allow a typical 18–22 year old to acquire a complete degree over electronic media from their homes and at their own pace. That is a remarkable event. Granted, many of these programs require some residency time, but often this is limited to short summer stints or a single semester culminating experience. Think of the implications of this shift. The advent of asynchronous learning disconnects college education from its traditional geography. Students are no longer bound by dislocation to distant schools. Students are no longer bound to full-time, highly inflexible programs. Learning, such a vital component today in the life of the individual, can now occur virtually anytime and anyplace. That flexibility is the hallmark of a new age in education.

The fluidity of information exchange facilitated by new means of technological communication has opened many new doors. Great Britain, a leading proponent of these new technologies, has invested heavily in their promise. The English government has strongly backed the development of the Open University, an educational program designed to provide a comprehensive variety of programs and courses electronically to individuals throughout the country. The investment is a recognition that asynchronous learning is not just a viable new means of learning, but in fact, a paradigm shift that will wholly revise our notion of education. The investment is also a highly provocative assertion that old modes of learning still cherished in the United States may be waning. As Sir John Daniel (Matthews, January 1998) put it in a recent article in the journal <u>Change</u>, "the U.S. system is peculiarly wedded to the technologies of real-time teaching and to the outmoded idea that quality in education is necessarily linked to exclusivity of access and extravagance of resource." In fact, the first argument often heard at universities when confronted with change, and particularly technological change, is that of the threat to quality! Little is often said about the limits of our own learning environment—for example, introductory courses with unwieldy enrollments (as many as 400–500 students for a general science class at some schools).

Indeed, the reception of asynchronous learning in the United States has been charged with controversy. Some decry the development of electronic learning, and particularly distance education, as the dismantling of our higher education system in favor of one less academically dynamic and more suited to economic manipulation. Other detractors look at electronic education as a commodification of knowledge which will result in the loss of academic diversity. Still others claim electronic education to be yet another magic pill aimed at solving social problems that are too complex for such simplistic and narrow solutions.

American higher education, however, has come to realize, despite the controversy and its many painful influences, that electronic learning is here to stay. Any large four-year university is now or will soon offer courses online. The allure to students of courses delivered to their homes, customized to their needs, and scheduled to their convenience is too great to ignore. Schools recognize that if they do not endorse electronic education by offering at least some classes via the computer, they will lose enrollment. That truth is punctuated by the speed with which technology is bringing ever more convenient and sophisticated forms of communication to our fingertips.

This last truth, a newly competitive enrollment environment for universities, is a sobering one for traditional institutions. With technology-mediated instruction becoming widely available, what loyalty does the student have to the regional university on which he or she would traditionally have relied for postsecondary education? The answer is simple: very little. Matthews (1998) sees the broad implementation of electronic instruction as the death of the regional comprehensive university. Why? Because geographic boundaries that insulated regional programs from competition no longer exist. A student in rural Minnesota is no longer limited to seeking admission to the nearest state university. That student could just as easily enroll in classes electronically distributed by the University of California at Los Angeles (a campus that has invested heavily in electronic instruction). For that matter, our student could enroll in a program distributed from a university in Sydney, Australia, or Madrid, Spain. The lesson is the same: electronic instruction will make the attraction of students a greater challenge for regional institutions of higher education.

Will some universities disappear in the ensuing decades as a result of this transformation? Perhaps. Will the university itself disappear as we know it? Never. Much overheated emotion surrounds the subject of technology-mediated instruction. I think the essential truth is this: new technologies for information transfer are marvelous and revolutionary tools for educators. However, they are simply that: tools. We still need to teach, to develop curricula, and to nurture students in the same way as we have always done. Technology is going to change much of the environment in which that vital work is done. Yes, some students of the future, maybe even many, will receive a majority of their postsecondary education electronically. Remember this, though. In our highly technical culture, postsecondary education has never been more important. Lifelong learning, both for general growth and professional viability, accompanies technology as landmarks of the new educational era. We will be teaching far <u>more</u> students for many <u>more</u> years than we do now. That is an important, and reassuring, realization.

One must also recognize that the physical university provides a culture that some students will recognize as essential to their education. You cannot take the culture of a Harvard or Berkeley or that of my own alma mater, the University of Nebraska, and distribute it electronically. Contrary to the exaggerated sentiments of some, technology does have numerous and tangible limitations. Yes, technology is an amazing tool for information transfer. Yes, technology can provide a whole new type of educational access. But, and this is crucial, technology, as a tool, cannot replace the fundamentally social aspects of higher education. Indeed, this is the principal disadvantage of technology-mediated instruction. Communication is interaction, and when we speak of interaction, I think we mean more than the digital exchange of bytes of information. Students will still like to meet with other students. Teachers will desire to have physical classrooms with live learners. For many subjects, the traditional ways of learning will remain the pedagogy of choice. The culture of the university will remain vibrant, albeit different, as a result of electronic instruction. I do not think, as I will repeat throughout our talk today, it will disappear.

What I think we must pay attention to when we speak of technology in education are the adaptations the university must make to effectively incorporate its influences into the fabric of higher education. I have already spoken of some of the enrollment issues that will arise in light of electronic education. Adapting to technology will also require other careful observations and actions. What about residency policies in light of the disappearance of geographic borders? What about our research libraries? How will they be administered in the face of constantly changing technology and modes of utilization? How are we budgeting for the implementation of the technological tools that are necessary to remain viable as teaching and research institutions? The Information Age will be exerting a profound effect on our institutions over the next few years. We must focus on making them prepared for that pressure. First in that task is realizing how the change will affect us—the professorate.

TREND THREE: THE CHANGING PROFESSORATE

The days of the Lone Ranger are over. Educational leaders of the future will catalyze the collaboration of others; they will have to engage, mobilize, inspire, partner, and delegate with skill to effectively implement educational policy. The Information Age is founded upon one dominant and defining element—speed. The traditional hierarchy of the past, with its time-consuming processes for decision making and implementation, has become debilitating. Soon, that hierarchy will be altogether archaic.

New management styles are resulting from the new ways of working that have emerged with changing times. Look at some of the terms that now describe labor in the workplace: there is flextime, telecommuting, the anytime/anyplace worker. Do you really think these terms are simply new management lingo for old ways of doing business? Think again. These new ways of working will forever change the nature of leadership. Leaders, be they supervisors in an industrial setting or professors in a university department, will no longer be able to manage by relying on old techniques.

The organization of the Information Age is a fluid one. That means the participants flow quickly from role to role as the organization responds to changing demands. Leadership is shared and increasingly determined not by hierarchy, but by the needs of the task at hand. An individual in charge one day will be subordinate the next as the organization adapts in a dynamic, speed-driven environment. Leaders are more likely to be mentors and coaches rather than traditional "bosses." This trend toward team-based management is fostering a growing movement toward shared leadership in organizations.

Because information flow is best managed collaboratively, collaboration will continue to be a landmark in the ongoing revolution in management style. For the professorate, that reality brings a number of truths. As managers of the educational enterprise, we will no longer find scholarly detachment a beneficial response. Collaboration requires involvement at an intimate level some of us may find obtrusive. I think that involvement will certainly be obtrusive to the old ways of working, but I again hold out the hope that the resulting change in our perspective will reinvigorate the university. We will be more involved in the direction of our departments, we will be more involved in the broader debate about the function of education, and we will be more involved with the students that we teach. And to be relevant to the students that we teach, we will need to be involved in partnerships related to external agencies and corporations. I can only see positive results from such involvement.

All these issues raise an extremely difficult question, though: How is the professorate going to preserve its culture along with the university culture on which it depends? I think we know some of that answer already. We won't be able to preserve our culture in quite the way it exists now. We are going to lose some pieces of the culture we are used to, even pieces that we cherish. However, I reassert my belief that this cultural revolution in academia can be stimulating and constructive if we are willing to face the challenge with courage and a willingness to learn new ways of thinking and working. As leaders, our fundamental priorities have not changed — we must be strong, visionary, and tirelessly dedicated to providing the environment best suited for our students. This requires acknowledging that change and flexibility mixed with agile effort is often chaotic.

Some of the most perplexing and challenging issues facing the professorate right now are curricular ones. In an age of rapid change in methods of knowledge transfer, how are we to design the curricula that are the blueprint for our work? How, for example, does one manage a virtual curriculum? How does a department track professors and students increasingly reliant on communication that is not always classroom-bound? How do we revisit the academic calendar in order to establish timelines for academic programs that are both sensible and responsive to changing demographics and to the new expectations of students? These questions are not easily addressed, but it is precisely these kinds of issues that present us with the opportunity to make good from the prospect of change. The curricula of tomorrow are going to be very difficult to outline, but we must begin to address closely these questions. After all, what we are to the student is largely demonstrated by the academic programs we prepare for them. Are we up for this challenge? I hope so.

The new professorate will also have to adjust to a new climate of assessment. Outcomes-based thinking will dominate how new academic programs are shaped and implemented. Students and policymakers are already looking at education in light of a skills-based rubric. Schools and universities will need to reassess their detachment from the vocational viability of their students. That detachment is unwise in today's climate; it was probably always unwise in retrospect. Graduating students blindly into the workplace is no longer a prudent path as universities are increasingly being assessed by the employment success of graduates. You can already see the response of universities to the emergence of outcomes-based assessment with the rise of innovative internship, interviewing, and placement centers. Only a decade ago, such centers, if they existed, were only a marginal activity devoted only passing attention. Today, these centers are becoming vital to the enterprise of higher education. I think that is good for our students.

Outcomes-based thinking, however, should also worry us a good deal. If we are increasingly assessed on the basis of functional outcomes like job placement, how do we preserve the parts of the curricula that remain important to us and our students, but which are not easily amenable to assessment? Already, we see this dilemma in a number of areas. What if career-motivated students don't want to take traditional liberal arts courses? Should we just lift these requirements? None of us are foolish enough to equate education with a simple checklist of acquired skills. Higher education provides a myriad of benefits to its students; we must retain the spirit of that environment by preserving programs not easily assessed and measured, but which broaden the educational experience of our students. Our leadership will be required to strike a balance between the desire for skills-based instruction and the need for more liberal forms of study.

The demands of change are also accompanied by unexpected rewards. Our schools of education, surprising as it may be to some, have already begun to benefit from new educational models. The overly compartmentalized university is coalescing once again under the demand of collaborative influences. Certainly, for schools of education, the fragmentation of the university into often warring academic departments has not been a good development. On this battlefield, funding and clout often followed those departments with lots of public relations glamour and grant-attracting muster. Schools of education, in these measures, have not faired well. The field of education has not been enthralling for university funding campaigns, and our grant collecting activities, while significant, are not of the caliber of more visible departments. Our service, however, has always been vital. As academic programs become more responsive to broader social needs, teaching is being accorded a renewed importance. One has only to look at the recent legislative frenzy in California, a state desperate for new teachers, to see why schools of education are becoming more prominent members of the university.

So what is to become of us? Dramatic scenarios aside, I think the professorate in higher education will emerge from this change very much intact. We will look different, we will work in different ways, and our universities will operate under a changed mandate. With all that, though, we will still be teachers. And, along the spectrum that is our world in the Information Age, I think teachers will represent one of the most vital linkages between the various interests of education, business, society, politics, and even the family. Education is a social function; that will always make it a unique profession; that will always assure its vitality.

TREND FOUR: PUBLIC/PRIVATE PARTNERING

The current educational system has been compared to the health care system of twenty or thirty years ago. Dominated by public and voluntary organizations, the health care industry was then a fragmented, high-cost, technologically lagging industry. Few business partnerships developed because health care was thought to be innately unprofitable or even inappropriate for profit-seeking organizations. Today, the health care industry has been dramatically changed through business partnerships. It is tightly organized into sectors, is more efficient, has a deep technological infrastructure, and enjoys strong growth. The education industry is second only to health care in size—and is now undergoing a revolution of a similar nature for similar reasons.

International Data Corporation estimates that the 13% share private industry currently has in the education market will double in the next two decades. As with the health care industry, the revolution in private industry involvement is being driven by broad trends, primarily technological advance and demographic change. In the new knowledge economy, information is king. Business depends on knowledge transfer now more than ever. Being the traditional distributor of knowledge, the education industry has become a prized economic arena (U.S. News & World Report, July 26, 1999).

That arena is huge and growing. Fully 10% of the U.S. Gross Domestic Product is spent on education—that is roughly $740 billion dollars a year. With that kind of money involved, and the promise of extended growth indefinitely, business has certainly taken notice of the opportunities presented by the education industry. Many of the businesses investing in education are familiar: Microsoft, Oracle Systems, Apple Computer. How many of you, however, recognize Advanced Learning Systems, DeVry Inc., Educational Management, and Provant? These companies are emblematic of the businesses that are reshaping the educational landscape. These are companies in the business of education with whom we will be partnering in the future in our commitment to serve students in an effective and relevant fashion.

The increased involvement of private industry in education delivery has alarmed many educators. That concern is justifiable. Private industry is changing education, and with that change will come the loss of some venerable educational traditions. For example, the four-year university dedicated to the 18–22-year-old student is probably nearing the end of its useful life. Private businesses like the University of Phoenix have hastened the emergence of that reality. The loss of the traditional four-year university is a dramatic shift, and one that will not be without painful adjustments. Cherished ways of living and learning will disappear.

Peter Drucker (1993) has claimed that the university will not exist thirty years from now because it cannot compete with business in the new knowledge-based economy. In his mind, that result is a positive one since greater efficiencies are achieved as a consequence of competitive influence. My intuition tells me that those of us here today would see things differently. The loss of the university would be for us unacceptable.

To counter the alarm over private industry involvement in education, however, I would ask you to examine Drucker's claim more closely. No doubt the university is going to change. No doubt that change will be dramatic. For some individuals, that change will certainly be painful. But this change does not mean the death of the public higher education system. More likely, the change will be a transformative one that reinvents the university rather than replaces it. Higher education has gone through many historical evolutions: from limited aristocratic institutions, from agrarian-based schools, from teachers colleges, from the influence of the GI Bill. I think this time, the university will adapt once again. Adapting this time may be the greatest challenge yet, but the results will be positive and constructive.

Our concern is best directed at fostering from all this change the optimal educational system for the student. After all, that is why we are all here—for the student. The involvement of private industry in higher education will help us serve students better. Let me give you an example from the company I work for now—Sylvan Learning Systems. And please remember, I come from a long line of dedicated service to traditional education. I have been an elementary teacher, a principal, a private school superintendent, and, more recently, a professor and academic vice chancellor. The vast majority of my career has been with public education, something I value immensely. I am a devoted advocate of the social importance of public education.

Now, to my example. Sylvan Learning Systems is very interested in remedial education. As you may know, many universities are not. Given finite resources, most institutions of higher education would like to devote their energy toward subjects they are best designed to teach. Remedial education, while a necessity, is not high on that list. After all, that was never meant to be the mission of the college or university. By partnering with Sylvan, as some universities do, a school can provide a remedial program that is more effective and less costly. Sylvan can specialize in remediation to assist universities that do not want to handle the program themselves, helping to better serve the overall needs of incoming students while allowing the university to improve its overall effectiveness.

Public/private partnering of this kind has become common as schools adapt under the influence of far-reaching social and economic changes. The result, I believe, is a system with greater capacity to serve the needs of students. The demise of the four-year university dedicated to 18–22 year olds is not the fault of the private education industry. That change has been in the works for years as a result of our transitioning to the Information Age. The University of Phoenix, by targeting a student population not served well by the traditional university (adult learners), has shown the limitations of our old model. In the end, revealing that weakness will help those universities with the courage and vision to change. The university of the future will not look at all like the university of today. Many will lament that loss. I share in some of their sentiments. However, the university of tomorrow, with the influence of private industry, will better serve students. I think, with cautious optimism, that change is to be welcomed.

TREND FIVE: LEADERSHIP IN THE GLOBAL EDUCATION ARENA

"Nothing of importance happened today."
—George III (King of England), diary entry, July 4, 1776. (Cerf & Navasky, 1998, p302).

The timing of George III's incredible diary entry has tremendous historical humor, but also serves as a good lesson for us against complacency during times of change. Today, with the pace of change in education, one would be, like George III, foolish to assume that nothing of importance has happened during the day simply because one did not see anything of consequence out the office window. The influences affecting our landscape are numerous, persistent, and gaining momentum. Little revolutions are breaking out daily in the once seemingly stable empire of education. Ignore them at your peril.

Perhaps the most unique element of this era of turmoil for the educational empire is the sheer scope of the change that is occurring. The influences affecting education are not just local, regional, or national. They are, without question, also global. At no other time in history has there been such potential for genuine global influences to assert themselves in as dramatic and rapid a fashion. Subsequently, I bring to the floor a word I must use with caution—globalization.

The term globalization is troubling to some. There are two causes: one, the term is weighted with millennial hype and subsequently lacks substantive meaning, and two, the term has gained political prominence as a catchall term for unfocused and often damaging educational policy. Globalization, for our purposes, is best left as a word describing simply that influence that is causing customary cultural, social, and geographic borders to disappear as we move into an age dominated by rapid, seamless information transfer. Governments often like to use the term to explain why the public educational universe is being dismantled. In this respect, the usage is more a shirking of responsibility than a description of influences bearing down on the educational arena.

The loose usage of the term globalization is significant for the educational leaders of tomorrow. Again, change is going to occur regardless of our personal desire for it. How that change occurs, though, is where we, as leaders, have a genuine say. Globalization is altering the educational enterprise. However, that does not justify a policy of abandonment concerning the existing educational system. Globalization, like the advent of business partnerships, does not mean the end of the university or of public education. Rather, globalization is a force that will profoundly reshape education. As such, globalization has great potential value. We, as stewards of education, must assure that potential is realized.

Often when one reads about globalization in education, one comes across the chilly Newspeak term "disintermediation" (Taylor, October 27, 1998). Literally, the word means "getting rid of the middle." The downsizing of companies is a well known form of "disintermediation." Prognosticators frequently use the term in tandem with globalization to map the decline of educational institutions. Indeed, educational organizations, from school boards to administrative bodies, are suffering a form of "disintermediation." The cause, however, is not globalization itself, but the use of globalization as an excuse by reformers to trim the educational tree of its "excesses." I, like you, would find value where these others would find excess. I would find vital structure where these others would see the needless middle.

Education is not like any business. Businesses can help education. Businesses can even educate. However, education can never simply become a business; its policies can never be driven by models purely political or economic. Education is fundamentally a social force and has all the complications that occur in a social environment. Globalization is also a social force; it is also very complicated. The influence of globalization on education, therefore, must be gauged carefully. Higher education will need to adapt; educational leaders must be at the forefront to direct the nature of that adaptation. Without vigilant leadership education will suffer loss. Now is a time both of opportunity and vulnerability. Since education is a social phenomenon, and because education is under the influence of globalization, the broad social health of the world becomes important. We must now look at some challenging social trends with a global eye. Here are some sobering ones that will challenge higher education in the future:

- The world's 200 richest people together have more money than the combined wealth of 40% of the world's population.
- Canada, Norway, and the United States are the richest countries in the world; the poorest twenty-two countries all occur in Africa.
- An average American worker could buy a computer with one month's salary; an average worker in Bangladesh would require eight years of salary for the same purchase (Geewax, July 25, 1999).

Globalization brings to education monumental challenges. As our arena expands inevitably toward an international scope, how should we adapt to best serve our students?

In summary, whom, then, do we look to for help in shaping the future? Lots of service arenas have adapted to change. We have looked at the health care parallel. We could also look at the legal industry, which has adapted from a more staid existence as an advocacy profession to one that is highly competitive and visible (how often do we see legal advertisements these days?). I think the service model that both health care and the legal profession have followed, with its plusses and minuses, is instructive. Higher education is a social service, after all. How can we direct that service through times of change so that its primary function, to help people, is best preserved?

The notion of service industry reminds me of a story I heard recently. A news organization in an American city wanted to test the response time of ambulances (clearly an outcomes-based assessment). They decided they would request an ambulance to be sent to a residence, and see how long it would take. They simultaneously called four different ambulance companies. And to make it interesting, they also called Domino's pizza. In the end, guess who arrived the quickest? That's right, Domino's; and the pizza was hot!!

The story illustrates the nimbleness required of even the most basic service profession. To survive today as a pizza delivery company, one really does need to rival the speed of an ambulance. Education will have to look at its enterprise in a similar way. Speed of instructional delivery may not be the dominating factor defining educational success in the future, but speed of adaptation to emerging needs certainly will. Adaptation looms large on the new educational landscape.

I began this presentation with a bit of history. The history of higher education is marked with dramatic changes. Often, we forget this history and come to think of higher education as a monolithic enterprise. That was never the case. Much of the highly charged language used to decry emerging educational adaptations (distance learning, for example) are the same arguments used fifty years ago when the two-year teacher colleges were transforming into four-year comprehensive universities (Morrison, 1998). That change occurred despite objections. The change of today will also.

The new reality for the educational leaders of tomorrow is dictated by three main forces: technology, globalization, and adaptation. The leaders of tomorrow's educational arena will have passion, will be willing to have their level of service measured (not, one hopes, against Domino's, though), will have innovative ideas about instruction, will have a deep sense of ownership in the emerging university, and will be dedicated lifelong learners. Professors can no longer be the "sage on the stage." The illiterate of the twenty-first century will not be just those who cannot read; they will also be those who cannot learn and relearn in a constantly changing environment. In a word, those who cannot adapt.

Leadership requires us to have vision, adaptability, and a dedication to lifelong education. To stay ahead of detrimental "disintermediating" influences, we must forge from change a new model of higher education. We must be prepared to constantly reinvent ourselves at a moment's notice. We must embrace true partnering with a variety of agencies and corporations. We must be prepared to endure repeated change to serve the needs of students who are entering a world in flux.

John F. Kennedy, speaking to the political and social challenges facing his new administration, used words appropriate to the work ahead for our "administration," the university professorate: *"All this will not be finished in the first one hundred days. Nor will it be finished in the first one thousand days, nor in the lifetime of this administration, nor even perhaps in our lifetime on this planet. But, let us begin."* (Bartlett, 1968, *Inaugural Address, January 20, 1961*).

Thank you.

REFERENCES

Abramson, Mark A. (May 1996). First Teams.http://www.govexec.com/reinvent/ articles/0596s6.htm, 4–5.

(September 1996). In Search of The New Leadership. http://www.govexec.com/archdoc/0996/0996s4.htm, 5.

(Spring 1997). Leadership for the Future: New Behaviors, New Roles, and NewAttitudes. http://www.leadership.com/leader.htm, 1–2.

Bartlett, J. (1968). Bartlett's familiar quotations, 14ᵗʰ edition. Emily M. Beck (Editor). Boston: Little, Brown & Co.

Bracey, G. W. (April 1999). Research-The Demise of the Asian Math Gene. Phi Delta Kappan, 620.

Cerf, C., & Navasky, V. (1998). The experts speak: The definitive compendium of authoritative misinformation. New York: Villard.

Clark, R.W., & Wasley, P.A. (April 1999). Renewing Schools and Smarter Kids-Promises for Democracy. Phi Delta Kappan, 591–595.

Cyberscape. (July 1996). Cybergovernment on display. http://www.govexec.com/tech/ cscapes/0796exe5.htm, 1.

Daniel, J. (1997). Why universities need technology strategies. Change, 29(4), 10–17.

Drucker, P. (1993). Post-capitalist society. New York: Harper Collins.

Friel, B. (August 25, 1997). Contract cybernauts. http://www.govexec.com/dailyfed/0897/08259b1.htm, 1.

Geewax, M. (July 25, 1999). The george jetson lifestyle in the info age. Perspective, Atlanta, Journal-Constitution.

Goodlad, J. I. (April 1999). Flow, Eros, and Ethos in Educational Renewal. Phi Delta Kappen, 571–578.

Immerwahr, J. (January 1999). Taking Responsibly—Leaders' Expectations of Higher Education. The National Center for Public Policy and Higher Education.

Matthews, D. (January 26, 1998). The transformation of higher education through information technology. Western Interstate Commission for Higher Education, 1–4.

Morrison, J. L. (September/October, 1998). The role of technology in education today and tomorrow: An interview with Kenneth Green. On the Horizon, 6 (5).

Mullan, C. (May/June 1999). New Technologies Give Rise To Distance Learning. Ed Fund "Focus", 1–10.

Murphy, J. (Spring 1999). Reconnecting Teaching and School Administration: A Call for a Unified Profession. UCEA Review.

Noddings, N. (April 1999). Renewing Democracy in Schools. Phi Delta Kappen, 580–583.

Robertson, H.J. (June 1999). Shall We Dance? Phi Delta Kappan, 733.

Schrag, P. (March 24, 1999). Old traditions vs. new markets. The Sacramento Bee, B9.

Smith, W. F. (April 1999). Leadership for Educational Renewal. Phi Delta Kappan, 603.

Soder, R. (April 1999). When Words Find Their Meaning. Phi Delta Kappan, 570.

Taylor, P. (October 27, 1998). Middleman deleted as word spreads. The Financial Times Newspaper. www.freespace.virgin.net/www.3.org/dis.htm

The Atlanta Journal-Constitution. (July 25, 1999). Global village: Fantasy and reality bliss, L1, L5.

The Chronicle of Higher Education. (July 30, 1999), B3.

Theobald, P. & Rochon, R. (April 1999). Orchestrating Simultaneous Renewal. Phi Delta Kappen, 587–588.

The Sacramento Bee. (July 4, 1999). Computers: Suddenly it's a whole new world. Forum, I1, I3.

U.S. News & World Report. (July 26, 1999). To have and have less: Don't look now, but the gap between rich and poor is widening. D. Gergen, Editorial, 127 (4), 64.

The Quest for a Center: Notes on the State of the Profession of Educational Leadership*

JOSEPH MURPHY

I. INTRODUCTION

> Whatever the causes, the profession is confronted with fragmentation; the challenge facing the field is how to deal with it.
>
> (Campbell, Fleming, Newell, & Bennion, 1987, p. 207)

> Patently, the assessments one makes of educational administration depend in great part on what one values and sees as important and on whether one tends to be optimistic or pessimistic in looking at the world.
>
> (Willower, 1988, p. 729)

First of all, I would like to thank AERA President Alan Schoenfeld and AERA Program Chair Geoffrey Saxe for the opportunity to speak here today. I would also like to thank you for coming to the session. Finally, I want to thank my colleagues on the stage—Karen Seashore Louis, Martha McCarthy, and Diana Pounder—who have agreed to participate in this session. The objective of AERA for this session is twofold: (1) to highlight critical issues regarding the needs and development of the profession of school administration and (2) to build a base for dialogue and action around the preparation and professional development of school administrators. My hope is that you will conclude that the presentation and the accompanying paper help meet these goals.

*Reprinted with permission from the University Council of Educational Administration (UCEA). The text of this lecture was originally presented as an invited address at the American Educational Research Association Annual Meeting, April 1999, Montreal, Canada. Subsequently, the text was published by UCEA as a monograph. The topic and substance of Dr. Murphy's Corwin Lecture was taken from this text.

Joseph Murphy, Vanderbilt University

Let me complete three additional tasks in this introduction. First, an advance organizer for the paper in the form of a thesis is established. Second, the structure of the paper is exposed.

Third, some general contextual notes are provided. The thesis is as follows:

1. We are in the midst of an era of ferment in the development of the profession of school administration.
2. We are on the way and traveling fast. Unfortunately, while some important progress has been realized, we have not always had a clear sense of where we are going.
3. We need a new center of gravity for the profession. Indeed, much of the work in this period of ferment can be characterized as a search for a much needed, defining core for the profession.
4. There is some evidence that the new core for the profession may grow from the seeds of school improvement and social justice.
5. For reasons discussed later, school improvement provides a particularly appropriate foundation for school administration.

The paper itself is comprised of five sections. Following this introduction, we examine the era of ferment in educational administration, looking particularly at the causes of unrest in the field. Next, we outline key markers on the path to reform in the academic arm of the profession since the release of the 1987 National Commission on Excellence in Educational Administration (NCEEA) report, Leaders for America's Schools. Following that, we analyze major changes in the profession in general and in the way school leaders are educated in particular. In the closing section, we apply a critical lens to developments in the field and to reform work over the last dozen years, and in the process, we posit a new core for educational leadership.

In terms of contextual notes, at least three issues merit attention. First, while there has been a good deal of legitimate critique about the profession, the storyline is not all bleak. It is important to remember that the profession of school administration is only about 50 years old, or as Achilles (1994) captures it, "The tradition of E[ducational] A[dministration] is relatively brief" (p. 10). As with other professions at a similar point in development, it is premature to make summative assessments. In short, I agree with Campbell and his colleagues (1987): "There is more reason for hope than despair. But there is much work to be done" (p. 213). My guess is that we probably have enough critique piled up about the state of the profession at its transition point of development. Critical analysis has become almost a cottage industry—a new area of study, if you will. We should heed Larry Cremin's (1961) reminder that "a protest is not a program" (p. 334). Second, I want to make it explicit that my understanding about this evolving new core for school administration is that it does not necessitate revolutionary change in the profession. I agree with Dan Griffiths (1999) that change in school administration will almost always be incremental. At the same time, you can have random incremental change or focused incremental change. And you can focus incremental change in a variety of ways. In short, we do need to take one step at a time. Yet it matters profoundly in which direction we start walking. Third, as Linda Lotto (1983) has reminded us, "Believing is seeing." I have tried to attend to that bit of wisdom throughout the analysis. At the same time, I am well aware that others may reach different conclusions as they sift through the information exammined for this report. In short, I acknowledge freely that my beliefs about what is best for the profession color the analysis, especially in the concluding part of the paper.

II. THE ERA OF FERMENT[1]

It appears to some analysts of school administration that we are in the midst of [a] round of great ferment—one that is accompanying the transition from the scientific to . . . the dialectic era.

(Murphy, 1993a, p. 1)

Recent major developments in educational administration may reasonably be characterized as a succession of attempts to challenge one or more of the assumptions of traditional science of administration.

(Evers & Lakomski, 1996b, p. 383)

A central theme of our work over the last 15 years has been that school administration is in the intersection between its past and its future, that it is struggling to loosen the bonds and routines that defined the profession from the mid-1950s to the mid-1980s during the theory movement (Murphy, 1992; 1993a; 1999b). While it is not clear to what extent those ties will be broken and, if they are, how the profession might be reconfigured, what is certain is that considerable effort applied in a relatively concerted manner has been directed to the reform of school administration over the last two decades. Indeed, we argue that the period defining the transition from the behavioral science era has been the most intense time of reform activity we have seen in school administration. It is also our position that although the current era of turmoil was foreshadowed by analysts almost at the same time that the theory movement broke over the profession (Culbertson, 1963; Harlow, 1962) and although it began to pick up momentum in the 1970s with the publication of T. B. Greenfield's (1975) insightful critique, it was not until the mid-1980s that the balance was tipped toward widespread critique and large-scale reform. Here, we briefly overview the reasons why the comfort of the status quo was thrown into question—borrowing freely from our earlier analyses in this area (Murphy, 1992; 1996; 1999b). Arguments are grouped into two clusters, those focusing on reform pressures brought about by the changing environment and those emanating from critical analyses of the profession itself.

The Changing Environment of School Administration

> One of the important things we know about leadership is that how we answer some of the most frequently asked questions about it depends on our assumptions about the nature of society and social organizations.
>
> (Slater, 1995, p. 469)

> To fully understand . . . university programs that prepare school leaders, it is necessary to explore the external forces that have helped to shape them.
>
> (McCarthy, 1999, p. 119)

In the next section, we examine forces internal to the academic arm of educational administration that are encouraging the profession to redefine itself. While that is where the bulk of reform attention has been focused to date, it is important to emphasize that school administration is also finding it necessary to reshape itself in response to changing conditions in the environment—forces that regardless of the internal health of the profession, demand a rethinking of the business known as school leadership. We review two sets of dynamics in this section—environmental forces associated with the evolution to a postindustrial world for the education industry and forces changing the nature of schooling of which school administration is a part.

The Evolution to a Postindustrial World

The Changing Economic Fabric

It is almost a fundamental law that the economy is undergoing a significant metamorphosis as we head into the twenty-first century. There is widespread agreement that we have been and continue to be moving from an industrial to a postindustrial or information economy (Cibulka, 1999). Key aspects of the new economy include: the globalization of economic activity, the demise of the mass-production economy, a privileging of information technology, an increase in the skills required to be successful, and an emphasis on the service dimensions of the marketplace (Marshall & Tucker, 1992). It is also becoming clear to many analysts that with the arrival of the postindustrial society, "we are seeing the dissolution of the social structure associated with traditional industrialism" (Hood, 1994, p. 12). The ascent of the global economy has brought an emphasis on new markets, "a loosening of the constraints of the labor market" (Dahrendorf, 1995, p. 21), and a "break[ing] of the state monopoly on the delivery of human services so that private enterprise can expand" (Lewis, 1993, p. 84). Along with these have come increasing deinstitutionalization, deregulation, and privatization.

There is a growing belief that "free market economics provide the path to prosperous equilibrium" (Thayer, 1987, p. 168)—a belief in "the assumption that left to itself economic interaction between rationally self-interested individuals in the market will spontaneously yield broad prosperity, social harmony, and all other manner of public and private good" (Himmelstein, 1983, p. 16). Supported by market theory and theories of the firm and by the public choice literature, there is a "new spirit of enterprise in the air" (Hardin, 1989, p. 16)—a renewed interest in "private market values" (Bailey, 1987, p. 141) and in the "virtues of private property" (Hirsch, 1991, p. 2) and a "promarket trend" (President's Commission on Privatization, 1988, p. 237) in the larger society. A view of individuals as "economic free agents" (Murnane & Levy, 1996, p. 229) is finding widespread acceptance.

While analysts are quick to point out the fallacy of this emerging belief in the infallibility of markets, there is little doubt that current alterations in the economic foundations of society are anchored firmly on a "belief in the superiority of free market forms of social organization over the forms of social organization of the Keynesian welfare state society" (Ian Taylor, cited in Martin, 1993, p. 48). As Starr (1991) notes, this expanding reliance on the market moves individuals in the direction of "exercis[ing] choice as consumers rather than as citizens" (p. 27). This evolution from government to markets has profound implications for education writ large and for emerging conceptions of schooling and school leadership.

Shifting Social and Political Dynamics

In the previous section, we addressed the changing economic substructures of a postindustrial state. In this section, we examine the shifting social and political foundations of the democratic welfare state that in turn act to help redefine the education industry and our understanding of school leadership.

The political and social environment appears to be undergoing important changes. There has been a loosening of the bonds of democracy (Barber, 1984). Thus, according to a number of scholars, "our American democracy is faltering" (Elshtain, 1995, p. 1), with a concomitant "loss . . . to our ways of living and working together and to our view of the worth of the individual" (Tomlinson, 1986, p. 211). The infrastructure of civil society also has been impaired. Analysts discern fairly significant tears in the fabric known as "modern civil society" (Dahrendorf, 1995, p. 23).

As a consequence of these basic shifts—the weakening of democracy and the deterioration of civil society, especially in conjunction with the ideological space that they share with economic fundamentalism—important sociopolitical trends have begun to emerge: (1) "a growing sense of personal insecurity" (Dahrendorf, 1995, p. 26), "unrest in the populace at large" (Liebman & Wuthnow, 1983, p. 3), and a less predictable "worldlife" (Hawley, 1995, pp. 741–742); (2) "the destruction of important features of community life" (Dahrendorf, 1995, p. 26); (3) shifts in the boundaries—both real and symbolic—between the state and alternative sociopolitical structures (Liebman, 1983a); and (4) an expanding belief that the enhancement of social justice through collective action, especially public action, is unlikely (Whitty, 1984).

The composite picture of self-destruction has been labeled "The Disunity of America" by Dahrendorf (1995, p. 23) and characterized as "the weakening . . . of the world known as democratic civil society" by Elshtain (1995, p. 2). One strand of this evolving sociopolitical mosaic is plummeting public support for government (Cibulka, 1999). In many ways, Americans "have disengaged psychologically from politics and governance" (Putnam, 1995, p. 68): "The growth of cynicism about democratic government shifts America toward, not away from, a more generalized norm of disaffection" (Elshtain, 1995, p. 25). As Hawley (1995) chronicles, "Citizens are becoming increasingly alienated from government and politics. They do not trust public officials" (p. 741), and they are skeptical of the bureaucratic quagmire of professional control.

A second pattern in the mosaic is defined by issues of poverty (Cibulka, 1999; Reyes, Wagstaff, & Fusarelli, 1999). Many analysts, for example, have detailed the "concept and the phenomenon of the underclass" (Dahrendorf, 1995, p. 24) or the "trend toward private wealth and public squalor" (Bauman, 1996, p. 627). According to Dahrendorf (1995), this economically grounded trend represents a new type of social exclusion—the "systematic divergence of the life chances for large social groups" (p. 24). He and others are quick to point out that this condition seriously undermines the health of society: "Poverty and unemployment threaten the very fabric of civil society. . . . Once these [work and a decent standard of living] are lost by a growing number of people, civil society goes with them" (pp. 25–26).

Consistent with this description of diverging life chances is a body of findings on the declining social welfare of children and their families (Reyes et al., 1999). These data reveal a society populated increasingly by groups of citizens that historically have not fared well in this nation, especially ethnic minorities and citizens for whom English is a second language. Concomitantly, the percentage of youngsters affected by the ills of the world in which they live, for example, poverty, unemployment, illiteracy, crime, drug addiction, malnutrition, poor physical health, is increasing.

According to Himmelstein (1983), society is best pictured as "a web of shared values and integrating institutions that bind individuals together and restrain their otherwise selfish, destructive drives" (p. 16). Some reviewers have observed a noticeable attenuation of these social bonds, or what Elshtain (1995) describes as a "loss of civil society—a kind of evacuation of civic spaces" (p. 5). The splintering of shared values and the accompanying diminution in social cohesiveness have been discussed by Dahrendorf (1995) and Mayberry (1991), among others. Few, however, have devoted as much attention to the topic of changing patterns of civic engagement and political participation as Robert Putnam (1995). According to Putnam, the "democratic disarray" (p. 77) that characterizes society and the polity can be "linked to a broad and continuing erosion of civic engagement that began a quarter-century ago" (p. 77). After examining citizen involvement across a wide array of areas, e.g., participation in politics, union membership, volunteerism in civic and fraternal organizations, participation in organized religion, he drew the following conclusion:

> By almost every measure, Americans' direct engagement in politics and government has fallen steadily and sharply over the last generation, despite the fact that average levels of education—the best individual-level predictor of political participation—have risen sharply throughout this period. Every year over the last decade or two, millions more have withdrawn from the affairs of their communities. (p. 68)

Another piece of the story, related to the themes of declining social cohesion and political abstinence but even more difficult to ignore, is the issue of "social breakdown and moral decay" (Himmelstein, 1983, p. 15) or rents in the "sociomoral" (Liebman, 1983b, p. 229) tapestry of society. Of particular concern is the perception that state actions have contributed to the evolution of social mores that are undermining the adhesiveness that has traditionally held society together—that "the welfare bureaucracy is irreversibly opposed to the established social morality" (Gottfried, 1993, p. 86).

The ideological footings of the emerging sociopolitical infrastructure are only dimly visible at this time. The one piece of the foundation that shines most brightly is what Tomlinson (1986) describes as the "ascendancy of the theory of the social market" (p. 211)—a theory that is anchored on the "supreme value [of] individual liberty" (p. 211). This emerging "high regard for personal autonomy, or liberty" (Gottfried, 1993, pp. xiv-xv) is both an honoring of individualization and a discrediting of collective action (Donahue, 1989; Katz, 1971). Social market theory suggests a "reduced role for government, greater consumer control, and a belief in efficiency and individuality over equity and community" (Bauman, 1996, p. 627). According to Whitty (1984), it includes the privileging of private over public delivery and "the restoration of decisions that have been made by professional experts over the last few decades to the individuals whose lives are involved" (p. 53). While critics of social market theory and glorified individualism foresee "a weakening of democratic participation [and] social cohesion" (Tomlinson, 1986, p. 211), advocates contend that "the individual pursuit of self interest is not a threat to the social bond, but its very basis" (Himmelstein, 1983, p. 16).

The Changing Nature of Schooling

As is the case with other organizations, schools are currently fighting to transform the way they think and act. From the collective effort of those who describe this change, a new vision of education quite unlike the "center of production" (Barth, 1986, p. 295) image that has shaped schooling throughout the industrial age is being portrayed. Embedded in this emerging view of tomorrow's schools are three central alterations: (a) at the institutional level, a rebalancing of the equation that adds more weight to market and citizen control while subtracting influence from government and professional actors; (b) at the managerial level, a change from a bureaucratic operational system to more communal views of schooling; and (c) at the technical level, a change from behavioral to social-constructivist views of learning and teaching. Each of these fundamental shifts leads to different ways of thinking about the profession of school administration and the education of school leaders (Louis & Murphy, 1994; Murphy & Louis, 1999).

Reinventing Governance

Most analysts of the institutional level of schooling—the interface of the school with its larger (generally immediate) environment—argue that the industrial approach to education led to a "cult of professionalism" (Sarason, 1994, p. 84) and to the "almost complete separation of schools from the community and, in turn, discouragement of local community involvement in decision making related to the administration of schools" (Burke, 1992, p. 33) and helped "marginalize parents as co-producers of their children's learning" (Consortium on Productivity in the Schools, 1995, p. 57). Critiques of extant governance systems center on two topics: (1) frustration with the government-professional monopoly and (2) critical analyses of the basic governance infrastructure—bureaucracy.

Most chroniclers of the changing governance structures in restructuring schools envision the demise of schooling as a sheltered government monopoly heavily controlled by professionals (Murphy, 1999a; in press). In its stead, they forecast the emergence of a system of schooling driven by economic and political forces that substantially increase the saliency of market and democratic dynamics (see Murphy, 1996). Embedded in this conception are a number of interesting dynamics. One of the key elements involves a recalibration of the locus of control based on what Ross (1988) describes as "a review and reconsideration of the division of existing responsibilities and functions" (p. 2) among levels of government. Originally called "democratic localism" (p. 305) by Katz (1971), it has more recently come to be known simply as localization or, more commonly, decentralization. However it is labeled, it represents a backlash against "the thorough triumph of a centralized and bureaucratic form of educational organization" (p. 305) and governance and an antidote for the feeling that "America has lost its way in education because America has disenfranchised individual local schools" (Guthrie, 1997, p. 34).

A second ideological foundation can best be thought of as a recasting of democracy, a replacement of representative governance with more populist conceptions, especially what Cronin (1989) describes as direct democracy. While we use the term more broadly than does Cronin, our conception shares with his a grounding in: (1) the falling fortunes of representative democracy, (2) a "growing distrust of legislative bodies . . . [and] a growing suspicion that privileged interests exert far greater influence on the typical politician than does the common voter" (p. 4), and (3) recognition of the claims of its advocates that greater direct voice will produce important benefits for society—that it "could enrich citizenship and replace distrust of government with respect and healthy participation" (p. 48).

A third foundation encompasses a rebalancing of the governance equation in favor of lay citizens while diminishing the power of the state and (in some ways) educational professionals. This line of ideas emphasizes parental empowerment by honoring what Sarason (1994) labels "the political principle" and by recognizing the "historic rights of parents in the education of their children" (Gottfried, 1993, p. 109). It is, at times, buttressed by a strong strand of anti-professionalism that subordinates "both efficiency and organizational rationality to an emphasis on responsiveness, close public [citizen] control, and local involvement" (Katz, 1971, p. 306).

The ideology of choice is a fourth pillar that will likely support the rebuilt edifice of school governance (Bauman, 1996). Sharing a good deal of space with the concepts of localism, direct democracy, and lay control, choice is designed to "deregulate the demand side of the education market" (Beers & Ellig, 1994, p. 35) and to "enable parents to become more effectively involved in the way the school is run" (Hakim, Seidenstat, & Bowman, 1994, p. 13). It means that "schools would be forced to attend to student needs and parent preferences rather than to the requirements of a centralized bureaucracy" (Hill, 1994, p. 76).

Finally, it seems likely that something that might best be thought of as democratic professionalism will form a central part of the infrastructure of school governance in the postindustrial world. What this means is the gradual decline of control by elite professionals—by professional managers and more recently by teacher unions—that characterized governance in the industrial era of schooling. While schools in the industrial era have been heavily controlled by professionals, they have not provided a role for the average teacher in governance. Indeed, under elite democracy and managerial centralization that defined school governance for the past century, teachers were explicitly denied influence. This view of front line workers is inconsistent with both human capitalism and emerging portraits of postindustrial schooling. It is not surprising, therefore, that the call for an enhanced voice for teachers is a central element in much of the current reform debate. It is also likely to become a key pillar in school governance for tomorrow's schools.

Reinventing Systems of Organization

Over the last few decades, "critics have argued that the reforms of the Progressive Era produced bureaucratic arteriosclerosis, insulation from parents and patrons, and the low productivity of a declining industry protected as a quasi monopoly" (Tyack, 1993, p. 3). There is growing sentiment that the existing structure of administration is "obsolete and unsustainable" (Rungeling & Glover, 1991, p. 415), that the "bureaucratic structure is failing in a manner so critical that adaptations will not forestall its collapse" (Clark & Meloy, 1989, p. 293). Behind this basic critique is the belief that schools have become dominated by producers and that students are not being well served. It is increasingly being concluded that the existing bureaucratic system of education with its "dead hand of central administration" (Jenks, 1966, p. 27) is "incapable of addressing the technical and structural shortcomings of the public educational system" (Lawton, 1991, p. 4).

More finely grained criticism of the bureaucratic infrastructure of schooling comes from a variety of quarters. Some reformers maintain "that school bureaucracies, as currently constituted could [never] manage to provide high-quality education" (Elmore, 1993, p. 37) and that, even worse, "bureaucratic management practices have been causing unacceptable distortions in educational process" (Wise, 1989, p. 301), that they are "paralyzing American education . . . [and] getting in the way of children's learning" (Sizer, 1984, p. 206). Some analysts believe that bureaucracy is counterproductive to the needs and interests of educators within the school—"that it is impractical, and it does not fit the psychological and personal needs of the workforce" (Clark & Meloy, 1989, p. 293), that it "undermine[s] the authority of teachers" (Sackney & Dibski, 1992, p. 2), and that it is "incompatible with the professional organization" (p. 4). Still other critics suggest that bureaucratic management is inconsistent with the sacred values and purposes of education—they question "fundamental ideological issues pertaining to bureaucracy's meaning in a democratic society" (Campbell et al., 1987, p. 73). Finally, some analysts contend that the rigidities of bureaucracy, by making schools "almost impenetrable by citizens and unwieldy to professionals" (Candoli, 1991, p. 31), impede the ability of parents and citizens to govern and reform schooling (Sarason, 1994).

As might be expected, given this tremendous attack on the basic organizational infrastructure of schooling, stakeholders at all levels are arguing that "ambitious, if not radical, reforms are required to rectify this situation" (Elmore, 1993, p. 34), that "the excessively centralized, bureaucratic control of . . . schools must end" (Carnegie Forum, cited in Hanson, 1991, pp. 2–3).

In its place, reformers are arguing for decentralized decision making and greater local control (Murphy & Beck, 1995) and for "policies . . . that unleash productive local initiatives" (Guthrie, 1986, p. 306). The emerging alternative vision of administration for tomorrow's schools includes methods of organizing and managing schools that are generally consistent with the "quiet revolution [in] organizational and administrative theory in Western societies" (Foster, 1988, p. 71). In the still-forming image of schools for the twenty-first century, hierarchical, bureaucratic organizational structures give way to systems that are more organic and more decentralized—systems that "suggest a new paradigm for school organization and management" (Mulkeen, 1990, p. 105). Of particular salience in this domain has been the evolution to more community-anchored conceptions of school organizations (Beck, 1994; Beck & Foster, 1999;

Sergiovanni, 1993). As with governance, these changes in our understandings of school organizations have important implications for postscientific era conceptions of administration and for the education of school leaders.

Reinventing Learning and Teaching

From the onset of the industrial revolution, education in the United States has been largely defined by a behavioral psychology-based model of learning—a model that fits nicely with the bureaucratic system of school organization. This viewpoint in turn nurtured the development of the factory and medical practice models of instruction which have dominated schooling throughout the twentieth century. Under these two models, the belief that the role of schooling is to sort students into the able and less able—those who would work with their heads and those who would work with their hands—has become deeply embedded into the fabric of schooling. According to Osin and Lesgold (1996), the perspectives noted above have "left the world with a mal-adaptive view of learning" (p. 623).

What is important here is the growing belief that we are "in the midst of redefining, even recreating conceptions of learning and teaching in schools" (Prestine, 1995, p. 140), i.e., a shift in the operant model of learning is a fundamental dynamic of the struggle to redefine schools. Of real significance, if rarely noted, is the fact that this new model reinforces the democratic tenets embedded in the postindustrial views of governance organization discussed above. The behavioral psychology-based model that highlights the innate capacity of the learner is being challenged by notions of constructivism and situated learning (Cohen, 1988; Prawat & Peterson, 1999; Rowan, 1995) and by the components of authentic pedagogy (Newmann & Wehlage, 1995). As Prawat and Peterson (1999) inform us, "Social constructivism represents more than an addition to the traditional, individualistic perspective that has dominated research on learning for most of this century. It . . . represents a dramatically different approach to learning, requiring fundamental changes in how . . . educators think about the process" (p. 203). Under this approach to learning, schools which historically have been in the business of promoting student adaptation to the existing social order are being transformed to ensure that they "help the vast majority of young people reach levels of skill and competence once thought within the reach of only a few" (National Commission on Teaching & America's Future [NCTAF], 1996, p. 8).

The emerging redefinition of teaching means that teachers, historically organized to carry out instructional designs and to implement curricular materials developed from afar, begin to exercise considerably more control over their profession and the routines of the workplace. Analysts see this reorganization playing out in a variety of ways at the school level. At the most fundamental level, teachers have a much more active voice in developing the goals and purposes of schooling—goals that act to delimit or expand the conception of teaching itself. They also have a good deal more to say about the curricular structures and pedagogical approaches employed in their schools (Newmann & Wehlage, 1995)—"influences over the basic elements of instructional practice (time, material, student engagement, and so forth)" (Elmore, 1989, p. 20). Finally, teachers demonstrate more control over the supporting ingredients of schooling—such as budgets, personnel, and administration—that affect the way they carry out their responsibilities.

Advocates of transformational change also see teaching becoming a more collegial activity (Newmann & Wehlage, 1995). Isolation, so deeply ingrained in the structure and culture of the profession, gives way to more collaborative efforts among teachers (Hargreaves, 1994). At the macro level, teachers are redefining their roles to include collaborative management of the profession, especially providing direction for professional standards. At a more micro level, new organizational structures are being created to nurture the development of professional community (Louis & Kruse, 1996; Sykes, 1999)—to allow teachers to plan and teach together, to make important decisions about the nature of their roles, and to engage in school-based learning initiatives.

As was the case with governance and organization, new views of learning and teaching call for quite different understandings of school leadership and of the role of universities in preparing school administrators.

Consternation Within the Profession: Meltdown of the Core

> The criticism of present-day administrators and their preparation are loud and clear and the demand for reform is heard on all sides.
>
> (Griffiths, 1988b, p. 8)

In addition to pressures from the environment, a good deal of internal soul searching also anchored calls for the reform of school administration. As has been the case in other major periods of change in the profession, these concerns were centered on the two core dimensions of the academy: (1) the intellectual infrastructure supporting the profession, including the research methods used as scaffolding in the construction process, and (2) the methods and procedures used to educate school leaders.

Questions About the Intellectual Infrastructure

> Perhaps the most privileged trophy of all is the so-called "knowledge base" of the discipline, that defined "core" which represents the most sacred intellectual ground of all because it represents what the field believes itself to be.
>
> (English, 1997, p. 5)

In this section, we examine what appears to be an irreparable gash in the fabric of the profession that has acted as a catalyst for the rising turmoil in school administration as well as for the efforts to reshape the profession. We refer specifically to attacks from a variety of quarters on the administration-as-science intellectual foundations that grounded the profession from the mid-1950s through the mid-1980s.

Although over the life of the theory movement the profession "increased in formality, structure, and complexity, much as did the school system—from amateur to professional, from simple to complicated, and from intuitive to 'scientific'" (Cooper & Boyd, 1987, p. 7)—the outcomes of the quest for a science of administration were considerably less robust than had been anticipated (Donmoyer, 1999). By the mid-1970s, this failure of the theory movement to deliver on its promises was brought to a head in a landmark paper delivered by T. B. Greenfield (1975) at the Third International Intervisitation program in Bristol, England (Griffiths, 1988a). Although other scholars had been drawing attention to the limitations of a near-exclusive emphasis on a scientific approach to training for some time, Greenfield unleashed the first systemic broadside attack on the central tenets of the theory movement, especially on its epistemological roots and guiding values. In a word, he found the scientific era of educational administration to be impoverished. Greenfield's paper went a long way in galvanizing critique of the field that began to wash over the profession in the mid-1980s.

Over the past quarter century, other thoughtful analysts have joined the debate about the appropriate value structure and cognitive base for educational administration (see Donmoyer, 1999, for a review; also Donmoyer, Imber, & Scheurich, 1995). On the knowledge base issue, there has been increasing agreement—although with noticeable differences in explanations—that "a body of dependable knowledge about educational administration" (Crowson & McPherson, 1987, p. 48) did not emerge during the behavioral science era. This condition means that upon exiting the behavioral science era, there was not much "conceptual unity" to the field (Erickson, 1979, p. 9).[2] In practical terms, Erickson concluded that "the field consist[ed] of whatever scholars associated with university programs in 'educational administration' consider[ed] relevant. It is, to say the least, amorphous" (p. 9). In his review, Boyan (1988a) concurred, arguing that "the explanatory aspect of the study of administrator behavior in education over 30 years appears to be an incomplete anthology of short stories connected by no particular story line or major themes" (p. 93). Given this absence of conceptual unity, there has not been much common agreement about the appropriate foundation for the profession, either. Thus, as the behavioral science era drew to a close, Goldhammer (1983) reported that although there were "general areas of concern that might dictate to preparatory institutions the names of courses that should be taught, . . . there [was] less agreement on what the content of such courses should actually be" (p. 269).

At the same time, a pattern of criticism was forming about both the definition of legitimate knowledge and the accepted ways in which it could be generated. As Crowson and McPherson (1987) reported, during this transition phase, critics "questioned with increasing vigor the appropriateness of traditional research methods and assumptions as a guide to an understanding of practice" (p. 48). Analysts called for both relegitimization of practice-based knowledge and the acceptance of:

An increasing diversity of research methods, including attempts at qualitative ethnographic, naturalistic, phenomenological, and critical studies . . . [and] an effort to generate "theories of practice" that incorporate both objective and subjective ways of knowing, both fact and value considerations, both "is" and "ought" dimensions of education within integrated frameworks for practice.

(Silver, 1982, pp. 56, 53)

Finally, there was a deepening recognition that the knowledge base employed in preparation programs had not been especially useful in solving real problems in the field. This questioning of the relevance of theory to practice can be traced to a number of causes. Deeply ingrained methods of working that assumed that one could discover theory that would automatically apply itself to situations of practice was the first. A second was the emergence of a "parochial view of science" (Halpin, 1960, p. 6)—one in which social scientists became "intent upon aping the more prestigious physical scientists in building highly abstract, theoretical models" (p. 6) at the expense of clinical science. A third was the proclivity of educational researchers employing social and behavioral sciences to contribute to the various disciplines rather than to administrative practice—administrative "structure and process were studied mostly as a way of adding to disciplinary domains" (Erickson, 1977, p. 136). "Indeed, the evolution of the field of educational administration reveals a pattern of attempts to resemble and be accepted by the more mature disciplines on campus" (Björk & Ginsberg, 1995, p. 23). Along these same lines, during this entire era, there was a lack of effort on the part of professors to distinguish systematically those aspects of the social and behavioral sciences that were most appropriate for practitioners (Gregg, 1969). In particular, insufficient attention was directed toward educational organizations as the setting for administration and leadership (W. D. Greenfield, 1995). Largely because of the overwhelming nature of the task (Culbertson, 1965), the weakness of the theory movement noted by the American Association of School Administrators (AASA) in 1960—the failure "to work out the essentials in the social sciences for school administrators and to develop a program containing these essentials" (p. 57)—was still a problem as the sun set on the behavioral science era. It remains a problem for the field as we embark on a new millennium.

A number of critics have also pointed out that regardless of its usefulness, the knowledge base constructed during the scientific era gave rise to a "narrowly defined concept of administration" (T. B. Greenfield, 1988, p. 147). This line of analysis spotlights the failure of the profession to include critical concepts, materials, and ideas (Donmoyer, 1999). To begin with, by taking a "neutral posture on moral issues" (Culbertson, 1964, p. 311), the theory "actively de-centered morality and values in the quest for a science of organization" (English, 1997, p. 18). When the term value judgment did surface, it was "frequently as an epithet indicating intellectual contempt" (Harlow, 1962, p. 66). Throughout the behavioral science era, there was "little serious, conscious effort to develop demonstrably in students the skills or behavioral propensities to act in ways that could be considered ethical" (Farquhar, 1981, p. 199).

Attention to the "humanities as a body of 'aesthetic wisdom' capable of contributing its own unique enrichment to the preparation of school administrators" (Popper, 1982, p. 12) was conspicuous by its absence.

Also neglected during this period of administration qua administration were educational issues — a phenomenon exacerbated by efforts to professionalize administration and thereby distinguish it from teaching. What W. A. Anderson and Lonsdale reported in 1957 — that "few items in the literature of educational administration. . . say much about the psychology of learning" (p. 429) — and what Boyan concluded in 1963 — that "the content of the advanced preparation tends to focus on the managerial and institutional dimensions as compared to teaching, the technical base of educational organizations" (pp. 3–4) — were equally true in 1987.

In summary, by the early 1990s, a multifaceted assessment of the intellectual foundations of the profession had produced a good deal of disquiet in the profession (Donmoyer, Imber, & Scheurich, 1995). This unease, in turn, has continually fueled the turmoil which still characterizes the academic wing of the field. It has also served — both directly and indirectly — as a springboard for many of the reform initiatives that have sprung up in the current era of ferment in the profession.

Concerns About Preparation Programs

The time has obviously come, I submit, for a fundamental, sweeping reassessment of our training program.

(Erickson, 1977, p. 137)

Since the late 1980s there have been calls for reform in nearly every aspect of the preparation of school leaders and admonitions that universities may be replaced . . . unless their programs are substantially transformed.

(McCarthy, 1999, p. 135)

The need for critical examination of educational administration preparation programs is obvious. Although changes are being undertaken by some departments, they are minimal, incremental, and lack a wholistic, referent view of the field.

(Björk & Ginsberg, 1995, p. 19)

The current era of ferment is fueled not only by critique of the intellectual foundations of the profession but also by critical reviews of preparation programs for school leaders (see, for example, Griffiths, Stout, & Forsyth, 1988a; Murphy, 1990c, 1992). Reviewers have chronicled a system of preparing school leaders that is seriously flawed and that has been found wanting in nearly every aspect. Specifically, critics have uncovered serious problems in: (a) the ways students are recruited and selected into training programs; (b) the education they receive once there — including the content emphasized and the pedagogical strategies employed; (c) the methods used to assess academic fitness; and (d) the procedures developed to certify and select principals and superintendents. Our review focuses on concerns that helped fuel the emergence of the current era of ferment in the mid-to late 1980s.

Recruitment and Selection

Analysts of the recruitment and selection processes employed in the mid-1980s by institutions in the administrator training business consistently found them lacking in rigor. Procedures were often informal, haphazard, and casual. Prospective candidates were often self-selected, and there were few leader recruitment programs. Fewer than 10% of students reported that they were influenced by the recruitment activities of the training institutions. Despite well-documented, if commonsensical, reminders that training outcomes depended on the mix of program experiences and the quality of entering students, research on the recruitment of school administrators was quite anemic (American Association of Colleges for Teacher Education, 1988; Miklos, 1988).

Standards for selecting students into preparation programs were often perfunctory: "Most programs ha[d] 'open admissions,' with a baccalaureate degree the only prerequisite" (Griffiths, Stout, & Forsyth, 1988b, p. 290); "For too many administrator preparation programs, any body is better than no body" (Jacobson, 1990, p. 35). The University Council for Educational Administration (UCEA)–sponsored study of the mid-1970s (Silver, 1978a) discovered that the rejection rates to preparation programs were quite low — about 12% for master's students, 14% for sixth-year students, and 25% for doctoral students. In 1984, Gerritz, Koppich, & Guthrie found that only about 1 in 30 applicants was denied admission to certification programs in California. Part of the reason for this nonselectivity can be traced to the use of questionable methods and procedures and to poorly articulated standards for entry. If all one needed 50 years ago to enter a training program in educational administration was a "B.A. and the case to pay tuition" (Tyack & Cummings, 1977, p. 60), the situation was not much improved as the profession took stock of itself in the mid-1980s.

It is not surprising that the quality of applicants is, and has been for some time, rather low. In 1988, for instance, Griffiths (1988b) revealed that "of the 94 intended majors listed in [the] Guide to the Use of the Graduate Record Examination Program 1985–86 . . . educational administration is fourth from the bottom" (p. 12). This lack of rigorous recruitment and selection procedures and criteria has several negative effects:

> First, it lowers the level of training and experience possible, since courses are often geared to the background and intelligence of the students. Second, "eased entry downgrades the status of the students in the eyes of the populace." Third, the candidates themselves realize that anyone can get in and that nearly everyone will get the license if he or she just keeps paying for credits. In part, this lack of rigor at entry reflects a lack of clear criteria for training or clear vision of what candidates and graduates will look like, and the realization that the graduate school experience itself is not very demanding.
>
> (Cooper & Boyd, 1987, p. 14)

This lack of rigor was believed to be contributing to the serious oversupply of cre-
dentialed administrators in the United States.

Program Content

Turning to the content of preparation programs at the time the ferment in the profession was beginning to warm up, critical reviews revealed the following problems:
the indiscriminate adoption of practices untested and uninformed by educational values and purposes; serious fragmentation; the separation of the practice and academic
arms of the profession; relatively nonrobust strategies for generating new knowledge;
the neglect of ethics; an infatuation with the study of administration for its own sake;
and the concomitant failure to address outcomes.

Critics averred that in many preparation programs "course content [was] frequently
banal" (Clark, 1988, p. 5). Nor did training programs exhibit much internal consistency. Students often confronted a "confusing mélange of courses, without clear
meaning, focus, or purpose" (Cooper & Boyd, 1987, p. 14; see also Achilles, 1984).
There was an absence of a "continuum of knowledge and skills that become more sophisticated as one progress[ed]" (Peterson & Finn, 1985, pp. 51–52). What all this
meant was "that most administrators receiv[ed] fragmented, overlapping, and often
useless courses that add[ed] up to very little" (Cooper & Boyd, 1987, p. 13).

One of the most serious problems with the cognitive base in school administration
training programs in the mid-1980s was the fact that it did not reflect the realities of
the workplace (Lakomski, 1998; Murphy, 1990b) and, therefore, at best, was "irrelevant to the jobs trainees assume" (Mulkeen & Cooper, 1989, p. 1) and, at worst, was
"dysfunctional in the actual world of practice" (Sergiovanni, 1989, p. 18). As we reported earlier, scholars of the behavioral science era attempted to develop a science of
administration. One of the effects was an exacerbation of the natural tension between
the practice and academic arms of the profession. The nurturance and development of
the social sciences became ends in themselves. Professors, never very gifted at con-
verting scientific knowledge to the guidance of practice, had little motivation to improve. As a result, the theory and research borrowed from the behavioral sciences
"never evolved into a unique knowledge base informing the practice of school administration" (Griffiths, 1988b, p. 19).

Mann (1975), Bridges (1977), Muth (1989), Sergiovanni (1989, 1991), and others have all written influential essays in which they describe how the processes and
procedures stressed in university programs in the theory era were often diametri-
cally opposed to conditions that characterize the workplace milieu of schools. Other
thoughtful reviewers concluded that administrators-in-training were often "given a
potpourri of theory, concepts, and ideas—unrelated to one another and rarely useful
in either understanding schools or managing them" (Mulkeen & Cooper, 1989, p.
12). In their review of training programs at the end of the theory era, Crowson and

McPherson (1987) argued that institutions "that had emphasized a solid grounding in theory, the social sciences, [and] rational decision making . . . were discovered to be well off the mark as effective preparation for the chaotic life of a principal or superintendent" (p. 49).

Evidence from nearly all fronts led to the conclusion that the focus on the behavioral sciences during the scientific era of training resulted in a glaring absence of consideration of the problems faced by practicing school administrators (McCarthy, 1999). The pervasive antirecipe, antiskill philosophy that characterized many programs of educational administration resulted in significant gaps in the prevailing knowledge base: an almost complete absence of performance-based program components; a lack of attention to practical problem-solving skills; "a neglect of practical intelligence" (Sergiovanni, 1989, p. 17); and a truncated conception of expertise. Administrators consistently reported that the best way to improve training in preparation programs would be to improve the instruction on job-related skills (Erlandson & Witters-Churchill, 1988).

The clinical aspects of most preparation programs in educational administration at the end of the 1980s were notoriously weak. Despite an entrenched belief that supervised practice "could be the most critical phase of the administrator's preparation" (Griffiths, 1988b, p. 17) and a long history of efforts to make field-based learning an integral part of preparation programs, little progress has been made in this area. And despite concern over the impoverished nature of clinical experience for nearly 30 years, Pepper was still able to report as late as 1988 that "few, if any, university programs in school administration offer a thorough clinical experience for future school administrators" (p. 361). The field-based component continued to be infected with weaknesses that have been revisited on a regular basis since the first decade of the behavioral science revolution in administrative preparation: (a) unclear objectives; (b) inadequate number of clinical experiences; (c) activities arranged on the basis of convenience; (d) overemphasis on role-centered as opposed to problem-centered experiences; (e) lack of individualization; (f) poor planning, supervision, and follow-up; (g) absence of "connecting linkages between on-campus experiences and field-based experiences" (Milstein, 1990, p. 121); and (h) overemphasis on low-level (orientation and passive observation type) activities (McKerrow, 1998; Milstein, 1996).

Woven deeply into the fabric of "administration as an applied science" was the belief that there was a single best approach to educating prospective school leaders (Cooper & Boyd, 1987), including a dominant worldview of administration as an area of study (content) and method of acting (procedure). A number of thoughtful analysts maintained that this perspective has resulted in significant gaps in the knowledge base employed in training programs of the era. Missing was consideration of the diversity of perspectives that informed scholarship and practice. For example, in her review of the literature on women administrators, Shakeshaft (1988) discovered "differences between the ways men and women approach the tasks of administration" (p. 403). She concluded that, although "these differences have implications for administrative training programs . . . the female world of administrators has not been incorporated into the body of work in the field . . . [n]or are women's experiences carried into the literature on practice" (pp. 403–406). Similar conclusions were reached about racial minorities.

One of the most troubling aspects of preparation programs of the mid-1980s was that they had very little to do with education. Most programs showed "little interest in exploring the historical roots and social context of schooling" (G. L. Anderson, 1990, p. 53) and did "a very bad job of teaching . . . a wider vision of schools in society" (Mulkeen & Cooper, 1989, p. 12). Furthermore, there was ample evidence that the content in training programs was heavily influenced by the "pervasive managerial-administrative ethic" (Evans, 1998, p. 30) that undergirded the profession and that preparation programs largely ignored matters of teaching and learning, of pedagogy and curriculum (Murphy, 1992). Most of the interest and scholarly activity of the behavioral science era heavily reinforced the "separation of problems in administration from problems in education" (T. B. Greenfield, 1988, p. 144) and the emphasis on noneducational issues in training programs. As Evans (1991) astutely chronicles, the era sponsored discourse and training primarily on "the administration of education" (p. 3), or administration qua administration—a major shift from its formative years when the emphasis "was upon the adjective 'educational' rather than upon the noun 'administration'" (Guba, 1960, p. 115). The separation of educational administration "from the phenomenon known as instruction" (Erickson, 1979, p. 10) meant that the typical graduate of a school administration training program could act only as "a mere spectator in relation to the instructional program" (Hills, 1975, p. 4).

By the early 1960s, the second major root of the field—values and ethics—like education before it, had atrophied (Beck & Murphy, 1994). The result was reduced consideration of two issues: (a) organizational values, purpose, and ethics and (b) organizational outcomes. According to Greenfield (1988), "The empirical study of administrators has eluded their moral dimensions and virtually all that lends significance to what they do" (p. 138). Despite some early notices that "educational administration requires a distinctive value framework" (Graff & Street, 1957, p. 120), despite pleas to reorient administration toward purposing (Harlow, 1962), and despite clear reminders that education is fundamentally a moral activity (Culbertson, 1963; Halpin, 1960), the issue of meaning in school administration as a profession and in its training programs had taken a backseat "to focus upon the personality traits of administrators—upon the mere characteristics of administrators rather than upon their character" (T. B. Greenfield, 1988, pp. 137–138). Thus at the close of the theory era, administrators were exiting training programs unprepared to grapple with ethical issues or to address openly the values deeply embedded in schools that often hide behind "a mask of objectivity and impartiality" (p. 150).

As early as 1960, Chase was pointing out what was to become an increasingly problematic situation in educational administration in general and in training programs in particular—a lack of concern for outcomes. Seventeen years later, Erickson (1977) reported that studies in the field "between 1954 and 1974 provided no adequate basis for outcome-oriented organizational strategy in education" (p. 128). Two years later, Erickson (1979) expanded on the ideas of his earlier essay. He documented "the tendency to neglect the careful tracing of connections between organizational variables and student outcomes" (p. 12). He decried the focus on the characteristics of administrators at the expense of more useful work. He laid out his now famous line of attack on the problem: "The current major emphasis, in studies of organizational consequences, should be on postulated causal networks in which student outcomes are the bottom line" (p. 12). At the time of the NCEEA (1987) report, preparation programs had yet to resonate to this idea. Indeed, in their analysis using data available at the start of the current era of ferment (i.e., 1986–1987), Haller, Brent, and McNamara (1997) concluded that "taken collectively, graduate programs in educational administration seem to have little or no influence on the attributes that characterize effective schools" (p. 227; see also Brent, 1998).

Delivery System

The delivery system that shaped preparation programs at the tail end of the theory movement was marked by a number of serious problems, most of which have a long history. Looking at the profession as a whole, it is clear that there are too many institutions involved in the training business. At the time of the NCEEA (1987) report, there were 505 institutions offering coursework in educational leadership, with "less than 200 hav[ing] the resources and commitment to provide the excellence called for by the Commission" (p. 20). Many of these programs were cash cows for their sponsoring universities, kept open more for political and economic than for educational reasons. In 1983, Willower offered this assessment of the situation: Many "offer graduate study in . . . name only. They seriously stint inquiry and survive by offering easy credentials and by working hard at legislative politics. Their faculties neither contribute to the ideas of the field nor are they actively engaged with them" (p. 194). These institutions tended to be characterized by high student-faculty ratios and limited specialization among faculty.

A related problem was the framework in which students' educational experiences unfolded: "Administrator training . . . [was] most often a dilatory option, pursued on a convenience basis, part-time, on the margins of a workday" (Sykes & Elmore, 1989, p. 80). Programs had indeed drifted far from the traditional residency model: At the end of the 1970s, Silver (1978a) reported that "the ideal of one or two years of full-time student life at the graduate level seems to be disappearing from our preparatory programs, and with it the notions of time for scholarly objectivity, student life, and colleague-like interaction between professors and students" (pp. 207–208). As many as 95 percent of all students were part-timers (Griffiths et al., 1988b), and "many students complet[ed] their training . . . without forming a professional relationship with a professor or student colleague" (Clark, 1988, p. 5).

We entered the current era of ferment with the arts and science model of education firmly entrenched in schools of education and departments of school administration to, the critics held, the detriment of the profession. According to them, this arts and science framework emerged more to help professors develop "greater academic sophistication through their professional roles in order to gain acceptance by their peers in other departments" (Goldhammer, 1983, p. 256) than to respond to the needs of prospective administrators. Unfortunately, it was clear by the mid-1980s that the model had neither furnished professors the status for which they had hoped nor provided graduates with the tools they needed in order to be successful practitioners (Björk & Ginsberg, 1995). In addition, it had driven a wedge between professors and practitioners, creating what Goldhammer (1983) labeled the "university-field gap" (p. 265).

The emulation of the arts and science model had spawned a number of sub-problems in preparation programs. One of the most serious was that education designed for practitioners (Ed.D. programs) had been molded to parallel the training provided to researchers (Ph.D. programs), in terms of both research requirements (Silver, 1978b) and general coursework (Norton & Levan, 1987). This blurring of requirements and experiences for students pursuing quite distinct careers resulted in the development of ersatz research programs for prospective practitioners. Students, burdened with a variety of inappropriate activities, were being prepared to be neither first-rate researchers nor successful practitioners.

In attempting to address the need to develop intradepartmental balance between professor-scholars attuned to the disciplines and professor-practitioners oriented to the field, departments had by the mid-1980s generally produced the worst of both. Unclear about the proper mission of preparation programs, seeking to enhance the relatively low status afforded professors of school administration, and overburdened with multitudes of students, faculties in educational leadership were characterized by "a strong anti-intellectual bias" (Griffiths, 1997), weak scholarship (McCarthy, Kuh, Newell, Iacona, 1988), problematic connections to the field (Willower, 1988), and considerable resistance to change (Cooper & Muth, 1994; McCarthy et al., 1988). A number of reviewers concluded that "only a relatively small number of those in the field of educational administration [were] actively engag[ed] in scholarly activities" (Immegart, 1990, p. 11). Even more disheartening were the assessments of the quality of the scholarship at the time (Boyan, 1981). According to Hawley (1988), because of serious limitations in their own training, many professors were not qualified to supervise research. Coupling this deficiency in ability with the previously noted lack of effort resulted in a situation in which "very little good research was being conducted by [educational administration] faculty and students" (Hawley, 1988, p. 85) and in which students developed a truncated, academic view of scholarly inquiry.

It is probably not surprising, although it is distressing, that inappropriate content ineffectively packaged was also being poorly delivered in many training institutions. "The dominant mode of instruction continu[ed] to be lecture and discussion in a classroom setting based on the use of a textbook" (Mulkeen & Tetenbaum, 1990, p. 20). Although some progress was made during the behavioral science era to infuse reality-oriented instructional strategies into preparation programs, the change was hardly revolutionary, and the use of innovative pedagogical methods was not prevalent at the close of the theory movement in school administration. For example, in the Texas National Association of Secondary School Principals (NASSP) study (Erlandson & Witters-Churchill, 1988), principals reported "lecture and discussion" to be the primary instructional mode used for eight of nine skill areas examined—and the ninth skill, written communication, was a close second!

Standards

Thoughtful critique of preparation programs at the time of the NCEEA (1987) report revealed that the lack of rigorous standards was a serious problem that touched almost every aspect of educational administration. Previously, we noted the general absence of standards at the point of entry into preparation programs. According to critics, once students entered preparation programs, the situation did not improve: "The quality of [their] experiences [was] often abysmally low" (Mulkeen & Cooper, 1989, p. 1). They were not exposed to rigorous coursework: "Students mov[ed] through the program without ever seeing a current research study (other than a local dissertation), without ever having read an article in ASQ or EAQ or AJS [Administrative Science Quarterly, Educational Administration Quarterly, and American Journal of Sociology, respectively]. They [were] functionally illiterate in the basic knowledge of our field" (Clark, 1988, pp. 4–5). Because performance criteria were ill-defined, there was also very little monitoring of student progress (Hawley, 1988). Not surprisingly, very few entrants into certification programs failed to complete their programs for academic reasons. Most former students indicate that their graduate training was not very rigorous (Jacobson, 1990; Muth, 1989). The delivery system most commonly employed—part-time study in the evening or on weekends—resulted in students who came to their "studies worn-out, distracted, and harried" (Mann, 1975, p. 143) and contributed to the evolution and acceptance of low standards (Hawley, 1988). Exit requirements, in turn, were often "slack and unrelated to the work of the profession" (Peterson & Finn, 1985, p. 54). Compounding the lack of standards at almost every phase of preparation programs were university faculty who were unable or unwilling to improve the situation (Hawley, 1988; McCarthy et al., 1988). Even greater obstacles to improving standards were the bargains, compromises, and treaties that operated in preparation programs—the lowering of standards in exchange for high enrollments and compliant student behavior. By the end of the theory era, the NCEEA (1987) and the NPBEA (1989) reports and other reviews also concluded that the time had come to markedly elevate standards in school administration.

III. MARKERS ON THE PATH TO REFORM

While it is impossible to prejudge what future historians of educational administration will designate as the major events that helped shape the profession for the post-theory era, certain events appear likely to receive considerable attention. In this section, we provide an overview of significant events of the current era of ferment as an introduction to that work (see also Forsyth, 1999; McCarthy, 1999; Thomson, 1999).

One marker that will surely be singled out is the set of activities comprising the work of the National Commission on Excellence in Educational Administration. Growing out of the deliberations of the Executive Council of the University Council for Educational Administration, the Commission was formed in 1985 under the direction of Daniel E. Griffiths. Support for the Commission came from funds contributed by a variety of foundations in response to concerted efforts on the part of the UCEA staff. The NCEEA has produced three influential documents that have promoted considerable discussion both within and outside educational administration: the 1987 report Leaders for America's Schools; Griffiths' highly influential address to the 1988 annual meeting of the American Educational Research Association (AERA) (subsequently published as a UCEA paper [Griffiths, 1988b]); and a UCEA-sponsored edited volume containing most of the background papers commissioned by the NCEEA (Griffiths et al., 1988a). These three documents helped to crystallize the sense of what is wrong with the profession, to extend discussion about possible solutions, and, to a lesser extent, to provide signposts for those engaged in redefining school administration.

Following up on these activities, the UCEA Executive Director, Patrick Forsyth, initiated discussions with foundations and set about mustering support for one of the NCEEA recommendations—the creation of the National Policy Board of Educational Administration (NPBEA). After considerable work on the part of UCEA to forge a union among the executive directors of 10 groups with a deep-seated interest in school administration, the NPBEA was created in 1988. Its care was entrusted to David L. Clark, then a professor of Educational Leadership at the University of Virginia. The NPBEA has undertaken a series of activities designed to provide direction for the reconstruction of the academic arm of the profession. After a year of work supported by the UCEA, chaired by its Executive Director, Patrick Forsyth, and facilitated by the NPBEA Executive Secretary, David L. Clark, the NPBEA released its first report, titled Improving the Preparation of School Administrators: The Reform Agenda, in May of 1989. The report outlines an extensive overhaul and strengthening of preparation programs. Its recommendations were later adopted in slightly modified form by the 50–plus universities comprising the UCEA. Following the release of The Reform Agenda, the NPBEA published a series of occasional papers that were designed to inform the reform debate in educational administration. It also sponsored, in conjunction with the Danforth Foundation, national conferences to help professors discover alternatives to deeply ingrained practices in training programs. Its 1992 conference on problem-based learning drew nearly 150 participants from universities throughout the United States and Canada.

Building on earlier-noted documents, two national efforts to redefine the knowledge base of the field unfolded in the early 1990s. In 1990, the National Commission for the Principalship (NCP), under the leadership of Scott D. Thomson and funded by the National Associations of Elementary School Principals and of Secondary School Principals, published a report titled Principals for Our Changing Schools: Preparation and Certification. The document represents an attempt to unpack the functional knowledge base required by principals. Working from this document, Thomson, under the aegis of the NPBEA—of which he was at the time Executive Secretary—assigned teams to flesh out each of the 21 knowledge domains identified in the report. The resulting document, Principals for Our Changing Schools: The Knowledge and Skill Base (NCP, 1993) provides a comprehensive outline of the core knowledge and skills needed by principals to lead today's schools. A year later, the UCEA authorized six writing teams under the overall direction of Wayne K. Hoy to update the knowledge bases in educational administration preparation programs.

In addition to the reform reports described earlier, change efforts have been shaped by a series of volumes devoted to the analysis and improvement of the academic arm of the profession. Each of these books has helped focus attention on the problems of the field and has provided alternative visions for a post-theory world as well as solution paths to guide the voyage. Some of the most important of these volumes are: the first two handbooks of research in the field, AERA-sponsored volumes, edited by Boyan (1988b) and Murphy & Louis (1999)—the Handbook of Research on Educational Administration; two volumes on the professoriate, authored by Martha M. McCarthy and colleagues—a 1988 book titled Under Scrutiny: The Educational Administration Professoriate and the 1997 follow-up volume, with G. D. Kuh—Continuity and Change: The Educational Leadership Professoriate; the edited volume growing out of the NCEEA project—Leaders for America's Schools (Griffiths, Stout, & Forsyth, 1988a); the 1990 National Society for the Study of Education Yearbook—Educational Leadership and Changing Contexts of Families, Communities, and Schools (Mitchell & Cunningham, 1990); a volume resulting from the National Center for Educational Leadership conference on cognitive perspectives in school administration—Cognitive Perspectives on Educational Leadership (Hallinger, Leithwood, & Murphy, 1993); and a volume on school administration published by the Politics of Education Association and edited by Hannaway and Crowson (1989)—The Politics of Reforming School Administration.

Other books devoted primarily to the reform of the academic arm of the profession include those edited by: Murphy in 1993b—Preparing Tomorrow's School Leaders: Alternative Designs; Mulkeen, Cambron-McCabe, and Anderson in 1994—Democratic Leadership: The Changing Context of Administrative Preparation; Donmoyer, Imber, and Scheurich in 1995—The Knowledge Base in Educational Administration: Multiple Perspectives; and Leithwood and his colleagues in 1996—International

Handbook of Educational Leadership and Administration; and those authored by: Beck in 1994—Reclaiming Educational Administration as a Caring Profession; Beck and Murphy in 1994—Ethics in Educational Leadership Preparation Programs: An Expanding Role and in 1998 (Beck, Murphy, & Associates)—Ethics in Educational Leadership Programs: Emerging Models; Milstein and Associates in 1993—Changing the Way We Prepare Educational Leaders: The Danforth Experience; and Murphy in 1992—The Landscape of Leadership Preparation: Reframing the Education of School Administrators.

The initiatives of the Danforth Foundation will no doubt been seen as an important marker in this period of reform. In addition to its sponsorship of the NCEEA and its core support for the NPBEA, Danforth has underwritten four significant efforts designed to assist self-analyses and improvement efforts in educational administration, all of which capture multiple elements from the various reform volumes and documents of the late 1980s: (a) a Principals' Program to improve preparation programs for prospective leaders; (b) a Professors' Program to enhance the capability of departments to respond to needed reforms; (c) research and development efforts, such as the Problem-Based Learning Project under the direction of Philip Hallinger at Vanderbilt University, that are designing alternative approaches to understanding the profession and to educating tomorrow's leaders; and (d) a series of conferences and workshops created to help the professoriate grapple with important reform ideas in the area of preparing leaders for tomorrow's schools.

Two standards-defining activities are also likely to be heavily referenced in future reports of events shaping the evolution, and perhaps the transformation, of the profession as it moves into the twenty-first century. The first initiative was the development by the National Council for the Accreditation of Teacher Education (NCATE) of their curriculum guidelines for school administration. This work, completed under the aegis of the NPBEA over a three-year period, brought the best thinking of the Policy Board—via Principals for Our Changing Schools: The Knowledge and Skill Base (NCP, 1993)—and the various professional associations (e.g., National Association of Elementary School Principals, American Association of School Administrators, Association for Supervision and Curriculum Development) into a comprehensive framework to reshape preparation programs for school leaders. A second initiative conducted under the auspices of the Council of Chief State School Officers (CCSSO) and in cooperation with the NPBEA—the Interstate School Leaders Licensure Consortium (ISLLC)—produced the first universal set of standards for school leaders. Approved in late 1996, Standards for School Leaders sets about strengthening the academic arm of the profession primarily through the manipulation of state controls over areas such as licensure, relicensure, and program approval (ISLLC, 1996).

Finally, it is likely that two additional triggering events from AERA and UCEA during this last decade will stand the test of time when the history of the profession is written. For AERA, the important event was the establishment of the Special Interest Group on Teaching in Educational Administration. For UCEA, it was the development of an annual convention. Both of these catalyzing initiatives have helped create sustained work in the service of reshaping the academic arm of the profession.

IV. THE SHIFTING LANDSCAPE OF THE PROFESSION

> Unless we know where we are going there is not so much comfort in being assured that we are on the way and traveling fast. The result is likely to be that much of our progress is but seeming.
>
> (Boyd Bode, cited in Cremin, 1961, p. 222)

In this section, we outline some of the major changes that are occurring in the field of school administration. The focus is on the distillation of themes that have become visible since the engagement of the struggle to define a postbehavioral science era for educational leadership. Two sources of data inform the discussion. First, we completed a general review of the literature in the area of school administration over the last 15 years. Second, we analyzed responses to three surveys completed by colleagues in school administration—one by 44 chairs from leadership department in UCEA institutions, one by 19 senior scholars in educational administration who allocate some of their research agenda to the study of the profession, and one by 86 colleagues whose understandings of reform in educational administration grow primarily from the changes they experience as members of the profession, not from their scholarship (for more details, see Murphy & Forsyth, 1999, chapters 2 and 7). In analyzing both the literature and the surveys, the search was for highly visible patterns in the tapestry of school administration. We examine those patterns in condensed form in two subsections that parallel the analysis of the profession provided in Section II above: rebuilding the foundations of the profession and changes in preparation programs. As is generally the case with these broad reviews, considerable wisdom can be gleaned by attending to what is not well-illuminated by the analysis.

Rebuilding the Foundations: The Scaffolding

Macro-level Configurations

To begin with, there is a sense in the literature and in the answers of the survey respondents that considerable effort is being devoted to assembling the elements necessary for rebuilding the profession—the creation of blueprints, the stockpiling of construction tools and material, and the organization of the labor necessary to undertake the work. While it is clear that various sectors of the field are employing different, and often incompatible, designs, there is a palpable sense of reform energy in the profession writ large and there is a discernable emphasis in leadership departments on strengthening preparation programs. Some of the forces engaged here include: (1) the ongoing efforts to refurbish—if not demolish—the old structure, especially the continued critique of the status quo as well as the many reconstruction initiatives underway; (2) the presence of highly visible reform agents, especially the task forces, commissions, and policy boards that have been active over the last 15 years; (3) the active pursuit of reform by key agencies in the profession, especially NCATE, CCSSO, NPBEA, and UCEA; and (4) the dissemination of demonstration initiatives, such as those sponsored by the Danforth Foundation, to strengthen the preparation of principals and the robustness of departments of educational leadership.

The rebalancing of preparation programs is also a featured issue in macro-level analysis of the profession. Two dimensions of the issue are especially prominent. To begin with, there is the pattern that one survey respondent labeled the "de-eliting" of preparation programs. In the words of our respondents, this means that there is no longer "a group of 'elite' institutions carrying the field": "The decline and now death of the University of Chicago's once famous Midwest Administration Center; the closing of graduate programs at Yale, Johns Hopkins, and elsewhere—all signal a gradual decline in the prestigious universities and their Education Administration programs and the rise of the lesser-known, lower prestige, smaller colleges."

One also develops a sense in these data of an increase in competition between suppliers of educational administration courses. There is a feeling that more institutions with less well-staffed faculties were moving into the preparation business. Noted with concern among survey respondents were "the proliferation of vendors for quick, easy, pain-free administrator certification" and the expansion of executive-style programs with minimal residency requirements. Contrary to economic theory, there appears to be a widespread feeling that this "competition" is lowering standards across educational administration programs in general and in the traditional quality institutions in particular.

Other new elements are also shaping the rebuilding of school administration, although none can be characterized as a theme. Among the most important are: an increase in the amount of networking efforts across institutions and throughout the profession; the internationalization of the profession; the reemergence of UCEA as a force and the strengthening of ties between UCEA and AERA; and the homogenization of programs across different types of institutions. With the exception of this last issue—increasing homogeneity—which has been confirmed by McCarthy and Kuh (1997), each of these issues merits further attention.

Micro-level Configurations

At the micro level, the feminization of the field is perhaps the most dominant pattern in the still forming, postbehavioral science portrait of school administration. This trend, in turn, is defined by at least three related elements: (1) a significant increase in the number of women in the professoriate, including the rise of women to positions of influence in professional organizations such as AERA, UCEA, and NCPEA; (2) a dramatic influx of women into certification and doctoral programs; and (3) an expanding presence of feminist perspectives in departments of school administration and in preparation programs for school leaders—what one survey respondent labeled "the infusion of the feminist perspective, feminist concerns, and feminist views of leadership, organization, and the role of education into educational leadership departments."

A second well-developed theme centers on the topic of departmental reconfiguration. A number of survey respondents made the point that departments of school administration are being reorganized in many colleges—a finding reinforced by the literature in this area (McCarthy & Kuh, 1997). Specifically, they are being merged with other programs to form larger departments or united with other departments to form larger divisions. Some colleagues maintained that these mergers have influenced programs negatively—resulting in fewer faculty trained in educational leadership and in less focus on issues of school administration. On the other hand, the fact that mergers sometimes strengthen relationships between departments of educational administration and departments of curriculum was viewed favorably.

An additional thread of the storyline here was characterized by one faculty respondent as "the doctoralization of education"—a heightened focus on the awarding of doctoral degrees in response to the need for leaders to secure this professional credential to gain employment in more and more jobs. Other individuals described changes in residency requirements, emphasizing primarily the growth of alternatives to full-time, on-campus residences. Finally, there is some evidence across all our sources of data that the basic structure of preparation programs is being reshaped by the rapid expansion of cohort programs. (We say more about these issues below.)

Infrastructure

There is moderate support for the claim that the foundations of educational administration, if not actually being repoured, have been undergoing important changes over the last decade. Particularly noteworthy have been the efforts to reshape the definition of school administration as a profession and to redefine educational administration as an area of study. On the first issue, there is some agreement that the conception of the school administrator role is being reconstructed around central ideas of leadership (Beck & Murphy, 1993). At the most basic level, this has meant a movement away from a century-long preoccupation with management ideology and with the dominant metaphor of principal as manager.

Leadership is being recast with materials from the intellectual and moral domains of the profession. A key element of this emerging vision is a deeper understanding of the centrality of learning and teaching and school improvement within the role of the school administrator—"a shift in focus [in the words of one survey respondent] from educational administration as management to educational administration primarily concerned with teaching and learning." Although other qualities of this new school administrator are less clear, the literature does provide clues about what they might be: (a) an understanding of caring and humanistic concerns as a key to effective leadership, (b) knowledge of the transformational and change dynamics of the principalship, (c) an appreciation of the collegial and collaborative foundations of school administration, and (d) an emphasis on the ethical and reflective dimensions of leadership (see Murphy, 1999b, and Murphy & Louis, 1994).

In much the same way that the literature is beginning to sketch out a redefined role for school leaders, it also reveals shifts under way in the prevailing conceptions of educational administration as a field of study. Three issues dominate the landscape here: (1) the search for a post-theory-movement knowledge base, (2) the emergence of alternative methods of investigation, and (3) a rebalancing of the academic-practitioner scale. On the first issue, survey respondents and the bulk of the literature echo what reviewers have been arguing for over a decade—that the infrastructure supporting the knowledge base for the last 40 years has weakened considerably, that we have been witnessing the loss of the intellectual core of our profession (see Section II above). While it is inaccurate to suggest that there is an emerging consensus about the defining elements of a developing knowledge base, the data we examined suggests that it will be more critical and more general in nature than it has been in the past. There is some sense that a post-theory-movement knowledge base will feature educational issues, ethics and values, and social conditions of children and their families and communities.

Concomitantly, there is consistency in the evidence that new forms of research have been privileged during the last 15 years. In particular, it is clear that ethnographic and other qualitative methods have gained considerable legitimacy. The heterogeneity of methodology that Boyan (1981) noted in his review has increased.

A final theme in this area is the movement toward better integration of—or the development of more powerful linkages between—theory and practice. The struggle itself is defined by work that: (a) places more emphasis on constructing the knowledge base from the raw material of practice, (b) highlights "theory in action/practice" in research and preparation programs, (c) recognizes practitioners as legitimate contributors to the development of knowledge, and (d) legitimizes discourse about practice in educational leadership departments. The theme itself might best be described as the strengthening in some cases and the rebuilding in others of university connections with the field—linkages that have grown threadbare over the last fifty years. It represents new efforts to link the academic and practice arms of the profession through partnerships. As noted below, it also reflects the significance of field-based experiences for students and the importance of practice-based problems for shaping learning activities in classes. Part of the storyline is an underlying sense of greater willingness to acknowledge the applied nature of the profession and to share the spotlight with practitioner colleagues—a movement to what Clark (1997) calls "authentic educational leadership" (p. 1).

Changes in Preparation Programs

> After being directionless for a decade, the field of educational administration in the mid-1980s undertook some important efforts to improve school leadership and the preparation of school leaders.
>
> (McCarthy & Kuh, 1997, p. 12)

Based on the replies of our survey respondents and a rather comprehensive review of work over the last 15 years, it appears that the pressures for reform are having a noticeable influence on administrator preparation programs.

Recruitment

To begin with, there is evidence of more active recruitment of students than has historically been the case in the profession. One gets a sense that the calls for greater emphasis on student recruitment that pepper major reform reports (e.g., NCEEA, 1987; NPBEA,1989) and ribbon critiques of the field (Griffiths, 1988; Murphy, 1990c) are being heeded. Some of this enhanced attention can be traced to concerted efforts to secure more diverse student bodies, especially in terms of racial composition. Some of the change is attributable to the widespread implementation of cohort programs, a dynamic that seems to have both permitted and encouraged programs to be more thoughtful about recruiting students. More vigorous work in the recruitment vineyards can also be linked to the establishment of collaborative arrangements with colleagues in schools and school districts to identify quality candidates. These partnerships are both a motivating force in and an outcome of the quest to strengthen recruitment in educational leadership programs.

Finally, while harder to pin down, part of a new proactive stance in the area of student recruitment results from enhanced clarity about program goals and conceptions of leadership undergirding individual preparation programs. There is some evidence that departments of school administration are arriving at more coherent and more shared understandings of leadership as well as more robust knowledge about experiences necessary to nurture leadership among students. As they do so, the picture of the type of student who fits that vision becomes clearer. In turn, some programs are being more aggressive in seeking out these types of students rather than simply waiting for the traditional drop-in trade. It is important to emphasize that these visions of good leadership and portraits of appropriate students vary across programs. For example, some programs seek out students with demonstrated leadership experience in schools while others deliberately cast a wider net, looking for nontraditional, and in some cases maverick, candidates. The key ingredient seems to be the clarity of perspective in the department. It is this dimension that seems to encourage active recruitment.

In closing, it is noteworthy that although still not heavily emphasized, recruitment is being connected to funding issues in ways not on the radar screen in earlier analyses (Murphy, 1991). A number of programs have entered into collaborative arrangements with school districts that help defray the costs of schooling for students.

Selection

In the area of selection, there is evidence of strengthened standards and greater selectivity. In some places, traditional selection measures such as grade point average and Graduate Record Examination scores have been ratcheted up. More important, a theme that might best be thought of as a revitalization of existing selection measures and a broadening of the portfolio of selection tools is evident. In this regard, there appears to be movement on a number of fronts at the same time. On one front, there seems to be greater coherence about the relevant mix of measures to be employed in the selection process as well as renewed commitment to employ these tools in a thoughtful fashion in the service of collecting and assessing information about candidates. There is a sense of a shift in the use of screening tools as rituals to fill slots to the use of screening tools as part of more wholistic and vibrant systems of measures for securing more able students.

At the same time, the key issue, as with recruitment, seems to be a more thoughtful use of a variety of measures deemed appropriate at a given institution rather than the identification of a particular list of indices. In some cases, assessment center exercises are being employed. In other departments, more traditional measures are being used. The essential ingredient appears to be commitment by the faculty to a comprehensive set of measures that are consistent with the demands and expectations of their various programs.

One major theme defines the pattern of students served by school administration programs—they are more diverse than a decade before. This is most noticeable in the increased percentages of minorities and women in leadership programs.

Course Content

Analysts of the condition of the curriculum that defined preparation programs in the 1970s and 1980s are generally quite critical (see Murphy, 1992, for a review). Neither do reviewers discern much interest during that period on the part of faculty to engage systemic curricular revision (McCarthy et al., 1988). By 1999, however, program change and development has become an important thread in the fabric of school administration. Indeed, the curriculum in preparation programs has been evolving in discernable ways over the last decade. Most noticeably, there has been an increase in attention provided to the core technology of schooling—tighter linkages between leadership and learning or what one survey respondent characterized as a "refocus on student learning and curriculum as major content/skill areas for administrators." The notion of the school administrator as instructional leader appears to be taking hold across the landscape of the profession. The overall feeling one senses is that program curriculum is being configured to support instructional improvement. At the macro level, this has meant more consideration being devoted to unpacking and examining the purposes of education and the appropriate missions for schools. It has also led to the pursuit of deeper understandings of and commitment to school reform, educational change, and school improvement. At the micro level, throwing the spotlight on the core technology has underscored the importance of theories of learning and teaching in preparation programs and has promoted increased legitimacy for examining quality teaching. It has also enhanced the saliency of student outcomes in assessing organizational effectiveness.

Over the last decade, preparation programs also seem to be awakening to the need to attend more forcefully to the moral and ethical dimensions of schooling and to the political aspects of education. In the ethics area, the moral context of leadership and the moral dimensions of the administrator's role are receiving more attention. There also seems to be a growing recognition of the ethic of caring and the importance of values in schools. In the policy domain, there is a sense that the curriculum in preparation programs has been evolving to reflect what one survey respondent labeled the "ecology of organizations"; that is, the use of policy not as a managerial tool but as a vehicle for leaders to guide organizations with increasingly permeable boundaries.

There is also some evidence of increased attention to the social fabric of education in program curriculum. While this concept covers a good deal of ground, it unpacks into at least three clusters of ideas, all of which are anchored in what one respondent labeled "the human factors in school leadership." To begin with, expanded emphasis on the social aspects of education has meant more attention devoted to the relationships between school and community—to new attention on education as an aspect of the larger society and to preparing leaders to operate from this perspective. The social dimension of the curriculum also includes greater attention to issues of diversity and to its impact on schooling and school leaders. Diversity, in turn, is generally defined primarily in terms of race, income, gender, other cultures, and internationalization. There is also some suggestion that more consideration is being given to collaborative organizational processes in preparation programs today than was the case a decade ago. Learning experiences designed to help future school leaders understand the importance of empowerment and to develop skills in the exercise of shared decision making/leadership are central topics in this area. Related ideas include nurturing teacher professionalism, learning to lead from the center rather than the apex of the organization, and developing schools as learning communities and collaborative cultures.

Other curricular changes also dot the preparation landscape, but with less frequency than the attention devoted to the educational, moral, and social dimensions of leadership programs. Three concepts define this second-tier grouping of curriculum revisions: (1) the continuing trend to emphasize qualitative research methods in research courses and in assignments completed in other classes; (2) a focus on technology in coursework, primarily as a tool for better organizational management (i.e., technology applied to administration); and (3) renewed attention to curriculum grounded in "successful corporate practice" and "business management tools and techniques."

Clinical Experiences

A good deal of change seems to be unfolding in the clinical components of preparation programs as well. Two patterns emerge. First, the focus on clinically based experiences in these programs has increased; there has been a significant increase in the role of field work in administrator preparation. This enhancement can best be characterized as the strengthening of the full array of clinical components, from class-based activities to full-blown internships. The profession seems to be working to integrate clinical experiences into university-based courses in new ways, i.e., clinical experiences are becoming a more significant component of regular courses. The use of real-world problems in coursework also appears to be expanding. The firewall between field activities and university coursework is being dismantled in many programs. At the same time, it appears that traditional practicum activities are being fortified. More time is being devoted to the practicum, and it is being done in a more thoughtful fashion. Finally, and consistent with recent NCATE guidelines, it is clear that the internship is being lengthened and deepened in many places. The overall effect is that the profession seems to be taking the clinical dimension of preparation programs more seriously than they did when the theory era of school administration was coming to an end in the early 1980s. Consequently, these clinical components comprise a larger percentage of the program completed by today's students.

The second theme can be characterized as an upgrading of the quality of the expanded clinical component of preparation programs. The plethora of methods being employed to improve field-based experiences includes: providing more structure to assignments, especially in terms of expectations about what students need to learn; increasing the amount and the quality of faculty supervision; ensuring greater involvement of site supervisors; integrating field experiences and academic offerings more effectively; developing better forums for students to debrief on clinical experiences and to reflect on their learning; creating better systems of mentor advising; establishing more diverse, field-based learning opportunities; and monitoring clinical experiences more closely.

In summary, it seems that programs have seriously begun to address the well-documented weaknesses and nearly intractable problems that have plagued the clinical component of preparation programs for the last 30 years. A more aggressive integration of field-based activities into traditional university-based classes has been an especially noteworthy achievement in these programs over the last decade. The continuation of the earlier efforts of the late 1980s to extend and deepen clinical work and to upgrade the quality of field-based experiences also deserves to be acknowledged.

The one area on which the data fail to provide much information is the nature of the clinical experiences themselves. We need better information at a micro level about the activities in which students in these longer and improved field experiences are actually engaged.

Teaching

While not gainsaying the continued prevalence of traditional "talk and chalk" methods, there is some evidence that instruction in school administration preparation programs is richer and more multidimensional in 1999 than it was when the original calls for strengthening preparation programs were released in the mid- to late 1980s. Most noteworthy has been the infusing of more authentic material and more thoughtful and reflective methods into programs. Undergirding this shift has been an enhanced focus on active learning and a renewed interest in the raw material of practice. Indeed, the major theme in this area chronicles the story of how instruction has become grounded more firmly in issues of practice. A variety of elements, in turn, help define practice-anchored instruction, including increased cooperation with schools in the delivery of programs of study, a renewed emphasis on the engagement of school-based administrators in the delivery of programs and services, and a general reknitting of the connections between universities and local educational agencies around issues of administrator training. Practice-anchored instruction also includes the use of more case study inquiry and more problem-based learning strategies.

Structure

Evidence from the data we examined suggests that changes in preparation programs extend to the structures that house and support the learning activities and to the students engaged in these endeavors. Perhaps the most distinct piece of the structural mosaic has been the widespread implementation of cohort programs. At the same time, there appears to have been an increase in the number of alternative delivery structures, such as executive doctoral programs and distance learning models to deliver off campus programs. Some shifts in the composition of faculty are also becoming visible, including the presence of more women and more professors with school- and district-based experience in departments of school administration.

Summary

While it is difficult to locate the influences afoot with certainty, some or all of the forces discussed below may help explain the program changes just examined. On the one hand, time may be the salient variable (Murphy, 1991). That is, most of the reform reports in the area of leadership have had a chance to spread across the profession. There has also been sufficient time for programs to engage change initiatives and for some of those efforts to take root.

It may also be the case that the buffering these programs have historically enjoyed—buffering employed to fend off external influences—may be thinning considerably. In short, their option not to act may be being reduced. In particular, the resurgence of more vigorous state control over preparation programs may be propelling reform efforts. This has certainly been the case in the states of North Carolina, Ohio, Mississippi, and Kentucky (Van Meter, 1999). Concomitantly, the introduction of market dynamics into the licensure system may be influencing departments to strengthen their training programs. At least two such forces have surfaced over the last decade—the creation of alternative avenues for licensure and the growth of alternative providers of programs leading to licensure, especially those offered by professional associations and local educational agencies.

Professional forces may also lie behind the reform work noted by these department heads. The widespread complacency about preparation programs among professors of educational administration, which has been highlighted by McCarthy et al. (1988) and McCarthy and Kuh (1997), is perhaps being challenged as older members of the professoriate retire and new faculty begin to assume the reigns of the profession. If indeed we are witnessing a lifting of the veil of complacency, it may be attributable to the influx of more women professors and of more faculty members who are joining the professoriate from practice (McCarthy, 1999). There certainly appears to be more agitation for program improvement today than was the case in the mid-1980s.

The growth of professional groups dedicated to program reform such as the new AERA special interest groups on problem-based learning and on teaching and learning in educational administration are noteworthy markers in the professional area. So too has been the development of professional networks of reformers such as those nurtured through the Danforth initiatives of the late 1980s and early 1990s. In short, it may be that the rather inhospitable landscape of the profession is being remolded to be more receptive to the seeds of change. It is worth noting that many more colleagues than was the case fifteen years ago have staked at least part of their professional reputations on work related to preparation program development and reform.

Finally, it is possible that shifting norms in universities in general and in colleges of education in particular may be responsible for some of the increased attention to program reform uncovered in our review. Specifically, at least two forces operating in education schools may be directing, or at least facilitating, program improvement. The first is the increased emphasis being placed "on enhancing the quality of instruction [in] most colleges and universities" (McCarthy & Kuh, 1997, p. 245). The second is the demand by many colleges of education that meaningful connections to practice be established and nurtured. While sometimes offset by other forces (e.g., the press for research respectability), these two dynamics may be helping to energize efforts to strengthen preparation programs in the area of educational leadership.

V. A CALL FOR A NEW CENTER OF GRAVITY

If educational administration ever had a central core or intellectual cohesion, that era seems to be past.

(Campbell et al., 1987, p. 199)

There are . . . several freeways which run through the territory [of school administration] with only a few crossovers and intersections available.

(Boyan, 1981, p. 8)

Let us take stock of where we are. We proposed that we are in the midst of considerable ferment in the field. We provided an overview of the forces that have driven and continue to fuel change efforts. We also offered a quick snapshot of some of the key markers in the struggle to move us to a different place—efforts to redefine, if not reanchor, the profession. Finally, we pointed to some themes that help us see what is unfolding in the field of school administration writ large.

The question at hand is, Where exactly are we? Are we still mired in the ferment, or are we closer to breaking out and establishing new foundations for the profession? There are, of course, quite different views on this issue. Perhaps the best answer is one provided by Robert Hutchins, although in reference to a different topic: "The system is headed in no direction, or in the wrong direction, or in all directions at once." This assumes that there is a "right" direction, a highly inflammable position in the university wing of the profession. Nonetheless, I will argue that there is a right direction, a principle of correspondence (Kliebard, 1995) that allows us both to honor the diversity of work ongoing in school administration and to maintain a center of gravity for the profession.

A Framework of Possibilities

Since the early decades of this century, proponents of contrasting philosophical views have sought to shape the graduate experience. One view has placed administrative roles at the center of thought and teaching. . . . The other view has emphasized the centrality of ethical and intellectual qualities essential to leadership in the larger public domain and within schools and school systems themselves.

(Campbell et al., 1987, p. 192)

Before we get there, however, I would like to lay out the traditional possibilities for creating a new center for school administration as a profession in general and for the preparation and development of school leaders in particular. While there are a variety of ways to think about this task, let me present a roadmap that encompasses the four most well-traveled pathways: Primacy of mental discipline (processes), primacy of the administrator (roles, functions, tasks), primacy of content (knowledge), and primacy of method.

A focus on mental discipline posits that particular content is less important than the development of processes or metacognitive skills. With deep roots in the dominant seventeenth-and eighteenth-century understandings of learning, a mental discipline perspective views content as a vehicle for the development of important faculties such as observation, judgement, and perception (Herbst, 1996; Krug, 1964; Reese, 1995). In here, one might include work on: (1) processes—such as the early work of Griffiths (1958) on administration as decision making or the more recent research of Leithwood (Leithwood & Stager, 1989) on administration as problem solving; (2) thinking/reflection—such as the scholarship of Ann Hart (1993), Chuck Kerchner (1993), and Karen Osterman and Robert Kottkamp (1993); and, at least for our purposes here, (3) ethics and values—such as the writings of Jerry Starratt (1991) and Lynn Beck (1994). In the practice wing of the professional edifice, one need look no further than to the quite popular assessment centers of the National Association of Secondary School Principals and the National Association of Elementary School Principals to see the vitality of the mental discipline approach grounding the profession (see, for example, Sirotnik & Durden, 1996).

Highlighting the role of the administrator privileges issues relating to the activities of school leaders. A review of the literature reveals that the key constructs here are: (1) roles—such as the work of Arthur Blumberg (1985), Larry Cuban (1976), Susan Moore Johnson (1996) and Richard Wallace (1996) on the superintendency; Hartzell, Williams, and Nelson (1995) and Catherine Marshall (1992) on the assistant principalship; Terry Deal and Kent Peterson (1990), Ellen Goldring and Sharon Rallis (1993), Phil Hallinger and Charlie Hausman (1994), Ann Hart and Paul Bredeson (1996), Karen Seashore Louis (Louis & Miles, 1990), Nona Prestine (1994), Tom Sergiovanni (1987), and a host of others on the principalship; (2) functions—such as the work of Martha McCarthy, Nona Cambron-McCabe, and S. B. Thomas (1998) on law, Jim Guthrie (Garms, Guthrie, & Pierce, 1978) and David Monk and Marge Plecki (1999) on finance, and Phil Young (Young, Place, Rinehart, Jury, & Baits, 1997) and William Castetter (1986) in the personnel area; and (3) tasks—such as the writings of Daresh (1989) and Sergiovanni and Starratt (1988) on supervising employees.

Spotlighting content places knowledge at the center of the administrative stage. Historically, this approach features two epistemological axes—discipline-based (or technical) knowledge and practice-based knowledge—axes which are regularly portrayed as being under considerable tension (Donmoyer, 1999; Forsyth & Murphy, 1999). Reform efforts afoot in the current era of ferment tend to spotlight the knowledge sector of our four-part framework. Work in the technical or academic domain is of three types: (1) struggles over the meaning and viability of knowledge-based foundations for the profession (see Donmoyer, Imber, & Scheurich, 1995); (2) attempts to widen the traditional knowledge domains that define school administration, e.g., the infusion of ethics and values into the profession (Beck & Murphy, 1994; Beck et al., 1998); and (3) analyses and initiatives to either recast the knowledge base of the field for the dialectic era (e.g., the recent NPBEA and UCEA curriculum development work described earlier) or establish a new ground for the profession (e.g., policy analysis—see Boyan, 1981, for a description of efforts to establish the politics of education as a foundation for the profession). In the practice domain, one main thrust has been the religitimization of the craft aspects of the profession, including the recognition of ideas such as "stories" that came under heavy critique during the scientific era (Griffiths, 1988b). A second thrust has been the work of scholars like Paula Silver (1986, 1987) and Ed Bridges and Phil Hallinger (1992, 1993, 1995) to codify and make more systematic what has traditionally been available in only an ad hoc fashion.

Finally, the field of school administration can be conceptualized in terms of methods. As with the other three areas, methods can be viewed as a strategy for helping move the profession from the current era of ferment to the next stage of development (Boyan, 1981). As with the case of emphasis on mental discipline, privileging methods pulls processes into the foreground while often, but not always, pushing other issues into the background. One line of work in this area has focused on efforts to strengthen methods in educational administration research (see Boyan, 1981, for an analysis). In addition, as noted in Section IV above, much of the work in school administration in this domain has been in the service of developing a more robust portfolio of designs—in both the research and the application domains. On the issue of a more robust portfolio of research strategies, the works of qualitative methodologists such as Yvonna Lincoln (Lincoln & Guba, 1985) and of scholars employing nontraditional approaches (see Griffiths, 1991) are most noteworthy. In the application domain, the scholarship of Bridges and Hallinger (1992, 1993, 1995) on problem-based learning is becoming increasingly woven into the profession, as are a renewed emphasis on case studies and a bundle of instructional strategies such as journal writing, novels, films, reflective essays, and autobiographies (see, for example, Brieschke, 1990; English & Steffy, 1997; and Short & Rinehart, 1993).

The Need to Recast the Problem

> The problem [is] not choosing between existing alternatives as it [is] reconstructing the question as to present new ones.
>
> (Kliebard, 1995, p. 49)

A Single Break-Out Point

The central dilemma that we face is that none of the four avenues for regrounding the profession is likely to be successful, successful in the ability to take and hold the high ground for long. The ascendancy of any approach will by necessity be the result of power dynamics that legitimize a chain reaction of continual struggle, dominance, and fall from grace. Let me show how this is the case by examining how the most popular break-out strategy—the development of a more robust body of scholarship—is unlikely to carry us to the next phase of development. Similar cases can be made for the other three elements of the framework as well.

The central problem is that our fascination with building the academic infrastructure of school administration has produced some serious distortions in what is primarily an applied field. It is difficult to see how renewed vigor in this area will do much to extract us from these difficulties. As a matter of fact, a case can be made that such efforts may simply exacerbate existing problems and deepen the fissures that mark the profession. To begin with, since academic knowledge is largely the purview of professors, the focus on technical knowledge places the university in the center of the field—a sort of pre-Copernican worldview of the profession. This perspective also creates serious reference misalignment. It strongly suggests that the primary reference group for academics is other professors.

There are other reasons to believe that a primary focus on content, especially technical knowledge, is as likely to reenforce problems as it is to expose the foundations for a new era in school administration. On the one hand, if one believes that the best predictor of future behavior is past behavior, then a content-based attack on the problems of ferment and fragmentation will probably solidify the orientation of professors to the various academic disciplines rather than to the field of school administration with its problems and challenges. The quest for deeper and more robust knowledge becomes little more than academic trophy hunting. Under this scenario, new content, no matter how appealing the topics, is no more likely to improve the profession than did the content being replaced. I believe that there is evidence of this dynamic already in the more appropriate knowledge areas being mined today (e.g., ethics, social context, critical theory, and so forth) (see, for example, Willower, 1998, on postmodernism).

Keeping the spotlight focused on academic knowledge also leads to, or at least reinforces, the belief that better theories will be the savior of educational practice. That is, if we can just develop better theories, the educational world would be a better place, educational administration programs would be stronger, and graduates would be more effective leaders. This entire argument is a little like the case for cold fusion. The problem is that the development of better or more refined or more elegant theories in and of itself will have almost no impact on the practice of school administration. Such work has not had much impact in the past, it is not having much influence now, and it is unlikely to be more efficacious in the future (Bridges, 1982; Hills, 1975). Worse, this work often reinforces the centrality of the university, makes knowledge an end rather than a means for improvement, privileges knowledge over values, and, quite frankly, diverts energy from other much more needed work.

All of this has led us to spend considerable time constructing what can only be labeled charitably as "the bridge to nowhere." That is, having made academic knowledge the coin of the realm and seeing its inability to penetrate the world of schooling, we have been forced to develop strategies to try to transport knowledge from the academic to the practice community. The focus is on the development of knowledge in one place and the transfer of it to another. I think that if we have learned anything over the last 30 years, it is that this bridge metaphor is largely inappropriate. When one examines this issue in a clear light, one really does not see much interest in actually doing the work necessary to build this bridge. People on both sides of the river seem to be fairly content where they are. What's more, if through some type of magic, the bridge were ever constructed, I do not think it would end up carrying much traffic. Trying to link theory and practice has been for the last 30 years a little like attempting to start a car with a dead battery. The odds are fairly long that the engine will ever turn over.

A related case can also be developed against making practice-based knowledge the gold standard for reform. The central problem here is that the practice of educational leadership has very little to do with either education or leadership. Thus weaving together threads from practice to form a post-theory tapestry of school administration is a very questionable idea. A number of analysts have concluded that schools are organized and managed as if we had no knowledge of either student learning (Goodlad, 1984) or the needs of professional adults (Clark & Meloy, 1989; Weick & McDaniel, 1989). Others have discovered that schools are administered in ways such that educational goals are undermined and learning is hindered (McNeil, 1988; Sizer, 1984; Wise, 1989), especially for lower ability students (Cuban, 1989; Murphy & Hallinger, 1989). Still others have built a fairly strong case over the last 70 years that the profession has drawn energy almost exclusively from the taproot of management and the ideology of corporate America (Newlon, 1934; Callahan, 1962; Boyan, 1963; Murphy, 1992). The message, to perhaps state the obvious, is that this practice knowledge is not exactly the raw material with which to build a future for the profession.

The point in this section is not to dismiss knowledge as unimportant. Scientific inquiry, scholarly insights, and craft knowledge will offer useful substance in the process of forging a post-scientific era of school administration. As a matter of fact, we will not be able to create a future without these critical components. What we are suggesting, however, is that if we expect a concerted effort primarily on this front to provide sufficient material to construct a new profession, we will likely be disappointed. Worse, over-reliance on the cultivation of knowledge, either in the academic or practice vineyards, is likely to exacerbate deeply rooted problems in the profession. And what is true for a singular focus on content holds, we argue, for methods, processes, and administrator roles and functions.

A Collective Attack

If none of the four traditional ways we have thought about the profession looks promising as a vehicle to help us escape what Campbell and his colleagues (1987) refer to as a nontranquil scene in school administration, will not continued progress on all fronts guide us to a successful landing in a postbehavioral science era? It is possible, but I think not likely. The issue of dominance never really fades away, although it is possible to reenvision the evolution of productive tension among ideas that in turn fosters cycles of creative dialogue and action. While this is possible, the history of the field would, I think, encourage us to not be too sanguine about this collective strategy. There is little room to expect anything similar to unified action to result from this approach. Absent that, it seems more likely that we will have continued fragmentation (Boyd & Crowson, 1981; Immegart, 1977) and the absence of synergy necessary for the profession to progress to the next stage of development.

In addition, the more recent evidence on this strategy—what Donmoyer (1999) in his chapter in the just released Handbook of Research on Educational Administration calls the "big tent" (p. 30) philosophy and what Campbell and his colleagues (1987) characterize as "paradigm enlargement" (p. 209)—is not encouraging either. After 15 years or more of following this approach, school administration today looks a good deal like Weick's (1976) famous tilted soccer field or, perhaps even more aptly, like the typical American high school of the last half of the twentieth century, what Powell, Farrar, and Cohen (1985) labeled the "shopping malls." We have responded to the challenges of purpose and development largely by ignoring them, at least by failing to thoughtfully grapple with them. We have done exactly what high schools have done; we have created a plethora of specialty shops for everyone who wants to move into the big tent. And like the players and fans in Weicks' soccer game, we have allowed everyone to establish their own rules and their own definitions of success. Everyone has his or her own booth in the tent and goes about his or her business with very few tethers to anything like a core, with little concern for coherence, largely unencumbered by mutually forged benchmarks and standards, with considerable thoughtfulness—or at least politeness—and with very little real conflict. Autonomy and civility rule. School administration as a profession stagnates.

Doing Nothing

Here is the question which now surfaces. If traditional frameworks that define the field offer insufficient force—either on a strategy-by-strategy or on a collective basis—then to redefine the profession, where do we turn? Before moving on to Dewey and Kliebard and the principle of correspondence, let me review a third possibility that is seen increasingly in the literature. In short, it would be to dismiss the notion that an anchor for the profession is a worthwhile idea. Certainly the discussion of a center or a core for school administration will cause consternation if not alarm among some colleagues, especially to the extent that it highlights what Foster (1998) labels "the certainties that surround our field: our beliefs in instructional leadership . . . [and] in productivity as a goal" (p. 295). The very concept of a core carries the potential to privilege certain ideas while marginalizing others. Let me acknowledge at the outset that this is a quite legitimate concern and one that we had to struggle to address in developing the Interstate School Leaders Licensure Standards for School Leaders. Yet the concern is not sufficient, at least from where I sit, to negate action. I agree with Donmoyer (1999) and Evers and Lakomski (1996b) that this third avenue of response—rejection of the possibility of a center—is likely to lead to, to borrow a phrase from Evers and Lakomski (1996a), "skepticism and enfeebling relativism" (p. 342).

I would suggest that recognizing that all knowledge and action are political does not mean that all knowledge and action are equal. I believe that Willower (1998) provides the high ground here when he reminds us that "some constructions of reality are better than others" (p. 450). I would go further and suggest that in the world of ideas, diversity is not in and of itself a virtue. More important, I would encourage us to be skeptical of the viewpoint that a core will only advantage some ideas and marginalize others. Centers can empower as well as constrain. We hear too little of this dimension of coherence in our literature.

A Principle of Correspondence

> During a period of extraordinary environmental turbulence, a concern for practical relevance shows itself both in the press for a paradigm shift and at the core of an emerging synthesis.
>
> (Boyan, 1981, p. 11)

Viewing the Concept

So far, we have argued that doing nothing—giving up or resisting the search for a unifying center to the profession—is not a wise idea, nor is it necessary to protect the interests of scholars with diverse viewpoints. We have also suggested that a concerted effort to move to a new era for school administration by focusing on any given element of the professional framework, i.e., the production of new theoretical knowledge, will not likely serve us well either. Finally, we maintained that an eclectic or big tent strategy in this era of ferment is equally as likely to be ribboned with problems as to be marked with benefits. What is left? It seems to me that one answer—and the one I will advocate here—lies in the work of Herbert Kliebard (1995) in the area of curriculum. Building on the work of Dewey, Kliebard introduces a patched-together concept called "principle of correspondence" (p. 57). It is his way of describing Dewey's efforts to recast problems away from selecting among alternatives and toward "the critical problem of finding a principle" (p. 57) that provides correspondence between the valued dimensions of a profession. For us, it provides a way of recasting a dilemma that by definition is not solvable (Cuban, 1990, 1992) into a problem that is, or at least may be, solvable.[3] In effect, it provides a fifth way of defining the profession—a "synthesizing paradigm" (Boyan, 1981, p. 10) that focuses on defining aims rather than stirring the academic caldron or parsing out administrative activities, one that spotlights what Boyd (1983) refers to as "goal-directed management" (p. 4).

Developing Standards

How can we frame a principle of correspondence to meet our needs? There is a good deal of open space here. However, it probably is desirable to hold any principle of correspondence to the following seven standards:

- It should acknowledge and respect the diversity of work afoot in educational administration yet exercise sufficient magnetic force—or what Boyan (1981) refers to as "intellectual magnetism" (p. 12)—to pull much of that work in certain directions.
- It should be informed by and help organize the labor and the ideas from the current era of ferment.
- It should promote the development of a body of ideas and concepts that define school administration as an applied field.
- It should provide hope for fusing the enduring dualisms described by Campbell and his colleagues (1987) that have bedeviled the profession for so long (e.g., knowledge vs. values, academic knowledge vs. practice knowledge) and should, to quote from Evers and Lakomski (1996a), provide a "powerful touchstone for adjudicating rival approaches to administrative research" (p. 343).
- It should provide a crucible where civility among shop merchants in the big tent gives way to productive dialogue and exchange—to something akin to the conceptions of community so beautifully captured by Furman (1998) and by Beck and Foster (1999).
- It should be clear about the outcomes upon which to forge a redefined profession of school administration; in other words it should provide the vehicle for linking the profession to valued outcomes.

That is:

- It should establish a framework that ensures that the "standard for what is taught lies not with bodies of subject matter" (Kliebard, 1995, p. 72) but with valued ends.

School Improvement as a Model

School management and the preparation of school administrators need to be vigorously redirected toward the enhancement of the outcomes of schooling for children.

(Boyd, 1983, p. 4)

Where might we find such a principle of correspondence? A number of thoughtful colleagues have provided frameworks that offer the potential to meet Kliebard's (1995) criterion of "reconstructing the questions as to present new [alternatives]" (p. 49) and that fit at least some of the standards outlined above. My purpose here is not to develop a comprehensive listing. Nor is it to evaluate each of the examples. The limited objective is simply to show how some colleagues in the profession have made progress in helping us exit the current era of turmoil by employing strategies that fit into the broad categorization of principles of correspondence.

A number of such efforts stand out. At least four with a knowledge-base tincture deserve mention. To begin with, there is the recent work of Griffiths (1995, 1997) on what he refers to as "theoretical pluralism" (1997, p. 371), but theoretical pluralism that is intrinsically yoked to problems of practice. There is also the scholarship of Willower (1996) on naturalistic philosophy or naturalistic pragmatism. A related line of work which might be best labeled "pragmatism" has been developed by Hoy (1996). The scholarship of Evers and Lakomski (1996b) on "developing a systematic new science of administration" (p. 379)—what they describe as "naturalistic coherentism" (p. 385)—is a fourth example of a principle of correspondence at work. The most important example with a practice focus is the work of Bridges and Hallinger (1992, 1995) on problem-based learning. Ideas with feet in both the academic and practice camps have been provided by Donmoyer (1999) who introduces the concept of "utilitarianism" as a potential way to redefine debate and action in the profession and by Murphy (1992) who discusses a "dialectic" (p. 67) strategy.

Again, my purpose here is simply to reveal how colleagues have begun doing some of the heavy lifting to help us in the process of conceptualizing new ways to think about recentering school administration. Individually and collectively, they offer bundles of ideas and sets of elements—ideas such as a problem-solving focus, emphasis on the concrete, highlighting the sense of possibilities—that offer real promise to the profession.

At the same time, each of the approaches listed above falls short when measured against the standards for a principle of correspondence. In addition, with the possible exception of the latter two, each remains too closely associated with one or the other of the traditional ways in which we have framed the profession, in nearly every case a focus on knowledge production. If we take a step back, I think that we can build on these and other breakout ideas to move a little closer to our goal.

The question at hand is as follows: When we layer knowledge about the shortcomings of the profession (Section II) onto understandings developing in the current era of ferment (Sections III and IV) and then apply the notion of a principle of correspondence with its imbedded standards (Section V), what emerges? It seems to me that three powerful synthetic paradigms become visible: democratic community, social justice, and school improvement. Each of these offers the potential to capture many of the benefits revealed by the standards and, in the process, to borrow a phrase from Fullan, to reculture the profession of school administration. In the remainder of this paper, I focus on what it means to rebuild school administration on one of these principles—school improvement.

Before I do that, however, let me answer the question of why I picked door number three. To begin with, and in contrast to some of my colleagues (see for example Foster, 1998; Scheurich, 1995), I do not see major conflicts between these principles. As a matter of fact, I suspect that they can be nested without a great deal of discomfort. At the same time, for the field of school administration as an applied discipline, I believe that issues of community building and social reconstruction nest better within the principle of school improvement than vice versa. There is a danger in pushing any of these principles to the forefront. But, a review of the literature in our field leads me to conclude that school improvement has the intellectual magnetism to keep social justice in its orbit; whereas the opposite is open to question. In effect, democratic community and social justice complete our understanding of school improvement. The obverse may not hold. Second, I believe that school improvement as a principle of correspondence has a broader appeal, that is it is more accessible, to the practice and policy domains of the profession. It will be the most effective of the three, I believe, in rebalancing the relationship between the academic and practice wings of the profession. Third, I believe that school improvement fits the standards for a principle of correspondence more fully than do the alternatives. Fourth, it addresses what Halpin (1957) described during the early phase of the theory movement as the most fundamental concern of the field—a focus on the foundations of school effectiveness—a call that was echoed by Boyan (1963) in the 1960s, expanded on in the 1970s by Erickson (1977, 1979), and clarified in the 1980s and 1990s by a number of colleagues in the educational leadership field. Finally, I find school improvement to be such a valuable synthetic design because it links with my own research-based understanding of school administration and educational leadership.

Consequences

A few points are worthy of note before we explore the implications of having school improvement and education form the new foundations of the profession. First, analysis of the last dominant era of the profession, the behavioral science phase, should lead us to be humble in our pronouncements. It was a fairly heady time for claims (Goldhammer, 1983; Murphy, 1992), and the outcomes fell considerably short of the expectations—or as Campbell and his colleagues (1987) have deduced, the behavioral science movement "produced more heat than light" (p. 193). Second, as noted in the introductory section of the paper, changing the taproot, for instance, changing from management to education, can have profound implications for educational administration. Yet it guarantees nothing. School improvement as a principle of correspondence offers considerable promise to educational administration. Yet whether we achieve that potential will remain an open question for some time.

The principle of correspondence we suggest argues for school improvement as the new center of gravity for school administration, education as the foundation for the profession, and applied knowledge as the fuel to make the system run (see Table 1). At the most fundamental level, this new center holds, as Evans (1991) nicely phrases it, that "the deep significance of the task of the school administrator is to be found in the pedagogical ground of its vocation" (p. 17). Thus, at the most basic level, the consequence of having a school improvement core, as Foster (1988) has argued, is that "educational administration must find its mission and purpose in the purpose of schooling generally" (p. 69), a point echoed by Sergiovanni (1993) and others.

It means, as my colleague Phil Hallinger and I have argued over the years, that the profession of educational administration must be, first and foremost, educationally grounded. It honors what Iwanicki (in press) calls "learning-focused" leadership. An educational focus does much to allay fears raised by colleagues like Guba (1960), Erickson (1977, 1979), Bates (1984), and others over the last 40 years and to reverse what Callahan (1962) labeled an "American tragedy" (p. 246).

Privileging school improvement also suggests that "understandings of administration and leading will need to change" (Prestine, 1995, p. 140). More specifically, it legitimates Bill Greenfield's (1995) proposition that "although numerous sources might be cultivated, norms rooted in the ethos and culture of teaching as a profession provide the most effective basis for leadership in a school" (p. 75). It infuses what Evans (1998) nicely describes as "the pedagogic motive" (p. 41) into the lifeblood of school leadership. In short, it forces us to rethink the meaning of leadership. It requires, as Rowan (1995) has recorded, that leaders be "pioneers in the development and management of new forms of instructional practice in schools, and [that] they . . . [develop] a thorough understanding of the rapidly evolving body of research on learning and teaching that motivate these new practices" (p. 116). Elsewhere, we, and others, have outlined what educationally grounded leadership entails (see Hallinger & Murphy, 1985, 1986; Murphy, Hallinger, Weil, & Mitman, 1983; Murphy 1990d, 1994). The important point here, as Leithwood, Leonard, and Sharatt (1998) recently concluded, is the educational ground. Labels such as instructional and transformational leadership are of secondary importance.

Reformulating the foundations of the profession to school improvement, education, and applied knowledge also implies a reconceptualization of the preparation and pro-

TABLE I. Rethinking the Center for the Profession of School Administration.

Time Frame	Center of Gravity	Foundation	Engine
1820–1900 Ideology	Philosophy	Religion	Values
1901–1945 Prescription	Management	Administrative Functions	Practice Knowledge
1946–1985 Behavioral Science	Social Sciences	Academic Disciplines	Theoretical Knowledge
1986 ! Dialectic	School Improvement	Education	Applied Knowledge

fessional development functions in school administration. As the National Commission on Teaching and America's Future (1996) concludes, the onus will be to "prepare and retrain principals who understand teaching and learning and who can lead high-performing schools" (p. 28). Or as Evans (1998) postulates, with school improvement as the operational principle of correspondence, "we need to wonder how we can develop educators, especially principals, who can think educationally, and not just managerially, about life" (p. 46). For a variety of reasons, which we have described elsewhere (Murphy, Hallinger, Lotto, & Miller, 1987), this shift represents a daunting task for the profession of school administration in general and for university professors in particular.

Nonetheless, it is not difficult to tease out some of the alterations in how we conceptualize the education of school leaders that result from reanchoring the profession around school improvement. Three changes, in particular, stand out. To begin with, a greater proportion of time than has been the case traditionally (Murphy et al., 1987) will need to be devoted to issues of learning and teaching and to the principles of school improvement. The behavioral science era brought law, economics, sociology, anthropology, political science, and related disciplines to our preparation programs. With school improvement as the core, new sets of frameworks will occupy center stage. Learning theory, school change, curriculum theory, assessment, and data analysis strategies are areas that come readily to mind.

Second, and equally important, much of what currently unfolds in preparation programs will likely be redirected, i.e., linked to larger purposes and underlying values that characterize school improvement. Existing content will both draw meaning from and operate more explicitly in the service of school improvement. This is a good example of the channeling function of the core, which we described earlier in our treatment of standards for principles of correspondence. It is perhaps most evident today in the areas of educational finance and in the policy domain of the profession.

In addition, a reformulation of school administration will influence the venue of learning activities in preparation programs. School improvement research—whether from the emerging body of research on professional development (Sparks & Hirsh, 1997), from the work on leadership as an organizational phenomena (Pounder, Ogawa, & Adams, 1995), from the growing understanding of professional communities (Louis & Kruse, 1996), from work on school change (Fullan, 1991), or from scholarship on whole-school reform (Stringfield, Ross, & Smith 1996)—helps us see that a good deal of the learning in preparation programs needs to be school-based.

Finally, it should be obvious that the research agenda of a regrounded profession will be pulled in some new directions. While fragmentation in the research domain is not a critical problem (Boyan, 1981), it does complicate the task of accumulating wisdom. It also makes it cumbersome to marshal concerted initiatives on the problems faced by practicing administrators and to address the needs of those in policy positions. While it is difficult to discern the full storyline here, some strands of the narrative are visible. First, a research agenda growing from the soil of school improvement has considerable potential to link micro-, mid-, and macro-level theory building. Second, it offers a useful avenue to provide "additional meaning" (Campbell et al., 1987, p. 207) to the various lines of work in the profession by linking them to school operations (Campbell et al., 1987). Third, a research agenda grounded in school improvement will direct energy toward the repair of two of the most critical flaws in the profession: the lack of attention to the core mission of our industry (Boyan, 1963; Murphy, 1992) and our "tendency to neglect the careful tracing of connections between organizational variables and student outcomes" (Erickson, 1979, p. 12).

VI. CONCLUSION

It is perhaps best to close this manuscript the way we began, by reviewing the central theses and exposing the logic we pursued to illustrate them. We opened with the claim that for the past 15 years, we have been in an era of ferment in school administration. We revealed how this phase in our development has been marked with considerable energy and defined by numerous initiatives in all domains of the profession. Unfortunately, rather than helping us forge a consensus on the foundations of a postbehavioral science era for school administration, much of the work has led to the fragmentation of the profession on an array of dimensions.

For reasons outlined more fully above, we argued that the notion of a center or core for school administration is a good idea. We then described the array of strategies that have given meaning to the profession over time. We concluded that none of these approaches individually offer real promise of a breakout. We illustrated this proposition with reference to the most popular strategy currently in operation, i.e., attempts to redefine the profession through the development of a more theoretically sound knowledge base. We also concluded that a collective attack employing the full assortment of methods of understanding school administration will more likely lead to increased paradigm enlargement than to professional coherence.

In order to address the issue of a postscientific era of school administration more productively, the concept of principles of correspondence was introduced. We based that discussion on a set of standards that might allow us to weigh the value of various formulations of these principles. We also touched briefly on examples of scholarship that can be characterized as principle development work. From there, we developed the case for school improvement as an appropriate core for the profession of school administration in a postscientific era. We closed by revealing how this regrounding strategy channels thinking about the profession writ large as well as ideology in school administration about leadership, leadership training, and research.

NOTES

1. Sections 2 through 4 of this paper are drawn from Murphy and Forsyth (1999). For a more complete discussion of the issues raised there, see chapters 1, 2, and 7 of that volume.
2. Willower and Forsyth (1999), while acknowledging the diversity in the field, argue that "the unifying elements deserve greater attention than they have received" (p. 20).
3. This represents a shift from how I saw the resolution to the era of ferment in my earlier work (1992, 1993). In those pieces, I argued that a dialectic dynamic that fused conceptions of school administration dominating the landscape from 1990–1941 and from 1946–1985 would prevail and a new era of school administration would follow. While school improvement as a principle of correspondence is consistent with the outcome of the dialectic hypothesis, the process taken to get there is somewhat different.

REFERENCES

Achilles, C. M. (1984, Fall). Forecast: Stormy weather ahead in educational administration. Issues in Education. 2(2), 127–135.

Achilles, C. M. (1994, February). Searching for the golden fleece: The epic struggle continues. Educational Administration Quarterly, 30(1), 6–26.

American Association of Colleges for Teacher Education. (1988). School leadership preparation: A preface for action. Washington, DC: Author.

American Association of School Administrators. (1960). Professional administrators for America's schools (Thirty-eighth American Association of School Administrators Yearbook). Washington, DC: National Educational Administration.

Anderson, G. L. (1990, February). Toward a critical constructionist approach to school administration: Invisibility, legitimation, and the study of non-events. Educational Administration Quarterly, 26(1), 38–59.

Anderson, W. A., & Lonsdale, R. C. (1957). Learning administrative behavior. In R. F. Campbell & R. T. Gregg (Eds.), Administrative behavior in education (pp. 426–463). New York: Harper.

Bailey, R. W. (1987). Uses and misuses of privatization. In S. H. Hanke (Ed.), Proceedings of the Academy of Political Science: Vol. 36, No. 3. Prospects for privatization (pp. 138–152). Montpelier, VT: Capital City Press.

Barber, B. R. (1984). Strong democracy: Participatory politics for a new age. Berkeley: University of California Press.

Barth, R. S. (1986). On sheep and goats and school reform. Phi Delta Kappan, 68(4), 293–296.

Bates, R. J. (1984). Toward a critical practice of educational administration. In T. J. Sergiovanni & J. E. Corbally (Eds.), <u>Leadership and organizational culture: New perspectives on administrative theory and practice</u> (pp. 260–274). Urbana: University of Illinois Press.

Bauman, P. C. (1996, November). Governing education in an antigovernment environment. <u>Journal of School Leadership, 6</u>(6), 625–643.

Beck, L. G. (1994). <u>Reclaiming educational administration as a caring profession.</u> New York: Teachers College Press.

Beck, L. G., & Foster, W. (1999). Administration and community: Considering challenges, exploring possibilities. In J. Murphy & K. S. Louis (Eds.), <u>Handbook of research on educational administration</u> (2nd ed., pp. 337–358). San Francisco: Jossey-Bass.

Beck, L. G., & Murphy, J. (1993). <u>Understanding the principalship: Metaphorical themes 1920s-1990s.</u> New York: Teachers College Press.

Beck, L. G., & Murphy, J. (1994). <u>Ethics in educational leadership programs: An expanding role.</u> Newbury Park, CA: Corwin Press.

Beck, L. G., Murphy, J., & Associates. (1998). <u>Ethics in educational leadership preparation programs: Emerging models.</u> Newbury Park, CA: Corwin Press.

Beers, D., & Ellig, J. (1994). An economic view of the effectiveness of public and private schools. In S. Hakim, P. Seidenstat, & G. W. Bowman (Eds.), <u>Privatizing education and educational choice: Concepts, plans, and experiences</u> (pp. 19–38). Westport, CT: Praeger.

Björk, L. G., & Ginsberg, R. (1995, February). Principles of reform and reforming principal training: A theoretical perspective. <u>Educational Administration Quarterly, 31</u>(1), 11–37.

Blumberg, A., & Blumberg, P. (1985). <u>The school superintendent: Living with conflict.</u> New York: Columbia University, Teachers College.

Boyan, N. J. (1963). Common and specialized learnings for administrators and supervisors: Some problems and issues. In D. J. Leu & H. C. Rudman (Eds.), <u>Preparation programs for school administrators: Common and specialized learnings</u> (pp. 1–23). East Lansing: Michigan State University.

Boyan, N. J. (1981, February). Follow the leader: Commentary on research in educational administration. <u>Educational Research, 10</u>(2), 6–13, 21.

Boyan, N. J. (1988a). Describing and explaining administrator behavior. In N. J. Boyan (Ed.), <u>Handbook of research on educational administration</u> (pp. 77–97). New York: Longman.

Boyan, N. J. (Ed.). (1988b). <u>Handbook of research on educational administration.</u> New York: Longman.

Boyd, W. L. (1983, March). What school administrators do and don't do: Implications for effective schools. <u>The Canadian Administrator, 22</u>(6), 1–4.

Boyd, W. L., & Crowson, R. L. (1981). The changing conception and practice of public school administration. In D. C. Berliner (Ed.), <u>Review of research in higher education</u> (Vol. 9, pp. 311–373). Washington, DC: American Educational Research Association.

Brent, B. O. (1998, October). Should graduate training in educational administration be required for principal certification? Existing evidence suggests the answer is no. <u>Teaching in Educational Administration, 5</u>(2), 1, 3–4, 7–10.

Bridges, E. M. (1977). The nature of leadership. In L. L. Cunningham, W. G. Hack, & R. O. Nystrand (Eds.), Educational administration: The developing decades (pp. 202–230). Berkeley: McCutchan.

Bridges, E. M. (1982, Summer). Research on the school administrator: The state of the art. Educational Administration Quarterly, 18(3), 12–33.

Bridges, E. M., & Hallinger, P. (1992). Problem-based learning for administrators. Eugene: University of Oregon, ERIC Clearinghouse on Educational Management.

Bridges, E. M., & Hallinger, P. (1993). Problem-based learning in medical and managerial education. In P. Hallinger, K. Leithwood, & J. Murphy (Eds.), Cognitive perspectives on educational leadership (pp. 253–267). New York: Teachers College Press.

Bridges, E. M. & Hallinger, P. (1995). Implementing problem-based learning in leadership development. Eugene: University of Oregon, ERIC Clearinghouse on Educational Management.

Brieschke, P. A. (1990, November). The administration in fiction: Using the novel to teach educational administration. Educational Administration Quarterly, 26(4), 376–393.

Burke, C. (1992). Devolution of responsibility to Queensland schools: Clarifying the rhetoric critiquing the reality. Journal of Educational Administration, 30(4), 33–52.

Callahan, R. E. (1962). Education and the cult of efficiency. Chicago: University of Chicago Press.

Campbell, R. F., Fleming, T., Newell, L., & Bennion, J. W. (1987). A history of thought and practice in educational administration. New York: Teachers College Press.

Candoli, I. C. (1991). School system administration: A strategic plan for site-based management. Lancaster, PA: Technomic.

Castetter, W. B. (1986). The personnel function in educational administration (4th ed.). New York: Macmillan.

Chase, F. S. (1960). The administrator as implementor of the goals of education for our time. In R. F. Campbell & J. M. Lipham (Eds.), Administrative theory as a guide to action (pp. 191–201). Chicago: University of Chicago, Midwest Administration Center.

Cibulka, J. G. (1999). Ideological lenses for interpreting political and economic changes affecting schooling. In J. Murphy & K. S. Louis (Eds.), Handbook of research on educational administration (2nd ed., pp. 163–182). San Francisco: Jossey-Bass.

Clark, D. L. (1988, June). Charge to the study group of the National Policy Board for Educational Administration. Unpublished paper.

Clark, D. L. (1997, March). Searching for authentic educational leadership in university graduate programs and with public school colleagues. Paper presented at the annual meeting of the American Educational Research Association, Chicago, IL.

Clark, D. L., & Meloy, J. M. (1989). Renouncing bureaucracy: A democratic structure for leadership in schools: In T. J. Sergiovanni & J. A. Moore (Eds.), Schooling for tomorrow: Directing reform to issues that count (pp. 272–294). Boston: Allyn & Bacon.

Cohen, D. K. (1988, September). Teaching practice. (Issue Paper 88–3). East Lansing: Michigan State University, National Center for Research on Teacher Education.

Consortium on Productivity in the Schools. (1995). Using what we have to get the schools we need. New York: Columbia University, Teachers College, The Institute on Education and the Economy.

Cooper, B. S., & Boyd, W. L. (1987). The evolution of training for school administrators. In J. Murphy & P. Hallinger (Eds.), Approaches to administrative training (pp. 3–27). Albany: State University of New York Press.

Cooper, B. S., & Muth, R. (1994). Internal and external barriers to change in departments of educational administration. In T. A. Mulkeen, N. H. Cambron-McCabe, & B. J. Anderson, (Eds.), Democratic leadership: The changing context of administrative preparation (pp. 61–81). Norwood, NJ: Ablex.

Cremin, L. A. (1961). The transformation of the school: Progressivism in American education 1876–1957. New York: Vintage.

Cronin, T. E. (1989). Direct democracy: The politics of initiative, referendum, and recall. Cambridge: Harvard University Press.

Crowson, R. L., & McPherson, R. B. (1987). The legacy of the theory movement: Learning from the new tradition. In J. Murphy & P. Hallinger (Eds.), Approaches to administrative training in education (pp. 45–64). Albany: State University of New York Press.

Cuban, L. (1976). Urban school of chiefs under fire. Chicago: University of Chicago Press.

Cuban, L. (1989). The "at-risk" label and the problem of urban school reform. Phi Delta Kappan, 70(10), 780–784, 799.

Cuban, L. (1990, October). Reforming school administration: Theory and practice. Paper presented at the annual meeting of the University Council for Educational Administration, Pittsburgh, PA.

Cuban, L. (1992, January-February). Managing dilemmas while building professional communities. Educational Researcher, 21(1), 4–11.

Culbertson, J. A. (1963). Common and specialized content in the preparation of administrators. In D. J. Leu & H. C. Rudman (Eds.), Preparation programs for administrators: Common and specialized learnings (pp. 34–60). East Lansing: Michigan State University.

Culbertson, J. A. (1964). The preparation of administrators. In D. E. Griffiths (Ed.), Behavioral science in educational administration (Sixty-third National Society for the Study of Education Yearbook, Part II, pp. 303–330). Chicago: University of Chicago Press.

Culbertson, J. A. (1965). Trends and issues in the development of a science of administration. In Center for the Advanced Study of Educational Administration, Perspectives on Educational Administration and the Behavioral Sciences (pp. 3–22). Eugene: University of Oregon, Center for the Advanced Study of Educational Administration.

Dahrendorf, R. (1995, Summer). A precarious balance: Economic opportunity, civil society, and political liberty. The Responsive Community, 13–39.

Daresh, J. C. (1989). Supervision as a proactive process. New York: Longman.

Deal, T. E., & Peterson, K. D. (1990). The principal's role in shaping school culture. Washington, DC: U.S. Department of Education, Office of Educational Research and Improvement.

Donahue, J. D. (1989). The privatization decision: Public ends, private means. New York: Basic Books.

Donmoyer, R. (1999). The continuing quest for a knowledge base: 1976–1998. In J. Murphy & K. S. Louis (Eds.), Handbook of research on educational administration (2nd ed., pp. 25–43). San Francisco: Jossey-Bass.

Donmoyer, R., Imber, M., & Scheurich, J. J. (Eds.). (1995). The knowledge base in educational administration: Multiple perspectives. Albany: The State University of New York Press.

Elmore, R. F. (1989, March). Models of restructured schools. Paper presented at the annual meeting of the American Educational Research Association, San Francisco.

Elmore, R. F. (1993). School decentralization: Who gains? Who loses? In J. Hannaway & M. Carnoy (Eds.), Decentralization and school improvement (pp. 33–54). San Francisco: Jossey-Bass.

Elshtain, J. B. (1995). Democracy on trial. New York: Basic Books.

English, F. W. (1997, January). The cupboard is bare: The postmodern critique of educational administration. Journal of School Leadership, 7(1), 4–26.

English, F. W., & Steffy, B. F. (1997, February). Using film to teach leadership in educational administration. Educational Administration Quarterly, 33(1), 107–115.

Erickson, D. A. (1977). An overdue paradigm shift in educational administration, or how can we get that idiot off the freeway. In L. L. Cunningham, W. G. Hack, & R. O. Nystrand (Eds.), Educational administration: The developing decades (pp. 114–143). Berkeley: McCutchan.

Erickson, D. A. (1979, March). Research on educational administration: The state-of-the-art. Educational Researcher, 8, 9–14.

Erlandson, D. A., & Witters-Churchill, L. (1988, March). Design of the Texas NASSP study. Paper presented at the annual convention of the National Association of Secondary School Principals.

Evans, R. (1991, April). Ministrative insight: Educational administration as pedagogic practice. Paper presented at the annual meeting of the American Educational Research Association, Chicago.

Evans, R. (1998, Summer). Do intentions matter? Questioning the text of a high school principal. Journal of Educational Administration and Foundations, 13(1), 30–51.

Evers, C. W., & Lakomski, G. (1996a, August). Postpositivist conceptions of science in educational administration: An introduction. Educational Administration Quarterly, 32(3), 341–343.

Evers, C. W., & Lakomski, G. (1996b, August). Science in educational administration: A postpositivist conception. Educational Administration Quarterly, 32(32), 379–402.

Farquhar, R. H. (1981, June). Preparing educational administrators for ethical practice. The Alberta Journal of Educational Research, 27(2), 192–204.

Forsyth, P. (1999). A brief history of scholarship on educational administration. In J. Murphy & P. Forsyth (Eds.), Educational administration: A decade of reform. Newbury Park, CA: Corwin Press.

Forsyth, P., & Murphy, J. (1999). A decade of changes: Emerging themes. In J. Murphy & P. Forsyth (Eds.), Educational administration: A decade of reform. Newbury Park, CA: Corwin Press.

Foster, W. (1988). Educational administration: A critical appraisal. In D. E. Griffiths, R. T. Stout, & P. B. Forsyth (Eds.), Leaders for America's schools: The report and papers of the National Commission on Excellence in Educational Administration (pp. 68–81). Berkeley: McCutchan.

Foster, W. (1998, August). Editor's foreword. Educational Administration Quarterly, 34(3), 294–297.

Fullan, M. (1991). The new meaning of educational change. New York: Teachers College Press.

Furman, G. C. (1998, August). Postmodernism and community in schools: Unraveling the paradox. Educational Administration Quarterly, 34(3), 298–328.

Garms, W. I., Guthrie, J. W., & Pierce, L. C. (1978). School finance: The economics and politics of public education. Englewood Cliffs, NJ: Prentice-Hall.

Gerritz, W., Koppich, J., & Guthrie, J. (1984, November). Preparing California school leaders: An analysis of supply, demand, and training. Berkeley: University of California, Berkeley, Policy Analysis for California Education.

Goldhammer, K. (1983, Summer). Evolution in the profession. Educational Administration Quarterly, 19(3), 249–272.

Goldring, E. B., & Rallis, S. F. (1993). Principals of dynamic schools: Taking charge of change. Newbury Park, CA: Corwin Press.

Goodlad, J. I. (1984). A place called school: Prospects for the future. New York: McGraw-Hill.

Gottfried, P. (1993). The conservative movement (Rev. ed.). New York: Twayne.

Graff, O. B., & Street, C. M. (1957). Developing a value framework for educational administration. In R. F. Campbell & R. T. Gregg (Eds.), Administrative behavior in education (pp. 120–152). New York: Harper.

Greenfield, T. B. (1975). Theory about organization: A new perspective and its implications for schools. In M. G. Hughes (Ed.), Administering education: International challenge (pp. 71–99). London: Athlone.

Greenfield, T. B. (1988). The decline and fall of science in educational administration. In D. E. Griffiths, R. T. Stout, & P. B. Forsyth (Eds.), Leaders for America's schools: The report and papers of the National Commission on Excellence in Educational Administration (pp. 131–159). Berkeley: McCutchan.

Greenfield, W. D. (1995, February). Toward a theory of school administration: The centrality of leadership. Educational Administration Quarterly, 31(1), 61–85.

Gregg, R. T. (1969). Preparation of administrators. In R. L. Ebel (Ed.), Encyclopedia of educational research (4th ed., pp. 993–1004). London: MacMillan.

Griffiths, D. E. (1958). Administration as decision-making. In A. W. Halpin (Ed.), Administrative theory in education. Chicago: University of Chicago, Midwest Administration Center.

Griffiths, D. E. (1988a). Administrative theory. In N. J. Boyan (Ed.), Handbook of research on educational administration (pp. 27–51). New York: Longman.

Griffiths, D. E. (1988b). Educational administration: Reform PDQ or RIP (Occasional paper, No. 8312). Tempe, AZ: University Council for Educational Administration.

Griffiths, D. E. (Ed.). (1991). Special issue: Non-traditional research methods in educational administration. Educational Administration quarterly, 27(3).

Griffiths, D. E. (1995). Theoretical pluralism in educational administration. In R. Donmoyer, M. Imber, & J. J. Scheurich (Eds.), The knowledge base in educational administration: Multiple perspectives (pp. 300–309). Albany: State University of New York Press.

Griffiths, D. E. (1997, October). The case for theoretical pluralism. Educational Management & Administration, 25(4), 371–380.

Griffiths, D. E. (1999). Preface. In J. Murphy & P. Forsyth (Eds.), Educational administration: A decade of reform. Newbury Park, CA: Corwin Press.

Griffiths, D. E., Stout, R. T., & Forsyth, P. B. (Eds.) (1988a). Leaders for America's schools: The report and papers of the National Commission on Excellence in Educational Administration. Berkeley: McCutchan.

Griffiths, D. E., Stout, R. T., & Forsyth, P. B. (1988b). The preparation of educational administrators. In D. E. Griffiths, R. T. Stout, & P. B. Forsyth (Eds.), Leaders for America's schools: The report and papers of the National Commission on Excellence in Educational Administration (pp. 284–304). Berkeley: McCutchan.

Guba, E. G. (1960). Research in internal administration—what do we know? In R. F. Campbell & J. M. Lipham (Eds.), Administrative theory as a guide to action (pp. 113–141). Chicago: University of Chicago, Midwest Administration Center.

Guthrie, J. W. (1986, December). School-based management: The next needed education reform. Phi Delta Kappan, 68(4), 305–309.

Guthrie, J. W. (1997, October). The paradox of educational power: How modern reform proposals miss the point. Education Week, 17(7), 34.

Hakim, S., Seidenstat, P., & Bowman, G. W. (1994). Introduction. In S. Hakim, P. Seidenstat, & G. W. Bowman (Eds.), Privatizing education and educational choice: Concepts, plans, and experiences (pp. 1–15). Westport, CT: Praeger.

Haller, E. J., Brent, B. O., & McNamara, J. H. (1997, November). Does graduate training in educational administration improve America's schools? Phi Delta Kappan, 79(3), 222–227.

Hallinger, P., & Hausman, C. (1994). From Attila the Hun to Mary Had a Little Lamb: Principal role ambiguity in restructured schools. In J. Murphy & K. S. Louis (Eds). Reshaping the principalship: Insights from transformational reform efforts (pp. 154–176). Newbury Park, CA: Corwin Press.

Hallinger, P., Leithwood, K., & Murphy, J. (Eds.). (1993). A cognitive perspective on educational administration. New York: Teachers College Press.

Hallinger, P., & Murphy J. (1985, November). Assessing the instructional management behavior of principals. Elementary School Journal, 86(2), 217–247.

Hallinger, P., & Murphy, J. (1986, May). The social context of effective schools. American Journal of Education, 94(3), 328–355.

Halpin, A. W. (1957). A paradigm for research on administrative behavior. In R. F. Campbell & R. T. Gregg (Eds.). Administrative behavior in education (pp. 155–199). New York: Harper and Row.

Halpin, A. W. (1960). Ways of knowing. In R. F. Campbell & J. M. Lipham (Eds.), Administrative theory as a guide to action (pp. 3–20). Chicago: University of Chicago, Midwest Administration Center.

Hannaway, J., & Crowson, R. (Eds.). (1989). The politics of reforming school administration. New York: Falmer.

Hanson, E. M. (1991). School-based management and educational reform: Cases in the USA and Spain. (ERIC Document Reproduction Service No. ED 336 832).

Hardin, H. (1989). The privatization putsch. Halifax, Nova Scotia: The Institute for Research on Public Policy.

Hargreaves, D. H. (1994). The new professionalism: The synthesis of professional and institutional development. Teaching & Teacher Education, 10(4), 423–438.

Harlow, J. G. (1962). Purpose-defining: The central function of the school administrator. In J. A. Culbertson & S. P. Hencley (Eds.), Preparing administrators: New perspectives (pp. 61–71). Columbus, OH: University Council for Educational Administration.

Hart, A. W. (1993). A design studio for reflective practice. In P. Hallinger, K. Leithwood, & J. Murphy (Eds.), Cognitive perspectives on educational leadership (pp. 218–230). New York: Teachers College Press.

Hart, A. W., & Bredeson, P. V. (1996). The principalship: A theory of professional learning and practice. New York: McGraw-Hill.

Hartzell, G. N., Williams, R. C., & Nelson, K. T. (1995). New voices in the field: The work lives of first-year assistant principals. Newbury Park, CA: Corwin Press.

Hawley, W. D. (1988). Universities and the improvement of school management. In D. E. Griffiths, R. T. Stout, & P. B. Forsyth (Eds.), Leaders for America's schools: The report and papers of the National Commission on Excellence in Educational Administration (pp. 82–88). Berkeley: McCutchan.

Hawley, W. D. (1995, Summer). The false premises and false promises of the movement to privatize public education. Teachers College Record, 96(4), 735–742.

Herbst, J. (1996). The once and future school: Three hundred and fifty years of American secondary education. New York: Routledge.

Hill, P. T. (1994). Public schools by contract: An alternative to privatization. In S. Hakim, P. Seidenstat, & G. W. Bowman (Eds.), Privatizing education and educational choice: Concepts, plans, and experiences. Westport, CT: Praeger.

Hills, J. (1975, Autumn). The preparation of administrators: Some observations from the "firing line." Educational Administration Quarterly, 11(3), 1–20.

Himmelstein, J. L. (1983). The New Right. In R. C. Liebman and R. Wuthrow (Eds.), The New Christian Right: Mobilization and legitimation (pp. 13–30). New York: Aldine.

Hirsch, W. Z. (1991). Privatizing government services: An economic analysis of contracting out by local governments. Los Angeles: University of California, Institute of Industrial Relations.

Hood, C. (1994). Explaining economic policy reversals. Buckingham, England: Open University Press.

Hoy, W. K. (1996, August). Science and theory in the practice of educational administration: A pragmatic perspective. Educational Administration Quarterly, 32(3), 366–378.

Immegart, G. L. (1977). The study of educational administration, 1954–1974. In L. L. Cunningham, W. G. Hack, R. O. Nystrand (Eds.), Educational administration: The developing decades (pp. 298–328). Berkeley, CA: McCutchan.

Immegart, G. L. (1990). What is truly missing in advanced preparation in educational administration? Journal of Educational Administration, 28(3), 5–13.

Interstate School Leaders Licensure Consortium. (1996). Standards for school leaders. Washington, DC: Council of Chief State School Officers.

Iwanicki, E. F. (in press). ISLLC standards and assessment in the context of school leadership reform. Journal of Personnel Evaluation in Education.

Jacobson, S. L. (1990). Reflections on the third wave of reform: Rethinking administrator preparation. In S. L. Jacobson & J. A. Conway (Eds.), Educational leadership in an age of reform (pp. 30–44). New York: Longman.

Jencks, C. (1966, Winter). Is the public school obsolete? The Public Interest, 2, 18–27.

Johnson, S. M. (1996). Leading to change: The challenge of the new superintendency. San Francisco: Jossey-Bass.

Katz, M. B. (1971, Summer). From voluntarism to bureaucracy in American education. Sociology of Education, 44(3), 297–332.

Kerchner, C. T. (1993). The strategy of teaching strategy. In P. Hallinger, K. Leithwood, & J. Murphy (Eds.), Cognitive perspectives on educational leadership (pp. 5–20). New York: Teachers College Press.

Kliebard, H. M. (1995). The struggle for the American curriculum 1893–1958 (2nd ed.). New York: Routledge.

Krug, E. A. (1964). The shaping of the American high school. New York: Harper and Row.

Lakomski, G. (1998, Fall). Training administrators in the wild: A naturalistic perspective. UCEA Review, 34(3), 1, 5, 10–11.

Lawton, S. B. (1991, September). Why restructure? Revision of paper presented at the annual meeting of the American Educational Research Association, Chicago, IL.

Leithwood, K., Chapman, J., Corson, D., Hallinger, P., & Hart, A. (Eds.). (1996). International handbook of educational leadership and administration. Dordrecht, The Netherlands: Kluwer.

Leithwood, K., Leonard, L., & Sharatt, L. (1998, April). Conditions fostering organizational learning in schools. Educational Administration Quarterly, 34(2), 243–276.

Leithwood, K. A., & Stager, M. (1989, May). Expertise in principals' problem solving. Educational Administration Quarterly, 25(2), 126–151.

Lewis, D. A. (1993). Deinstitutionalization and school decentralization: Making the same mistake twice. In J. Hannaway & M. Carnoy (Eds.), Decentralization and school improvement (pp. 84–101). San Francisco: Jossey-Bass.

Liebman, R. C. (1983a). Introduction. In R. C. Liebman and R. Wuthnow (Eds.), The New Christian Right: Mobilization and legitimation (pp. 1–9). New York: Aldine.

Liebman, R. C. (1983b). The making of the New Christian Right. In R. C. Liebman and R. Wuthnow (Eds.), The New Christian Right: Mobilization and legitimation (pp. 227–238). New York: Aldine.

Liebman, R. C., & Wuthnow, R. (Eds.). (1983). The New Christian Right: Mobilization and legitimation. New York: Aldine.

Lincoln, Y. S., & Guba, E. G. (1985). Naturalistic inquiry. Beverly Hills, CA: Sage.

Lotto, L. S. (1983, Winter). Believing is seeing. Organizational Theory Dialogue, 31(6), 6–26.

Louis, K. S., & Kruse, S. D. (1996). Professionalism and community: Perspectives on reforming urban schools. Newbury Park, CA: Corwin Press.

Louis, K. S., & Miles, M. B. (1990). Improving the urban high school: What works and why. New York: Teachers College Press.

Louis, K. S., & Murphy, J. (1994). The evolving role of the principal: Some concluding thoughts. In J. Murphy & K. S. Louis (Eds.), Reshaping the principalship: Insights from transformational reform efforts (pp. 265–281). Newbury Park, CA: Corwin Press.

Mann, D. (1975, May). What peculiarities in educational administration make it difficult to profess: An essay. The Journal of Educational Administration, 13(1), 139–147.

Marshall, C. (1992). The assistant principal: Leadership choices and challenges. Newbury Park, CA: Corwin Press.

Marshall, R., & Tucker, M. (1992). Thinking for a living: Work, skills, and the future of the American economy. New York: Basic Books.

Martin, B. (1993). In the public interest? Privatization and public sector reform. London: Zed Books.

Mayberry, M. (1991, April). Conflict and social determinism: The reprivatization of education. Paper presented at the annual meeting of the American Educational Research Association, Chicago, IL.

McCarthy, M. M. (1999). The evolution of educational leadership preparation programs. In J. Murphy & K. S. Louis (Eds.), Handbook of research on educational administration (2nd ed., pp. 119–139). San Francisco: Jossey-Bass.

McCarthy, M. M., Cambron-McCabe, N. H., & Thomas, S. B. (1998). Public school law: Teachers' and students' rights. Boston: Allyn and Bacon.

McCarthy, M. M., & Kuh, G. D. (1997). Continuity and change: The educational leadership professoriate. Columbia, MO: The University Council for Educational Administration.

McCarthy, M. M., Kuh, G. D., Newell, L. J., & Iacona, C. M. (1988). Under scrutiny: The educational administration professoriate. Tempe, AZ: University Council for Educational Administration.

McKerrow, K. (1998). Administrative internships: Quality or quantity? Journal of School Leadership, 8(2), 171–186.

McNeil, L. M. (1988, January). Contradictions of control, part 1: Administrators and teachers. Phi Delta Kappan, 69(5), 333–339.

Miklos, E. (1988). Administrator selection, career patterns, succession, and socialization. In N. J. Boyan (Ed.), Handbook of research on educational administration (pp. 53–76). New York: Longman.

Milstein, M. M. (1990). Rethinking the clinical aspects of preparation programs: From theory to practice. In S. L. Jacobson & J. A. Conway (Eds.), Educational leadership in an age of reform (pp. 119–130). New York: Longman.

Milstein, M. (1996, October). Clinical aspects of educational administration preparation programs. Paper prepared for a workshop of the Mississippi professors of educational administration, Jackson.

Milstein, M., & Associates. (1993). Changing the way we prepare educational leaders: The Danforth experience. Newbury Park, CA: Corwin Press.

Mitchell, B., & Cunningham, L. L. (Eds.). (1990). Educational leadership and changing contexts of families, communities, and schools. (Eighty-ninth National Society for the Study of Education Yearbook, Part II). Chicago: University of Chicago Press.

Monk, D. K., & Plecki, M. L. (1999). Generating and managing resources for school improvement. In J. Murphy & K. S. Louis (Eds.), Handbook of research on educational administration (2nd ed.) (pp. 491–510). San Francisco: Jossey-Bass.

Mulkeen, T. A. (1990). Reinventing school leadership. Working memo prepared for the Reinventing School Leadership Conference. Cambridge, MA: The National Center for Educational Leadership.

Mulkeen, T. A., Cambron-McCabe, N. H., & Anderson, B. J. (Eds.) (1994). Democratic leadership: The changing context of administrative preparation. Norwood, NJ: Ablex.

Mulkeen, T. A., & Cooper, B. S. (1989, March). Implications of preparing school administrators for knowledge-work organizations. Paper presented at the annual meeting of the American Educational Research Association, San Francisco.

Mulkeen, T. A., & Tetenbaum, T. J. (1990). Teaching and learning in knowledge organizations: Implications for the preparation of school administrators. Journal of Educational Administration, 28(3), 14–22.

Murnane, R. J., & Levy, F. (1996). Teaching the new basic skills: Principles for educating children to thrive in a changing economy. New York: The Free Press.

Murphy, J. (1990a). The educational reform movement of the 1980s: A comprehensive analysis. In J. Murphy (Ed.), The educational reform movement of the 1980s: Perspectives and cases (pp. 3–55). Berkeley: McCutchan.

Murphy, J. (1990b, Fall). Restructuring the technical core of preparation programs in educational administration. UCEA Review, 31(3), 4–5, 10–13.

Murphy, J. (1990c). The reform of school administration: Pressures and calls for change. In J. Murphy (Ed.), The educational reform movement of the 1980s: Perspectives and cases (pp. 277–303). Berkeley: McCutchan.

Murphy, J. (1990d). Principal instructional leadership. In L. S. Lotto & P. W. Thurston (Eds.), Advances in educational administration: Changing perspectives on the school. (Vol. 1 Part B, pp. 163–200). Greenwich, CT: JAI Press.

Murphy, J. (1991, Spring). The effects of the educational reform movement on departments of educational leadership. Educational Evaluation and Policy Analysis, 13(1), 49–65.

Murphy, J. (1992). The landscape of leadership preparation: Reframing the education of school administrators. Newbury Park, CA: Corwin Press.

Murphy, J. (1993a). Ferment in school administration: Rounds 1–3. In J. Murphy (Ed.), Preparing tomorrow's school leaders: Alternative designs (pp. 1–17). University Park, PA: University Council for Educational Administration.

Murphy, J. (Ed.). (1993b). Preparing tomorrow's school leaders: Alternative designs. University Park, PA: University Council for Educational Administration.

Murphy, J. (1994). Transformational change and the evolving role of the principalship: Early empirical evidence. In J. Murphy & K. S. Louis (Eds.), Reshaping the principalship: Insights from transformational reform efforts (pp. 20–53). Newbury Park, CA: Corwin Press.

Murphy, J. (1996). The privatization of schooling: Problems and possibilities. Newbury Park, CA: Corwin Press.

Murphy, J. (1999a). New consumerism: Evolving market dynamics in the institutional dimension of schooling. In J. Murphy & K. S. Louis (Eds.), Handbook of research on educational administration (2nd ed., pp. 405–419). San Francisco: Jossey-Bass.

Murphy, J. (1999b). A decade of change: An overview. In J. Murphy & P. Forsyth (Eds.) Educational administration: A decade of reform. Newbury Park, CA: Corwin Press.

Murphy, J. (in press). Educational governance: The shifting playing field. Teachers College Record.

Murphy, J., & Beck, L. G. (1995). School-based management as school reform: Taking stock. Newbury Park, CA: Corwin Press.

Murphy, J., & Forsyth, P. (Eds.). (1999). Educational administration: A decade of reform. Newbury Park, CA: Corwin Press.

Murphy, J., & Hallinger, P. (1989, March-April). Equity as access to learning: Curricular and instructional treatment differences. Journal of Curriculum Studies, 21(2), 129–149.

Murphy, J., Hallinger, P., Lotto, L. S., & Miller, S. K. (1987, December). Barriers to implementing the instructional leadership role. Canadian Administrator, 27(3), 1–9.

Murphy, J. Hallinger, P., Weil, M., & Mitman, A. (1983, Fall), (1984, September). Instructional leadership: A conceptual framework. Planning and Changing, 14(3), 137–149.

Murphy, J., & Louis, K. S. (Eds.). (1994). Reshaping the principalship: Insights from transformational reform efforts. Newbury Park, CA: Corwin Press.

Murphy, J., & Louis, K. S. (Eds.). (1999). Handbook of research on educational administration (2nd ed). San Francisco: Jossey-Bass.

Muth, R. (1989, October). Reconceptualizing training for educational administrators and leaders: Focus on inquiry (Notes on Reform, No. 2). Charlottesville, VA: National Policy Board for Educational Administration.

National Commission for the Principalship. (1990). Principals for our changing schools: Preparation and certification. Fairfax, VA: Author.

National Commission for the Principalship. (1993). Principals for our changing schools: The knowledge and skill base. Fairfax, VA: Author.

National Commission on Excellence in Educational Administration. (1987). Leaders for America's schools. Tempe, AZ: University Council for Educational Administration.

National Commission on Teaching and America's Future. (1996). What matters most: Teaching for America's future (summary report). New York: Author.

National Policy Board for Educational Administration. (1989). Improving the preparation of school administrators: The reform agenda. Charlottesville, VA: Author.

Newlon, J. H. (1934). Educational administration as social policy. New York: Scribner.

Newmann, F. M., & Wehlage, G. G. (1995). Successful school restructuring. Madison: University of Wisconsin-Madison, Center on Organization and Restructuring of Schools.

Norton, M. S., & Levan, F. D. (1987, Winter). Doctoral studies of students in educational administration programs in UCEA member institutions. Educational Considerations, 14(1), 21–24.

Osin, L., & Lesgold, A. (1996, Winter). A proposal for the reengineering of the educational system. Review of Educational Research, 66(4), 621–656.

Osterman, K. F., & Kottkamp, R. B. (1993). Reflective practice for educators: Improving schooling through professional development. Newbury Park, CA: Corwin Press.

Pepper, J. B. (1988). Clinical education for school superintendents and principals: The missing link. In D. E. Griffiths, R. T. Stout, & P. R. Forsyth (Eds.), Leaders for America's Schools: The report and papers of the National Commission on Excellence in Educational Administration (pp. 360–366). Berkeley: McCutchan.

Peterson, K. D., & Finn, C. E. (1985, Spring). Principals, superintendents and the administrator's art. The Public Interest, 79, 42–62.

Popper, S. H. (1982, Winter). An advocate's case for the humanities in preparation programs for school administration. The Journal of Educational Administration, 20(1), 12–22.

Pounder, D. G., Ogawa, R. T., & Adams, E. A. (1995, November). Learning as an organization-wide phenomena: Its impact on school performance. Educational Administration Quarterly, 31(4), 564–588.

Powell, A. G., Farrar, E., & Cohen, D. K. (1985). The shopping mall high school: Winners and losers in the educational marketplace. Boston: Houghton Mifflin.

Prawat, R. S., & Peterson, P. L. (1999). Social constructivist views of learning. In J. Murphy & K. S. Louis (Eds.), Handbook of research on educational administration (2nd ed., pp. 203–226). San Francisco: Jossey-Bass.

President's Commission on Privatization. (1988). Privatization: Toward more effective government. Washington, DC: U.S. Government.

Prestine, N. A. (1994). Ninety degrees from everywhere: New understandings of the principal's role in a restructuring Essential School. In J. Murphy & K. S. Louis (Eds.), Reshaping the principalship: Insights from transformational reform efforts (pp. 123–153). Newbury Park, CA: Corwin Press.

Prestine, N. A. (1995). Crisscrossing the landscape: Another turn at cognition and educational administration. Educational Administration Quarterly, 31(1), 134–142.

Putnam, R. D. (1995). Bowling alone: America's declining social capital. Journal of Democracy, 6(1), 65–77.

Reese, W. J. (1995). The origins of the American high school. New Haven, CT: Yale University Press.

Reyes, P., Wagstaff, L. H., & Fusarelli, L. D. (1999). Delta forces: The changing fabric of American society and education. In J. Murphy & K. S. Louis (Eds.), Handbook of research on educational administration (2nd ed., pp. 183–201). San Francisco: Jossey-Bass.

Ross, R. L. (1988). Government and the private sector: Who should do what? New York: Crane Russak.

Rowan, B. (1995, February). Research on learning and teaching in K-12 school: Implications for the field of educational administration. Educational Administration Quarterly, 31(1), 115–133.

Rungeling, B., & Glover, R. W. (1991, January). Educational restructuring—the process for change? Urban Education, 25(4), 415–427.

Sackney, L. E., & Dibski, D. J. (1992, August). School-based management: A critical perspective. Paper presented at the Seventh Regional Conference of the Commonwealth Council for Educational Administration, Hong Kong.

Sarason, S. B. (1994). Parental involvement and the political principle: Why the existing governance structure of schools should be abolished. San Francisco: Jossey-Bass.

Scheurich, J. J. (1995). The knowledge base in educational administration: Postpositivist reflections. In R. Donmoyer, M. Imber, & J. J. Scheurich (Eds.), The knowledge based in educational administration: Multiple perspectives (pp. 17–31). Albany: State University of New York Press.

Sergiovanni, T. J. (1987). The principalship: A reflective practice perspective. Boston: Allyn and Bacon.

Sergiovanni, T. J. (1989). Mystics, neats, and scruffies: Informing professional practice in educational administration. The Journal of Educational Administration, 27(2), 7–21.

Sergiovanni, T. J. (1991, March). The dark side of professionalism in educational administration. Phi Delta Kappan, 72(7), 521–526.

Sergiovanni, T. J. (1993). Organizations or communities: Changing the metaphor changes the theory. Paper presented at the annual meeting of the American Educational Research Association, Atlanta, Georgia.

Sergiovanni, T. J., & Starratt, R. J. (1988). Supervision: Human perspectives (4th ed.). New York: McGraw-Hill.

Shakeshaft, C. (1988). Women in educational administration: Implications for training. In D. E. Griffiths, R. T. Stout, & P. R. Forsyth (Eds.), Leaders for America's schools: The report and papers of the National Commission on Excellence in Educational Administration (pp. 403–416). Berkeley: McCutchan.

Short, P. M., & Rinehart, J. S. (1993). Reflection as a means of developing expertise. Educational Administration Quarterly, 29(4), 501–521.

Silver, P. F. (1978a). Some areas of concern in administrator preparation. In P. F. Silver & D. W. Spuck (Eds.), Preparatory programs for educational administrators in the United States (pp. 202–215). Columbus, OH: University council for Educational Administration.

Silver, P. F. (1978b). Trends in program development. In P. F. Silver & D. W. Spuck (Eds.), Preparatory programs for educational administrators in the United States (pp. 178–201). Columbus, OH: University Council for Educational Administration.

Silver, P. F. (1982). Administrator preparation. In H. E. Mitzel (Ed.), Encyclopedia of educational research (5th ed., Vol. 1, pp. 49–59). New York: Free Press.

Silver, P. F. (1986, Summer). Case records: A reflective practice approach to administrator development. Theory Into Practice, 25(3), 161–167.

Silver, P. F. (1987). The Center for Advancing Principal Excellence (APEX): An approach to professionalizing educational administration. In J. Murphy & P. Hallinger (Eds.), Approaches to administrative training in education (pp. 67–82). Albany: State University of New York Press.

Sirotnik, K. A., & Durden, P. C. (1996). The validity of administrator performance assessment systems: The ADI as a case-in-point. Educational Administration Quarterly, 31(3), 449–472.

Sizer, T. R. (1984). Horace's compromise: The dilemma of the American high school. Boston: Houghton Mifflin.

Slater, R. O. (1995, August). The sociology of leadership and educational administration. Educational Administration Quarterly, 31(3), 449–472.

Sparks, D., & Hirsh, D. (1997). A new vision for staff development. Alexandria, VA: Association for Supervision and Curriculum Development.

Starr, P. (1991). The case for skepticism. In W. T. Gormley (Ed.), Privatization and its alternatives (pp. 25–36). Madison: The University of Wisconsin Press.

Starratt, J. (1991, May). Building on ethical school: A theory for practice in educational leadership. Educational Administration Quarterly, 27(2), 185–202.

Stringfield, S., Ross, S., & Smith, L. (Eds.). (1996). Bold plans for school restructuring: The New American Schools designs. Mahwah, NJ: Lawrence Erlbaum.

Sykes, G. (1999). The "new professionalism" in education: An appraisal. In J. Murphy & K. S. Louis (Eds.), Handbook of research on educational administration (2nd ed., pp. 227–249). San Francisco: Jossey-Bass.

Sykes, G., & Elmore, R. F. (1989). Making schools more manageable: Policy and administration for tomorrow's schools. In J. Hannaway & R. L. Crowson (Eds.), The politics of reforming school administrations (pp. 77–94). New York: Falmer Press.

Thayer, F. C. (1987). Privatization: Carnage, chaos, and corruption. In B. J. Carroll, R. W. Conant, & T. A. Easton (Eds.), Private means, public ends: Private business in social service delivery (pp. 146–170). New York: Praeger.

Thomson, S. D. (1999). Causing change: The National Policy Board for Educational Administration (NPBEA). In J. Murphy & P. Forsyth (Eds.), Educational administration: A decade of reform. Newbury Park, CA: Corwin Press.

Tomlinson, J. (1986). Public education, public good. Oxford Review of Education, 12(3), 211–222.

Tyack, D. B. (1993). School governance in the United States: Historical puzzles and anomalies. In J. Hannaway & M. Carnoy (Eds.), Decentralization and school improvement (pp. 1–32). San Francisco: Jossey-Bass.

Tyack, D. B., & Cummings, R. (1977). Leadership in American public schools before 1954: Historical configurations and conjectures. In L. L. Cunningham, W. G. Hack, & R. O. Nystrand (Eds.), Educational administration: The developing decades (pp. 46–66). Berkeley: McCutchan.

Van Meter, E. (1999). The evaluation of curriculum in preparation programs. In J. Murphy & P. Forsyth (Eds.), Educational administration: A decade of reform. Newbury Park, CA: Corwin Press.

Wallace, R. C. (1996). From vision to practice: The art of educational leadership. Thousand Oaks, CA: Corwin Press.

Weick, K. E. (1976). Educational organizations as loosely coupled systems. Administrative Science Quarterly, 21, 1–19.

Weick, K. E., & McDaniel, R. R. (1989). How professional organizations work: Implications for school organization and management. In T. J. Sergiovanni & J. H. Moore (Eds.), Schooling for tomorrow: Directing reforms to issues that count (pp. 330–355). Boston: Allyn & Bacon.

Whitty, G. (1984, April). The privatization of education. Educational Leadership, 41(7), 51–54.

Willower, D. J. (1983, Summer). Evolutions in the professorship: Past philosophy, future. Educational Administration Quarterly, 19(3), 179–200.

Willower, D. J. (1988). Synthesis and projection. In N. J. Boyan (Ed.), Handbook of research on educational administration (pp. 729–747). New York: Longman.

Willower, D. J. (1996, August). Inquiry in educational administration and the spirit of the times. Educational Administration Quarterly, 32(3), 344–365.

Willower, D. J. (1998, September). Fighting the fog: A criticism of postmodernism. Journal of School Leadership, 8(5), 448–463.

Willower, D. J., & Forsyth, P. B. (1999). A brief history of scholarship on educational administration. In J. Murphy & K. S. Louis (Eds.), <u>Handbook of research on educational administration</u> (2nd ed., pp. 1–23). San Francisco: Jossey-Bass.

Wise, A. E. (1989). Professional teaching: A new paradigm for the management of education. In T. J. Sergiovanni & J. H. Moore (Eds.), <u>Schooling for tomorrow: Directing reforms to issues that count</u> (pp. 301–310). Boston: Allyn & Bacon.

Young, I. P., Place, A. W., Rinehart, J. S., Jury, J. C., & Baits, D. F. (1997). Teacher recruitment: A test of the similarity-attraction hypothesis for race and sex. <u>Educational Administration Quarterly, 33</u>(1), 86–106.

PROFESSIONAL LEARNING IN LEADERSHIP PREPARATION

Toward a Learning-Oriented Instructional Paradigm: Implications for Practice[1]

RODNEY MUTH

Most school administrators function in highly stressful, ill-defined, ambiguous, and uncertain situations in which decisions made by them or their designees often carry considerable consequence—for students, parents, school staff, and the community. By contrast, most administrator preparation programs take place in controlled environments, usually classrooms, in which "problems of practice" are many steps removed from the intensity of day-to-day administrative life in schools. It is unlikely, if only for economies of scale and professorial survival, that all preparatory activities for administrative positions will be moved from the peaceful confines of classrooms to the cauldron of practice. Nevertheless, progress can be made in "bringing to life" the realities of administrative practice to prepare candidates more effectively for the vicissitudes of life in schools as educational "leaders." Such progress is more likely if current programs are adapted to focus clearly on student performance in authentic tasks. These tasks should be designed to address program goals and enable students to transfer their knowledge and skills effectively to practice settings.

AN EVOLVING MODEL

In response to the learning needs of administrators in training, a "paradigm" might reconceptualize how administrator preparation programs are organized and conducted. An initial version of this paradigm, Table 1, focuses on (a) foundational elements for a revised approach to learning processes in advanced programs in educa-

[1] An earlier version of this paper was presented at the annual meeting of the National Council of Professors of Educational Administration, Jackson Hole, Wyoming, August 1999, under the title *Integrating a Learning-Oriented Paradigm: Implications for Practice*. I am indebted to Marcia Muth for her helpful suggestions on trimming the original paper to its current form.

Rodney Muth, University of Colorado at Denver

TABLE I. An Evolving Paradigm for Learning-Oriented Programming.

Foundations	Learning/Teaching Strategies/Activities	Outcome Expectations
Constructivism (Duffy & Cunningham, 1996)	Experiential Education (Kolb, 1984)	Knowledge and Skills (Colorado Department of Education, 1997)
Collaborative Learning (Bruffee, 1993)	Problem-based Learning (Duffy & Cunningham, 1996)	Deliberative Action (Kennedy, 1987)
Student- or Learner-centered Learning (Hannafin & Land, 1997)	Action Learning/Action Research (Morely, 1989; Stringer, 1996)	Reflective Practice (Schön, 1983, 1987)
Principles of Adult Learning (Merriam & Caffarella, 1991)	Appreciative Inquiry (Barrett, 1995; Hammond, 1996)	Lifelong Learning (Brown, 1997)

Note: The columns are not causally related. Each column should be viewed as a whole and as supportive of the column to its right. Source: Muth et al. (1999, p. 9).

tional administration, (b) strategies or activities that professors and students might use to develop and engage in opportunities to learn, and (c) outcomes that a program might seek for its graduates (Muth et al., 1999).[2]

The first column in Table 1, *Foundations*, shows the principles or philosophical perspectives that might undergird a program's learning/teaching strategies or activities: constructivism, collaborative learning, learner centeredness, and an orientation to adult learning. While this model is evolving, it provides a starting point for expanded discussions of teaching-learning philosophies and practices that should be driven by the types of learning outcomes preferred—both by students and professors. The middle column, *Learning/Teaching Strategies/Activities*, outlines specific overlapping and complementary strategies—including experiential education, problem-based learning (PBL), action learning/action research, and appreciative inquiry—that can help students move toward desired programmatic outcomes. Finally, the right-hand column, *Outcome Expectations*, indicates what programs might strive to achieve: graduates who have attained definite skills and knowledge (as specified, for example, by the state of Colorado [Colorado Department of Education, 1997]), demonstrating them authentically through portfolios, and who will be deliberative, reflective practitioners and lifelong inquirers.

[2] Although the original material (Muth, 1999) for this chapter has been shortened considerably, I remain indebted to my coauthors—Debra Banks, Jean Bonelli, Barbara Gaddis, Harriet Napierkowski, Cason White, and Victoria Wood—for their substantial contributions to our original paper (Muth et al., 1999) on which the earlier paper was based.

TRANSLATING THE PARADIGM INTO PRACTICE

No matter how desirable these foundations, strategies, and outcomes, for most professors of educational administration the issue is how the use of such categories might affect the **organization and delivery of preparation programs**, including certificates, licenses, and degrees (Master's and doctorate). How might these components be explicated as performance expectations? What are some implications for professors and their students? To address these and other questions, the framework provided in Table 1 is very briefly examined below, starting with column three, outcome expectations. Initial "criteria" (underlined passages) for program and role reconceptualization are developed selectively throughout to elucidate potential changes in student, faculty, and program practices.

Detailing Knowledge and Skills

The first entry in Table 1, third column, is "Knowledge and Skills." In Colorado, a statewide effort that began in the early 1990s resulted in performance standards not only for elementary and secondary students but for teacher and administrator preparation as well. The standards for administrator and principal preparation helped faculties develop portfolio expectations (Muth, Murphy, Martin, & Sanders, 1996) and other performance assessments (Ford, Muth, Martin, & Murphy, 1996) for knowledge and skill development by providing faculty with clear outcomes and related assessments around which to develop opportunities to learn.

Our experience suggests that *preparation programs should develop program goals and objectives that detail their preferred outcomes for student performance*. In the absence of state standards, this can be accomplished readily by adopting the performance standards set forth by the Interstate School Leaders Licensure Consortium (1996), the National Association of Elementary School Principals (1997), the National Policy Board for Educational Administration (1995), or some combination of these. While clarifying goals and objectives requires considerable time and effort, the payoff is significant for program coherence, student assessment, and program evaluation and accreditation.

Focusing on Deliberative Action

After analyzing several perspectives on professional expertise, Kennedy (1987) concludes that "deliberate action" *requires that professionals reflect on their and other's actions and their consequences*, forming a means-ends repertoire (Kennedy, 1987, p. 148). While Kennedy's ideas are not new—Dewey (1933) articulated them early and Schön (1983) lately—their application to professional training is more recent. Deliberative action *requires professionals to be expert diagnosticians who blend knowledge with experience* to generate, in clinical parlance, "illness scripts" (Schmidt, Norman, & Boshuizen, 1990) that form the bases for diagnoses and are continually modified by experience. Research (Driver, Asoko, Leach, Mortimer, & Scott, 1994; Duckworth, 1987) suggests that the development of professional expertise *requires the vertical integration of experience with codified empirical knowledge* during preparation in order to assist practitioners in developing the equivalent of illness scripts.

Working on Reflective Practice

Becoming a deliberative actor is facilitated by reflective practices (Kennedy, 1987; Schön, 1983; Sergiovanni, 1991) which focus attention on what one is learning. Disciplined self-inquiry, however, does not come naturally. Like most things, however, it can be learned, refined, and extended through applications. Because of the importance that they attach to the role of reflection, Dewey (1944) and later Schwab (1978) and Schön (1983, 1987) contend that the *interaction of analysis and action* must be considered in program design. An individual's "ability to deliberate successfully about courses of action develops over time by observing one's own actions and their consequences" (Kennedy, 1987, p. 148) and is essential to effective professional practice. By *continuously reflecting on action*, "students become increasingly capable of performing complex 'mental experiments,'" defining complex problems, and critically evaluating outcomes of their actions (Murphy, Martin, & Muth, 1994, p. 6).

Supporting Lifelong Learning

Lifelong learning involves a predisposition to inquiry, problem solving, and continuous growth, attitudes that need to be encouraged and skills that can be learned. Lifelong learners are active, inquisitive, and goal oriented. Such characteristics have implications for their formal education (Livneh & Livneh, 1988): (a) they seek professional growth, wanting to relate what they know and do to what they learn; (b) they are self-motivated to learn and achieve; (c) they are ready for change; (d) they have specific goals when engaging in learning activities; and (e) they are oriented to the future.

Programs that expect to foster and support lifelong learning need to *focus on outcomes* as opposed to techniques, *use cooperative learning designs, let learners control their own learning, engage learners actively in creating their own learning environments, provide learners opportunities to complete projects that demand new skills and apply existing skills to new situations,* and *ensure that instructional materials support these strategies* (Brown, 1997). Becoming a lifelong learner enables any professional to grow and improve as conditions and expectations change.

Facing the Challenges of Constructivism

In a constructivist world (first column of Table 1), knowledge accrues to individuals through *negotiated social interactions* (Lambert et al., 1995), often producing "cognitive conflict" and individual reflections on and evaluations of personal understanding (Savery & Duffy, 1995): "learning is an active process of constructing rather than acquiring knowledge"; "instruction is a process of supporting that construction rather than communicating knowledge" (Duffy & Cunningham, 1996, p. 171).

This perspective has at least two implications. First, *active engagement with differing perspectives* (interpretations, preferences, etc.) leads to broader and more complex understanding among individuals. Learning, then, is an interactive process and personal knowledge bases are *socially constructed in a community of learners* through negotiation of beliefs, understanding, values, and experiences (Lambert et al., 1995). Second, a learner is not expected to acquire an expert's meaning; instead, knowledge is generated "not in the content but in the activity of the person in the content domain. That is, the active struggling by the learner with issues *is* learning" (Duffy & Cunningham, 1996, p. 174; emphasis in the original). Thus, in a constructivist orientation students are pushed to engage actively in and become more *responsible for their own learning*.

Encouraging Collaboration

Collaborative learning capitalizes on the constructivist perspective that people learn best when they are actively engaged in and responsible for their own learning (Bruffee, 1993). "Good learning, like good work, is collaborative and social, not competitive and isolated. Working with others often increases involvement in learning. Sharing one's ideas and responding to others' improves thinking and deepens understanding" (Chickering & Ehrmann, 1997, p. 2).

Collaborative processes also support learners' intentional learning, develop critical thinking skills, and enhance cognitive development (Duffy, Dueber, & Hawley, 1998). Further, collaborative learning promotes *active participation in learning* (Oliver & Reeves, 1994; Sharan, 1980) and *non-authoritarian styles of classroom interaction* (Johnson, Johnson, & Smith, 1991b), resulting in higher achievement, better relationships with peers, and greater social competence (Johnson, Johnson, & Smith, 1991a).

Shifting "Centeredness"

A constructivist approach clearly suggests that the learner is central in the learning process, not the teacher. Differing importantly from traditional perspectives, a student- or learner-centered approach places students in situations in which they can gather information, usually about a learning "problem," and construct knowledge in the context of their own experiences. Research suggests that student-centered learning encourages divergent reasoning, problem solving, and critical thinking—developing *"students as designers" of their own learning* (Hannafin & Land, 1997). Other benefits include increased motivation, greater retention of knowledge, deeper understanding of problems, more positive attitudes toward what is learned (Felder & Brent, 1996), increased interaction among learners, greater collaboration, and enhanced learner control (Merrill, 1997). Faculty, though, are challenged to redevelop their teaching practices, step away from center stage, place students at the heart of the learning process, and *create problems of practice and collaborative problem-solving strategies* that become the focal point for knowledge and skill acquisition.

Acknowledging Adult Learning

Supportive of learner centeredness, andragogy (Knowles, 1980, 1984), a widely accepted theory of adult learning, assumes that (a) mature adults are self-directed, (b) adults accumulate a reservoir of experience, (c) adults' readiness to learn is closely related to the developmental tasks of their social role (i.e., if I need to know it, I will learn it), (d) mature adults are more concerned about solving problems than simply acquiring knowledge, and (e) adults are motivated to learn by internal factors (Merriam & Caffarella, 1991). Further, the locus of control over actual learning lies within a learner's distinctive mental processes (Berger, 1988).

To accelerate adult-oriented programming, faculty need to develop *aids that assist* students in organizing and relating new information to previously stored information. These supports (e.g., learning guides, scenarios, standards-linked learning goals, cases, detailed "program syllabi") can decrease student anxiety about learning something new. They also facilitate *self-directed and self-designed* (not isolated but cooperative or collaborative) learning projects in place of "talking head" teaching.

To ensure that adults learn effectively, instructors further need to plan learning opportunities in "rich environments for active learning" (*real problems in real situations*) (Grabinger, Dunlap, & Duffield, 1997) rather than identify exactly how something is to be learned. Moreover, faculty need to facilitate the *application of what is learned* as part of an activity. In such situations, faculty become guides, facilitators, mentors, or coaches, and learners necessarily assume more responsibility for and leadership of their learning.

"Experiencing" Education

The second column ("Learning/Teaching Strategies/Activities") in Table 1 initially focuses on conceptions of education that date from Dewey (1938), Freire (1970), and Kolb (1984) who say that learners need to be involved directly and actively in their learning. By accepting this view of learning by doing, experiential education supports problem solving, curiosity, and inquiry. As an active rather than a passive or vicarious process, experiential education has four components: action, observation (including reflection and dialogue), formation of knowledge, and testing and refinement of knowledge (Kolb, 1984). While "traditional" education assumes that knowledge exists "outside" an individual learner, constructivist orientations assume that knowledge is created within individual learners, usually in interaction with others. Monson's (1991) transaction model deems learning a *self-directed process of making meaning and solving problems* in which all (students, teachers, and other community members) are learners with diverse backgrounds and interests. *Learners build upon their existing knowledge and skills*, reflecting on what and how they are learning. Given this perspective, teachers become primarily responsible for *designing learning opportunities* that foster active, collaborative engagement.[3]

In order to shift from teacher-centrism to student-centrism, teaching strategies must change, transforming the roles of teachers and learners. In the transaction model, teachers facilitate student learning "by acting as a catalyst for problem-solving" while students, no longer blank slates or empty vessels to be filled, interact cooperatively with each other and with instructors, sharing responsibility for both teaching and learning (Kolb, 1984, p. 53).

Implementing Problem-Based Learning (PBL)

As one strategy for achieving desired programmatic outcomes, PBL starts with an authentic problem of practice or content, challenging students to develop content expertise and skills within a knowledge domain. Instead of presenting content, after which students confront related problems, a teacher "presents students with ill-structured problems *before* they receive instruction" (Grabinger et al., 1997, p. 8; emphasis in the original). Faced with a problem, students must analyze the issues involved and seek useful, often cross-disciplinary, knowledge to generate helpful solutions. As a result, students use collaborative problem solving to build knowledge relevant to specific instructional settings and outcomes desired.

PBL has five major features: (a) learning begins with a problem, (b) students are encouraged to develop definitions of the problem while discovering possible solutions, (c) faculty members serve as resources and coaches, (d) learning how to learn is emphasized rather than learning facts, and (e) clinical skills are learned along with academic theories (Murphy et al., 1994, p. 7). The problems on which students focus can be constructed specifically for a learning experience, or they may occur naturally in the field. For instance, students may use cases or simulations, which are typical of classroom PBL applications, or they may focus on real-life and real-time problems in schools or other educational agencies.

---

[3] Simply providing students with problems of practice, or "presented problems" (Getzels, 1979) which are "well formed and defined" (Rehm & Muth, 1998, p. 289) is insufficient, according to Getzels (1985). Getzels suggests that problems need to be "discovered" or "created" to ensure that students are fully involved, that problems are meaningful and real, and that learning is lasting and useful.

PBL supports Kennedy's (1987) perspective on professional expertise as deliberative action, and opportunities to learn need to enable aspiring practitioners to develop the necessary knowledge and skills (Murphy et al., 1994, pp. 8–9). This development can be managed best by (a) *developing authentic problems of practice*; (b) *engaging with faculty in joint experiments*; (c) *developing skills in collaboration, discourse, and teamwork*; (d) *seeking and evaluating information about the results of actions*; and (e) *deliberating with others* on the appropriateness of decisions according to normative and evolving criteria, including values, ethics, and cultural appreciation.

Using Action Learning

Action learning (Morley, 1989) is a tool for helping any system adapt effectively to its environment. Action learning focuses on using problems of practice to encourage "collaborative learning as a basis for initiating strategies for change" (p. 182). The context for learning is the system and its broader social environment. Based in action research (Argyris, Putnam, & Smith, 1987; Trist, 1981), action learning is collaborative and "is about change because the result is a system that is adaptive in its environment" (Rehm & Muth, 1998, p. 295).

Action learning seeks to *empower clients*, involving them in a collaborative, *exploratory process of discovery learning* that respects their local context and their need to own both the process and the outcomes. Action learning also helps clients gain the knowledge and skills needed to address future problems of practice, most often without intervention from outside the system.

Starting with Appreciative Inquiry

Appreciative inquiry (Barrett, 1995; Hammond, 1996) is a positive process for improving organizations, their components, and the systems in which they are embedded. Appreciative inquiry is a particularly useful approach for "knowledge workers" for whom deliberation, collaboration, and effective application of knowledge are inherent to their work (Pasmore & Purser, 1993). An appreciative inquiry perspective recognizes the *importance of understanding context*, viewing organizations as wholes within larger environments, and *valuing the people* within an organization, *treating them with dignity and respect*, and seeing them as the creative essentials that produce effective outcomes.

CURRENT LICENSING PROGRAM

The context for the above analysis is a program developed by the Administrative Leadership and Policy Studies (ALPS) faculty at the University of Colorado at Denver (UCD).[4] The faculty began experimenting in 1991 with knowledge "domains" as replacements for courses, reasoning that (a) disparate courses, offered smorgasbord,

---

[4] This section comes primarily from an ALPS program brochure (Administrative Leadership and Policy Studies, n.d.).

placed the entire burden for synthesis and integration of knowledge on students; (b) knowledge cannot be conveniently packaged in time-bound "courses"; (c) the world of practice in educational administration does not begin and end with a "semester"; and (d) knowledge acquisition and skill building need to be integrated to create seamless, long-term opportunities to learn.

Through focused appraisal and modifications, a thirty-one-semester-hour licensing program has emerged. This licensing program prepares people to assume leadership roles in elementary and secondary education in Colorado. It is standards based and meets the preparation program requirements of Colorado's Department of Education (1997). Individuals who complete the licensing program, receive faculty endorsement, and pass the state-approved assessment test are eligible to receive a Colorado Provisional Administrator License or Colorado Provisional Principal License. (A Master's or Educational Specialist degree can be completed with at least nine additional credits.) Following district-sponsored induction and endorsement, a provisional licensee can apply for the Colorado Professional License for Administrator or Principal.

The program's credits are organized into four "domains" which incorporate broad knowledge and skill areas and are connected to one-hour internships. Thus, the domain and internship credits each semester constitute a seven-hour block, and students generally meet once a week for 5 hours (see Table 2). An intensive internship, usually developed for a summer term, allows students to apply knowledge in practice settings for extended periods.

The domain requirements for licensing are:

TABLE II. Administrator and Principal Licensing Program and MA/EdS.

License	Fall	Spr	Sum	Fall	Spr	MA/EdS Hours	Tot.
5700	6						6
5710					6		6
5720		6					6
5730				6			6
5930	1	1	3	1	1		7
Tot.	7	7	3	7	7		31
MA/EdS						9	9
Tot.	7	7	3	7		9	40

Note: The pattern outlined represents one way of arraying the domains. Depending on the semester in which the program begins, the pattern may vary. Source: Division of Administration, Supervision, and Curriculum Development at the University of Colorado at Denver program brochure.

CONTENT AREAS

EDUC 5700, Administrative Leadership in Educational Organizations (6 credits): focuses on key concepts, theories, and research related to leadership in educational organizations, including organizational behavior, leadership, culture and change, and power as they relate to administrative practice

EDUC 5710, Administering the Environment of Public Schools (6 credits): focuses on problems and issues external to schools and their impact on developing effective schools; issues include law, finance, planning, culture, governance and politics, and school/community relations

EDUC 5720, Supervision of the Curricular and Instructional Program of the School (6 credits): focuses on supervision, instructional leadership, and administration of instruction and curriculum, including teacher appraisal, assessment processes, curriculum design, and instructional effectiveness

EDUC 5730, Administering the School Improvement Process (6 credits): focuses on problems and issues related to developing effective schools, including organizational behavior and leadership, planning and assessing school improvement programs, and empowering teachers to improve school outcomes

FIELD PRACTICE

EDUC 5930, Internship in Administration and Supervision (7 credits): focuses on integrating classroom and field activities to ensure ongoing knowledge applications to problems of practice

The licensing program is a collaborative effort in which student cohorts are jointly recruited, selected, and trained by UCD faculty and field practitioners from district consortia. "Coursework" occurs in the four domains which are connected to field experiences in schools. The program (a) uses a PBL approach that connects learning activities to problems of practice, (b) involves practitioners and university faculty in instruction and field supervision, (c) integrates the internship throughout the four semesters of the program to provide ample opportunities for field projects and action research, (d) applies adult learning theories to facilitate a learner-centered orientation, (e) uses portfolios to assess performance, and (f) focuses on the state's licensing standards and preparation to complete the state's PLACE™ test successfully. PBL provides content as well as process ways of thinking about problems of professional practice and emphasizes learning in settings that most resemble the conditions of practice. Thus, students gain clinical skills (the capacity to recognize and solve problems of professional practice) through the integration of content learning and field applications. Most program graduates are hired as principals or assistant principals or for other administrative positions closely following completion of the program.

PROGRAM RE-"CONSTRUCTION"

While redesigning the ALPS program to create a constructivist, student- and adult-centered, collaborative learning environment, many questions arose. What would such a preparation program in educational administration look like? Would it work effectively for students and faculty? How would their roles change from conventional models? How could these changes be encouraged and supported? What are the implications of various instructional strategies (e.g., problem-based learning, action learning) for faculty work and student learning? How can program implementors assure that students become knowledgeable and skilled practitioners? What role can knowledge and skill standards play? Why are deliberative action, reflection on the consequences of one's work, and lifelong learning essential to effective practice? How can these outcomes facilitate continuous professional growth and self-improvement of program graduates? Using criteria selectively drawn from sections above, the implications of these questions for program development and for student and faculty roles are outlined in the Appendix.

Implications for Program Development

The material in the Appendix is intended to start conversations about ways to make programs more responsive to the needs of students, facilitate preparation experiences which more effectively use problems of practice, and ensure that the knowledge base in educational administration and the skills required of effective school administrators are fully addressed. The "criteria" outlined in the left-hand column of the Appendix have been pulled from the preceding text and constitute some of the factors that might be used to restructure preparation programs and student and faculty roles in these programs. For example, C5, "Integrate analysis and action," comes from the section above on reflective practice, and is viewed by Dewey (1944), Schwab (1978), and Schön (1983, 1987) as essential to effective program design.

If problem- or practice-based learning is most successful when it capitalizes on ill-structured, ill-defined (indeterminate) problems of practice (Grabinger et al., 1997), then a problem-based program must articulate clearly the *types of learning outcomes expected and the types of problems that lend themselves to such learning*. Without such specifications, learning would be random and idiosyncratic, and programs would be subject to many of the accusations appropriately leveled at education generally. Nevertheless, being specific about outcomes leaves wide open the means by which such outcomes are achieved, thus suggesting that a program should (a) be flexibly structured, (b) be organized around the problems of practice that students are expected to understand and master, and (c) emphasize authentic assessments of learning outcomes. In this design, a program is conceptualized not as a loose confederation of courses, perhaps capped by an internship experience, but as an integrated whole. Except for the accounting demands of the university, such a program is structured as a series of ongoing, mutually reinforcing strands that bridge theory and practice, integrate content and field experience, and treat students as active, engaged, mature learners.

Implications for Program Orientation

The Appendix also helps define the implications of overall program orientation. For example, a program in educational administration might decide to encourage deliberative action, including reflection on personal actions and those of others, diagnosing situations based on experience and knowledge, and integrating knowledge with experience. Such a decision would then require program builders to (a) expect and provide feedback to oral and written reflections on learning activities (cf. P2, P6, P32),[5] (b) expect detailed problem analyses that call on experience and research (cf. P3, P5, P21, P33), and (c) expect learning activities that involve field action (cf. P4, P5, P24).

Implications for Student Roles

Student roles become clearer once a program orientation, such as deliberative action, is defined. This orientation might require that students (a) analyze their own actions, comparing them to those of others (both peers and experienced practitioners) (cf. S2, S6, S11, S32); (b) contrast these actions to literature on administrative practice in order to build successively more sophisticated "action scripts" (cf. S3, S19, S25, S33); (c) write analyses of situations, issues, and problems that invoke experience and related research to sharpen both thinking and writing skills (cf. S5, S14, S28); (d) present and defend these analyses, taking and integrating feedback (cf. S9, S10, S17); and (e) engage individually, with peer teams, faculty, and field personnel (in various combinations) in consequential field projects informed and driven by research (cf. S4, S13, S20, S21, S24, S31, S35).

Implications for Faculty Roles

Finally, an orientation to deliberative action would define specific roles for faculty. First, faculty would need to develop protocols for reflection that help guide students to attain both the process skills and the desired outcomes of deliberative action (cf. F2, F5, F10). Second, faculty would need to structure time—perhaps in face-to-face or online discussions—for students to develop, practice, and hone their skills (cf. F14, F16, F22, F33). Third, faculty would have to develop and articulate guidelines for

---

[5] Some items are taken from areas other than deliberative action to show the overlap and reinforcement inherent in this way of thinking about program coherence.

written or oral analyses of action strategies, perhaps including the development of norms for interaction with clients, working in groups, and the like (cf. F3, F5, F6, F32, F35). Further, faculty would need to create resource bases for field activities, including clinical faculty who could supervise, mentor, and work with individual students and teams during their field experiences (cf. F4, F12, F22, F37). Additional resources could include expert faculty advice and counsel, research and other written resources (e.g., Web, library, and legal), and feedback sessions (peer, field, and faculty) that might support particular problems of practice (cf. F9, F11, F16, F25).

THE CHALLENGE AHEAD

The above story, like many others, is unfinished. Similarly, the design ideas presented here are still unfolding. As future stories are constructed, faculty will revise the program to respond to the latest research, student concerns, and their own observations. With each iteration, they learn more about themselves, teaching, student learning, and program development and implementation. Part of this learning involves significant introspection about the role of faculty as instructional developers. For example, if ideas outlined above—particularly those about adult learning and learner centeredness—are essential to effective professional development, then faculty need to engage students more productively and collaboratively in constructing their own professional knowledge. This actually should free faculty to focus more explicitly on instructional design and learning facilitation. Doing so, however, would require fundamental shifts in current conceptions and practices in professional preparation of educational administrators.

For example, even though learner-centered instruction focuses on a learner's needs, professional responsibility requires instructors, as "institutional assessors," to determine the knowledge and skills for which learners are accountable when completing a certificate, license, or degree. Historically, the role of faculty as assessors has weakened as courses have come to define programs and degrees and completion of courses has come to define competence. While defining expected program outcomes, instructors do not have to determine just how students learn what is to be learned. Rather, they should determine what is to be learned, develop multiple ways to guide learning activities, focus explicitly on relating these opportunities to learn to outcome expectations, and craft authentic assessments that clearly connect learning activities to these outcomes. In addition, they can, as Goodland (1999) suggests, focus on "materials development" instead of information dispensing, and take "pride in developing [materials] that teach people" (p. 4).

Shifts in faculty roles like these necessitate explicit examination of current practices, professional expectations, and preferred futures. It is in this process, examples of which are outlined here, that faculty—and aspiring administrators—can reconceptualize and redevelop teaching and learning to improve professional practice in school administration. It is this collaboration toward mutually beneficial futures that might be the most significant outcome of extended conversations about the future of preparation in educational administration.

APPENDIX

RESTRUCTURING PROGRAMS AND ROLES

CRITERIA	IMPLICATIONS FOR PROGRAM	IMPLICATIONS FOR STUDENTS	IMPLICATIONS FOR FACULTY
Knowledge and Skills			
C1.Specify outcome expectations for student performance	P1.Develop detailed goals and objectives for student performance and corresponding assessments, so that the total program is the focus	S1.Track and reflect on learning activities; prepare documents and other exhibits that demonstrate performance in specified areas	F1.Formulate learning outcomes consistent with external and internal expectations that are reinforced throughout program
Deliberative Action			
C2.Reflect on own and others' actions	P2.Require oral and written reflections on learning activities	S2.Analyze actions, compare to others, compare to literature	F2.Develop protocols for reflections; provide time for practice
C3.Diagnose situations based on experience and knowledge	P3.Require detailed analyses that call on experience and research	S3.Write analyses which invoke experience and research	F3.Articulate guidelines for analyses
C4.Integrate knowledge with experience	P4.Expect learning activities that involve field action	S4.Engage in field activities guided by research	F4.Create resource bases for field activities
Reflective Practice			
C5.Integrate analysis and action	P5.Expect reality-based exercises that require analysis and action	S5.Sharpen analytical skills and apply to practice	F5.Clarify expectations for analyses and their applications
C6.Reflect continuously on actions	P6.Expect reflective-practice journal that focuses learning	S6.Keep reflective-practice journal	F6.Devise sample journaling methods

CRITERIA	IMPLICATIONS FOR PROGRAM	IMPLICATIONS FOR STUDENTS	IMPLICATIONS FOR FACULTY
Lifelong Learning			
C7.Focus on outcomes	P7.Publish explicit outcome expectations	S7.Track activities as they relate to outcomes	F7.Develop rubrics for assessing outcomes
C8.Use cooperative learning	P8.Expect group products	S8.Learn to cooperate, delegate, lead, and follow	F8.Construct group activities with product outcomes
C9.Empower students to control own learning	P9.Expect students to create own learning opportunities	S9.Take responsibility for own learning	F9.Specify what is to be learned and provide supports
C10.Engage learners in creating learning environments	P10.Require self-assessments of proficiencies	S10.Acknowledge strengths and weaknesses and develop action strategies	F10.Create self-assessment tools and individual learning contracts
C11.Facilitate challenging skill-building projects	P11.Require intensive and extensive internships connected to content areas	S11.Use self-assessments and discussions with field personnel to develop projects	F11.Determine skills and self-assessments
C12.Develop opportunities to learn and supportive materials	P12.Expect a wide range of learning activities	S12.Expect assistance and guidance in developing individual	F12.Develop resources to support specified learning activities
Constructivism			
C13.Provide opportunities to "negotiate" knowledge	P13.Require group products that fairly allocate responsibilities	S13.Engage in group activities, take responsibility, and produce fair share	F13.Develop group- and skill-building activities

CRITERIA	IMPLICATIONS FOR PROGRAM	IMPLICATIONS FOR STUDENTS	IMPLICATIONS FOR FACULTY
C14.Engage actively with diverse views	P14.Expect multiple viewpoints to be debated	S14.Balance opinions with other perspectives and argue opposing views	F14.Create opportunities for defense of controversial viewpoints
C15.Develop community of learners	P15.Expect resource sharing and use	S15.Share resources with group	F15.Develop teams and other interdependent groups
C16.Shift responsibility for learning to students	P16.Require student development of learning goals	S16.Develop individual learning goals	F16.Develop and use self-assessments to counsel students
Collaboration			
C17.Promote active participation in learning	P17.Expect students to participate in program development	S17.Engage with peers and faculty to develop program, group, and personal learning objectives	F17.Facilitate student participation in program development and revision
C18.Equalize power	P18.Expect participants to work as equals in learning	S18.Expect to be treated as equals in learning	F18.Recognize that practice is ill-structured and that all have much to learn
Recentering			
C19.Support student-designed learning	P19.Expect student products beyond program requirements	S19.Use experiences and past learning to demonstrate knowledge and skills	F19.Expect students to use experience as part of their learning
C20.Create problems of practice	P20.Adopt a problem orientation	S20.Engage in field and other problem-solving activities	F20.Establish problem types that attend to program goals
C21.Create problem-solving activities	P21.Expect active engagement in problem solving	S21.Engage in field and other problem-solving activities	F21.Develop activities that stimulate and encourage problem solving

CRITERIA	IMPLICATIONS FOR PROGRAM	IMPLICATIONS FOR STUDENTS	IMPLICATIONS FOR FACULTY
Adult Orientation			
C22.Develop learning aids	P22.Acknowledge the importance of materials development	S22.Expect support for learning activities	F22.Develop support resources that extend students' ability to learn
C23.Develop self-directed activities	P23.Expect students to define objectives and complete learning	S23.Become confident about capabilities	F23.Create opportunities for self-directed learning
C24.Promote interaction with "real" problems	P24.Require involvement in consequential problems of practice	S24.Engage in internship and group learning in field settings	F24.Develop range of engagements with field problems
C25.Encourage knowledge and skill applications	P25.Expect applications of knowledge and skills	S25.Acquire and document knowledge and skills during problem solving	F25.Articulate knowledge base and skills needed
Experiential Education			
C26.Encourage self-direction	P26.Expect individually developed learning activities	S26.Design own learning experiences	F26.Assess individual experiences
C27.Validate and use experience	P27.Engage students in facilitating learning of others	S27.Assist peers with their learning needs	F27.Encourage students to share expertise
C28.Design opportunities to learn	P28.Specify types of learning expected	S28.Negotiate learning opportunities according to needs	F28.Provide range of opportunities for each outcome
Problem-based Learning			
C29.Seek authentic problems	P29.Expect problems to be the impetus for learning	S29.Engage with practice	F29.Identify variety of problems matched to outcomes and assessments

CRITERIA	IMPLICATIONS FOR PROGRAM	IMPLICATIONS FOR STUDENTS	IMPLICATIONS FOR FACULTY
C30.Student-faculty collaboration	P30.Expect collaborative learning	S30.Develop collaboration skills	F30.Design activities that require collaboration
C31.Develop skills in group work	P31.Emphasize group work and products	S31.Participate in group activities	F31.Construct group experiences and skill-building activities
C32.Engage in self-appraisal	P32.Specify periodic self-assessments	S32.Perform self-assessments and track progress	F32.Develop self-assessment procedures
C33.Expect sound rationales for perspectives	P33.Require articulation of perspectives on issues	S33.Develop clear understanding of values and beliefs	F33.Challenge student perspectives
C34.Encourage group discourse	P34.Expect group activities and products	S34.Engage with others in building consensus	F34.Design products that require group agreements
Action Learning			
C35.Engage relevant participants	P35.Require group field work	S35.Work with stakeholders to clarify outcomes	F35.Develop with students "contract" expectations for work with clients
C36.Engage in discovery learning	P36.Pose ill-structured problem situations	S36.Be open and inquisitive	F36.Exploit ambiguous situations
Appreciative Inquiry			
C37.Clarify contexts	P37.Expect contextual thinking	S37.Use knowledge base to develop broad overviews	F37.Ensure that knowledge base has sufficient resources
C38.Treat people with dignity and respect	P38.Demand valuing of others	S38.Develop tolerance of and respect for others	F38.Create indeterminate situations that elicit multiple "voices"

REFERENCES

Administrative Leadership and Policy Studies (n.d.). Administrator and principal licensing program with Master's or educational specialist degrees. Denver: Author, School of Education, University of Colorado at Denver [revised March 2000].

Argyris, C., Putnam, R., & Smith, D. M. (1987). Action science: Concepts, methods, and skills for research and intervention. San Francisco: Jossey-Bass.

Barrett, F. J. (1995). Creating appreciative learning cultures. Organizational Dynamics, 24(2), 36–49.

Berger, K. S. (1988). The developing person through the life span (2nd ed.). New York: Worth.

Brown, B. L. (1997). New learning strategies for generation X. Columbus, OH: Eric Clearinghouse on Adult, Career, and Vocational Education.

Bruffee, K. (1993). Collaborative learning: Higher education, interdependence and the authority of knowledge. Baltimore: Johns Hopkins University Press.

Chickering, A. W., & Ehrmann, S. C. (1997, August 28). Implementing the seven principles: Technology as lever. American Association for Higher Education. [On-line]. Available: http://www.aahe.org/technology/ehrmann.htm [1998, May 15]

Colorado Department of Education. (1997, September). Rules for the administration of the Educator Licensing Act of 1991. Denver, CO: Author.

Dewey, J. (1933). How we think: A restatement of the relation of reflective thinking to the education process. Boston: Heath.

Dewey, J. (1938). Experience and education. New York: Collier Books.

Dewey, J. (1944). Democracy and education. New York: Free Press.

Driver, R., Asoko, H., Leach, J., Mortimer, E., & Scott, P. (1994, October). Constructing scientific knowledge in the classroom. Educational Researcher, 23(7), 5–12.

Duckworth, E. R. (1987). "The having of wonderful ideas" and other essays on teaching and learning. New York: Teachers College Press.

Duffy, T. M., & Cunningham, D. J. (1996). Constructivism: Implications for the design and delivery of instruction. In D. H. Jonassen (Ed.), Handbook of research for educational communications and technology (pp. 170–198). New York: Macmillan.

Duffy, T. M., Dueber, W., & Hawley, C. L. (1998). Critical thinking in a distributed environment. In C. J. Bonk & K. King (Ed.), Electronic collaborators: Researching the discourse of learner-centered technologies for literacy, apprenticeship, and discovery. Mahwah, NJ: Lawrence Erlbaum.

Felder, R., & Brent, R. (1996). Navigating the bumpy road to student-centered instruction. [On-line]. Available: www2.ncsu.edu/lockers/f/felder/public/Papers/Resist.html [1998, May 6]

Ford, S., Muth, R., Martin, W. M., & Murphy, M. J. (1996, October). Performance assessment: The real world of educational leadership. Paper presented at the annual meeting of the University Council for Educational Administration, Louisville, KY.

Freire, P. (1970). Pedagogy of the oppressed. New York: Continuum.

Getzels, J. W. (1979). Problem-finding and research in educational administration. In G. L. Immegart & W. L. Boyd (Eds.), Problem-finding in Educational Administration (pp. 5–22). Lexington, MA: D. C. Heath.

Getzels, J. W. (1985, September). Problem finding and the enhancement of creativity. NASSP Bulletin, pp. 55–61.

Goodland, M. (1999, July 22). Faculty roles differ at Open University: UCB's Lewis details new higher ed model from England. Silver & Gold Record, pp. 1, 4.

Grabinger, S., Dunlap, J. C., & Duffield, J A. (1997). Rich environments for active learning in action: Problem-based learning. Alt-J, 5(2), 5–17.

Hammond, S. A. (1996). The thin book of appreciative inquiry. Plano, TX: Kodiak Consulting.

Hannafin, M. J., & Land, S. M. (1997). The foundations and assumptions of technology-enhanced student-centered learning environments. Instructional Science, 25(3), 167–202.

Interstate School Leaders Licensure Consortium (1996). Standards for school leaders. Washington, DC: Council of Chief State School Officers.

Johnson, D. W., Johnson, R. T., & Smith, K. A. (1991a). Active learning: Cooperation in the college classroom. Edina, MN: Interaction.

Johnson, D. W., Johnson, R. T., & Smith, K. A. (1991b). Cooperative learning: Increasing college faculty instructional productivity. ASHE-ERIC Higher Education Report No. 4. Washington, DC: George Washington University.

Kennedy, M. M. (1987). Inexact sciences: Professional education and the development of expertise. In E. Z. Rothkopf (Ed.), Review of research in education, vol. 14 (pp. 133–167). Washington, DC: American Educational Research Association.

Knowles, M. (1980). The modern practice of adult education: From pedagogy to andragogy (2nd ed.). New York: Cambridge Books.

Knowles, M. (1984). The adult learner: A neglected species (3rd ed.). London: Gulf Publishing.

Kolb, D. (1984). Experiential learning: Experience as the source of learning and development. Englewood Cliffs, NJ: Prentice-Hall.

Lambert, L., Walker, D., Zimmerman, D. P., Cooper, J. E., Lambert, M. D., Gardner, M. E., & Slack, P. J. F. (1995). The constructivist leader. New York: Teachers College Press.

Livneh, C., & Livneh, H. (1988). Factors differentiating high and low participants in lifelong learning. Educational and Psychological Measurement, 48(3), 637–646.

Merriam, S. B., & Caffarella, R. S. (1991). Learning in adulthood: A comprehensive guide. San Francisco: Jossey-Bass.

Merrill, M. D. (1997). Learning-oriented instructional development tools. Performance Improvement, 36(3), 51–55. [On-line]. Available: http://www.coe.usu.edu/it/id2/ DDC297.htm

Monson, P. (1991). Charting a new course with whole language. Educational Leadership, 48(6), 51–53.

Morley, D. (1989). Frameworks for organizational change: Towards action learning in global environments. In S. Wright & D. Morley (Eds.), Learning works: Searching for organizational futures (pp. 163–190). Toronto: ABL Group, Faculty of Environmental Studies, York University.

Murphy, M. J., Martin, W. M., & Muth, R. (1994, October). Matching performance standards with problems of practice: Problem-based learning in a standards environment. Symposium presentation on Problem-based Learning, Performance Standards, and Portfolios at the annual meeting of the University Council for Educational Administration, Philadelphia, PA.

Muth, R. (1999, August). Integrating a learning-oriented paradigm: Implications for practice. Paper presented at the annual conference of the National Council of Professors of Educational Administration, Jackson Hole, WY.

Muth, R., Banks, D., Bonelli, J., Gaddis, B., Napierkowski, H., White, C., Wood, V. (1999, April). Toward an instructional paradigm: Recasting how faculty work and students learn. Paper presented at the American Educational Research Association, Montreal, Canada.

Muth, R., Murphy, M. J., Martin, W. M., & Sanders, N. (1996). Assessing knowledge and skills through portfolios. In J. Burden (Ed.), Prioritizing instruction (pp. 216–231). Fourth Annual Yearbook of the National Council of Professors of Educational Administration. Lancaster, PA: Technomic.

National Association of Elementary School Principals. (1997). Proficiencies for principals: Elementary and middle schools. Alexandria, VA: Author.

National Policy Board for Educational Administration. (1998). NCATE curriculum guidelines: Advanced programs in educational leadership for principals, superintendents, curriculum directors, and supervisors. In National Council for Accreditation of Teacher Education (Ed.), NCATE Curriculum Guidelines (pp. 183–204). Washington, DC: National Council for Accreditation of Teacher Education.

Oliver, R., & Reeves, T. C. (1994). Dimensions of effective interactive learning with telematics for distance education. Educational Technology Research and Development, 44(4), 45–56.

Pasmore, W. A., & Purser, R. E. (1993, July/August). Designing work systems for knowledge workers. Journal for Quality Participation, 16(4), 78–85.

Public School Forum of North Carolina. (1987). The condition of being an educator: An analysis of North Carolina's public schools. Raleigh: Public School Forum of North Carolina.

Rehm, R., & Muth, R. (1998). Toward a theory of problem-based learning for the preparation of educational administrators. In R. Muth with M. Martin (Eds.), Toward the year 2000: Leadership for quality schools (pp. 289–299). Sixth Annual Yearbook of the National Council of Professors of Educational Administration. Lancaster, PA: Technomic.

Savery, J. R., & Duffy, T. M. (1995). Problem based learning: An instructional model and its constructivist framework. In B. G. Wilson (Ed.), Constructivist learning environments: Case studies in instructional design (pp. 135–148). Englewood Cliffs, NJ: Educational Technology.

Schmidt, H. G., Norman, G. R., & Boshuizen, H. P. A. (1990). A cognitive perspective on medical expertise: Theory and implications. Academic Medicine, 65(10), 611–621.

Schön, D. A. (1983). The reflective practitioner: How professionals think in action. New York: Basic Books.

Schön, D. A. (1987). Educating the reflective practitioner: Toward a new design for teaching and learning in the professions. San Francisco: Jossey-Bass.

Schwab, J. J. (1978). The practical: A language for curriculum. In I. Westbury & N. J. Wilkof (Eds.), Science, curriculum and liberal arts: Selected essays (pp. 287–321). Chicago: University of Chicago Press.

Sergiovanni T. J. (1991). The principalship: A reflective practice perspective (2nd ed.). Boston, MA: Allyn & Bacon.

Sharan, S. (1980). Cooperative learning in small groups: Recent methods and effects on achievement, attitudes and ethnic relations. Review of Educational Research, 50(2), 315–342.

Stringer, E. T. (1996). Action research: A handbook for practitioners. Thousand Oaks, CA: Sage.

Trist, E. (1981, June). The evolution of socio-technical systems: A conceptual framework and an action research program. Occasional paper no. 2. Ontario, Canada: Ontario Quality of Working Life Centre.

The Professional Studies Model (PSM) and Professional Development for Practicing Administrators in the New Millennium

JOHN R. HOYLE and ARNOLD D. OATES

In keeping with the 2000 Yearbook theme, the focus of this chapter is on a preparation model that is best suited to strengthen the abilities of school leaders to face the challenges in the new millennium. According to Hoyle, English, and Steffy (1998), this preparation model is the Professional Studies Model (PSM) which was one of the most significant changes in administrator preparation programs in the last decade. The PSM centers on a cohort of students who are practicing or aspiring administrators selected by a committee consisting of both university professors and practicing administrators from school districts who work collaboratively with universities. Research in group dynamics and group process gave rise to the cohort concept for graduate study.

Gloria Murray (1998) makes a strong case for the use of cohorts to facilitate the development of transformational leaders for schools. Murray says it this way: "First of all, cohorts can be viewed as laboratories for researching, learning, and practicing the collaborative, interactive and social nature of transformational leadership. . . . Experiences found in group processing and reflection found in cohort preparation programs better prepare aspiring school leaders for facilitating transformation in all work groups" (pp. 23, 24). While medical schools have used student cohorts for decades, it is a recent addition to graduate programs in educational administration. The authors agree that the cohort model is superior to the traditional one in terms of team-building skills, moral leadership, sharing, and mentoring. Dr. John Taylor, Director of Staff Development in Conroe, Texas ISD, believes that professional development through cohorts has been a positive and enriching experience for participants. Cohort members have raised the level of dialogue relating to issues facing educational administrators. Murray (1998) sums the use of cohorts by writing, "Cohort groups can add mightily to the knowledge base for education administration and provide insight into the effect of transformational leadership in schooling" (p. 26).

John R. Hoyle, Texas A&M University
Arnold D. Oates, Texas A&M University

This chapter includes a description of the Professional Studies Model and its strengths and concerns. Selected research studies are presented on the impact of the PSM and cohort system at East Carolina University, the University of Georgia, the University of Missouri-Columbia, and eight California universities. Finally, research findings are presented from a sub-set of students from three doctoral cohorts at Texas A&M since 1990. The primary focus of the study was to investigate the perceived relationships between the PSM and the professional development of each cohort member.

THE PROFESSIONAL STUDIES MODEL (PSM)

The PSM requires students to undergo a one-year program to earn a Master's or Specialist's degree and a three- to four-year program for the Ed.D. or Ph.D. Efforts are made to teach knowledge "domains" rather than traditional courses that follow no sequence. The faculty usually consists of both university and clinical faculty (i.e., superintendents and principals) who plan and teach together. The focus of this paper in on PSM programs for the Ed.D. or Ph.D.

Classes are conducted over "extended weekends," intensive summer sessions running two to five weeks, or semester courses that meet for three to five hours one night a week. This PSM was brought about by the general perception that school administrator preparation programs were out of touch with the changing nature of schools and schooling. Failing to tie the abstract theoretical issues of school management to the primary functions of teaching, learning, and school improvement, preparation programs became targets of criticism by practicing administrators, state departments, and university administrators. The ground-breaking report produced by the National Commission on Excellence in Educational Administration (1987) reinforced the need to change the role of administrator from managing things to the primary function of instructional leadership and school improvement. Also *Leaders* recommended that administrator preparation should be housed in professional schools rather in colleges of arts and sciences. The professional school model encourages student cohort groups and programs that combine intellectual development with the world of practice braced by carefully planned field experiences under the tutelage of skilled mentors (Forsyth, 1987).

While the professional school model, which has become commonly called the Professional Studies Model (PSM), has become the most popular and widely used model, critics remain. Professors have expressed concern about a lowering of standards at the expense of intellectual rigor. Some believe that the balance of theory and practice leans in favor of practice without a strong theoretical and research base. Wesson (1996) questioned if collusion among doctoral cohort members at Arkansas State University was detrimental to learning and the overall success of the PSM. Wesson concludes that any negative signs of collusion gave way to cohesion as a result of well designed cohort learning experiences that created team work and high levels of learn-ing. In spite of the criticisms and potential problems with the PSM, most professors of educational administration agree with practicing administrators and professional administrator associations that traditional doctoral programs which require full-time graduate study are no longer a viable option for most potential and practicing admin-istrators who desire to pursue a degree and licensure. Most students with family re-sponsibilities have financial difficulties recovering from the loss of salary for one year or one semester. Also, some who choose a year of full-time residency and complete a doctorate experience difficulty landing a position commensurate with their academic credentials and advanced training. Most practicing administrators seek doctoral pro-grams that allow them to keep their jobs, and steady income, with the hope of being promoted within their local system. School superintendents and personnel adminis-trators are expressing concerns about the growing shortage of qualified young school administrators to fill the number of principalships.

The growing shortage of qualified and talented candidates to fill the growing number of principalships, especially in urban areas, is a call for alarm. Paul Hous-ton (1998), the executive director of the American Association of School Adminis-trators, reports that national studies reveal a shortage of candidates for leadership positions in schools in America and that the most critical shortage is in the urban secondary schools where the role of principal has become more demanding and dangerous. The better candidates prefer suburban or rural schools where there is less violence, more community support, and less stress. Houston (1998), says it this way:

> There are those who may not see this as a problem because they do not see a need for ad-ministrators. Others think that anyone who has ever run anything can do the job. While most people in America have come to accept the proverb that "it takes a village to raise a child," not all have recognized that it takes a leader to create and nurture the village. Vir-tually every piece of educational research recognizes that effective schools and school dis-tricts start and end with strong leaders. (p. 44)

Thus the nurture and care of talented school leaders to fill this void is not only the concern of administrator preparation programs, but also the entire university and so-ciety itself. It takes a committed "village" of professors, university administrators, policy makers, state and national professional associations, and legislators to recruit and prepare the "best and brightest" for leadership roles in the schools of the twenty-first century. Preparation programs must be closely linked with the schools to provide relevant degree programs and state-of-the-art staff development for busy school lead-ers. This link between the degree program and professional development must center on the enhancement of scholarly practice and ethical praxis for each member of the cohort. The PSM is proving to be the best vehicle to make this important link from preparation to professional development

The PSM as a competency and skill-driven degree program with greater empha-sis on field-based learning is closely linked to the needs of the public schools and those who lead them (Fulmer & Marcano, 1997). While changes are being made in preparation programs, much of the content, social justice emphases, and instructional delivery are not connected to professional development needs of America's school leaders.

RESEARCH AND THE PSM

Progress has been made in designing more relevant and "student friendly" Master's and doctoral programs that serve a more diverse student population. Berry (1995) believes that the major reason that graduate students fail to graduate from educational administration programs is that the faculty is insensitive to the personal "spirit" and professional concerns of the students. However, student evaluations of new PSM doctoral programs reveal that most students in the cohort model perceive their program to be relevant, sensitive to their personal and professional lives, and academically rigorous. Doctoral students at East Carolina University indicated that the academic rigor, faculty advising, faculty and student interactions, and the structure and sequence of the program were all effective. The students express concerns over the quality and relevance of the research and methodology and dissertation proposal components of the program and racial insensitivity was cited by some as a concern. Researchers also found that improvements are needed in the interpersonal dynamics between students and the professors to further enrich the program (Bell, McDowelle, Lanier, & Lanier, 1996).

A cohort program developed at the University of Georgia incorporated principles of problem-based learning and student-based learning to help strengthen the link between academic content and professional practice. Although the students gained new skills and knowledge as self-directed learners and in building trust, taking risks, and in problem finding and solving, the adjustment to "changing interpersonal dynamics between professors and students" was necessary for successful implementation of the new PSM. Faculty were learning new skills to encourage and lead students in gaining increased confidence in problem-based and self-learning, and were eventually able to "step back" to allow the students to take control of their own learning. Faculty are looking at the time and energy required and ways to create the problem-based curriculum and are seeking the best ways to use their energies and resources to upgrade the program in the years ahead (Pajak, Tanner, Rees, & Holmes, 1995).

A 1996 study conducted by Hatley, Arrendondo, Donaldson, Short, and Updike, revealed that students enrolled in a PSM cohort doctoral program at the University of Missouri-Columbia were positive about their experience. They saw the experience as both "challenging and exhilarating" and "an excellent learning experience." The students also had high praise for the cohort model which promoted collaboration and friendships (p. 10). The following preliminary conclusions were drawn from the study.

- The program has had positive impact on students' cognitive growth as well as on their professional practice.
- Content, instructional strategies, and experiential learning activities . . . were well received by students. Students feel free to express both their positive and negative comments about the program, with the belief that they can influence both the content and context of their own learning within the doctoral program.
- Faculty members and campus administrators' perceptions of the program's impact on their own practice and on the department's on-campus instructional program vary with their level of involvement with the cohort program. (pp. 26–27)

Shelly Dorn and Rosemary Papalewis (1997) analyzed the perceptions of 108 doctoral students from eight California universities. Their research suggests that group cohesiveness and persistence to complete their degrees are significantly correlated (p. 3). This finding reinforces the general findings that the cohort model provides support and creates cohesive teams which collaborate to identify and solve educational problems. A student in the first cohort doctoral program at Texas A&M University commented that, "This experience will prepare us to be collaborative leaders with the vision to build exemplary schools for all of our children (Bratlien, Genzer, Hoyle, & Oates, 1992).

While the successes of PSM doctoral programs are many, questions about their usefulness in the ongoing professional development of the cohort participants have received little attention in the literature. The following study focuses on the professional development dimension.

PURPOSE OF THE STUDY

The purpose of this study was to investigate the relationship between the curriculum in the Professional Studies Model doctorate at Texas A&M University and the professional development needs of those who have completed or are currently enrolled in the program. The belief that a PSM doctorate will prepare a school leader for life is a false one. Once a student becomes "doctor," most preparation programs lose contact and the student is on his or her own to solve the problems of schools and schooling. Based on this common practice of "severing" the umbilical cord between the student and the preparation program, the researchers surveyed former and current doctoral students who have had the "cohort" experience.

A 23-item forced-choice and open-ended Doctoral Cohort Questionnaire was developed and reviewed by faculty and research assistants. The questionnaires were mailed to 42 former or current cohort members in April 1998. Twenty-two of the 42 returned their questionnaires and 2 were returned because of no forwarding address. Phone interviews were conducted as follow-up for corroborating data to help analyze on the primary question about the relationship between the PSM and its effect on the daily job performance of each participant.

FINDINGS AND IMPLICATIONS

The overall impression of the PSM cohort students was very positive with some caveats. In response to the general research question about the relevance of the PSM doctorate to ongoing professional development of the participants, Item number 6, "The course of study met or is meeting my professional expectations to prepare me for the next level of my career," had a mean score of 3.41 out of 4.00 with only one response below 3 (see Table 1). For Item eight, "The course of study balances theory and practice," cumulative responses revealed a mean score of 3.50 with two respondents scoring a 2.00. Item nine, "The course of study places appropriate emphasis on curriculum and instruction," was slightly lower with a mean of 3.04 with five cohort members registering a 2.00, "disagree moderately." The last item that relates directly to the professional development issue, number 14, "The course work in educational technology was adequate to meet your professional needs," was the lowest of any score at 2.26. Seven respondents reported a 1.00 and three others recorded a 2.00.

Responses to the open-ended questions relating to the professional development issue closely aligned with the items listed above. Among these responses are the following:

- Courses with more school visitations would be productive. These proved helpful to me.
- One of the two choices of courses should be allowed, like electives, to meet special needs of individuals.
- Let each student design his/her own internship (IEP) based on present job status.
- Allow students to select an elective that could help in the job/position.
- More emphasis on management/intern in higher leadership roles.
- The course requirements fit job descriptions.
- The cohort model allowed discussions relevant to problems directly related to our own districts.
- Well-planned instruction, continuous instructional atmosphere, use of theory and practice.
- Improve the internship, mine was too much busywork notebook activity.
- Finance and curriculum need to be updated.
- Too much emphasis on preparation for the superintendency, more emphasis on instructional leadership.

Dr. Taylor, Director of Staff Development in Conroe, Texas ISD, observed that cohort members asked "probing and important questions relating to curriculum, instruction, and leadership issues" at district staff meetings. Cohort members who were interviewed stated that the program evaluation course allowed them to apply theory and research to the application of addressing identified problems in the district.

A recent cohort graduate shared the following concerning job performance: "I had always considered myself to be a top performer. I am now a better time manager, can

TABLE I. Results—Cohort Questionnaire.

Item No.	SA	A	D	SD	Mean	Std. Dev.
4. The most difficult element of the admissions criteria was the presentation portion in the interview.	0	6	13	3	2.13	.639
5. The written exercise was the most difficult element of the admissions criteria.	1	7	11	3	2.27	.767
6. The course of study met or is meeting my professional expectations to prepare me for the next level of my career.	12	8	1	1	3.40	.796
7. The sequence in the course offerings is appropriate without too much overlap in the content.	5	14	3	0	3.09	.610
8. The course of study balances theory with practice.	12	9	1	1	3.50	.597
9. The course of study places appropriate emphasis on curriculum and instruction.	6	11	5	0	3.04	.722
10. The course of study includes the appropriate number of tools courses, i.e., evaluation, statistics, tests and measurement, and research	10	11	1	0	3.40	.590
11. The summer courses are as convenient as possible to meet the demands of your job responsibilities.	6	7	5	4	2.68	1.08
12. Most courses were offered at a time that best fit your work schedule.	15	7	0	0	3.68	.476
13. The district (superintendent and board) was/is supportive of your efforts to complete the degree requirements.	11	9	2	0	3.40	.666
14. The coursework in educational technology was adequate to meet your professional needs.	3	6	3	7	2.26	1.14
15. The cohort members usually bonded and assisted each other in the learning process.	17	4	1	0	3.72	.550
16. Your mentor/advisor was usually available when you needed him/her.	13	9	0	0	3.59	.503
17. Your were adequately prepared for the written and oral comprehensive/preliminary (San Antonio and Conroe-Willis I only).	11	0	0	0	4.00	.000
18. You were given ample assistance in identifying a research topic for your record of study (if applicable to you).	9	10	0	1	3.35	.745

put information together in a more comprehensive manner for presentations, and recognize the importance of research and planning when making decisions."

All cohort interviewees related the teamwork and camaraderie that existed among the doctoral cohort. One person stated, "These members have become family to me."

Other Items Relating to PSM Program

The students tended to believe that neither the eight-minute oral presentation nor the written exercise was the most difficult part of the admissions process with mean scores of 2.13 and 2.27. (See Items 4 and 5 in Table 1.) The cohorts believe that the course offerings are appropriate without too much overlap in the content (Item 7, mean 3.09). The students feel that the tools courses in evaluation, statistics, tests and measurement, and research were appropriate in number and content (Item 10, mean 3.40). However, responses to the open-ended questions produced some valuable suggestion for improvement. The suggestions were as follows:

- Offer stat courses before the education research courses.
- More emphasis on program evaluation and data group process ideas.
- Proper sequence of courses should have statistics before tests and measurements and offer the research class along with the first stat course.
- Stat class should be taught in a lab setting.

Responses to whether or not the summer class schedule was convenient as possible are mixed. Twelve of the respondents strongly agreed or agreed while nine disagreed or strongly disagreed (Item 11, mean 2.68). A related item stating "Most courses were offered at a time that best fit your work schedule," was viewed as favorable (Item 12, mean 3.68). The contrast in the mean scores on these related items is interesting. Perhaps one reason is the summer classes which meet three or four times a week create a state of frenzy for the commuting student, while the fall and spring semester classes meet one night a week or on selected weekends. Since the faculty are on 10.5 month contracts, most of the classes are held during the first summer session and with very few the second session. This creates problems for the students who are required to be on the job as school administrators for most of June and part of July. No solution to this ongoing problem has been found at this writing. While the one 90-minute commute for the students from the Conroe, Texas, area is not easy, every effort is made to schedule the night classes on campus or in Conroe to best fit student schedules. Most professors have been willing to make the drive to the school district to conduct some of the classes each semester. Students in the Duquesne Interdisciplinary Doctoral Programs for Educational Leaders (IDPEL) PSM in Pittsburg, Pennsylvania, praise the faculty for their willingness to commute to their homesites and their ease of communication with distance learning via satellite TV, e-mail, faxes, the web, and video conferencing (Henderson, 1995).

The district superintendents and boards were viewed by the cohorts as "supportive of your efforts to complete the degree requirements." (See Item 13, Table 1.) This positive response is no surprise since the superintendent and his top associate superintendents were directly involved in the identification and selection of each cohort member. A key to the past success of the Texas A&M University PSM is this close collaboration between the department and the district superintendent in identifying candidates with the talent and interest in school leadership and in planning field-based experiences which will benefit both the district and the students. The first cohort PSM between our department and three San Antonio Texas school districts led to national recognition by The American Association of School Administrators in 1991 for Outstanding Achievement in Leadership Preparation.

The most positive response from each cohort was the item which stated, "The cohort members usually bonded and assisted each other in the learning process." The mean score on this item number 15 is 3.72 which supports similar findings in the studies described above which were conducted at the University of Georgia, University of Missouri, East Carolina University, Arkansas State University and in eight California universities. In each study the cohort model's primary strength is the bonding and friendships that occur as a result of sharing the "ordeal" and working as teams to identify and solve problems and to lean on each other to stay the course to completion of the degree. Students in this study offer the following comments on the value of the cohort model.

- Strong collegial support, coordination of efforts with district.
- The cohort provided a built-in safety net, I have received life time relationships as a result of the cohort.
- Support from cohort members, faculty support.
- Support from other cohort members, offering classes in the school district.
- Core group ID.
- Support of cohort members, development of professional relationships with professors.
- Development of professional relationships with peers, the group keeps us all moving forward.
- Carpooling and extra help, social aspects, team work.
- Individual faculty and department office staff.

Weakness of the Cohort Mode

The students indicated that the cohort model tends to isolate them from the other doctoral students. Another concern expressed was that some individuals have higher standards than the others which can cause stress and a problem with the balance of work in a team project. This balance and the potential problem of too much collusion among cohort members are other concerns that need attention by program monitors. Collusion among four of the cohort members on recent comprehensive written exams created a problem for the faculty. The collusion surfaced during the oral part of the exams when students gave the same pat answers to questions related to naturalistic inquiry and educational foundations. The four students were required to undergo remediation on selected topics and be re-examined. The faculty will alter the exam process in the future by giving exam questions to examine each student in more confidential ways.

The final three items on the questionnaire that focused on the availability of mentors/advisors (Item 16), adequate preparation for oral and written comprehensive exams (Item 17) and assistance in identifying a research topic for the record of study (Item 19) all received a very favorable response of with a mean of 3.59, 4.00, and 3.35 respectively (see Table 1).

CONCLUSIONS

The results of this first comprehensive evaluation of the past and current PSM doctorate at Texas A&M University produced valuable data to assist faculty in improving the program. The impressions formed by those who have completed the program will prove helpful to those currently enrolled. While many of the responses by cohort members were not surprising, some of the positive and negative impressions were. The students perceived that the curriculum in the PSM doctoral program was relevant to their staff development needs as practicing school administrators with the exception of the course in educational technology. However, after analysis of the data, the researchers realize that the questionnaire was inadequate to fully answer the professional development question. Only four items were directed to the primary focus of this study, thus leaving the researchers and the reader asking more questions about the value of the cohort model in assisting the student in professional growth and success on the job. To strengthen the database, a follow-up to the study was conducted through interviews which directed questions toward the professional development issue and moral consciousness and ethical praxis in their shared experiences.

The overwhelming support of the cohort model for its positive impact on the professional and personal lives of the students and the overall positive impression of the sequencing of the classes and the professors were somewhat surprising based on conversations with some of the students over the past year. The problems related to the sequence of the statistics, tests and measurement, and research classes were more serious than program planners thought they were. Perhaps this problem emerged because planners did not thoroughly assess each cohort member's background in statistics. The expectation was that students would have a basic knowledge of statistics. There was little surprise that the educational technology class was viewed as somewhat irrelevant due to the nature of the course content and focus.

The students are sensitive to the problems of scheduling classes which are convenient for them and the professor. Program planners have an especially difficult time scheduling professors in curriculum and instruction, statistics and tests and measurements. While the PSM is a high priority for professors in educational administration, the same priority is rarely found in the other departments. Planners attempt to identify professors in other departments who have interest in school improvement and administration and enjoy working with practicing school administrators. This problem may explain the one-on-one relationship with the planners of the program and professors in supporting disciplines seems to be more successful than merely working through proper administrative procedures.

The findings of this study add support for the PSM doctorate that centers on cohorts of students. Not only is the knowledge base presented in a more sequential and accountable manner, but the students are more engaged in problem-based, self-directed learning and team building than is found in most traditional programs. These learning opportunities were very relevant to the daily job requirements of each student. The networking of students in class, via e-mail and fax, the closer and more frequent communication with professors and the district central administration, and the benefits to the district are all hallmarks of the PSM doctorate. There is little doubt that America's schools are facing more social, political, and financial turmoil each year. It is therefore vital to the welfare of America's children and youth that universities and school districts invest time and money in identifying and training the best, brightest, toughest and most compassionate school leaders. The PSM does not solve all of the financial, political, and personnel problems facing schools and schooling, but given serious thought and careful planning, the model is the best vehicle available to carry the preparation of school leaders into the next millennium. However, the greatest benefit of the PSM shared in the follow-up interviews was summed up in this statement: "I grew mentally and spiritually from my participation in the doctoral cohort program. With the support I received from the professors and my fellow cohort members, I don't believe I would have finished my degree. You see, I never felt alone. That meant everything."

The faculty, graduate students, and school leaders agree that the professional studies model is proving to be the best process to prepare moral and democratic leaders who can march confidently into the new millennium.

REFERENCES

Bell, E., McDowelle, J. O., Lanier, S. P., & Lanier, M. K. (1996, November). A case study of an ed.d. in educational leadership, school of education, East Carolina state university. Paper presented at the southern regional council on educational administration annual conference.

Berry, M. D. (1995) Why our doctoral students drop out: A challenge to educational administration professors. In P. Bredeson and J. Scribner (Eds.), The Professoriate: Challenges and

Promises. The third yearbook of the National Council of Professors of Educational Administration. Lancaster, PA: Technomic Publ. Co.

Bratlien, M., Genzer, S. M., Hoyle, J. R., & Oates, A. (1992). The professional studies doctorate: Leaders for learning. Journal of school leadership, 2(1), 75–89.

Dorn, S. H., & Papalewis. R. (1997, March). Improving doctoral student retention. Paper presented the annual meeting of the American Educational Research Association, Chicago, IL.

Forsyth, P. (1987, November). Revamping the preparation of school administrators. Paper presented at the annual conference of the southwest development laboratory, Albuquerque, NM.

Fulmer, C., & Marcano, R. L. (1997). Rethinking learning cultures: Themes from educational leadership cohort stories. In School Administration: The New Knowledge Base. The fifth yearbook of the National Council of Professors of Educational Administration. Lancaster, PA: Technomic Publ. Co.

Hatley, R. V., Arrendondo, D. E., Donaldson, J. F., Short, P. M., & Updike, L. W. (1996, October). Evaluating the design, implementation, and impact of a non-traditional cohort ed.d. program in educational leadership and policy analysis. Paper presented at the annual meeting of the University Council for Educational Administration, Louisville, KY.

Henderson, J. (1995, Spring). Translating theory into practice: Preparing school leaders with mentoring and practice experience. The AASA Professor, 17(4), 1–4.

Houston, P. (1998, June 3). The ABCs of administrative shortages. Education week. 44 & 32.

Hoyle, J., English, F, & Steffy, B. (1998). Skills for successful 21st century school leaders. Arlington, VA: The American Association of School Administrators.

Murray, G. J. (1998). New leaders for restructured schools: Can cohort models meet the challenge? The AASA Professor, 21(3/4), 22–27.

National Commission on Excellence in Educational Administration (1987). Leaders for America's schools. Tempe, AZ: Arizona State University.

Pajak, E., Tanner, C. K., Rees, F., & Holmes, C. T. (1995, April). Using a pbl student-centered approach to doctoral study. Paper presented at the annual meeting of the American Educational Research Association, San Francisco, CA.

Wesson, L. H. (1996, April). Cohesion or collusion: Impact of a cohort structure on educational leadership doctoral students. Paper presented at the annual meeting of the American Educational Research Association, New York, NY.

Jubilee Justice: Educating the Ethical Imagination through Literature

RITA E. GUARE

PRELUDE

> *When you open your eyes*
> *We'll walk, once more*
> *among the hours and their inventions.*
> *We'll walk among appearances*
> *and bear witness to time and its conjugations.*
> *Perhaps we'll open the day's doors.*
> *And then we shall enter the unknown.*
> *(Bishop, 1983, p. 274)*

In the poem "January First," Elizabeth Bishop wrote about the year's doors opening and about having to create meaning upon entering a new world. Crossing the threshold of a new millennium invites educational administrators in similar ways to "bear witness to time," to "open the day's doors," and to enter more open spaces where we become more fully ourselves by engaging and enlarging the work of justice.

Warnings about Y2K disasters and promises of stunning celebrations to mark this historic moment of time are far behind us now. What remains is the lingering belief that the coming of the new millennium is about so much more. Historically, the end of one time cycle and the beginning of another is a period exposing intense vulnerability and surfacing unrealized promise. The Greeks called it a kairos, a critical time for seeking Ultimate Meaning. For educational leaders searching for deeper purposes, the year 2000 marks a great Jubilee. It is a time to change our lives, to renew our hearts, and to celebrate a new vision of justice.

In the Hebrew scriptures, the Jubilee was one of the holy years, a sacred time, to "sound the trumpet," to "let the land lie fallow," to proclaim "liberty in the land for all, to forgive debts, and to make relationships right" (Leviticus 25: 10–17). The

---

Rita E. Guare, Fordham University

biblical tradition of Jubilee is not some pious religious custom from the past. Rather, Jubilee is an ideal that includes a tradition of memory, a tradition of forgiveness and action. At the heart of Jubilee is a spiritual and ethical call to justice, one that urges us to start over, to reconcile our relationships with one another, and to renew the work we do as school leaders.

The solemn opening of the Holy Door to Saint Peter's Basilica in Rome marked the beginning of Jubilee 2000. In Western Europe the custom of passing through the Holy Doors dates back to the sixteenth century with pilgrims marching over sacred thresholds to remember, to realize, and to renew their commitment to living Jubilee justice.

For educational leaders, Jubilee may be just as significant and symbolic if we pay attention to the poet who invites us to open our eyes and "walk, once more, among the hours," opening doors and crossing thresholds to deeper meanings and purposes. In the spirit of those early pilgrims, who marched into futures of challenge and promise, educational administrators can walk in the company of others: remembering the past, celebrating and critiquing the present, and committing to a future of acting justly in the name of the other.

It is a kairos. This crucial time for seeking "more open territory" (Heidegger, 1968, p. 13), beyond the custody of "the established order of things" (Foucault, 1973, p. XXI), calls for inner renewal and reconciliation. For many, the tradition of Jubilee with its intent to reestablish relationships rooted in justice may not be well-known. Nevertheless, I want to frame this chapter and explore the possibilities of reeducating the ethical imaginations of administrators within the historical and spiritual context of Jubilee.

PURSUING PURPOSE

> The questions that we have to ask and to answer . . . during this moment of transition are so important that they may well change the lives of all men and women forever. For we have to ask ourselves, here and now, do we wish to join that procession, or don't we? On what terms shall we join that procession? Above all, where is it leading us. . . .
>
> (Woolf, 1966, pp. 62–63)

This chapter has a dual purpose. First, it raises the question of what really matters in the preparation of educational administrators for tomorrow's schools. Despite the consensus that leadership counts, deep philosophical and political disagreements remain about what kind of educational administrators are needed; where should they come from; and, how should educational administrators be prepared for a future of challenges that we can only dimly imagine.

The idea that strong administrative leaders are essential for good schools is not new. A rich tradition of research exists in the field to support this claim (Fullan, 1993; Goodlad, 1984; Goodlad, Soder, & Sirotnik, 1990; Lawrence-Lightfoot, 1983; Sizer, 1992; Vaill, 1989). The renewed focus on administrative leadership, however, reflects a belated recognition that national and local standards alone are not enough to inspire what is deepest in us, a life lived from the center of our being (Beck & Murphy, 1994;

Boyer, 1995; Groome, 1998; Noddings, 1992; Sergiovanni, 1992, 1994, 1996; Sizer, 1996; Starratt, 1994, 1996).

In *Here and Now*, Henri Nouwen (1994) describes that kind of living in this way:

> Wheels help me remember how important a life lived from the center is. When I move along the rim, I can reach one spoke after another, but when I stay at the hub I am in touch with all the spokes at once. (p. 18)

In spite of the many distractions, the diversity of the many strokes, that claim our time and energy as administrators, Nouwen (1994) urges a more focused, life-giving attention to all that we intend as leaders.

In order for administrative leaders to help restore integrity to education, energize dispirited teachers, create futures of hope and promise for all children, and bring parents and community leaders to the table as partners in a common enterprise, preparation programs must address ways to nurture and sustain a vision lived from the center. What counts as administrative leadership? What is at the hub of the preparation programs we design? These are questions "we have to ask and to answer . . . during this moment of transition" (Woolf, 1966, p. 62), during this historic and spiritual moment of Jubilee. These are questions of the utmost importance precisely because they bear within themselves the unrealized possibility of changing lives forever.

In pursuing these questions, I intend to examine the boundaries of the postmodern condition, which intersect with and are sympathetic to a Jubilee Year that calls for deeper meanings of justice. These boundaries reveal a discontent with things as they are, expose oppressions and injustices, and suggest new understandings of the self in relation to the human community.

In form, this work is an aesthetic essay suggesting the second purpose of the chapter, namely, the importance of the literary arts in illuminating paths toward justice. Literature is a rich resource for educating the ethical imaginations of administrators. The interpretation of literature can be a form of critical inquiry into administrative processes and actions (Brieschke, 1990). Such diagnosis can help administrators set new agendas for research and reflection, invite less authoritarian modes of teaching and learning, and catalyze insights about our own moral visions (Patrick, 1998). This chapter may hint at a posture for administrative leaders in this postmodern season and may be an opportunity for those involved in preparation programs to consider the place of literature in reeducating ethical imaginations.

MAPPING THE DIVIDE: MODERNISM AND POSTMODERNISM

> For fragmentation is now very widespread, not only throughout society, but also in each individual; and this is leading to a kind of general confusion of the mind, which creates an endless series of problems and interferes with our clarity of perception so seriously as

to prevent us from being able to solve most of them. . . . The notion that all these fragments are separately existent is evidently an illusion, and this illusion can not do other than lead to endless conflict and confusion.

(Bohm, 1980, p. 10)

The modern worldview is rapidly giving way to what is being called postmodernism, a worldview that is still largely unarticulated and notoriously imprecise. In fact, some writers reject the term postmodern altogether and replace it with the term postessentialist, denoting a world, which has lost its ability and its desire to think or speak about essences. In this chapter postmodernism will be used as a "term for a time in clear contradistinction to those that sought and believed in the notion of essences" (Beatham, 1991, p. 10). Postmodernism, more than any other body of current theoretical writings, has resulted in a profound shift creating radical changes in contemporary thought and experience.

Characteristic of this emerging worldview is the unmistakable feeling that we no longer lay claim to the Enlightenment ambitions of unity, certainty, and predictability. A postmodern philosophy rejects what Jean Francois Lyotard has called the metanarrative, that is, any master or universal code that assumes the validity of its own truth claim (1984, p. XXIV). At its deepest level, postmodernism represents not just another crisis in the ebb and flow of history. Rather, it represents a new crisis of the modernist culture itself. The poet, Matthew Arnold captures the turning tides of this crisis when he wrote:

> The Sea of Faith
> Was once, too, at the full, and round earth's shore
> Lay like the folds of a bright girdle furled.
> But now I only hear
> Its melancholy, long, withdrawing roar,
> Retreating, to the breath
> Of the night-wind, down the vast edges drear
> And naked shingles of the world.
> *(1986, pp. 597–598)*

Many believe that the outgoing tide of modernism has nearly run its course. However, the feeling that the modern period has reached its end is not new. Revelations about epochal changes in the social, political, economic, and cultural contexts of our lives were disclosed nearly three decades ago. In the 1970s the historical limits of modernism came into sharp focus. Since then, there has been growing belief in the following ideas: we are not bound to complete what Habermas has called the "project of modernity"; we are beginning to recognize that chaos rather than "man-made" order is the natural language of the universe, and, we need not pursue the arts as some telos of abstraction, but rather as pathways toward plurality, solidarity and justice. The combined wisdom of these intuitions has opened up a host of undreamed possibilities for creative endeavors today. Instead of being bound to one version of the one best history that is directed toward some logical and unfolding goal, a more dynamic historical pattern has spiraled. We are beginning to explore openly the contradictions and unrealized promises of the Enlightenment project. That project advanced by human reason and science, and later coupled with the rise of the Industrial Revolution, advocated rugged individualism, a devaluing of nature, and an unrelenting march toward progress. This ideology removed any possibility for shared human experience and knowledge particularly for those who were not privileged.

Modern narratives, however, are disclosing that cultures and contemporary times hold the tensions of this great paradox. The intellectual legacy from seventeenth- and eighteenth-century liberal, enlightenment thinking has conditioned us to behave in ways that make absolute the limitless possibilities and efficacy of reason and science. Yet, twentieth-century events, including world wars, holocausts, ethnic cleansings, disease, and hungers of all kinds have compelled us to question the bounds of such reason. We lament over what T.S. Eliot has called a century with its heap of broken images. At the same time, we need to push beyond the limits of reason that have created the kinds of myths and narratives, which have become occasions for oppression. What I am pressing for in this chapter is a vision of the ethical imagination as a metaphor for releasing the full flourishing of the human community.

John Dewey believed that a democratic society requires a community in which there is real uncertainty and contingency, with people who are still incomplete, who are still becoming all that we cherish, hope, and love (Westerbrook, 1991). It seems to me that what Dewey was calling for was an awakening of the human imagination so that life can always be seen "in the making." Only the imagination has the power and the passion to evoke visions that have the capacity to stir what is deepest in the human soul: a hunger and thirst for justice and mercy.

In spite of the distinctively pragmatic beliefs that shape our lives, the American liberal democratic myth of justice and human rights is persistently and inspirationally rendered in Enlightenment language, which we find embedded in the independence text of Thomas Jefferson. As a people, we share belief in Jefferson's self-evident truth that rights are naturally occurring, inherent, and intrinsic to the human condition. Enlightenment philosophical thought justified this moral position as residing in the essence of human nature. Enlightenment philosophers were of one mind and one voice in believing and in proclaiming that human reason alone would achieve moral truth through reason's appeal to conscience. Moreover, Enlightenment thinkers held that in the presence of free and open discussion human reason would arrive at the one right answer to all moral and scientific questions.

This line of reasoning has led Western democratic institutions to engage in open and deliberative exchanges in pursuit of answers consistent with a single essentialist definition of human nature, a definition which identified those faculties of heart and mind common to all humanity. These Enlightenment beliefs rooted in essentialist thought moved entire societies away from absolute religious sources of justification for moral action and toward absolute individual-based reasons for moral decisions.

The metanarratives of Enlightenment thinking, grounded in the individual human conscience informed and guided by reason, have been discredited by the critiques of some postmodernists. For them, one essential truth is an Enlightenment value and subject to critical reflection. Some postmoderns suggest more radically that there is no such thing as truth in itself. Rather, truth exists in abundance; it is always multiple; it is always plural.

Michel Foucault (1984) broadens and deepens postmodern discourse by shifting the focus of the argument. Foucault understands the postmodern project as one intended "to give new impetus, as far and wide as possible to the undefined work of freedom" (1984, p. 46). At the heart of postmodernism is an interrogation of modernity in the service of greater freedom. From his perspective, the Enlightenment search for objective truth has distracted us from the real work of freedom needed today. Foucault (1984) rejects the notion that meaning and truth are transcendent goals which human beings discover through abstract reflection. Rather, he stresses the role of free persons choosing and acting in order to open more just and lovelier ways of being in the world. The hope of postmodernism is that such attention to the present will lead to greater self and social understanding so that we may know more clearly the limitations of the modern world.

Postmoderns begin with a heightened sense of the historical context of all human knowing and acting. They build on the belief that there is no ground, no inquiry or action that is not situated, embedded in the human community. According to Foucault, "We must try to proceed with the analysis of ourselves as beings who are historically determined, to a certain extent, by the Enlightenment" (1984, p. 43). Unavoidably modern, postmodernists seek to move beyond the limits of modernity. According to James Bernauer, one of Foucault's ultimate aims is to transgress "the prisons of a particular historical determinism" (1990, p. 180). At the same time, Foucault wants to restore to the center of thought and action the "imaginative creativity" that was exiled by modernity so that once again it becomes possible to re-create new understandings of the human self at higher levels of complexity and at deeper levels of intimacy (Bernauer, 1990, p. 181).

The postmodern critical investigations of reason in her most exalted mood, essential truth, and power-knowledge claims occur through the interrogation of systems of thought and practices that may appear on the surface to be liberatory. However, when the systems are confronted, when the layers of institutions are pulled back, what we often see are living stories of oppression and not freedom. Far from gentle in their critique, postmodern thinkers cut to the marrow of the bone, leaving exposed to gaping, wondering eyes the unfulfilled promises of the Enlightenment project.

These postmodern shocks have caused fissures in the central morality tales of our culture, tales that have lost their power in stirring what is deepest in the human spirit. In *Murder in the Cathedral*, T.S. Eliot captured something of this loss and the price we would pay for hearts no longer awake, hearts hardened and disinterested to the secret terrors of others:

There have been oppression and luxury.
There have been poverty and license,
There has been minor injustice,
Yet we have gone on living,
Living and partly living . . .
We have seen births, deaths and marriages,
We have been afflicted with taxes,
We have had laughter and gossip,
Several girls have disappeared
Unaccountably, and some not able to.
We have all had our private terrors,
Our particular shadows, our secret fears.
(1958, pp. 180–181)

In spite of the lost legacy that many of us experience today, "we have gone on living, living and partly living." For well over two hundred years, seventeenth- and eighteenth-century metanarratives, grounded in Lockean liberal democracy and buttressed by the essentialist philosophy of Descartes and Kant, have guided inquiry and theory and have shaped educational practices and values. Today, postmodern thinkers, in search of a larger freedom and more generous acts of justice for all people are challenging the assumptions beneath these practices and values. Preparation programs interested in shaping a different kind of history for administrative practice, a history that does not destroy or privilege one form of inquiry as the exclusive way of knowing, will explore multiple ways for administrators to identify and deepen their core values.

THE HUB OF ADMINISTRATIVE PREPARATION

There is a central quality which is the root criterion of life and spirit . . . this quality is objective and precise, but it cannot be named. . . . The search which we make for this quality in our own lives is the central search of any person, and the crux of any individual person's story. It is the search for those moments and situations when we are most alive.
(Alexander, 1979, pp. 19ff.)

Leaders need a kind of whole-sightedness, a vision of the world in which what is unique, particular, and profoundly personal informs what is common, plural, and deeply communal. Mikhail Bakhtin (1981) explores the dialogic relationship between the individual and others, between the particular and the plural. Bakhtin (1981) believes that each human person understands his or her uniqueness only against the knowledge of other selves. Uniqueness presents itself because of the ability to see one's life from a particularly situated horizon, a singular space unreachable to any other. According to Bakhtin (1981) this results in what he calls an "excess of seeing," that is one person will always see and know something about the other, which from her place she cannot know herself. This "excess of seeing" invites solidarity with the other; through empathy, one can fill in the horizon of the other.

In this chapter, I have suggested that the hub represents that singular space unreachable to any other. Ethical persons live and lead from "a central quality, which is the root criterion of life and spirit" (Alexander, 1979, pp. 19ff.). The great paradox of this kind of living is that the most personal is most universal, the most intimate is most communal, the most contemplative is most active (Nouwen, 1994). The dialogical exchange that occurs by filling in one anothers' horizons creates the story of our lives together. An aesthetic vision of ourselves emerges at the same time that bonds of solidarity are created between us.

I am suggesting that preparation programs for administrators cultivate awareness and encourage patterns of action for remembering the bonds that we share with one another, for critiquing structures and processes that violate those bonds, and for recommitting to visions of justice that reconcile us with each other. Imaginative literature is rich with texts for illuminating awareness and encouraging actions, which I am suggesting administrators develop within themselves and in the learning communities that they lead. Experiences with works of literature have the power to prompt and provoke the continued fresh thinking our craft desperately needs.

What I am pressing for is the continual expansion of human capacities when we see and promote literature as enlarging preparation programs to include the aesthetic as a way of reeducating the ethical imagination. I have in mind three literary works that reveal ways of being and acting in the world worthy of critical and creative reflection. The Greek tragedy, *Antigone*, by Sophocles calls us to remember the high price of courage when the ideals of authority and responsibility harden into absolutes. Albert Camus's novel, *The Plague* (1948) helps us to see things as they are and summons the only hope in times of pestilence, critical action. Ralph Ellison's, *Invisible Man*, (1952), takes us beneath the city life of New York to find the rage and resignation of racism. In times like these, silence must be broken, oppression exposed, and the story of justice and mercy retold. Each of these novels has the capacity to make one "see, finding encouragement, consolation, fear, charm—all you demand—and, perhaps, also that glimpse of truth for which you have forgotten to ask" (Conrad, 1967, pp. IX-X).

It is not my attempt to explicate the rich meanings that each of these works holds. All I hope is to invite us to cross thresholds into worlds of imaginative literature, to open doors to multiple meanings, and to act from that central quality that is the root of our lives and spirits.

TRADITIONS OF REMEMBERING

Memory in all of its complexity and potency makes us more fully human. Memories are neither true nor false but often are incomplete and inadequate visions of the past. Essentially, the nature of memory is shifty, creating movements of consolation and discomfort of an outgrown self. To remember, then, is a way of constantly revising the human self. If we allow memory the space that it needs to re-vision and reconstruct reality, it will display the ambiguities, contradictions, and surprises that keep us open to the future.

Literature is rich with texts for learning to remember with multiple visions and perspectives. In particular, tragic drama reveals what happens in life when people fail to reconsider their actions in favor of more generous alternatives. The Greek tragedy *Antigone* offers readers any number of perspectives; however, I remember drawing specific insights that became defining for me.

Antigone, the daughter of Oedipus and Jocasta and the heroine of Sophocles' play, risks, and, ultimately, loses her life in order to bury her brother's body. With little thought about saving her own life, she openly refuses to obey King Creon's order that her brother, Polynecies, remain unburied as punishment for opposing Creon. Creon's law forbidding the burial of her brother's body strikes fire in Antigone's soul. She will not obey. When the guards discover Antigone breaking the King's law to honor her brother's dead body, she does not hide nor deny her actions. Rather, she acts to redeem a law that violates the unwritten law of God which is carved in every human heart and which cries out for justice.

Thich Nhat Hanh (1987) noted that purity of heart is the desire to will one thing and one thing alone. Antigone desired to be faithful to the memory of her brother. She lived her life against forgetting that memory. While Creon's concerns were not insignificant, his perceptions of his duty and authority as a ruler led him to act unjustly. Creon's action did not permit Antigone the kind of diseased complacency that may grip our lives. Rather her single-hearted response witnessed to Divine Justice and ruptured Creon's clearly controlled values that upheld the supreme authority of the state.

The ethical power of the play as a whole invites us beyond the intense conflict of values between these two characters to deeper realities about life and love and choosing to act in the name of the other for the sake of justice. Typically, Greek tragedy enacts a reconciliation of the human with the Divine made visible through human choice. The complexity of the play and the intricacies of human hearts making ethical choices can be found in the song lines, the lyrical narratives woven throughout *Antigone*. According to philosopher, Martha Nussbaum (1986), these lyrics not only guide the interpretation of the play, but they offer a vision of human understanding. Shortly after Antigone's act of transgression but before her capture, the chorus announces:

> *Numberless are the world's wonders,*
> *but none*
> *More wonderful than man . . .*

Singing about all man's powers and his supremacy over all creatures, the chorus adds:

> *He has made himself secure - from all*
> *But one:*
> *In the late wind of death he cannot stand.*

Finally, the chorus reflects:

> *O clear intelligence, force beyond all measure!*
> *O fate of man, working both good and evil!*
> *When the laws are kept, how proudly*
> *His city stands!*
> *When the laws are broken, what of his city then?*
> *(Sophocles, Antigone, Scene I, Ode I)*

The ethical choices in Antigone are never neutral. What is at work in the play is a view of human understanding straining toward justice. As Nussbaum explains:

> The lyrics both show us and engender in us a process of reflection and (self) discovery that works through a persistent attention to and (re) - interpretation of concrete words, images and incidents. We reflect on an incident not by subsuming it under a general rule, not by assimilating its features to the terms of an elegant scientific procedure, but by burrowing down into the depths of the particular, finding images and connections that will permit us to see it more truly, describe it more richly. (1986, p. 69)

Nussbaum advances a powerful understanding of life directed toward justice. In the compelling image of a spider sitting in the middle of its "web of connections responsive to the pull of each separate thread," the human person understands life and chooses to act justly by "hovering in thought and imagination around the enigmatic complexities of the seen particular" (1986, p. 69).

Hannah Arendt (1958) uses that same beautiful image of weaving a "web of human relationships" in describing how our actions and speech constitute what often lies between us. It is this "in-between" character of our lived lives where the almost invisible nature of the spider's threads bind us in communion and solidarity. "But for all its intangibility, this in-between is no less real than the world of things we visible have in common. We call this reality the 'web of human relationships,' indicating by the metaphor its intangible quality" (1958, p. 183). Antigone acts within this web of human relationships with the soulful strength of one whose love is "a full measure, pressed down, shaken together, and running over" (Luke 6:39–40).

In classic Greek style, Antigone incarnates the tragedies of those who reduce and restrain the meaning of justice and illuminates the spirit at work when the "just one justices." History remembers Antigone's heroic resistance in the face of oppression, injustice, and death. She lives for all those who hunger and thirst for justice. We who love the play hover in thought and imagination around the complexities of her particular single-hearted and dramatic gesture that restored integrity.

According to Nussbaum (1986), tragic literature can be a rich resource for critical reflection precisely because it touches both the cognitive and emotional levels of human experience. Further, it illuminates the complexity of what may be going on in any difficult situation. In the difficult situations that leaders face everyday, we cross thresholds into realms of multiple meanings when we listen, paying strict attention to the differences we hear. When leaders acknowledge that truth and goodness are always beyond our personal understandings, we demonstrate our willingness to be influenced by the horizons of others. When we act out of traditions of memory that honor justice and courage, we are witness to the generous possibilities of the human spirit. Virtue lies in that "web of human relationships" (Arendt, 1958) between leaders and followers especially when we remember the bonds we share with others in human communities and when we are willing to critique those structures and processes that violate that solidarity.

TRADITIONS OF CRITIQUE

Literary artists intensify attentiveness to the concrete world within which we all live and move and have our being. They hover in thought and imagination about every moving thing, and their singular focus hollows life. Attending to things as they are, artists pursue paths that deeply honor local knowledge with all its character, color, and contours, while, at the same time, evoking a kind of sympathetic or tacit knowing that acknowledges the meanings which lie just below the surface of all things.

In powerful ways, literature lures us to examine the promise and the paradox that reside in particularities, to explore other perspectives and possibilities, and to imagine lovelier and more just ways of living in the world. On another level, literature can open us to feelings of immediacy, posture us for moves toward solidarity, and engage us in critiquing social situations that dehumanize. Such actions have moral and ethical dimensions, require thoughtfulness and enlarge visions.

> Learning to be thoughtful is not learning to perform a particular action nor is it acquiring a method of obtaining a particular result; it is developing a 'second nature' which transforms heart and mind.
>
> (Schrag, 1988, p. 80)

We see that "second nature" developing in Dr. Rieux, a leading character in Camus's novel, *The Plague* (1948). In the beginning of the story, when the pestilence hits the little French town, the people are cast about, hopeless and resigned to the incurable and inevitable death-dealing disease. At first, Dr. Rieux fights the disease dispassionately simply because that is what his job requires. Only later when he sees in the faces of his patients the horror of the plague's devastation does he discover something deeper about his craft. Instinctively, he knows he must rethink the manner of his work, re-vision the meaning and purpose of his practice. With renewed commitment, Dr. Rieux decides to fight vigilantly against the plague rather than conspire in its merciless mission against life. In his thoughtful effort to reclaim his craft of healing, we hear him speak of those "unable to be saints but refusing to bow down to pestilences," those who "strive their utmost to be healers" (Camus, 1948, p. 278).

I am reminded of certain administrators who do their jobs, dutifully but dispassionately, the way Dr. Rieux first approached his work. After all, what more can we do when crisis threatens the very enterprise to which we have committed ourselves. Tarrou helped Dr. Reiux see how together they could empower a people grown weary and hopeless to fight against the power of the plague. Thus, Dr. Reiux came to understand his craft in a deeper way. In rereading this novel, I wonder what are the "pestilences" in our schools today to which some of us will refuse to bow. I wonder what it will cost us "to strive" our "utmost to be" educators.

TRADITIONS OF RECOMMITMENT

Literature has the power to nurture and nourish the life of the imagination. Without the ability to imagine, we are incapable of creating communities of solidarity with the poor, the oppressed, and the unloved. We need what Ralph Ellison's narrator was calling a reconstruction of our inner eyes, a recreated imaginative vision, so that we may see the kind of invisibility that accompanies injustice.

In reading *Invisible Man* (1952), I remember questioning the meaning of history especially for those whose lives were silenced by acts of hate, aggression, and violence. Ellison subtly suggests that meaning might be restored through the creative work of art. The protagonist's personal pain finds expression in and through his writing. What he discovers in that process is that he has a story to tell. Compelled to leave the solitary confinement of his cellar, he is prepared to reenter the world of others, the web of human relationships. The protagonist transcends the limits of injustice and widens his particular angle of vision to include others who suffer invisibility and voicelessness. In the end, he comes to a deeper level of consciousness and a new understanding of his work for justice when he says: "Who knows but that, on the lower frequencies, I speak for you?" (1952, p. 439). The story triumphs not because hate is eliminated from the web of human relationships but because a heart bent towards justice wants to love again. Like Tarrou in *The Plague* who "resolved always to speak-and to act-quite clearly" and who "decided to take in every predicament, the victim's side so as to reduce the damage done" (Camus, 1948, p. 230), the nameless narrator, by the end of his story, has crafted his mission, too.

I believe that it is important that at the same time administrators are leading reform efforts, we confront the challenge of reconstructing our "inner eyes" by which we understand reality and question our visions and practices. We need to know what to resist and what to embrace especially from those who advertise the best practices and sure solutions to complex issues. We may need to ask ourselves every once in a while, "on the lowest frequencies" for whom do I speak?

Literature can clarify and sharpen reality drawing our attention to what we might have forgotten, violated, or simply missed. The works of Sophocles, Camus, and Ellison have the capacity to take us into new and unexpected worlds where pain and sorrow are transformed into life-giving lessons. The pathways that these and other literary works open involve excursions of possibility for renewing and recreating the face of Jubilee justice.

EPIGRAM

In this chapter, I have attempted to sketch what may be at the hub of administration preparation programs. Historically, I have identified this as a kairos, a time when the Judeo-Christian event of Jubilee intersects with postmodern concerns for a larger freedom and a greater justice. Within this context, I have urged that those of us who are involved with administrators recognize that the sustaining quality of their leadership lies in their ability to identify "a central quality which is the root criterion of life and spirit" (Alexander, 1979, pp. 19 ff.). The search for this central quality is at the hub of preparation programs. I have proposed that releasing the ethical imaginations of administrators by honoring and enlarging the place of the literary arts in their preparation is one way of remembering, critiquing, and recommitting to a life lived from the center.

These are but a handful of ideas. Reformers, researchers, and reflective practitioners may have other helpful suggestions for designing preparation programs for administrators. All I hoped to do was to draw on the life of imaginative literature to help us consider:

What does it mean to live life from the center?

How can literature re-educate the ethical imagination of leaders?

Do traditions of memory, critique and commitments enliven our search for those moments and situations when we have been most alive as administrators?

I raise these questions because I believe "it is important that everything we love be summed up into something unforgettably beautiful. . . . " (Leiris, 1988, p. 201). This Jubilee Year demands nothing less.

REFERENCES

Alexander, C. (1979). The timeless way of building. OUP: New York.

Arendt. H. (1958). The human condition. Chicago: University of Chicago Press.

Arnold, M. (1986). "Dover Beach" In R.D. Yanni (Ed.). Literature. New York: Random House.

Bakhtin, M.M. (1981). The dialogic imagination. Austin: University of Texas Press.

Beatham, M. D. (1991). Brawling between heaven and earth. (Doctoral dissertation, University of Cincinnati, 1991).University Microfilms International, 1416.

Beck, L. G., & Murphy, J. (1994). Ethics in educational leadership programs: An expanding role. Thousand Oaks, CA: Corwin.

Bernauer, J. (1990). Michel Foucault's force of flight: Toward an ethics for thought. New Jersey: Humanities Press International.

Bishop, E. (1983). The collected poems. New York: Farrrar Straus and Giroux.

Bohm, D. (1980). Wholeness and the implicate order. London: Ark Paperbacks.

Boyer, E.L. (1995). The basic school: A community for learning. Princeton, NJ: Carnegie Foundation for the Advancement of Teaching.

Brieschke, P. (November, 1990). The administrator in fiction: Using the novel to teach educational administration. Educational Administration Quarterly, 26 (4), 376–393.

Camus, A. (1948). The plague (S. Gilbert, Trans.). New York: Knopf.

Conrad, J. (1967). Preface to The nigger of the narcissus. In Great works of Joseph Conrad. New York: Harper Collins.

Eliot, T. S. (1958). The complete poems and plays, 1909–1950. New York: Harcourt, Brace & Co.

Ellison, R. (1952). Invisible man. New York: Signet Books.

Foucault, M. (1973). The order of things. New York: Vintage Books.

Foucault, M. (1984). The Foucault reader. New York: Pantheon Books.

Fullan, M. (1993). Change forces: Probing the depths of educational reform. New York: The Falmer Press.

Goodlad, J. I. (1984). A place called school. New York: McGraw-Hill.

Goodlad, J. I., Soder, R., & Sirotnik, K. A. (Eds.). (1990). The moral dimensions of teaching. San Francisco: Jossey-Bass.

Groome, T. (1998). Educating for life. Allen, TX: Thomas More Press.

Hanh, T. N. (1987). The miracle of mindfulness: A manual on meditation. Boston: Beacon Press.

Heidegger, M. (1968). What is called thinking? (J.C. Gray, Trans.). New York: Harper Collins.

Lawrence-Lightfoot, S. (1983). The good high school: Portrait of character and culture. New York: Basic Books, Inc.

Leiris, M. (1988). "Faire-part." In E.C. Oppler (Ed.) Picasso's Guernica (p. 201). New York: Norton.

Leviticus. 25: 10–17. (1966). The Jerusalem Bible. Garden City, New York: Doubleday.

Luke 6:39–40. (1966). The Jerusalem Bible. Garden City, New York: Doubleday.

Lyotard, F. (1984). The postmodern condition. Minneapolis: University of Minnesota Press.

Noddings, N. (1992). The challenge to care in schools: An alternative approach to education. New York: Teachers College Press.

Nouwen, H. (1994). Here and now. New York: Crossroad.

Nussbaum, M. (1986). The fragility of goodness. New York: Cambridge University Press.

Patrick, A. E. (May, 1998). Imaginative literature and the renewal of moral theology. New Theology Review, 11 (2), 43–55.

Schrag, F. (1988). Thinking in school and society. London: Routledge.

Sergiovanni, T. J. (1992). Moral leadership: Getting to the heart of school improvement. San Francisco: Jossey–Bass.

Sergiovanni, T. J. (1994). Building community in schools. San Francisco: Jossey–Bass.

Sergiovanni, T. J. (1996). Leadership for the school house: How is it different? Why is it important? San Francisco: Jossey–Bass.

Sizer, T. (1992). Horace's school: Redesigning the American high school. Boston: Houghton Mifflin.

Sizer, T. (1996). Horace's hope: What works for the American high school. New York: Houghton Mifflin, Co.

Sophocles. (1967). Antigone. In Sophocles, the oedipus cycle: An English version. New York: Harcourt Brace & Co.

Starratt, R. J. (1994). Building an ethical school: A practical response to the moral crisis in schools. Washington, DC: Falmer.

Starratt, R. J. (1996). Transforming educational administration: Meaning, community, and excellence. New York: McGraw-Hill.

Vaill, P. (1989). Managing as a performing art. San Francisco: Jossey-Bass.

Westerbrook, R.B. (1991). John Dewey and American democracy. Ithaca: Cornell University Press.

Woolf, V. (1966). Three guineas. New York: Harcourt Brace.

CONNECTING PREPARATION AND PRACTICE

The Use of Simulations in Principal Preparation Programs: A Bridge Between the Classroom and Filed-Based Experiences[1]

EDWARD W. CHANCE and PATTI L. CHANCE

How well graduate programs in educational administration prepare students for the real world of the principalship is a topic of much debate and dialogue (Brent, Haller, & McNamara, 1997; Downey, 1998; Griffiths, Stout, & Forsyth, 1988; Murphy, 1992; Schneider, 1998). The National Commission for the Principalship (1990) recommended that curriculum in educational administration preparation programs consist of a common core of knowledge and skills grounded in the problems of practice. Their recommendations suggested that the following elements be included in the common core of knowledge:

1. Societal and cultural influences on schooling
2. Teaching and learning processes and school improvement
3. Organizational theory
4. Methodologies of organizational studies and policy analysis
5. Leadership and management processes and functions
6. Policy studies and politics of education
7. Moral and ethical dimensions of schooling

The Interstate School Leaders Licensure Consortium (ISLLC) developed standards which address not only knowledge that school leaders must possess but also the dispositions and performances essential to school leadership (Council of Chief State School Officers, 1996).

Principal preparation programs have been challenged to employ instructional strategies and delivery systems that are learner-centered, stress active learning, and

[1]The text of this chapter was presented at the NCPEA 53rd Annual Conference in Jackson Hole, Wyoming, and is published here in memory of Edward W. Chance.

Edward W. Chance, University of Nevada Las Vegas
Patti L. Chance, University of Nevada Las Vegas

utilize cooperative approaches (Murphy, 1992). Wilson (1993) suggested that instruction in educational administration programs should be shaped by a "constructionism" paradigm, "requiring not only individual reflection but also interaction with others" (p. 223). The use of simulations in principal preparation programs allows school administration students to utilize their knowledge in practical applications and to develop an understanding of how values and beliefs guide actions (Griffiths, Stout, & Forsyth, 1988; Hoelscher, 1996; Paul, 1990). Simulations provide an instructional tool to teach concepts and theory within a contextual framework and furnish an engaging venue through which students can explore and reflect upon specific leadership issues.

Two significant trends holding particular implications for school leadership are the increasing cultural diversity in America and the shift from an industrial- to an information-based society. This article discusses two specific simulations, used in the principal preparation program at the University of Nevada Las Vegas, to engage students in these issues through a constructionist approach. These simulations represent both traditional and computer-based applications. Bafa Bafa (Shirts, 1977) is a traditional simulation that requires students to reflect upon their leadership roles in building relationships within a diverse, multicultural community. The Information Environment for School Leader Preparation [IESLP] (University Council of Educational Administration, 1998) is a web-based environment with many instructional applications. The simulation activity conducted in conjunction with IESLP requires students to access and analyze data via computer-based technology and provides students practice in decision making, problem solving, communication, and group dynamics.

MULTICULTURAL SIMULATION IN PRINCIPAL PREPARATION

Toward the goal of developing school leaders who possess the knowledge, dispositions, and skills for leadership in culturally diverse settings, the Department of Educational Leadership at the University of Nevada, Las Vegas, utilizes a cross-cultural simulation entitled Bafa Bafa in its administrative preparation program. This type of simulation allows students to examine their own cultural perceptions and to think about how people behave when they are faced with action and expectations that differ from theirs (Hoelscher, 1996, p. 39). The simulation offers a high level of involvement yet allows an atmosphere of personal detachment due to the use of imaginary cultures and situations.

Bafa Bafa, developed by R. Garry Shirts, introduces the notion of cultures and allows students to become involved in a cross-cultural experience. Bafa Bafa engages students in a simulation of two imaginary cultures, the Alpha society and the Beta society. Initially, participants are placed in either the Alpha or Beta society. The Alpha and Beta societies are separated from one another and participants spend the beginning of the simulation learning to become an Alphan or a Betan. Once participants have been inducted into their society, each society is slowly introduced to the other through observations and visitations. All social contact during the simulation must be done as an Alphan or a Betan, including language, customs, and behavior. Neither society is told anything about the other, the task being to learn about the other society through observation and interaction. The simulation is concluded after all members of each society have had the opportunity to visit the other. A most important aspect of the experience is the debriefing after the simulation. It is during the discussion after the simulation that "cultures are unraveled and the participants compare perceptions of one another's culture" (Shirts, 1994, p. 4).

In order to gauge the effectiveness of the Bafa Bafa simulation regarding student sensitivity to multicultural issues, instructors administered a pre- and postsimulation questionnaire to forty-three graduate students who participated in the simulation. The questionnaire and entitled "Culture and Values" developed by Edward W. Chance and Porter Troutman, consisted of fifteen statements geared to measure students' understanding of culture and intercultural relations. Participants were asked to respond to each statement utilizing a Likert scale in which one represented strong disagreement and five represented strong agreement. Participants were also asked to write a personal response to the Bafa Bafa experience.

The presimulation questionnaire indicated that students had an understanding of culture, cultural differences, and cultural tolerance. Participants indicated that culture is created by human beings, with a mean response of 4.42, and that each group develops its own culture (mean response of 4.02). Participants agreed that we compare other cultures to our own cultural values (M=4.23) and that one's own cultural values influence perceptions (mean response of 4.42) and behaviors (mean response of 4.51). Responses to the preactivity questionnaire showed that participants strongly agreed that tolerance for diversity is important for improving relations with others, with a mean response of 4.70.

The presimulation questionnaire found the participants' mean response to the statement, "As an educated person, I am not prejudiced to other cultures," was 3.23, indicating neutrality or slight agreement. Participants responded similarly to the statement, "Adapting to another culture is easier for better educated individuals," with a mean response of 3.21.

The questionnaire asked participants to respond to several statements regarding attitudes toward comparing cultures and intercultural relations. Prior to the simulation, participants indicated slight disagreement with the statement that everyone is ethnocentric, with a mean response of 2.78. Participants were neutral (mean response of 3.19) to the statement, "Each culture thinks its own ways are superior." Participants indicated slight agreement, with a mean response of 3.51, to the statement that adaptation is one way to work with another culture. Prior to the simulation, participants indicated agreement that all cultures have biases and prejudices (mean response of 4.21) and that all cultures respond to respect and disrespect.

After students participated in the Bafa Bafa simulation, participants were given the same questionnaire. Table 1 summarizes pre- and postsimulation mean responses.

Participants showed stronger agreement to statements concerning culture after the simulation. While participants agreed prior to the simulation that each group develops its own culture, after the activity participants indicated strong agreement. After the sim-

TABLE I. Mean Responses to "Culture and Values" Questionnaire.

Statement	Presimulation Mean	Postsimulation Mean	Difference
Culture is created by human beings	4.42	4.82	0.40
Each group develops its own culture	4.02	4.76	0.74
Everyone is ethnocentric	2.78	3.63	0.85
We compare people and events based on our own cultural value systems	4.23	4.66	0.43
Our culture and values influence what we see, hear, and feel as well as how we process what we see, hear, and feel	4.42	4.70	0.28
There is no universal intercultural problem-solving method	3.26	3.62	0.36
Cultural conflict does not disappear because we decide to ignore it	4.51	4.45	-0.06
Tolerance for diversity and an open mind are important for improving our relations with others	4.70	4.84	0.14
In every culture, people respond to respect and disrespect	4.30	4.37	0.07
All cultures have biases and prejudices	4.21	4.63	0.42
Cultural values and beliefs influence attitudes and behaviors	4.51	4.71	0.20
One way to work with another culture is to adapt to that culture	3.51	4.29	0.78
Adapting to another culture is easier for better educated individuals	3.21	3.68	0.47
Each culture thinks its own ways are superior	3.19	4.03	0.84
As an educated person, I am not prejudiced to other cultures	3.23	3.29	0.06

ulation, participants generally agreed with the statement that everyone is ethnocentric, in contrast to a general disagreement with this statement prior to the Bafa Bafa activity. While participants had indicated neutrality toward the statement "Each culture thinks its own ways are superior" before the simulation, they generally agreed with this statement after the activity. Similarly, participants more strongly agreed with the statement that all cultures have biases and prejudices after the simulation than they did before.

One student commented, "It was interesting how much hostility was created between the two cultures, and this was among educated, culturally aware adults." Others made statements such as, "Feelings of superiority set in much quicker than I ever thought possible" and "We became defensive and proud of our new identities."

Regarding statements of intercultural relations, participants more strongly agreed that adaptation is a way to work with another culture after the simulation. They also indicated stronger agreement with the statement, "Adapting to another culture is easier for better educated individuals." In reference to the other culture in the Bafa Bafa simulation, one student admitted after the activity, "I didn't even want to understand their culture because I felt so uncomfortable, was instantly turned off and thought they were rude."

The debriefing after the simulation allowed participants to discuss their feelings and reactions to coping with a foreign culture. "I learned that I put my guard up naturally when faced with new norms," reflected one student. Another commented, "I realized how unsettling it is to be faced with trying to understand a culture where no one is willing to help you fit in. I can see why students in the classroom are willing to go to extreme lengths in order to get out of uncomfortable situations."

USING TECHNOLOGY IN A SIMULATION ABOUT SCHOOL IMPROVEMENT

Schools today can ill afford to hire principals and other administrators who are not equipped with the skills of computer-based technology. School leaders must be comfortable with utilizing technology for gathering information and analyzing data for better decision making. Computer literacy in and of itself, however, is not adequate. School leaders must be able to apply these skills to issues and problems within the context of a specific setting or environment. The Information Environment for School Leader Preparation (IESLP) developed under the auspices of the University Council for Educational Administration (1998) provides just such a tool for educational administrative preparation programs.

IESLP is a web-based instructional system that gives students and instructors access to data from a virtual school district and community. A variety of exercises, which are presented in a problem-based approach and are relevant to the virtual school environment, are available to users. Problem exercises are similar to in-basket simulation problems or case studies. Students work on problems through face-to-face group interaction, while utilizing computer technology to retrieve and manipulate information from the virtual school databases in order to make decisions that are relevant and appropriate to the given context.

The Department of Educational Leadership at the University of Nevada, Las Vegas, participated in beta testing of the IESLP program in the spring semester of 1999. Twenty-four students in a master's degree cohort program for principal preparation engaged in an IESLP simulation related to curriculum, school improvement, and community concerns about standardized test scores (Chance & Chance, 1998). The IESLP virtual environment upon which the problem was based was a small, rural school district. Students were grouped into "administrative teams" of four, where two individuals were assigned roles as elementary principals and two were given roles as secondary principals. Students were given the task of developing recommendations for a school improvement plan to be presented to the Superintendent and ultimately to the Board of Education.

Prior to introducing students to IESLP, a presimulation questionnaire was administered. Students were asked to respond to questions about problem solving, decision making, and information sources as well as to rate themselves on their utilization of specific computer technology tools. Students rated their professional use of nine computer-based tools on a scale from one to five, where one represented no use and five represented consistent use.

Presimulation responses indicated that students were most comfortable with the computer technology tools of e-mail and word processing with mean responses of 3.96 and 4.76 respectively. The lowest presimulation responses were in the use of electronic spreadsheets and databases, with a mean rating of 2.10 and 2.29 respectively. Students' use of these tools also showed the highest gains in the postsimulation survey. After using IESLP, students' mean response to their use of electronic spreadsheets was 2.96, an average gain of .86, and the mean response to using databases was 3.17, an average increase of .88. Substantial growth was also reported in the use of accessing government and professional organization's web sites for gathering information. Table 2 summarizes the pre- and postquestionnaire responses regarding students' utilization of various technological tools.

It is important to note that during the course in which IESLP was introduced and executed, students were not formally trained in the use of specific electronic tools, although some incidental teaching occurred on an as-needed basis. Thus, students were immersed into the problem and information environment and were forced into a hands-on, experiential learning situation. Powerful learning occurred through students' own collaborative efforts, a mode of adult learning style that has been well-documented (Wood, Thompson, & Russell, 1990).

Students' personal reflections regarding IESLP as a learning tool pointed out its benefits in areas such as problem identification, problem solving, decision making, data analysis, and collaboration. One student team observed that the IESLP simulation "provided a safe environment in which to practice our skills . . . and let us make mistakes

TABLE II. Mean Responses to Professional Use of Computer-based Tools.

Tool	Presimulation Mean	Postsimulation Mean	Difference
E-mail	3.96	4.38	+.42
Spreadsheet	2.10	2.96	+.86
Database	2.29	3.17	+.88
Word Processor	4.67	4.96	.29
ERIC Search	2.52	3.00	.48
Web Search	3.29	3.85	.56
Searching Government Web Sites	2.50	3.13	.63
Using Professional Web Sites	2.73	3.52	.79
On-line Library Databases	2.56	2.79	.23

without impacting students." Regarding specific technological tools, one group wrote: "IESLP was a valuable learning experience as a future administrator as it allowed us to utilize a database to gather information. We used a spreadsheet to organize and analyze test scores and student data." Another team stated that "the application of technology forced us to learn how to access data, create a spreadsheet, and design graphs."

The effect of IESLP, however, went beyond technological application. One team noted: "IESLP was a real world experience that placed us in an administrative role incorporating realistic challenges and decision-making opportunities." Another team noted the benefits of collaboration and critical feedback: "We presented our collaborative projects in a simulated administrative-superintendent meeting where our supervisor gave us critical feedback and caused us to rethink our decisions."

CONCLUSIONS AND REFLECTIONS

Activities like Bafa Bafa and web-based environments such as IESLP provide useful instructional tools for school administration preparation programs by actively engaging prospective principals in simulations that focus on specific problems and issues of school leadership. Bafa Bafa encourages aspiring principals to reflect upon their personal values and their understanding of other cultures before they are faced with serious issues "on the firing line" of the principalship. Simulation exercises such as those presented through IESLP allow educational leadership students to practice decision making, problem solving, and technology applications prior to meeting such challenges in their first administrative appointment. In essence, simulations, like case studies and in-basket exercises, help bridge the gap between theory and practice.

Recommendations for educational administration preparation reform emphasize field-based experiences (McCarthy, 1999; Milstein, 1993; Murphy, 1992). Although aspiring principals must be exposed to the problems of practice through field-based activities, educational leadership programs need to provide students with a foundation of conceptual knowledge and leadership skill training that will prepare them for field experiences. Simulations can serve as a bridge or transition between the classroom and the field by allowing students the opportunity to "try on" the leadership role in a safe environment prior to practicing newly learned skills in an actual school setting.

REFERENCES

Brent, B. O., Haller, E. J., & McNamara, J. H. (1997). Does graduate training in educational administration improve America's schools? Phi Delta Kappan, 79 (3), 222–227.

Chance, P. L., & Chance, E. W. (1998). Community involvement: A two-edged sword in Crawford Public Schools. [On-line]. Available at http://ieslp.coe.missouri.edu.

Council of Chief State School Officers. (1996). Interstate school leaders licensure consortium Standards for school leaders. Washington, D.C.: Author.

Downey, C. J. (1998). Is it time for us to be accountable too? The AASA Professor, 22 (1), 12–17.

Griffiths, D. E., Stout, R. T., & Forsyth, P. B. (1988). The preparation of educational administrators. In D. E. Griffiths, R. T. Stout, & P. B. Forsyth (Eds.), Leaders for America's Schools (pp. 284–304). Berkeley, CA: McCuthchan.

Hoelscher, K. (1996). Using simulations to develop cultural sensitivity in preservice teachers: The Heelotia experience. Multicultural Education, 3 (3), 39–43.

McCarthy, M. M. (1999). The evolution of educational leadership preparation programs. In J. Murphy & K. S. Louis (Eds.), Handbook of research on educational administration (2nd ed.). San Francisco: Jossey-Bass.

Milstein, M. M. (Ed.). (1993). Changing the way we prepare educational leaders: The Danforth experience. Newbury Park, CA: Corwin Press.

Murphy, J. (1992). The landscape of leadership preparation: Reframing the education of school administrators. Newbury Park, CA: Corwin Press.

National Commission for the Principalship. (1990). Principals for our changing schools: Preparation and certification. Fairfax, VA: Author.

Paul, R. (1990). Critical thinking. What every person needs to survive in a rapidly changing world. Rohnert Park, CA: Center for Critical Thinking and Moral Critique.

Schneider, J. (1998). University training of school leaders isn't the only option. The AASA Professor, 22 (1), 6–7.

Shirts, R. G. (1977). Bafa Bafa: A cross culture simulation. Del Mar, CA: Simulation Training System.

Shirts, R. G. (1994). Bafa Bafa: A cross culture simulation. In Simulation Training System Products Catalog. Del Mar, CA: Simulation Training System.

University Council for Educational Administration. (1998). IESLP: The Information Environment for School Leadership Preparation: Instructor Guide. [On-line]. Available at http://ielsp.coe.missouri.edu.

Wilson, P. T. (1993). Pushing the edge. In M. M. Milstein (Ed.), Changing the way we prepare educational leaders: The Danforth experience (pp. 219–234). Newbury Park, CA: Corwin Press.

Wood, F. H., Thompson, S. R., and Russell, F. (1990). Designing effective staff development programs. In B. Dillon-Peterson (Ed.), Staff development/organizational development (pp. 59–91). Alexandria, VA: Association for Supervision and Curriculum Development.

Assessment of Interns' Performance: A Key to Enhance School Leader Preparation for the New Millennium

MARTHA N. OVANDO

The value of learning through field-based experiences has been widely recognized in the field of educational administration preparation (Anderson, 1988; Balanoff, King, and Ovando, 1995; Björk & Ginsberg, 1995; Daresh, 1987; Milstein, 1990; Morgan, Gibbs, Hertzog, and Wylie, 1997; Ovando, 1990; Richardson, 1992). As a result, most preparation programs include a format that provides students with an opportunity to relate theory to practice in diverse settings, because "intellectual knowledge, in and of itself, is not enough" (Milstein, Bobroff, & Restine, 1991, p. 5). However, the assessment of such experiences for program enhancement continues to be a challenge. Additionally, questions relative to its potential to enhance preparation programs have also emerged.

School leader preparation programs in the new millennium will need to respond to a changing environment—an environment which "will definitely demand a particular principal preparation program, one focused on context and process, rather than content" (Herman and Herman, 1993, p. 91). Consequently, preparation institutions should respond to the renewed interest and calls for better preparation of educational leaders (Clark & Clark, 1996). Further, recommendations for quality preparation of school leaders suggest that there is a need for

> a balance between learning about and learning how, rooted in a solid foundation of learning why. In the process, students should have multiple opportunities to demonstrate mastery of those skills and knowledge traditionally required of administrative positions as well as those which have not yet been clearly identified but which may be required in the future. (Milstein, 1990, p. 122)

The internship has become the most common strategy to achieve such a balance in the field of school leader preparation; however, questions challenging its merit continue to be raised.

Martha N. Ovando, The University of Texas at Austin

Thus, it becomes imperative that we assess the internship experience and interns' performance to generate feedback for the individual and the preparation institution. The assessment of interns' field experiences may provide key information to enhance school leader preparation. As Milstein, et al., (1991) remind us, "evaluation lets us know how close we have come to meeting our purposes and provides information needed to make decisions that can improve our performance. As such, it is an important aspect of the planning and management of internship programs" (p. 101). One way to generate relevant information to enhance school leader preparation programs is through the assessment of interns' performance with the collaboration of field supervisors (site administrators). Field supervisors interact with school administration interns within the context of diverse schools, and they have a unique opportunity to observe how prospective school leaders apply educational administration knowledge, skills and attitudes as they attempt to address complex issues and demands of the classrooms and the challenging conditions in schools.

An intern's performance assessment can be conducted at different points of his or her field-based experiences to generate specific information for the purpose of continuous improvement. Promising methodological approaches include "document analysis, interviews, observations, and questionnaires" (Milstein, et al., 1991, p.112). For example, *The Assessment of Interns' Performance Form* used in a school leader preparation program with the assistance of field supervisors has the potential to highlight the intern's strengths and needs for further development as well as generate meaningful feedback to improve preparation programs.

The remainder of this paper describes the process and results of a study using content analysis (Krippendorff, 1980) of the Assessment of Interns' Performance completed by school administrators who supervise interns in a variety of school settings as part of a university-based school leader preparation program. The focus of this study was on the interns' actual field-based experiences, the areas in which interns are involved, their overall performance, their potential as future administrators, their strengths and areas for further development, and recommendations for school leader preparation program enhancement.

BACKGROUND

As we enter a new millennium, school leader preparation programs are challenged to respond to calls for higher standards and excellence for all students. Similarly, these programs "face mandates for change as a result of national, state and local policies that demand institutional reform and accountability" (Morgan, Gibbs, Hertzog, & Wylie, 1997, p. 3). Consequently, preparation institutions, namely universities, are in the process of developing initiatives toward improving the preparation of school leaders. These institutions are also in search of innovative arrangements which include effective field-based learning experiences to equip prospective school leaders with the knowledge, skills, and attitudes that will enable them to better serve all students.

Improving the preparation of school leaders

The need to improve school leader preparation for the new millennium echoes the criticism and calls for higher standards (Applebome, 1996, Griffiths, 1988; Kempner, 1991; Thurrston, Clift, & Schacht, 1993), and the "the importance of educational leadership in bringing about desired change and to the development of leaders who are able to create effective learning communities" (Clark & Clark, 1996, p. 18). Further, traditional school leader preparation programs are being questioned as a way to equip school leaders who will face the complex issues and challenges of the twenty-first century. For instance, Herman and Herman (1993) assert that principals will have to "combine the skills of the specialist with the perspective of the generalist, working with diverse groups to integrate ideas aimed at solving a continuous stream of problems. This demands preparing school leaders to formulate goals collectively, to set and maintain direction with groups and to jointly develop organizational procedures" (p. 91).

Similarly, school leader preparation programs must reflect the extensive body of research that recognizes the principal's leadership role as an essential role in realizing success for all students. For instance, Murphy (1995) suggests that three important themes emerged from investigations of school improvement efforts in which the principal was a key individual. These included "defining and sustaining educational purpose; developing and nurturing community; and fostering personal and organizational growth" (Murphy, 1995, p. 2). Further, it is important to recognize that the attributes of transformational leadership are also supported by school leadership research (Cavazos, 1999; Clark & Clark, 1994; Leithwood & Steinbach, 1995; Louis & Murphy, 1994; Marek, 1999) as the most promising and effective school leadership of the future. Previous research also suggests that there is a high level of agreement relative to the knowledge, competencies and attributes of effective transformational leaders. As Carlson states "there is a consensus view that the organization of the future . . . will need leaders and followers invested in a transformational process" (1996, p. 137).

While there is apparent agreement about the dimensions of transformational leadership required to lead the schools of the twenty-first century, Teitel (1996) reminds us that we must also consider how to equip school leaders for the twenty-first century. Consequently, preparation institutions would need to incorporate research-based leadership dimensions into school leader preparation programs and develop, implement and evaluate innovative approaches. According to Clark and Clark (1996), improved school leader preparation "calls for renewed efforts on the part of school district and university administrators, professional administrator organizations, and state and federal government officials to collaborate in the improvement of and support of educational leadership preparation programs" (p.18). Further, as preparation institutions consider how to improve school leader preparation programs collaboratively, at least two important issues should be addressed: "the nature of these programs and the challenges for implementing them" (Clark and Clark, 1996, p. 19).

Implementing collaborative initiatives requires connecting two different worlds for the shared purpose of improved school leader preparation, as well as consideration of "the cultural differences between faculties in schools of education and those in K-12 schools that must be negotiated in order to create the ultimate professional continuum" (Howey and Zimpher, 1999, p. 297). Moreover, collaborative endeavors should be based on the common understanding that school leaders play a key role in achieving success for all students, and that there is a need for shared commitment and responsibility to design, implement and evaluate better school leader preparation programs. Such programs should not only incorporate current research-based leadership knowledge, skill and disposition, but should also include meaningful field-based experiences in diverse school settings. The literature suggests that some institutions have initiated collaborative endeavors with school districts in an effort to support financially a year-long paid internship to offer prospective school leaders field-based experiences that go beyond traditional formats (Yates and Wagstaff, 2000). Field-based experiences provide school leader candidates with opportunities to enhance their school leadership capacity and to reflect on the complexities and the contextual nature of schooling.

The Internship as a Field-Based Experience

The field-based experience commonly referred to as internship is not new in the field of education preparation programs. However, a renewed emphasis on field-based learning suggests that the school leader's internship may satisfy new standards and serve as a vehicle to enhance school leader preparation for the new millennium (Daresh, 1998; Morgan, et al., 1997; Yates and Wagstaff, 2000).

On the other hand, Short and Price remind us that "concern about the role of the clinical experience in administrative preparation appeared as early as the late 1940s" (1992, p. 4). As a vehicle to enhance school leader preparation, the internship has been the focus of much debate, discussion and reform. For instance, according to Campbell and colleagues (1987), early internship arrangements were similar to student teaching experiences as a field study mechanism. This was later modified to differentiate preparation programs for school administrators from teacher preparation programs. Initially, the purpose was "to apply content, presumably taught and learned in the classroom, to a field experience jointly supervised by college-based faculty and senior practitioners" (Morgan, et al., 1997, p. 4).

While only two universities (the University of Chicago and the University of Omaha) had an internship requirement by the end of the 1940s, interest in field-based experiences expanded and gained support from the National Conference of Professors of Educational Administration (NCPEA), and a branch of NCPEA that later became the University Council of Educational Administration (UCEA) (Milstein, et al., 1991). During the 1950s, several universities embraced and advanced the internship as a result of support from the Kellogg Foundation. By the 1960s, the American Association of School Administrators (AASA) expressed strong support for field-based experiences through the AASA Yearbook by stating that "the internship is so important that it is the sine qua non of a modern program of preparation of educational administrators. If an institution cannot provide internship training, it should not be in the business of preparing educational administrators" (AASA, 1960, p. 82).

Further, it was reported that by 1962, at least 117 universities incorporated internships into their administrator preparation programs (Hencley, et al., 1963). As the number of universities embracing the internship concept increased in an effort to improve school leader preparation, the need to develop guidelines to enhance the quality of internship experiences emerged. Hence, UCEA and AASA (1964) formed a task force to establish a set of principles that would guide universities in their efforts to design internships. The spirit of the guidelines emphasized the need to balance the study of educational administration theory and the application of school administration competencies, and the value and promise of the internship experience (Short & Price, 1992). Further, these guidelines emphasized the need for collaboration between universities and schools and supported the idea of joint efforts to determine the effectiveness of the field-based experiences, as well as the need to share resources (Short & Price, 1992).

During the 1970s, learning through field-based experience was recognized as a promising instructional strategy for undergraduate programs in other fields as well. While there were various combinations in internship program descriptions, Duley (1978) found that there were at least seven broad educational goals. These goals were:

1. Put theory into practice, develop higher cognitive skills: learn how to apply, integrate, and/or evaluate knowledge and/or the methodology of a discipline or a field.
2. Acquire knowledge: engage in research, analyze the organizational structures.
3. Acquire and develop specific skills: problem solving, interpersonal, group process, coping and/or psychomotor
4. Increase personal growth and development: increase self-understanding, self-confidence, self-reliance, and/or clarify values.
5. Learn how to learn independently: develop the ability to use experiential learning theory or engage in cross-cultural learning.
6. Explore careers: develop self-understanding and acquire and use career exploration skills.
7. Become responsible citizens: develop a firsthand understanding of the political system. Identify issues of concern, and develop the political and social action skills appropriate to citizenship. (p. 315)

The 1980s witnessed an increase in the number of institutions, which included an internship as an important component of school leader preparation programs. Skalski and associates (1987) report that at least 220 universities included some form of field-based learning experience to meet both university requirements and state certification requirements. However, as the number of universities requiring internships increased, great variations in format, nature, requirements, and timeframe became apparent, which in turn generated considerable criticism. For instance, Pitner observed that "the nature of the appropriate tasks of school administration and the proper setting for developing requisite skills remains the subject of considerable disagreement among clinical training advocates" (1988, p. 382). Similarly, others report that a number of preparation programs continued to be the focus of criticism "for not providing the field-based experiences necessary for developing outstanding principals" (Anderson, 1989, p. 56).

During the 1990s, the internship appears to have gained legitimacy as an avenue to enhance the quality of school leader preparation. Currently, professional organizations such as UCEA and AASA as well as state certification bodies and school districts (Wagstaff and Yates, 2000) support the significance of the internship. However, questions that challenge the quality and appropriateness of the internship experience have also emerged. As Milstein recognized:

> Too often field sites are chosen haphazardly and/or are not closely monitored. The potential for interns being constraint to passive observation, being placed in roles which do not fit closely with their career goals or being used as "go-fers," is great when clear and agreed upon expectations are not developed. Likewise, campus-based practicums and seminars on a regular basis are rarely available or required and clinical experiences are often isolated from the rest of a students' program flow. Finally, the connecting linkages between campus experiences and field-based experiences are rarely adequately developed. (1990, p. 121)

Consequently, to enhance the success of field-based learning experiences and to make clear connections between theory and practice, school leader preparation programs need to include internships that are designed, implemented and evaluated with the participation of students, university faculty and successful school leaders. Emphasizing the need for planning, Milstein, et al., (1991) state that "when they (clinical experiences) are planned with care and when interns are given opportunities to work with exceptional leaders, these clinical experiences can have a positive impact on interns' confidence and their ability to perform as leaders" (p. 6). The value of collaboration between university faculty and school leaders for the purpose of designing meaningful field-based experiences was also supported by the National Commission on Excellence in Educational Administration which argued that:

> the logic of professional preparation, which introduces students to theory and research and then guides them into the world of practice, is well-suited for the important work of school administration. The necessary close working relationship between the university and the world of practice will benefit the quality of research and the quality of administrator preparation. In addition, public interests are served by the fact that administrators have studied school administration in the university and have been mentored by a team of research and clinical professors prior to independent practice. (1987, p. 20)

During the 1990s, school preparation programs included well-defined goals for the internship. According to Balanoff, et al. (1995) internship goals clarified the expectations for the intern, the faculty and the field supervisor. Further, in an effort to inform and guide interns as well as field supervisors who play the role of mentors, researchers and practitioners have developed manuals and handbooks that describe the nature and the requirements of the internship (Balanoff, et al., 1995; Morgan, et al., 1997; The University of Texas, 1997).

The mentors (site administrators) play a key role during the internship experience. They provide guidance and support as interns engage in a variety of administrative functions, such as they learn to lead schools. They also have the opportunity to observe and interact with prospective school leaders in real situations within diverse school contexts. More importantly, "when the university and site administrator work together to prepare interns as potential school leaders for leading-in-learning, there is a high likelihood that the outcome will be a rich internship experience which ultimately benefits the profession of school leadership" (The University of Texas, 1997, p. 2.). Mentors actually see how interns interact with other professionals in the field, how they respond to problems, how they make decisions, and how they contribute to the education of children in diverse contexts. Therefore, "the role of the mentor is important, is personally and professionally rewarding and it requires planning" (The University of Texas, n.d., p. 3). Thus, information generated through the assessment of interns' performance completed by mentors "provides the basis for decision making about the future, both for continuing development of individual interns and program graduates, and for modifications and changes that guarantee the continued integrity and relevance of the program itself" (Milstein, et al., 1991, p. 116).

The literature suggests that in order for the internship to be an effective culminating experience, general administrative knowledge needs to be developed prior to placement of interns. In addition, a supportive mechanism should be in place so that interns have an opportunity for reflection, and continuous monitoring and assessment of skill application should be completed. (Herman & Herman, 1993; Milstein, et al., 1991; NASSAP, 1992; Balanoff et al., 1995; The University of Texas, n.d.). While there appears to exist some agreement about the substantive components of the internship, its purpose, nature, relevance, supervision, financial support, prior preparation, timeframe, and evaluation (Griffiths, 1988; Morgan, et al., 1997; Murphy & Hallinger, 1987; Pitner, 1988; Short & Price, 1992) continue to be challenged and debated. In support, Short and Price (1992) assert that "little evaluative data exist regarding the impact of clinical experiences, particularly the internship, on students' subsequent administrative effectiveness and success. It is imperative that such an inquiry be initiated and findings disseminated to those responsible for administrator preparation" (p. 7). Moreover, the need to evaluate interns' field-based experiences becomes most relevant as we attempt to respond to challenges associated with the better preparation of school administrators for the new millennium. Therefore, assessing interns' performance with the collaboration of field supervisors may constitute a significant step toward enhancing school leader preparation.

METHODOLOGY AND PROCEDURES

The evaluation of an administrative internship, which seeks to generate meaningful feedback for the intern and the preparation program, can be accomplished at different stages and using a variety of techniques. The purpose of this study was to determine the activities in which the interns were involved, overall performance ratings, the intern's role potential, the intern's areas of strengths and further development needs, as well as recommendations to enhance the internship program. Therefore, this chapter is based on data obtained at the end of the internship experience of a university-based preparation program. This section describes the internship program and the process followed to collect information.

The Internship Experience

The department of educational administration of a major public university located in central Texas embraced the belief that the internship (as a field-based learning experience) is one of the most valuable components of the school leader preparation program and certifying process. It provides prospective school leaders with an opportunity to "link intellectual knowledge and competence with successful performance, and to assure that students develop leadership skills required to create nurturing learning environments for all students" (Balanoff, et al., 1995, p. 3). However, given the emerging new demands for better school leader preparation programs, a revision of the internship was undertaken, and new guidelines were developed. As a result

> students undertake a variety of academic challenges in the university's administrator preparation program. Among them are courses in curriculum development, human development, foundations of educational administration, school law, instructional leadership, research, administration of organizations, and problem solving in educational organizations. The courses together with the internship experience are directed toward improving the knowledge and skills of school leaders. (The University of Texas, 1997, p. 2)

Further, students interested in completing an administrative internship must have completed at least 30 hours of graduate studies. By fulfilling the requirements of these graduate studies, students become competent in concepts and knowledge areas required for the complexity and demands of school leadership. Students also complete the required training and certification to perform certain specialized functions such as instructional leadership and teacher appraisal. The current handbook for the program includes

> two major types of arrangements in the internship program: 1) school-based and 2) central/support office-based. In both cases, the goals of the internship are the same: To promote experiential learning through a personal relationship for the purpose of professional instruction and guidance of the administrative intern. (The University of Texas, 1997, p. 3)

As students engage in a yearlong internship experience, they also enroll in a Reflective Seminar. This seminar is designed to bring together all students completing an internship, for the purpose of introspection and discourse. A faculty member facilitates this seminar and students are provided with opportunities to synthesize coursework and field experiences. Selected administrative areas are revisited or expanded as needed to make sure students have a comprehensive grasp of school leadership. In addition, students share concerns, learn from one another, and give and receive constructive feedback. When these three major components are linked together (graduate studies, administrative internship, and reflective seminar), a three-dimensional foundation for school leader preparation emerges. Thus, it can be affirmed that theoretical knowledge, field experiences and reflection may lead to school leader capacity development (see Figure 1).

As stated earlier, the mentor (field supervisor) plays an essential role in the internship. In cooperation with the faculty advisor, the mentor formulates site-relevant program objectives, activities and duties, as well as general time lines for achieving these objectives (Balanoff, et al., 1995). Further, the mentor "enhances the intern's professional growth by presenting increasingly complex administrative challenges to the intern . . . by modeling, communicating and providing feedback" (The University of Texas, 1997, p. 9). Thus, it is expected that the mentor will meet with the intern to clarify expectations, provide relevant information about school policies and procedures, offer office space and the necessary resources, connect the intern with appropriate personnel, and evaluate the intern's performance (Balanoff, et al., 1995).

At the completion of the internship experience, the mentor evaluates the intern's performance and completes the *Assessment of Intern's Performance Form*. The purpose of the assessment of intern's performance is to "make accurate judgments about the intern's ability to perform administrative and instructional leadership activities, to provide useful feedback to interns, to identify the potential of interns as future administrators, as well as to identify areas for further development" (Balanoff, et al., 1995, p. 8). Once the form is received by the faculty supervisor, a meeting is sched-

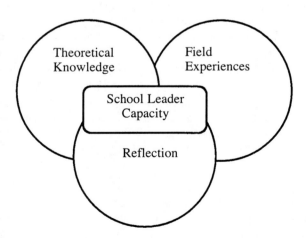

FIGURE 1. Three-dimensional Foundation of School Leader Capacity

uled with the intern for feedback purposes. Most students welcome the opportunity to review their assessment and usually agree with field supervisor comments. Finally the form is placed in the intern's file for future reference when students request letters of recommendation.

Participants

This study included school administrators who performed the role of mentors. These mentors supervised interns in a variety of settings as part of a university-based educational administrator preparation program. A total of 46 administrators completed the *Assessment of Intern's Performance Form*. A majority (74%) of these "field supervisors" were school principals, others were superintendents (7%), assistant superintendents (9%), coordinators of special education (7%), and director of special programs (4%). Both central office and campus levels were represented. All three levels of schools (elementary, middle and high school) were also represented.

Data sources and analysis

The *Assessment of Intern's Performance Form* falls within the document and records category known as "nonhuman sources" (Lincoln & Guba, 1985). It was selected following the Milstein, et al. (1991) selection criteria for accessibility, relevance, accuracy, economy of resources, skill, and time. Additionally, the assessment form was found to be a stable, rich and non-reactive source of information (Lincoln & Guba, 1985). Data analysis was completed following Krippendorf's (1980) guidelines for content analysis.

The assessment form included identification information such as intern's name, internship position, field supervisor name and position, school, and district. It also included a list of areas of activities in which interns were involved, ranging from budgeting to special programs; an overall rating of intern's performance using a scale of 1 to 5, with 1 meaning outstanding performance and 5 meaning poor performance; a rating of interns' demonstrated ability in areas such as planning, organization, time management, human relations, communications, and others using a scale from 1 to 5, with 1 meaning low ability and 5 meaning high ability. Additionally, open-ended questions requested field supervisors' perceptions of the interns' potential, strengths, areas for further development; suggestions for improvement; general comments and willingness to continue working with the program. These forms are valid sources of information because they "represent data that are thoughtful in that informants have given attention to completing, and therefore enabled the researcher to obtain the language and words of informants" (Creswell, 1994, p. 151).

A total of 46 actual intern's assessment forms were analyzed. The researcher reviewed, sorted and coded the information contained in these forms using quantitative and qualitative procedures. Frequencies, percentages and means were computed to organize and analyze interns' positions, school districts, areas of involvement and interns' performance ratings. Data relative to interns' demonstrated ability were analyzed by computing the frequency of ratings by each respondent. Respondents assigned a rating using a scale ranging from 1 to 5, with 1 labeled as "low" and 5 labeled as "high." The mean rating for each ability was computed by multiplying the frequency total by its scaled value to produce a weighted rating, and all weighted ratings were added for each ability. Then, the total of weighted ratings was divided by the number of responses for each ability. Additionally, qualitative research guidelines for content analysis (Krippendorff, 1980) were followed. Such analysis enabled the researcher to "isolate patterns and processes, commonalties and differences, and to gradually elaborate a set of generalizations" (Miles & Huberman, 1984, p.9).

RESULTS

This section presents the findings of the content analysis of the *Assessment of Intern's Performance Form*. It describes the interns' positions, school districts, areas of activities in which interns were involved, overall performance ratings, role potential, areas of strength, areas for further development, recommendations for enhancing the internship experience, additional comments, and willingness to continue providing internship opportunities.

Interns were placed in different positions and levels. More than half of the interns (54%), were placed as "administrative assistants." From these administrative interns, a majority (76%), were placed at campus levels (elementary, middle and high school), and only a few (24%) were placed at central office. On the other hand, less than half of the interns (28%), were placed as "assistant principals" at elementary and middle schools, and only a few (7%) were placed as elementary school "principals."

A total of 14 school districts were represented. Some of these schools were located within geographical proximity to the university. However, the local urban independent school district placed a majority (30%) of the interns. Two other districts, one located about 30 miles south and the other one located about 45 miles north of the university, placed a few (11% & 13%) interns, while the other 11 districts located at further distances (50 to 100 miles) placed at least one to three interns.

According to the respondents, interns engaged in a number of activities or programs. However, most of them (85%) engage in special programs such as Gifted and Talented, Chapter I, English as a Second Language, research projects, special education and others that focus on specific campus needs and priorities. More than half of the interns also (80%) engage in curriculum related-activities and policy and regulations, and others (78%) engage in instructional supervision. Instruction-related activities and school law appear to be areas with least involvement on the part of the interns (see Table 1).

TABLE I. Interns' Areas of Activities.

Areas	Number of Interns	Percentage
Special programs	39	85
Curriculum	37	80
Policies and regulations	37	80
Instructional supervision	36	78
Personnel	35	76
Community relations	35	76
Student services	34	74
Budgeting	34	74
Predictions and projections	30	65
Records	30	65
Parent programs	30	65
Instruction	29	63
School law	26	57

Note: Total percentage is higher than 100 because respondents checked all that applied.

Field supervisors completing the assessment forms appear to have high regard for interns' performance. A majority (67%) of interns' overall performance was rated as "outstanding." Less than half (28%) of the interns' overall performance was rated as "above average," and the overall performance of very few (4%) was rated as "average" (see Table 2).

Interns' demonstrated ability, as reported by the field supervisors, included effective planning, organization, time management, human relations, oral communications, written communication, taking directions, use of organization's policies and procedures, and application of theory in educational administration. Findings revealed that interns' demonstrated ability was highly rated in all of these areas, as can be observed in Table 3.

According to field supervisors, interns have the potential to perform a variety of administrative roles. Data also revealed that interns have the potential to perform both central office and campus level roles. The following roles emerged at central level: coordinator of a variety of programs (20%), instructional supervisor (17%), resource manager (7%), superintendent (2%) and assistant superintendent (2%). On the other

TABLE II. Interns' Overall Rating.

Rating	Number of Interns	Percentage
Outstanding	31	67
Above average	13	28
Average	2	4
Below average	—	—
Poor	—	—

TABLE III. Interns' Demonstrated Ability Rating.

Ability	Ratings					Total Responses	Mean Ratings
	5	4	3	2	1		
Effective planning	155	48	9			46	4.61
Organization	160	48	6			46	4.65
Time management	135	60	12			46	4.33
Human relations	160	40	12			46	4.61
Oral communication	145	52	12			46	4.54
Written communication	145	60	12			46	4.59
Taking directions	190	28	3			46	4.80
Use of organization's policies & procedures	150	42	6			46	4.22
Application of theory in educational administration	140	60	9			46	4.41

hand, the following roles emerged at campus level: principal or instructional leader (26%), assistant principal (26%), student discipline manager (7%), and student, teacher, and parent mediator (9%). Three additional roles that emerged were researcher (11%), planner (13%), and organizer (9%), as can be observed in Table 4.

Field supervisors indicated that interns have several strengths. From these, interpersonal skills (50%) and organization skills (43%) emerged as the most common. Other strengths included comprehensive knowledge (26%), communication, both oral and written (13%), creativity (13%), self-motivation (11%), task orientation (11%), cooperation (9%), sense of humor (7%), and student-centeredness (7%). Additionally, at least one field supervisor identified problem solution, conceptualization, bilingual, work ethics, common sense and willingness as additional strengths.

On the other hand, field supervisors identified specific areas for interns' further development. The following emerged as areas of need: additional experience (24%), budgeting (17%), personnel management (15%), physical plant management (7%), curriculum knowledge (7%), discipline management (4%), time management (4%), assertiveness (4%), ability to handle multiple responsibilities simultaneously (4%), and district knowledge (4%). Additionally, at least one field supervisor identified program design, delegation, problem solving, objectivity, scheduling, initiative, and development of a bank of ideas as areas of need.

Furthermore, field supervisors made specific recommendations to enhance the internship experience, and to improve the school leader preparation program. The emerging recommendations were clustered in the following categories.

Communication

According to respondents the internship experience can be enhanced, by increasing the level of communication between the university and the school dis-

TABLE IV. Interns' Potential Roles.

Roles	Number	Percentage
Central office level		
Coordinator	9	20
Instructional supervisor	8	17
Resource manager	3	7
Superintendent	1	2
Assistant superintendent	1	2
Facilitator of staff dev.	1	2
Campus level		
Principal	12	27
Assistant principal	12	27
Student disc. manager	3	7
Mediator (student, teacher, parent)	3	7
Other		
Planner	6	13
Researcher	4	9
Organizer	4	9

Note: Total is more than 100 percent because field supervisors indicated more than one role.

tricts. Specifically, more communication between the faculty advisor and the campus administrator is needed to clarify expectations and school leader preparation outcomes. The following field supervisor comments support the need for clearer communication:

> Provide information in an orientation conference that involves the intern, principal, and university supervisor for a better overall understanding of program outcomes.

> Provide more opportunities to discuss this assessment.

> More communication between university faculty and campus supervisor would strengthen the program.

> It would be helpful to know a week or so ahead of time of placement of intern. It would also be helpful to have a list or guide regarding tasks/responsibilities to be provided to the intern.

Length of Internship

Respondents' comments suggest that one-semester internships are limiting and may not necessarily provide interns with the amount of time required to develop a comprehensive understanding of school leadership and to have more practical experience. As a field supervisor said, "I believe a whole year along with course work would allow the intern to see the whole picture. This is necessary before assuming responsibilities for a school." Another field supervisor expressed the need for additional time as follows:

This internship experience was short lived. It would be my recommendation that an internship should consist of a full year program to allow the prospective administrator to experience the interactions of running a school with the community and Central Administration, PTA, partners in education, school board, special programs, special education, counseling, library, food service, transportation, maintenance, technology, health services, housekeeping, media services, printing services, staff development, textbooks and finance.

Assessment and feedback

Periodic formative evaluations or assessments emerged as an important tool for program development. According to these field supervisors, collecting information about the actual accomplishments of interns may provide relevant information to highlight the benefits for the participating schools and to improve the role of the field supervisor in assisting the intern. As a field supervisor expressed, "A summary of the internships over recent years, and what these interns accomplished for the cooperating agency, should be provided." Another expressed this need when raising the following question: "Is there a way for your program to give feedback to us regarding adjustments or improvements we (I) should make in assisting/leading the intern through the process?"

Balance

Field supervisors believe that there is a need to create a balance between predetermined activities and flexibility to engage in other areas, as well as between theory and practice. As one field supervisor commented, "Continue the balance that exists between faculty supervisors contacts and the freedom to explore the campus experience." Another said, "Do not allow them (interns) to take too many courses while completing their internship." Similarly, a field supervisor said, "Program needs balance between theory and practice. I still believe your program is very theory oriented and perhaps there could be a better balance to what actually goes on in the field."

The additional comments provided by the field supervisors fell within two main categories: the internship program and the intern. The following comments reflect field supervisors' satisfaction:

The university is doing a good job of placement and follow-up.

The internship relationship between the university and the school district was excellent.

Working with the intern and the university internship program has been a most rewarding experience for me, and I trust for the intern as well.

The internship experience is outstanding. The best way to learn is on the job. Keep a balance between theory and practice.

The internship program is excellent preparation for the awesome responsibility of managing a school effectively.

We have had an excellent experience with the Department of Educational Administration, and hope to continue a placement of interns.

It has been a pleasure to work with the program—support and cooperation from university was always available.

Field supervisor's comments about the interns and their contributions to the school were generally positive. The following statements reflect their impressions:

Continue to provide excellent caliber of interns to the profession through proper screening.

Intern was an outstanding intern and will make a fantastic principal. The district needs to keep her.

Intern has become an asset and has become a very valuable part of the staff.

Intern is a very skilled/practical future administrator.

Intern was an asset to the high school.

There is an amazing difference from the time the intern arrives to when he or she leaves. The growth is very rewarding. The intern spends the first three months in shock because of so many different aspects in one job. I realize this can only be learned on the job.

The intern was outstanding. Please send me more just like her.

The intern is an exceptional professional. She has provided an invaluable service to the American Institute of Learning.

Further, as field supervisors made suggestions to improve internships and school leader preparation programs, at least four areas of concern emerged: the scope of the internship areas, the true value of additional academic assignments, the need to develop problem-solving skills, and the involvement of the faculty. As field supervisors remarked:

Provide more opportunities to experience campus level and district-wide budgeting and finance; use of federal and state monies.

By providing for real-life experiences such as school projects to count for credit. The individual papers for class are time-consuming and not as effective as using what they produce for the daily work assignment.

Cut back on demand of research papers and focus practical, realistic experiences.

Provide real-life situations which present opportunities for problem solving, and stimulate continued growth and knowledge.

Spend more active involvement time with the intern on the job and not just interview the intern.

Finally, respondents were asked whether they would be interested in continuing to provide opportunities for other interns in the future. A majority of the field supervisors (93%) responded affirmatively, indicating that "yes" they would be willing to work with other interns, and very few (7%) were doubtful.

CONCLUSION

School administration internships have gained legitimacy as field-based experiences; however, new concerns and questions have emerged. Similarly, generating information for the purpose of providing feedback to interns as well as the preparation programs continue to be a challenge as we attempt to equip principals for the new millennium through better preparation of educational leaders (Clark & Clark, 1996). This chapter focused on the assessment of interns' performance in a university-based internship program. Following both qualitative and quantitative research guidelines, this study utilized interns' assessment forms completed by 46 field supervisors in order to determine the activities in which the interns were involved, overall performance ratings, interns' role potential, intern's areas of strengths and further development needs, as well as recommendations to enhance the internship program.

Findings suggest that field-based learning experiences enhance prospective school leaders awareness level relative to the demands and complexity of school leadership in changing and diverse settings. This finding supports Thurston, Clift, and Schacht (1993) and Thomson's (1993) assertion that we must prepare school leaders for changing schools, and that as schools experience shifts in student populations, principals are expected to be prepared to lead successful change. Findings also indicate that interns are usually involved in special programs that tend to address campus-specific needs and priorities, which might require additional skill development. Supporting the need for additional skill development, researchers suggest that a knowledge base should be drawn from school administration practice (Clark & Clark, 1996; Thomson, 1993; Thurston et al., 1993) in order to better respond to the practical challenges of school leadership.

While the interns in this study exhibit potential to perform several administrative roles at both campus and central office levels, they appear to be prepared to become principals and assistant principals. Therefore, we should focus on the evolving role of the school principal, rethink traditional programs, and develop alternative designs to prepare school leaders for the new millennium (Louis & Murphy, 1994; Murphy, 1993, 1995; Rost, 1991).

Further, findings suggest that interns are very strong in interpersonal skills and organization. On the other hand interns need additional experience and further development in management areas such as budgeting, personnel, and physical plant. These findings support the notion that it is important to provide interns with opportunities to experience a full range of experiences which include both traditional and new dimensions of school leadership and that school leader preparation institutions specify competencies to be developed (Balanoff, et al., 1995; Milstein, et al., 1991; Morgan, et al., 1997; The University of Texas, 1997).

According to field supervisors in this study, enhancement of the internship experiences requires clear communication between the university and cooperating school district, as well as clarification of expectations: a longer timeframe, continuous assessment and feedback for the intern, the campus administrator and the university as well. Furthermore, better balance between theory and practice, greater flexibility, expanding the scope of the internship, reducing academic assignments and opportunities to develop problem-solving skills may contribute to a more meaningful internship experience and the development of school leaders for the new millennium.

This study was limited to one university-based internship and one source of information. While wide generalizations are not possible, it can be asserted that the assessment form completed by field supervisors may be a promising vehicle to generate information that can be used to enhance the quality of the interns' field experiences and school leader preparation program. Further, such information has potential as a source of future reference when students apply for administrative positions. Therefore, school leader preparation programs should select the most effective means to assess intern's performance and to generate constructive feedback in order to enhance preparation of school leaders.

Finally, it is important to affirm that while benefits and shortcomings associated with the internship as a field-based learning experience were highlighted here to some extent, and that this study focused on the assessment of interns' performance as a mechanism to generate information for program improvement purposes, additional questions and challenges for the internship and the implementation of school leader preparation programs remain. Further, as Clark and Clark (1996) affirm, emerging challenges "can be overcome through the collaborative efforts of educators, community/business leaders, and government officials. The preparation of outstanding educational leaders is too critical to the reform of American education for us not to join together" (p. 20). Consequently, it is imperative that preparation institutions search for effective strategies to engage in collaborative initiatives that may lead to joint planning, implementation and evaluation of alternative and creative designs to enhance school leader preparation programs for the new millennium.

REFERENCES

Anderson, G. (1988). Practice as inquiry: The professional knowledge of the principal. Unpublished document, Department of Educational Administration, University of New Mexico.

Anderson, M. E. (1989). Training and selecting school leaders. In S. C. Smith and P. K. Piele (Eds.), School leadership (pp. 53–84). Eugene, OR: ERIC Clearinghouse on Educational Management, University of Oregon.

Applebome, P. (1996, March 27). Education summit calls for tough standards to be set by states and local school districts. The New York Times, B7.

Baciliuos, Z. (1987, March). A proposal for the reconstruction of the administrative internship. Paper presented at the annual meeting of the American Educational Research Association, Washington, D.C.

Balanoff, H., King, K. & Ovando, M. N. (1995). Administrative internship manual. Unpublished manuscript, Department of Educational Administration, College of Education, The University of Texas, Austin, TX.

Björk, L., & Ginsberg, R. (1995). Principles of reform and reforming principal training: A theoretical perspective. Educational Administration Quarterly, 31(1), 11–37.

Campbell, R. F., Fleming, T., Newell, L. J. & Bennion, J. W. (1987). A history of thought and practice in educational administration. New York: Teachers College Press.

Carlson, R. (1996). Reframing and reform: Perspectives on organization, leadership, and school change. White Plains, NY: Longman Publishers.

Cavazos, M. (1999). The instructional leadership of high school principals in successful hispanic majority high schools. Unpublished doctoral dissertation, University of Texas, Austin, TX.

Clark, D. C. and Clark, S. N. (1994). Restructuring the middle level school: Implications for school leaders. Albany, NY: State University of New York Press.

Clark, D. C. and Clark, S. N. (1996). Better preparation of educational Leaders. Educational Researcher, 25(9), 18–20.

Creswell, J. W. (1994). Research design: Qualitative and quantitative approaches. London: SAGE publications.

Daresh, J. (1987, October). Administrative internship and field experiences: A status report. Paper presented at the annual meeting of the University Council of Educational Administration, Charlottesville, VA.

Daresh, J. (1998, April). Are field based programs the answer to the reforms of administrator preparation programs? Paper presented at the annual meeting of the American Educational Research Association, New Orleans, LA.

Duley, J. S. (1978). Learning through field experience. In O. Milton and Associates (Eds.), On college teaching (pp. 314–339). San Francisco: Jossey-Bass Publishers.

Griffiths, D. (1988). Educational administration: Reform PDQ or RIP (University Council for Educational Administration, Occasional Paper No. 8312). Tempe, AZ: Arizona State University.

Hencley, S.P. (Ed.). (1963). The internship in administrative preparation. Washington, DC: The Committee for the Advancement of Educational Administration.

Herman, J., & Herman, J. L. (1993). School-based management: Current thinking and practice. Springfield, IL: Charles C Thomas, Publisher.

Howey, K. R., and Zimpher, N. L. (1999). Pervasive problems and issues in teacher education. In G. A. Griffin, (Ed.), The education of teachers, Ninety-eight yearbook of the national society for the study of education, Part I (pp. 279–305). Chicago, IL: The University Chicago Press.

Jick, T. D. (1984). Mixing qualitative and quantitative methods: Triangulation in action. In T. S. Bateman & G. R. Ferris (Eds.), Methods and analysis in organizational research (pp. 364–372). Reston, VA: Reston Publishing Company.

Kempner, K. (1991). Getting into the castle of educational administration. Peabody Journal of Education, 66(3), 104–123.

Krippendorff, K. (1980). Content analysis: An introduction to its methodology. Beverly Hills, CA: Sage Publications.

Leithwood, K., & Steinbach, R. (1995). Expert problem solving: Evidence from school and district leaders. Albany, NY: State University of New York Press.

Lincoln, Y. S., & Guba, E. G. (1985). Naturalistic inquiry. Newbury Park, CA: Sage Publications.

Louis, K., & Murphy, J. (1994). The evolving role of the principal. In J. Murphy & K. Louis (Eds.), Reshaping the principalship: Insights from transformational reform efforts (pp. 265–279). Thousand Oaks, CA: Corwin Press, Inc.

Marek, S. (1999). The role of the principal in achieving and sustaining academic success in high-poverty elementary schools. Unpublished doctoral dissertation, University of Texas, Austin, TX.

Miles, M. B., & Huberman, A. M. (1984). Qualitative data analysis. Beverly Hills, CA: Sage Publications.

Milstein, M., Bobroff, B. & Restine, L. N. (1991). Internship programs in educational administration: A guide to preparing educational leaders. New York: Teachers College Press.

Milstein, M. (1990). Rethinking the clinical aspects in administrative preparation: From theory to practice. In S. L. Jacobson & J. Conway (Eds.), Educational leadership in an age of reform. New York: Longman.

Morgan, P. L., Gibbs, A. S., Hertzog, C. J., & Wylie, V. (1997). The educational leader's internship: Meeting new standards. Lancaster, PA: Technomic.

Murphy, J. (1993). Alternative designs: New directions. In J. Murphy (Ed.), Preparing tomorrow's school leaders: Alternative designs (pp. 225–253). University Park, PA: The University Council for Educational Administration.

Murphy, J. (1995). Rethinking the foundations of leadership preparation: Insights from school improvement efforts. Design for Leadership: The Bulletin of the National Policy Board for Educational Administration, 6(1), 1–4, 6.

Murphy, J., & Hallinger, P. (1987). Emerging views of the professional development of school administrators: A synthesis with suggestions for improvement. In J. Murphy & P. Hallinger (Eds.), Approaches to administrative training (pp. 245–281). Albany: SUNY Press.

National Commission on Excellence in Educational Administration. (1987). Leaders for America's schools. Tempe, AZ: University Council for Educational Administration.

Ovando, M.N. (1990). Internship follow-up report. Unpublished manuscript, Department of Educational Administration, The University of Texas at Austin.

Pitner, N. J. (1988). School administrator preparation: The state of the art. In D. Griffiths, R. Stout, & P. Forsyth (Eds.), Leaders of American's schools (pp. 367–402). Berkeley, CA: McCutchan.

Richardson, J. (1992, November 4). Revisions in teacher training for middle grades urged. Education Week, p. 11.

Rost, J. (1991). Leadership for the twenty-first century. New York: Praeger.

Short, P. M. & Price, H. J. (1992). Clinical experience in administrators preparation programs: Are we there yet? UCEA Review, 23(3), 4–7.

Skalski, J., Lohman, M., Szcepanik, J., Barratta, A., Bacilious, Z., & Schulte, S. (1987, April). Administrative Internships. Paper presented at the annual meeting of the American Educational Research Association, Washington, DC.

Teitel, L. (1996). Leadership in professional development schools: Lessons for the preparation of administrators. UCEA Review, 37(1), 10–11, 15.

The University of Texas at Austin (1997). Handbook for students and mentor administrators, The University of Texas, Department of Educational Administration, Austin, TX.

Thomson, S. (Ed.). (1993). Principals for our changing schools: Knowledge and skill base. Lancaster, PA: Technomic Publishing Company.

Thurston, P., Clift, R., & Schacht, M. (1993). Preparing leaders for change-oriented schools. Phi Delta Kappan, 75(3), 259–265.

Yates, J., & Wagstaff, J. (2000). Building partnerships between universities and school districts. Paper presented at the Conference Within a Conference of The American Association of School Administrators National Conference of Education, San Francisco, CA.

A Comparison of Full- and Part-time Internships in an Administrator Preparation Program

LYNN K. BRADSHAW and KERMIT G. BUCKNER

Debates continue over the preparation of school administrators. Some question the need for university training (Haller, Brent, & McNamara, 1997; Brent, 1998), and others describe the continuing need to define the most appropriate content for principal preparation and the most effective forms of instructional delivery (Daresh, & Playko, 1997). McCarthy (1999) described a range of state initiatives to improve preparation programs. Some initiatives focused on reviewing, eliminating, or redesigning existing programs while others explored possibilities for alternative licensure.

Relatedly, the debate continues over the desired relationship between theory and practice in the preparation of school administrators. As the focus of preparation programs has shifted from management to leadership preparation and school improvement, there was increased interest in incorporating "field-based instruction that applies research to problems faced on the job and brings practitioners and researchers together to seek solutions" (McCarthy, 1999, p. 128). Daresh (1999) emphasized the need for future educational leaders to promote teaching and learning as the core activity of the school, to manage change, and to work collaboratively with diverse stakeholder groups. In proposing school improvement as the "center" for the profession of educational leadership, Murphy (1999) observed that school-based programs would force students to examine connections between organizational variables and student outcomes. There is growing interest in job-imbedded training (Daresh & Playko, 1997; Wood & McQuarrie, 1999) and the roles of formal and informal mentors in administrator development (Barnett, 1995; Crow & Matthews, 1998; Gooden, Carrigan, & Ashbaugh, 1999; Kraus & Cordiero, 1995; Wood & Killian, 1998). When applicants are in short supply, it is not unusual for school administrators to be hired before they complete a preparation program and are licensed by the state. Early in the current wave of reform in preparation programs for school administrators, Duke (1992) suggested the possibility of allowing local districts to orient, train, and provisionally

Lynn K. Bradshaw, East Carolina University
Kermit G. Buckner, East Carolina University

license new school administrators and requiring applicants for university programs to demonstrate on-the-job success with basic administrative tasks. Students with administrative experience "would be more likely than preservice students to bring with them specific questions about the effectiveness of certain practices as well as a wealth of practical experiences against which to compare theory and research" (p. 770).

As preparation programs for school administrators have been redesigned, they generally include more substantial clinical experiences and internships (Cordiero & Sloan-Smith, 1996; Clark & Clark, 1996; Glasman & Glasman, 1997; NPBEA, 1995; Short & Price, 1992). Murphy (1991) called for more information about "the activities in which students in these longer and improved field experiences are actually engaged" (p. 55). There is a perception among educators and education decision makers that full-time internships are preferable to part-time internships because they will allow principal candidates to be fully immersed in an administrative role. In addition, there is an expectation that principal interns should be paired with only the most successful and experienced principals. However, there is support for the idea that there is much that can be learned from leaders, both good and bad (Mc-Call, 1997; McCall, Lombardo, & Morrison, 1988). The purpose of this study was to examine the internship experiences of full-time and part-time administrative interns in a school administrator preparation program at East Carolina University. Not all interns are in full-time internships, and although university professors are able to influence the placement decision, the interns tend to be placed by the districts to meet district needs.

THE CONTEXT FOR THE STUDY

New Master of School Administration (MSA) programs for preparing school leaders in North Carolina were implemented in 1996. The initial legislation called for full-time yearlong internships, but in response to shortages of candidates for administrative positions, universities were soon required to develop internship options for part-time students. MSA students at East Carolina University fall into several categories based on their reasons for enrollment and their employment status. Some have been encouraged by their principals or superintendents to become licensed as school administrators, and they may have already participated in district staff development for future school leaders. A few have already been hired in administrative positions and must enroll in university preparation programs and complete licensure requirements. Others have chosen, on their own, to pursue a degree and licensure in school administration as a means of professional advancement.

Each year, there is a cohort of full-time MSA students who have been selected as North Carolina (NC) Principal Fellows. The Principal Fellows are granted leave from their teaching positions and receive financial support to pursue full-time study for two years. They complete a full-time yearlong internship during the second year. A few students pursue full-time study without the support of the Principal Fellows Program. However, the majority of students who are not Principal Fellows enroll on a part-time basis, taking courses in the evenings and during the summers, completing the internship requirements while they are employed as teachers or in administrative roles.

Students enroll in the internship for two semesters, fall and spring. The Principal Fellows are in their assigned schools four days each week, and they spend the fifth day on campus taking one course and participating in an intern seminar. Interns who are employed as teachers or administrators are in the schools five days each week, and they take courses and attend intern seminars at night. Part-time interns who are continuing to teach, "log" administrative hours whenever possible and continue to seek administrative opportunities during the summer months.

Early in the internship, all interns assess their knowledge, skills, and professional perspectives against state and national standards for school administrators. Using the self-assessment results, interns develop a growth plan that includes strategies for building skills during the internship. They develop a Leadership Portfolio containing the internship log, evidence of growth activities within each standard, and reflections about what they have learned. The comprehensive examination is an oral defense of the portfolio.

RESEARCH DESIGN AND METHODOLOGY

A survey was developed to gather information from the full- and part-time administrative interns regarding the quantity and quality of the internship activities. Respondents included 39 interns enrolled in the MSA internship during the 1998–1999 academic year. Fourteen were full-time interns completing the Principal Fellows Program, and 10 were full-time interns employed in administrative positions by their districts. The remaining 15 were part-time interns who sought administrative opportunities and logged internship hours while they continued to teach. Often, the part-time interns performed administrative activities during planning periods, hours before and after school, extended day initiatives, and weekend programs, and they sought additional opportunities during the summer months to meet the minimum 500-hour requirement. Interns responded to the survey at the beginning of the spring 1999 semester. Most respondents had begun logging internship hours during the summer of 1998.

The survey asked the interns to project the average number of hours each week spent in various types of activities: resolving discipline issues, working with buses, parent contacts, teacher observations, teacher conferences, meetings, and other activities. Open-ended questions asked about their opportunities to work with the instructional programs, interaction with parent and community groups, experiences with teacher evaluation, and progress toward the completion of the Leadership Portfolio. Finally, interns were asked to make recommendations for new interns including one strategy that had helped them become a valuable part of the school administrative team.

Quantitative data were analyzed using descriptive statistics, and trends were noted. Responses to open-ended questions were compared, and matrices were developed to identify themes.

RESULTS AND MAJOR FINDINGS

Of the 39 interns in the study, 10 were male and 29 were female. The interns were assigned to elementary (21), middle (6), and high school (10) settings with 16 to 95 teachers (see Table 1). Two interns were in positions that served entire districts directing English as a Second language and Exceptional Children's Programs. Two interns worked in high schools where there were three other assistant principals, 9 worked with two other assistant principals, and 15 worked with one other assistant principal. Twelve interns, including six full-time interns serving in administrative roles, were the only "assistant principal" in the school.

Reported Hours per Week in Administrative Activities

Although there were large differences in the number of hours each week that interns reported being engaged in administrative activities (see Table 2), it is important to note that the numbers reflect the interns' perceptions when they completed the survey and are not necessarily accurate. A few totals were unrealistically high, and others were surprisingly low, suggesting that major activities were not reflected in the report.

As expected, the part-time interns who were continuing to teach reported the smallest number of administrative hours per week, an average of 17.9. The range was from 8 to 34 hours each week, with bus duty, after-school remediation programs, school improvement and curriculum development meetings, and textbook responsibilities providing the most common opportunities for those logging the larger numbers of hours.

The Principal Fellow interns reported the next largest number of administrative hours, with an average of 38.1 and a range of 15 to 90. For Principal Fellows, who were in the schools four days each week, discipline issues consistently required the most time.

TABLE I. Participant Characteristics.

	Gender		School Level			
	Male	Female	Elem.	MS	HS	All
Part-time Interns	3	12	9	0	5	1
Full-time Interns						
Nonprincipal Fellows	4	6	4	2	3	1
Principal Fellows	3	11	8	4	2	0
All Participants	10	29	21	6	10	2

TABLE II. Average Number of Hours per Week Engaged in Administrative Activities.

| | Part-time Interns | | Full-time Interns | | Principal Fellows | | All |
	Average	Range	Average	Range	Average	Range	Average
Resolving discipline issues	2.70	0–7	16.1	3–30	12.9	2–35	9.76
Working with buses	3.03	0–10	6.2	0–12	4.93	0–15	4.53
Parent contacts	2.23	0–10	7.6	3–20	4.5	1–15	4.45
Teacher observations	1.20	0–12	3.7	0–10	3.0	1–6	2.49
Teacher conferences	1.33	0–10	4.6	1–10	3.36	1–15	2.90
Meetings at school	3.40	1–10	5.2	2–10	3.36	2–7	3.87
Meetings away from school	2.00	0–6	3.5	0–15	2.71	0–6	2.65
Other activities	2.00	0–20	5.1	0–25	3.71	0–27	3.42
Total	17.9	8–34	52.0	15–82	38.4	15–90	34.1

The full-time interns who were hired by the districts in administrative roles reported an average number of 52 administrative hours per week, with a range of 15 to 82. Discipline issues and parent contacts accounted for a large portion of those hours.

Experience with Teacher Observation and Evaluation

In separate questions, interns were asked to describe their opportunities to observe, conference with, and evaluate teachers. There were striking differences within and across all groups of interns in their opportunities in these areas. Only one part-time intern, five full-time interns, and three Principal Fellows reported conducting classroom observations with a mentor administrator. Two of those interns, 1 full-time intern and 1 Principal Fellow, reported conducting 10 to 20 observations with their mentors. Part-time interns reported minimal opportunities to observe, conference with, and evaluate teachers alone. Seven of 15 part-time interns reported working with 1 to 6 teachers in the evaluation process, and in many cases those teachers were beginning teachers and the intern was serving as a mentor. Three full-time interns and 6 Principal Fellows also reported limited opportunities in this area, working with 0 to 6 teachers.

The remaining full-time interns and Principal Fellows reported considerable activity in this area. Many were assigned to complete a percentage of the teacher observations or to evaluate a specific group of teachers for the year. At the high end, 1 Principal Fellow reported being responsible for the evaluation of 25 teachers throughout the year. In addition to courses in supervision and curriculum leadership, 27 of the 39 interns reported having completed the state training program in the use of the state teacher evaluation instrument, and 14 had completed the state training program for mentors. Only 1 of the interns assigned to evaluate large numbers of teachers had not completed the state training program, and he did not consider the lack of training a problem. "I have not had the formal course in using the state teacher evaluation instrument, but the county and other administrators have various formats available for my use. I prefer the narrative variation inputted directly into the word processor."

Opportunities to Work with the Instructional Program

Interns in all groups reported a variety of opportunities to work with the instructional program:

- Analyzing test data
- Helping teachers with instructional timelines and pacing guides
- Helping develop programs in specific curriculum areas
- Reviewing lesson plans and progress reports
- Supporting beginning teachers
- Visiting classrooms and conducting teacher observations and evaluation
- Selecting textbooks and other instructional materials
- Providing staff development
- Attending grade level meetings
- Working with alternative education programs
- Helping with the accreditation (SACS) process

The reported activities were similar across the three groups, but the time spent with the instructional program was obviously less for the part-time interns.

Opportunities to Work with Parents and Community Groups

Similar patterns were noted in the interns' activities with parents and community groups. Interns in all groups reported working with parents to resolve student discipline issues, and many mentioned PTO meetings, Parent Advisory Councils, Booster Clubs, fundraisers, and committee work. Several worked with other community agencies to develop special programs for students.

Preparation for the Internship

When asked what experiences in their preparation program had helped them prepare for the internship, many cited field experiences and shadowing. Several courses were felt to be particularly valuable: supervision, law, ethics, strategic problem solving, and finance. Students who had participated in the LEAP assessment center and the Springfield/SAS simulation felt that those opportunities were helpful, expressing appreciation for in-baskets and hands-on activities.

Students identified additional experiences that they felt were needed. They wanted more information about financial issues, exceptional children's programs, time management strategies, and dealing with angry or difficult people. They were concerned about the instructional program and wanted more strategies for helping teachers improve their classroom instruction. Students also expressed needs for information and help with the internship and the licensure exam. They wanted to clarify the requirements for the internship and see sample Leadership Portfolios.

Technology Competence

Interns in all groups tended to rate themselves proficient in the technology standards set by the state. On a scale of 0 to 3, the overall average rating was 2.3, and the average rating for each of the three groups was similar: part-time interns (2.2), full-time interns (2.4), and Principal Fellows (2.36). All interns rated themselves at least proficient with some standards, and 17 interns gave themselves a "3," the highest rating.

Interns were interested in knowing more about the software packages used in the schools, particularly the student information management system (SIMS) and the programs used to analyze student performance data. Several mentioned the need to be familiar with Apple/MAC technology, and a number of interns were interested in knowing more about how to help teachers integrate technology into the instructional program.

Suggestions for Success

Interns in all groups were able to identify strategies for becoming part of the administrative team. Suggested strategies included:

- Choose your school carefully, and work in a place where you are needed so that you will have to jump in and take responsibility.
- Start early. Learn the office staff and the school before the teachers start.
- Establish and define your role with the principal in the beginning.
- Use your down time at the beginning to start the internship log and to read school handbooks.
- If you don't have time to make daily entries in your log, keep notes on your calendar and update it weekly.
- Spend as much time as possible researching curriculum needs, shadowing administrators, visiting other classrooms. See the whole school.
- Observe, observe, observe. Get into the classrooms on a regular basis.
- Be visible and available.
- Don't be afraid to ask questions and seek help!
- Take the initiative. Volunteer to help, and ask to do things on your own.
- Make plans to involve yourself. Don't wait for the principal to involve you.

- Ask yourself what you can do to improve the school and then do everything possible to accomplish your goals. Take ownership and become concerned about your school.
- Look at the whole picture—what's best school-wide.
- Work collaboratively. Share information so that we can all be consistent. Never let your partners be blind-sided by an issue or something you should have told them about. Include many members of the school community to reach consensus about what is best for students.
- Show respect to all individuals. Listen. Support the teachers. Keep your word.
- Networks are helpful. Communicate with your cohort and with your professors.
- Take care of family and personal needs, especially your health.

Part-time interns recognized the challenge of completing the internship while continuing to teach. Several pointed out that full-time internships were a "plus." One part-time intern described a need to "stay in the middle—being a teacher with other teachers and being an administrator with the administrators." Another noted, "Trying to teach and get experiences during the year is difficult. Summer gave me the opportunity to be involved in situations that were almost impossible during the year." A particularly dedicated part-time intern expressed these concerns: "Although I have almost survived, I do feel at times that I have missed out on 'office things' that an administrator does. Also, I don't have time to 'walk and talk' with the administrative team." An intern who was seldom given "important" assignments observed, "Have a principal who is just as enthusiastic about having your help as you are about completing the program."

CONCLUSIONS AND IMPLICATIONS

The results of the study confirmed that although there were differences between full- and part-time internships, both could be positive development opportunities. The supervising principal played an important role in the internship, but interns learned from both good and bad examples.

Differences between Full- and Part-time Internships

As expected, full-time interns experienced more administrative opportunities than part-time interns, but there was considerable variation within both groups. A full-time internship did not guarantee a balance of administrative opportunities, and interns were most likely to have quality development opportunities when they were able to recognize leadership opportunities and to respond to them successfully. When the supervising principal believed that the intern was a good administrative candidate, the principal was more likely to provide authentic assignments whether the intern was full or part time. Part-time interns with full teaching responsibility for a self-contained elementary or exceptional children's classroom experienced the greatest difficulty when trying to obtain administrative experiences.

Intern experiences with teacher evaluation were particularly uneven. Some districts had established unique training requirements for teacher evaluators, and principals were reluctant to allow interns without the required training to evaluate teachers. University faculty and interns must identify local training requirements early so that interns can obtain the necessary training, particularly if they are planning to seek permanent employment in the district after graduation. As an alternative, supervising professors found that principals were willing to allow "untrained" interns to shadow them during teacher evaluation activities. Teacher evaluation is important in instructional leadership, and university faculty must work with principals and district administrators to assure that interns have quality opportunities to develop skills in this area.

The Value of a Skilled Mentor

The host principals were important players in the internship experience, and orientation and training were provided in group and individual sessions. Additional efforts are needed to clarify expectations for the internship, including the Leadership Portfolio. University supervisors must continue to work with principals and interns to assure that interns are engaged in varied administrative activities and develop needed skills. Increased communication with the principal mentors seemed to be particularly needed for part-time interns.

Helping the Interns Take Charge of Their Own Professional Development

In addition to the strategies listed above, interns will be more likely to have a balance of quality administrative experiences if they are able to identify their needs for growth and to recognize opportunities for developing them. The program can prepare the interns to take responsibility by continuing to foster a developmental frame of mind.

Assessment

In response to the survey, several modifications have occurred or are being planned for the internship at East Carolina University. The Principal Fellows who began their internships in the fall of 1999 participated in an assessment center at the end of the spring semester. The National Association of Secondary School Principal's Developmental Assessment Center (DAC) was modified for student use. The assessment provided students opportunities to deal with time management, teacher evaluation, and other issues the survey indicated were needed in the preparation program.

Earlier attempts to use assessment center methodology to assess students had been difficult due to the cost of providing assessors and the time required for assessment data analysis and reporting by faculty or others. The Developmental Assessment Center was modified to include self- and peer assessment. This modification encouraged reflection and produced high quality data on student performance with minimal cost and faculty involvement.

Based on modifications resulting from the study, the analysis of strengths and developmental needs from the assessment has become the basis for initial development planning during the internship. Relatedly, data will be collected during the internship to determine the accuracy and utility of the assessment prior to the internship experience.

Development planning

Development planning is an essential part of any meaningful growth experience. There are a number of factors that influence the development of an effective school administrator. The opportunities provided by a supervising principal are important, but knowledge of self, combined with a flexible plan for one's own development, is essential. Additionally, learning occurs within a context that must be a part of the planning. And finally, learning should be grounded in well-established expectations or standards.

Based on the findings from this study, the development planning expected of students was modified. Consequently, interns begin their internship by developing a plan that reflects their assessed or perceived strengths and development needs. The plan includes strategies to build on strengths as well as to strengthen weaknesses, and describes specific situations and assignments that will provide opportunities for growth. In addition, the plans, as they are developed, reflect the goals and improvement plans of the schools to which the interns are assigned, allowing them to respond to the context within which they are working. The plans are also tied to the Interstate School Leaders Licensure Consortium Standards (ISSLC) for school leaders.

The impact of this planning and the intern's ability to follow the plan will be monitored. During the intern seminars students are now encouraged to discuss the plans, make adjustments, and evaluate their progress.

Reflecting

Interns report that reflecting on experiences is one of the most difficult things they are asked to do. A typical reflection consists of a description of what happened and what the intern did to "handle" the problem or issue. Beginning in the fall of 1999, East Carolina interns are expected to reflect more deeply on their experiences. This "deep" reflection will be encouraged in the seminars all interns are required to attend and in the portfolio each intern must submit. Intern reflections revolve around four questions:

1) What happened?
2) What did you do?
3) What did you learn?
4) How will you use what you learned in future situations?

The intern's ability to reflect will be monitored during visits by supervising professors and at seminars. The portfolio will also provide data on the quality of reflection.

SUMMARY

The administrative internship continues to be an important component of leadership preparation programs. While full-time internships might be ideal, they are not always feasible, and even if mentors could be hand-picked, there is no guarantee that a specific principal will be a positive role model for a specific intern. This comparison of the experiences of full- and part-time interns found that interns learned and developed important skills in both types of internships with a variety of supervising principals. Although the full-time internship provided a larger quantity of opportunities than part-time internships, the full-time internship did not guarantee a balanced internship experience, especially when the supervising principal was more concerned with the efficient operation of the school than with the development of the intern. Part-time interns sought and obtained many valuable development opportunities. It was also not necessary to place the interns with "excellent" principals in order for them to develop. The support of the university supervisor and peer support through the intern seminars and peer reflection groups helped interns learn from "mistakes" and from practice that was less than best. The development of a leadership portfolio based on standards for school leaders was a powerful learning experience. It allowed students to reflect across an entire year, compare their experience and learning with the standards, recognize what they had learned, and set goals for future growth. The modified comprehensive exam became an authentic task based on questions specifically tied to portfolio evidence.

Efforts to develop the interns' ability to take charge of their own development were successful and should be strengthened. University faculty can support the intern by helping the supervising principals understand the purpose and design of the internship and by facilitating collaborative needs assessment and planning of developmental activities throughout the internship. As a result, the interns' development during the internship will provide a strong base for continuing professional development throughout their careers as school leaders.

REFERENCES

Barnett, B. G. (1995). Developing reflection and expertise: Can mentors make the difference? Journal of Educational Administration, 33(5), pp. 45–59.

Brent, B. O. (1998). Should graduate training in educational administration be required for principal certification? Existing evidence suggests the answer is no. Teaching in Educational Administration Newsletter, 5(2), 1–7.

Clark, D. C., & Clark, S. N. (1996). Better preparation of educational leaders. Educational Researcher, 25(9), 18–20.

Cordiero, P. A., & Sloan-Smith, E. (1996). Administrative interns as legitimate partners in the community of practice. Journal of School Leadership, 6(1), 4–29.

Crow, G. M., & Matthews, L. J. (1998). Finding one's way: How mentoring can lead to dynamic leadership. Thousand Oaks, CA: Corwin Press, Inc.

Daresh, J. C. (1999). Preparing school leaders to "break ranks." Connections, 2, 29–32.

Daresh, J. C., & Playko, M. A. (1997). Beginning the principalship: A practical guide for new school leaders. Thousand Oaks, CA: Corwin Press, Inc.

Duke, D. L. (1992). The rhetoric and the reality of reform in educational administration. Phi Delta Kappan, 73, 764–770.

Glasman, N., & Glasman, L. (1997). Connecting the preparation of school leaders to the practice of school leadership. Peabody Journal of Education, 72(2), 3–20.

Gooden, J. S., Carrigan, J. K., & Ashbaugh, C. R. (1999, October). Training principal interns: Analyzing the experience. Paper presented at the annual meeting of the Southern Regional Council on Educational Administration, Charlotte, NC.

Haller, E. J., Brent, B. O., & McNamara, J. F. (1997). Does graduate training in educational administration improve America's schools? Another look at some national data. Phi Delta Kappan, 79(3), 222–227.

Kraus, C. M., & Cordiero, P. A. (1995, October). Challenging tradition: Re-examining the preparation of educational leaders for the workplace. Paper presented at the annual meeting of the University Council for Educational Administration, Salt Lake City, UT.

McCall, M. W. Jr. (1997). High flyers: Developing the next generation of leaders. Cambridge, MA: Harvard Business School Press.

McCall, M. W. Jr., Lombardo, M. M., & Morrison, A. M. (1988). The lessons of experience: How successful executives develop on the job. Lexington Books.

McCarthy, M. M. (1999). The evolution of educational leadership preparation programs. In J. Murphy, & K. S. Louis (Eds.), Handbook of research on educational administration (pp. 119–139). San Francisco: Jossey-Bass Publishers.

Murphy, J. (1991). The effects of the educational reform movement on departments of educational leadership. Educational Evaluation and Policy Analysis, 13(1), 49–65.

Murphy, J. (1999, April). The quest for a center: Notes on the state of the profession of educational leadership. Paper presented at the annual meeting of the American Educational Research Association, Montreal.

National Policy Board for Educational Administration (NPBEA). (1995). NCATE guidelines: Curriculum guidelines for advanced programs in educational leadership for principals, superintendents, curriculum directors, and supervisors. Alexandria, VA: Educational Leadership Constituent Council.

Short, P. M., & Price, H. J. (1992). Clinical experience in administrator preparation programs: Are we there yet? UCEA Review, 33(3), 4–7.

Wood, F. H., & Killian, J. E. (1998). Job-embedded learning makes the difference in school improvement. Journal of Staff Development, 19(1), 52–54.

Wood, F. H., & McQuarrie, F. (1999). On-the-job learning. Journal of Staff Development, 20(3), 10–13.

Preparing Tomorrow's Leaders: Grounding Programs in National Standards

RONALD D. WILLIAMSON
MARTHA B. HUDSON

Demand for school reform continues unabated at the start of the new millennium. Nearly every reform agenda includes a call for improved leadership—leadership which embraces teaching and learning as the central role of schools, thrives on accountability, and values parent and community participation (Boyer, 1995; National Association of Secondary School Principals, 1996).

School leaders play a critical role in the complex life of their school. They work with faculty and parents to articulate a vision and set priorities. They cultivate and nurture parent and community support. Leaders' skills, attitudes and predispositions significantly impact the way in which their school responds to student and community needs.

In response to the recognition of the vital role of leadership in school reform, a debate emerged about both the purpose and design of school leadership preparation programs (Achilles, 1998; Haller, Brent & McNamara, 1997; Thomson, 1993) and their effectiveness (Kempner, 1991; Thurston, Clift, & Schacht, 1993; Van Meter & Murphy, 1997). Dissatisfaction with the amorphous nature of such programs led to development of recommendations for their modification (Griffiths, Stout & Forsyth, 1988; National Policy Board for Educational Administration, 1989) and articulation of the knowledge, skills and predispositions required of contemporary school leaders (Council of Chief State School Officers, 1996).

Dissatisfaction was not limited to the structure and content of preparation programs. Serious questions were also raised about the role of universities in training school leaders (Achilles, 1994; Haller, Brent & McNamara, 1997; Schneider, 1998).

Left unanswered these questions will continue to dominate the discourse about school leadership preparation and have the potential to erode the role of universities in preparing leaders for the new millennium. Despite the nearly universal recognition of the need for reform, it has been slow to develop.

Ronald D. Williamson, University of North Carolina at Greensboro
Martha B. Hudson, University of North Carolina at Greensboro

Many school leadership programs, however, responded to this debate and launched initiatives to examine their programs and make modifications based on both the standards for school leaders and the recommendations for relevant and meaningful preparation programs. While individual programs vary, they often incorporate several similar components including:

- a strong sense of purpose developed in collaboration with prospective students, local school district personnel, practicing school leaders, and state policymakers (Achilles, 1994; Clark & Clark, 1996);
- a knowledge base which incorporates issues confronted by contemporary school leaders and which reflects an integration of theory, research and practice (Murphy, 1991; Thomson, 1993; Thurston, Clift, & Schacht, 1993);
- an appreciation that teaching and learning are the central function of schools and that school leaders must be knowledgeable about successful practice and skillful at engaging the school community in examining its teaching practices (Achilles, 1998; Council of Chief State School Officers, 1996; Murphy, 1999a);
- a greater use of clinical activities including school-based internships which focus on confronting the problems faced by school leaders today (Leithwood, Jantzi, & Coffin, 1995; Milstein & Krueger, 1997; National Policy Board for Educational Administration, 1989).

Programmatic changes, once launched, become quickly institutionalized and often remain in place simply because that is "the way we do things around here" (Achilles, 1999). Faculty adjust and the altered program becomes the new norm. Students, on the other hand, confront different realities—do the changes meet their perceived needs, will the knowledge and skills they develop be applicable in the "real" world of schools?

Standards for School Leaders

From this debate emerged an initiative to delineate those attributes central to school leadership. As a result of discussion among practitioners, professional organizations and university faculty the Council of Chief State School Officers (1996) identified a set of national standards for school leaders (See Table 1). The standards emphasized the complexity of the leadership role (Bolman & Deal, 1991), the importance of moral and ethical grounding (Sergiovanni, 1992), the value of working closely with parents and community (Prestine, 1991; Sergiovanni, 1994), and the importance of student learning as the primary function of schools (Newman, 1991).

Concurrent with national activity, the North Carolina General Assembly called for major reforms in principal preparation and supported creation of new programs. Students must now complete an approved Masters of School Administration (MSA) degree and receive a satisfactory score on the Interstate School Leaders License Assessment (Educational Testing Service, 1997), based on the standards, in order to be issued a principal's license. MSA programs were redesigned to ensure that core knowledge was grounded in problems of practice. Program approval was contingent on commitment to a problem-based pedagogy and clinical opportunities, including the equivalent of a full-time internship.

A systematic investigation of the impact of the redesigned program on student perceptions of program value was initiated in 1997 (Williamson & Hudson, 1998). Since the new program addressed nearly all recommendations for improved principal preparation, the results of this study may prove informative to others responding to the calls for reform in university programs.

METHODOLOGY

In order to investigate the impact on students of new content standards and revised instructional practices and to gather student perspectives and insights on these initiatives, a study was designed to incorporate the student voice as one measure of the im-

TABLE I. Interstate School Leaders Licensure Consortium Standards.

Standard 1	A school administrator is an educational leader who promotes the success of all students by facilitating the development, articulation, implementation, and stewardship of a vision of learning that is shared and supported by the school community.
Standard 2	A school administrator is an educational leader who promotes the success of all students by advocating, nurturing, and sustaining a school culture and instructional program conducive to student learning and staff professional growth.
Standard 3	A school administrator is an educational leader who promotes the success of all students by ensuring management of the organization, operations, and resources for a safe, efficient, and effective learning environment.
Standard 4	A school administrator is an educational leader who promotes the success of all students by collaborating with families and community members, responding to diverse community interests and needs, and mobilizing community resources.
Standard 5	A school administrator is an educational leader who promotes the success of all students by acting with integrity, fairness, and in an ethical manner.
Standard 6	A school administrator is an educational leader who promotes the success of all students by understanding, responding to, and influencing the larger political, social, economic, legal, and cultural context.

Council of Chief State School Officers (1996). Interstate School Leaders Licensure Consortium: Standards for School Leaders. Washington, DC: Author.

pact of program reform (Williamson & Hudson, 1999). It afforded students the opportunity to, in their own words, demonstrate how new standards were integrated into their attitudes and their practices. Further, it allowed them to assess how both the content and the pedagogy influenced their preparedness.

Data were gathered in three ways: from a short survey of students providing demographic data and information about program value, from student writing samples, and through a series of interviews with students exiting the program (Stake, 1995; Yin, 1994). Questions which guided this study are summarized in Table 2. Complementing one another, these data sources provided both quantitative and qualitative responses and allowed for a more holistic assessment of the program's potential to impact the thinking and the practice of future school leaders.

TABLE II. Study Questions and Data Sources.

Questions	Survey	Writing Samp	Interview	Incidentn Rpt	Artifacts
		Data Sources			
1. What do students believe about leadership when they begin their preparation program?	X	X			
2. How do student beliefs about leadership change during their time in the MSA program?		X	X		
3. What critical events mold and shape student thinking about leadership?			X	X	
4. What elements of the MSA program do students find most useful? of greatest value?			X	X	X

X–Item covered by this data source

Reporting and analysis of the data used qualitative methods suggested by Creswell (1998) and Stake (1995). Lightfoot (1983) suggested that the researcher use words to capture the essence of the subject of the research. In this investigation, the subject was one principal preparation program and the multiple perspectives of students provided insights into the impact of that program on their preparation.

Such personal understanding is the goal of case study research. Relatedly, Stake (1991) notes, "people recognize the value of something inferentially and simultaneously as the come to know it, not apparently comparing it to real or abstract standards" (p. 73). Practitioners attend to experiential accounts, the stories of people in situations similar to their own. Such vicarious experiences may lead to improved practice. Therefore, case study methodology can help practitioners reach new understandings, ones that emerge when readers recognize similarities in cases of interest to them. According to Stake, such understandings validate research findings and are, ultimately, the source of social change.

FINDINGS

This investigation revealed a number of important findings about the impact of program changes. Student voices offer important insights into the value and importance of a program. These insights contributed significantly to the discourse surrounding the organization and priorities of school leadership preparation.

The survey data gathered as students exited the program asked them to consider standards-based program elements. Each element was rated on importance and how well the MSA program helped students achieve that particular aspect of school leadership. The combined responses from two years of graduates are included in Table 3. These data demonstrated that students perceived all program elements as important and that they felt prepared.

Analysis of additional data revealed four areas as most relevant to student thinking about themselves as leaders and their practice of school leadership. They included perceived resolution of the tension between theory and practice, the centrality of teaching and learning to the practice of school leadership, the incorporation of more democratic practices in school life, and the use of a field-based experience to complement and give meaning to traditional course work.

Theory vs. Practice

Nowhere is the dichotomy between earlier conceptions of leadership preparation and new notions more evident than around the tension between theory and practice. Questions frequently asked by students such as "Will I ever use this when I become a school administrator?" capture the tension that has long existed. Perennial comments from graduates that their preparation programs were disconnected from the real world of schools were part of the mounting evidence that reform was needed (Clark & Clark, 1996; Daresh, 1988; DeSpain & Livingston, 1997).

The tension between theory and practice is not just one of "book learning" vs. "real-problems." It reflects an ongoing examination of ways in which the knowledge base for school leaders must reflect and appreciate the realities of contemporary school life. It further reflects a need to make the knowledge base relevant and useful to aspiring school leaders. They need to see that it can inform and improve their practice.

The debate is not new. Achilles (1985) suggested that viable leadership programs incorporate three components: what to do, how to do it, and why a particular thing should or should not be done. This notion that practice should be guided by research gets at underlying assumptions about leadership. Is it learning what to do or learning ways of learning what to do (Dembowski, 1999)?

TABLE III. Exit Responses of MSA Students.

Activity	How important?	How prepared?
Acting with integrity, fairness, and in an ethical manner	4.00	3.89
Understanding the issues and problems faced by school leaders	4.00	3.87
Advocating, nurturing and sustaining a school culture and instructional program conducive to student learning and staff professional growth	3.97	3.77
Opportunity to interact with practitioners	3.97	3.55
Development, articulation and implementation of a vision of learning shared and supported by the school community	3.90	3.77
Grounding in the social, ethical, and moral context and leadership	3.87	3.77
Understanding, responding to, and influencing the larger political, social, economic, legal, and cultural context	3.84	3.78
Responding to diverse community interests	3.84	3.35
Preparation for the licensure exam	3.84	3.68
Collaborating with families and community interests	3.81	3.35
Ensuring management of the organization, operations, and resources for a safe, efficient and effective learning environment	3.74	3.32
Knowledge of state standards for school leaders	3.74	3.71
Mobilizing community resources	3.68	2.87
Understanding the theory on school leadership	3.63	3.73

4=high value	2=more low than high value
3=more high than low value	1=low value

The standards for school leaders developed in the 1990s reflect an appreciation for problems of practice. The Council of Chief State School Officers (1996) suggested that sound preparation programs consist of core knowledge but should be grounded in the realities of school life.

Additional questions emerged about the background and training of those who teach in school leadership programs. Students are aware of and appreciate the experience of their professors (Williamson & Hudson, 1999). A recent study revealed that students in school leadership preparation programs value professors who have "a wide range of leadership experiences as well as academic preparation" (DeSpain & Livingston, 1997, p. 13). Students perceived that such professors performed more effectively in all traditional professorial roles—teaching, service, and research.

The redesigned MSA program sought to address this tension. Students suggested that it was possible for university preparation programs to integrate theory and practice in ways that honor both the knowledge base and the realities of school life. As one student explained, "This program is focused on our success as practitioners. We learned the theory, don't get me wrong, but it was always connected to schools and real problems in schools."

Another student suggested that the program had succeeded in doing what Achilles (1985) called for—that it had taught him not only what to do and how to do it, but how to decide why a particular thing should or should not be done. This student maintained that,

> There are two things MSA programs ought to do: give [students] the philosophical and theoretical base from which to make their decisions and provide the hands-on, practical everyday sorts of skills or exposure that administrators need on the job. I would tell anyone coming into the program that [this university] does a wonderful job of both.

In another student's words, "Understanding key principles that guide our behavior was essential."

Some students spoke of how exposure to the knowledge base, to the theory, helped them challenge their own assumptions about the purposes of schooling and appropriate leadership behavior. One graduate, for instance, cited an example from her internship of choosing students to participate in a school remediation program. She was told to select students who had the best chance of improving their test scores. This student related that, prior to her studies, she would not have questioned the request. After exposure to the theory, however, she challenged the assumptions behind that recommendation and raised, within herself and with her mentor, questions about the purpose of schooling and for whom and why schooling was provided. In the end, decisions were made based on student need rather than the potential to raise the school's scores.

Students attributed their ability to understand theory in the context of practice, to see beyond the immediate "how-tos" to the "whys" to what they were taught, how they were taught, and by whom. As one student expressed it, "One of the most valuable parts of the MSA program is the fact that the professors have been in situations where we are planning to go. Thus their teachings are based on theory, but tempered with a strong dose of reality." Another shared a similar appreciation with, "They [professors] have asked us to focus on and revisit our beliefs about children and the culture of schools, and they speak from practical experience as well as theory." That experience made a difference to students. As one summarized, "[Professors] have projected a philosophy toward teaching that has really enriched my experience."

This investigation suggested that one way to resolve the tension between theory and practice is to teach in ways that emphasize the integration rather than separation (Murphy, 1999a; Thurston, Clift & Schacht, 1993). According to these students, this was best accomplished by professors with experience as educational leaders and who used pedagogy that grounded theory in the context of practice (Leithwood, Jantzi & Coffin, 1995; Milstein & Krueger, 1997).

Centrality of Teaching and Learning

Placing greater emphasis on the importance of teaching and learning has emerged as an important part of both proposals for educational reform (Boyer, 1995; National Association of Secondary School Principals, 1996) and reform in the preparation of school leaders (Council of Chief State School Officers, 1996). These dynamics led to calls for greater emphasis on incorporating such knowledge into leadership preparation (Achilles, 1999). Murphy (1999a) argued for reconnecting teaching and school administration. He suggested that the field of educational administration ought to define its "center of gravity" as school improvement. Such a center would involve recognizing the school as the unit of change and focusing policy and practice on the integration of learning and organization. The school leader in this scenario would know about teaching and learning and would apply that knowledge in ways that lead to school improvement (Murphy, 1999a).

Results from this study suggested that students appreciated the centrality of teaching and learning to schools and understood that their primary function as school leaders was to improve schools, not just for some, but for all. This parallels the emphasis of the national standards (Council of Chief State School Officers, 1996). Students repeatedly cited students and their success as the center of their future work as school leaders.

One student, for instance, looked back on his development over time and pointed out that his increased learning and experience,

> paired with thought and self-inspection, have led me to adopt a more holistic platform. I still recognize the importance of the principal in determining the success of a school; however, I now see the student as the focus of all education.

What is in the best interests of students, what supports success for all, what creates and maintains a culture focused on teaching and learning—these are the principles that graduates said will guide their practice. They acknowledged the complexity of the job, but were steadfast in their commitment to remain focused on what was most important. As one said, "As a leader, if I keep the students' interests ahead of politics, personalities, and community agendas, I will be successful. I will also be able to complete my duties and meet my responsibilities with a clear conscience and with integrity."

Student writing revealed how their beliefs changed while in the program. In an analysis of their personal platform, one student reported that,

> With each class I have been in and through my internship experiences, I have refined my guiding principles and narrowed them from many broad goals to five specific areas which will aid me in my administrative endeavors. I feel these five areas will be the backbone of my work as a school administrator and I am proud that children are at the top of my list.

Preparation programs may seek to increase the knowledge, to influence the dispositions, and to improve the practice of future school leaders in many ways. It is hard to imagine, though, that anything could be more important than producing future leaders who have students "at the top of their lists" and who, through a focus on teaching and learning, seek to make schools better places for those students. Clearly an emphasis on teaching and student learning resonates with students and reflects growing appreciation for this as a central role of school leaders (Achilles, 1998; Murphy, 1999b).

Democratic Schools

The calls for reform of principal preparation programs consistently support a different kind of school leader, one who is more democratic than autocratic, more collaborative than authoritarian. The Interstate School Leader Licensure Standards for instance, call for leaders who develop, articulate, and implement a vision of learning that is shared and supported by the school community. Tomorrow's leaders must collaborate with families and communities and must respond to diverse community interests. These leaders' success will be embedded in the realization that teachers and other staff members are part of the school community. They will be expected to create environments and build cultures characterized by shared commitment to student learning (Council of Chief State School Officers, 1996).

The findings from this study revealed that students saw themselves becoming a more democratic type of leader. They saw themselves changing over time—from leaders who have the answers and tell others what to do to leaders described as democratic, inclusive and collaborative.

One student, for instance, indicated that he initially saw school leadership as largely managerial, consisting of the day-to-day routines. During his studies a different picture emerged. He explained that he began to see the larger cultural issues and shifted from perceiving the principal as manager to seeing the complexities and intricacies of school leadership:

I was more 'full of myself' when I came here. Thought I had the answers and was just putting time in the program. Wow! Have I changed. I'm much more humble and appreciate the complexity and ambiguity of school leadership.

One part of this perceived complexity is the need to work with others, both inside and outside the school. One student summarized a common learning:

It [MSA program] took the picture I had of what a principal is and turned it all around to seeing you need to be a person who's able to work with other people, not tell other people how to work.

Another student commented on the change in her personal platform while in the program:

my (current) language is much warmer and more human. . . . I have gained a deeper understanding that people make a school, with all our abilities and our faults, and that a good leader can channel the first and help address the second.

Students learned that democratic practices are an essential part of school improvement. As one student expressed it, "I have learned that there are multiple ways to get things done in education, and if you try to do it all by yourself with your own ideas, you will more than likely fail." Real improvement requires collaboration of the key players. Another student said he used to believe that "leader meant boss," but now understood that, "Leadership is much more than telling people what you want done. It is about leading people to change. It's also about helping people gain efficacy during that change."

Students in this study demonstrated a clear shift in thinking about democratic behavior. One summarized the change:

I have seen that the leader not only shouldn't but can't run a school alone. I have also come to believe that, in fact, the school is less a building than a collection of people who are there to help children.

Such findings came from the integration of program experiences with opportunities for reflection. Another student described the experience:

I believe that what the program has given me the most is a chance to stop and look at myself as a leader and realize how important ownership, empowerment, and effectiveness are to the faculty and staff of a school.

Students did not lose sight of the fact that schools exist within the context of a larger community, within larger social, cultural, and political contexts (Achilles, 1994; Council of Chief State School Officers, 1996). One student described it as new "insight into schools as they are inextricably interwoven with society." That society contains persons whose voices are too often ignored by schools. Attending to these persons is another part of students' new commitments. Another student talked at length about her concern for "social equity," especially in working with a diverse, urban student population. She described her own keen awareness of how the decisions and choices of school leaders directly affect social equity.

Such awareness was frequently connected to issues of teaching and learning. What pointed to a more inclusive attitude were multiple references to success, to learning, to achievement for all students. In addition, there was recognition that achieving that goal was inextricably linked to collaboration with families and communities. Students exited the program committed to such practices, committed to creating democratic processes in their schools (Achilles, 1998; Murphy, 1999a).

Time in the Field

An almost universal recommendation for reform of leadership preparation was participation in a comprehensive internship program (National Commission for the Principalship, 1990; National Policy Board for Educational Administration, 1989). Incorporating an opportunity for students to learn while doing has long been a feature of leadership preparation (Chance, 1990; Foster & Ward, 1998). Often, however, the internship has failed to build links between the university experience and that in the field (Bass, 1990).

While not universal, many internships asked students to select a school, often the one in which they taught, as a place for hands-on experience with school leadership. Such an approach often disconnected the field-based experience from the knowledge and skills learned in the classroom.

Daresh (1988) and others have suggested that field-based components to leadership programs must not only develop competence and confidence in handling the day-to-day regularities of schools, they must also provide an opportunity for students to think about and reflect on their personal development as school leaders. He suggested that such reflection occurs best in a setting where students can raise questions, challenge current practice, and explore their own evolution as a leader. The internship site, due to its close connection to their teaching careers, often fails to offer such opportunity.

The university setting, with opportunity for seminars, site visits, and a growing network of colleagues with whom students can process their experiences, was identified by this study as an important element of the internship experience. Combined with exposure to the real problems and regularities of schools, these opportunities to critique, process, problem solve, and dream made the internship the most meaningful aspect of the program for many students. It was the place where connections were made—between theory and practice, between the ideal and the real, between professors and students, and with one another.

Several students pointed to the connection between theory and practice that emerged in the internship. One reported that, "the internship experiences have given me a chance to test the theoretical aspects of my classwork in a real setting." Another commented,

I have always believed that the opportunity to put theory into practice is the most crucial step in understanding. . . . The opportunity to work with administrators as they have gone about their tasks, as well as the opportunity to perform those tasks, has been by far the most helpful of all the experiences associated with the MSA program.

Still another student described the experience as "a case of the ideal affecting practice." This student reported using information from MSA classes to solve real school problems and pointed out that,

> Without the background provided by the MSA program, the internship would have been meaningless. Armed with knowledge concerning the major concepts that administrators must deal with, however, I am able to make heads-and-tails of what goes on in schools.

The locale for many of these connections was a weekly seminar for students completing internships. One student appreciated the "many opportunities I have had to reflect on my experiences and to share my growing beliefs as well as my hopes and disappointments with my classmates." Another student appreciated the seminar because it was, "immeasurably helpful and comforting to 'check up' with each other and to know that we are not alone in some of the difficulties and rewards we have faced."

Some students had excellent mentors who both modeled good practice and processed thinking, decisions, and actions with students. As one reported:

> I was fortunate to be able to work with my principal. . . . She treated me with the same respect and confidence she affords her administrative team. . . . She entrusted me with many of the administrative responsibilities. . . . Her leadership and encouragement have increased my confidence as a potential administrator.

Another commented that,

> The amount of time that has been devoted to my development as an administrator by my principal has been astonishing, and I don't think I would want to trade any other experience for the opportunity to have seen real issues through the eyes of experience as they unfolded around us.

Such opportunities also gave students greater understanding of schools different from their own. As one student saw it:

> One of the strengths of this program is that we had a chance to interact with students from different types of schools. The students represented a lot of geographical areas and perspectives. That helped us to learn about all sorts of problems, issues, and considerations.

Thus, it was not simply being in the field that contributed to graduates' potential as leaders. It was also the opportunity to individually and collectively reflect on real problems of practice and generate new possibilities for dealing with them. Opportunities for reflection emerge as a central feature of the field-based experience and align with recommendations for improved preparation programs (Leitwood, Jantzi, & Coffin, 1995; Milstein & Krueger, 1997). In such settings, students were able not only to critique existing practices, but to dream of what might be. To see themselves as capable of making such dreams happen was a powerful finding.

IMPLICATIONS

Questions abound about whether or not university preparation programs can adequately prepare leaders for contemporary schools (Achilles, 1994; Brent & McNamara, 1997; Murphy, 1999a; Schneider, 1998). The way in which universities respond to those questions will determine the viability of their programs in the new millennium.

Reform must be highly visible, deeply felt, and responsive to the needs of school districts, the people who work in those schools, and the clients they serve (Schneider, 1998; Thomson, 1993). This study indicated that embracing the reforms articulated over the past two decades can successfully prepare students who perceive themselves as able to meet current standards for school leadership and who believe that the primary role of school leaders is to improve teaching and learning.

Developing school leaders committed to changing leadership practices is the foundation of school reform (Boyer, 1995; Van Meter & Murphy, 1997). Students in this study reported that they were ready to "make a difference." They were comfortable advocating for students and student achievement, at ease challenging long-standing norms about the organization and structure of schools, and untroubled by those resistant to change.

When asked about their goals as a school leader, students most frequently reported the need "to focus on student learning, not adult needs," and to recognize the importance of working collaboratively with school constituent groups. One student said, "I believe that . . . democratic leadership is the most effective way to implement real and lasting change." Still another remarked, "I've come to appreciate that to make real progress with students I have to trust those who work most closely with them, and be confident that they will do the 'right' thing."

Programs that adopt a pedagogy and select faculty that facilitate the integration of theory and practice, that build explicit links between course work and clinical experiences, and that emphasize a focus on teaching and learning in democratic settings reflect recommendations for sound leadership programs (National Policy Board for Educational Administration, 1989; Thomson, 1993). This investigation revealed that students value such approaches and perceive that they are well prepared to confront the realities of school leadership.

Questions continue about whether or not school leadership preparation programs can adequately prepare leaders for tomorrow's schools (Achilles, 1994; Schneider, 1998). The student voices reported here say the answer is "yes." They valued the opportunity for critical reflection, to "dream," and to work in a supportive environment to anticipate the possibilities of reformed schools. These students also valued the explicit pedagogical links between practice, the "how to" and the focus on "why." This grounding of pedagogy in practice was seen as a vital link in their preparation.

Programs such as those described by these student voices can and do facilitate the integration of theory and practice. They promote the centrality of teaching and learning and assist students in developing an intense commitment to their schools. In so doing, they contribute to the creation of principals with the knowledge, skills and pre-dispositions needed for tomorrow's schools.

REFERENCES

Achilles, C. M. (1985, August). Building principal preparation programs on theory, practice and research. Paper presented at the National Conference of Professors of Educational Administration, Starkville, MS (ERIC Document Reproduction Service No. ED 308 592).

Achilles, C. M. (1994). Searching for the golden fleece: The epic struggle continues. Educational Administration Quarterly, 27(1), 5–29.

Achilles, C. M. (1998, Summer). How long? The AASA Professor, 22(1). Retrieved December 8, 1999, from World Wide Web: http://www.aasa.org/TAP/summer9804.htm

Achilles, C. M. (1999, February). Are training programs in educational administration efficient and effective? Paper presented to the AASA Conference within a Conference, New Orleans, LA.

Bass, G. (1990). The practitioner's role in preparing successful school administrators. NASSP Bulletin, 74(529), 27–30.

Bolman, L. & Deal, T. (1991). Reframing organizations. San Francisco: Jossey-Bass.

Boyer, E. (1995). The basic school. Princeton, NJ: The Carnegie Foundation for the Advancement of Teaching.

Chance, E. W. (1990, August). The administrative internship: Effective program characteristics. Paper presented at the annual meeting of the National Council of Professors of Educational Administration, Los Angeles, CA.

Clark, D. & Clark, S. (1996). Better preparation of educational leaders. Educational Researcher, 25(8), 18–20.

Council of Chief State School Officers (1996). Interstate school leaders licensure consortium: Standards for school leaders. Washington, DC: Author.

Creswell, J. W. (1998). Qualitative inquiry and research design: Choosing among five traditions. Thousand Oaks, CA: Sage

Daresh, J. (1988). "Learning at Nellie's elbow": Will it truly improve the preparation of educational administrators? Planning and Changing, 19(3), 178–187.

Dembowski, F. (1999, Winter). Rigor and relevance in the training of educational administrators. The AASA Professor, 23(1). Retrieved December 8, 1999, from World Wide Web: http://www.aasa.org/TAP/fall99dembowski.htm

DeSpain, B. C. & Livingston, M. (1997). The importance of school administrative experience for the educational leadership professor: A view of student perceptions. The AASA Professor, 29(4), 7–14.

Educational Testing Service (1997). Candidate information bulletin for the school leaders licensure assessment. Princeton, NJ: Author.

Eisner, E. (1976). Educational connoisseurship and criticism: Their forms and functions in educational evaluation. Journal of Aesthetic Education, 10, 135–150.

Eisner, E. (1991). Taking a second look: Educational connoisseurship revisited. In M. W. McLaughlin & D. C. Phillips (Eds.), Evaluation and education: At quarter century (pp. 169–187). Chicago: National Society for the Study of Education.

Foster, L. & Ward, K. (1998). The internship experience in the preparation of higher education administrators: A programmatic perspective. The AASA Professor, 22(2), 14–18.

Griffiths, D. E., Stout, R. T. & Forsyth, P. B. (1988). Leaders for America's schools: The report and papers of the National Commission on Excellence in Educational Administration. Berkeley, CA: McCutchan.

Haller, E., Brent, B. & McNamara, J. (1997). Does graduate training in educational administration improve America's schools? Phi Delta Kappan, 79(3), 222–227.

Kempner, K. (1991). Getting into the castle of educational administration. Peabody Journal of Education, 66(3), 104–123.

Leithwood, K., Jantzi, D., & Coffin, G. (1995). Preparing school leaders: What works? Connections, 3(3), 1–7.

Lightfoot, S. (1983). The good high school: Portraits of character and culture. New York: Basic Books.

Milstein, M. & Krueger, J. (1997). Improving educational administration preparation programs: What we have learned over the past decade. Peabody Journal of Education, 72(2), 100–116.

Murphy, J. (1991). The effects of the educational reform movement on departments of educational leadership. Educational Evaluation and Policy Analysis, 13(1), 49–65.

Murphy, J. (1999a, April). The quest for a center: Notes on the state of the profession of educational leadership. Paper presented at the annual conference of the American Educational Research Association Annual Meeting, Montreal, PQ, Canada.

Murphy, J. (1999b). Reconnecting teaching and school administration: A call for a unified profession. UCEA Review, 15(2), 1–4.

National Association of Secondary School Principals (1996). Breaking ranks: Changing an American institution. Reston, VA: Author.

National Commission for the Principalship. (1990). Principals for our changing schools: Preparation and certification, Fairfax, VA: Author.

National Policy Board for Educational Administration (1989). Improving the preparation of school administrators: An agenda for reform. Charlottesville, VA: Author.

Newman, F. (1991). Linking restructuring to authentic student achievement. Phi Delta Kappan, 72, 458–463.

Prestine, N. (1991). Shared decision-making in restructuring essential schools: The role of the principal. Planning and Changing 23(3/4), 160–177.

Schneider, J. (1998, Summer). University training of school leaders isn't the only option. The AASA Professor, 22(1). Retrieved October 9, 1999, from World Wide Web: http://www.aasa.org/TAP/summer98.03.htm

Sergiovanni, T. (1992). Moral leadership: Getting to the heart of school improvement. San Francisco: Jossey-Bass.

Sergiovanni, T. (1994). Building community in schools. San Francisco: Jossey-Bass.

Stake, R. (1991). Retrospective on "The countenance of educational evaluation": In M. W. McLaughlin & D. C. Phillips (Eds.), Evaluation and education: At quarter century (pp. 67–88). Chicago: National Society for the Study of Education.

Stake, R. (1995). The art of case study research. Thousand Oaks, CA: Sage.

Thomson, S. D. (1993). Professionalizing the principalship. International Journal of Educational Reform, 2(3), 296–299.

Thurston, P., Clift, R. & Schacht, M. (1993). Preparing leaders for change-oriented schools. Phi Delta Kappan, 75(3), 259–265.

Van Meter, E. & Murphy, J. (1997). Using ISLLC standards to strengthen preparation programs in school administration. Washington, DC: Council of Chief State School Officers.

Williamson, R. & Hudson, M. (1998, February). Identifying value in administrator preparation programs: Varying perspectives. Paper presented at the annual conference of the Eastern Educational Research Association, Tampa, FL.

Williamson, R. & Hudson, M. (1999, April). Preparing tomorrow's principals: Meeting emerging challenges. Paper presented at the annual conference of the American Educational Research Association, Montreal, PQ, Canada.

Yin, R. (1994). Case study research: Design and methods (2nd ed.). Newbury Park, CA: Sage.

MEETING CHALLENGES OF
GENDER AND DIVERSITY

Millennial Challenges for Educational Leadership: Revisiting Issues of Diversity

LUCRETIA D. PEEBLES

The future of American public education is a stake. At the dawn of the millennium the improvement of K-12 public education remains an issue of primary importance for the nation, its states, and their respective cities and communities. As a uniquely American invention, the public school was developed during the 1840s to meet the demands of an economy that desperately needed skilled workers with a rudimentary understanding of citizenship to work in newly developed jobs in an industrialized society. Since its inception, this model has proven to be resilient, changing only incrementally to accommodate societal needs (The Council of State Governments, 1997; Tyack & Cuban, 1995). Hence, the pressing need to make changes in the present model of education has become more pronounced, and legislators, corporations, and taxpayers are exerting pressure to make schools more accountable for ensuring that each student graduates armed with the critical knowledge and skills to compete successfully in a global society. And equally as important as the mastery of knowledge and skills, is the expectation that schools produce students who demonstrate an appreciation for diversity and the ability to engage in positive social interactions that respect the personhood and dignity of every human being.

Of no less importance to the future of education in America, is the current crisis in educational leadership (Malone & Caddell, 2000). The title of a report released by The California Commission on the Teaching Profession (1985) poses a critical and timely question: "Who Will Teach Our Children?" Considering the crisis in public education, this question might be appropriately appended to include two additional inquiries that also merit consideration: Who will lead our schools? More specifically, given the critical issues facing education, why would anyone choose to become a teacher, even more a leader in a public school?

The report What Matters Most: Teaching for America's Future (1996) reveals that urban schools will experience a shortage of teachers during the next decade. The short-

Lucretia D. Peebles, University of Denver

age, due in large part to retirements and rising enrollments, will require the hiring of one million teachers in the next five years and two million teachers over the next ten years (Krei, 1998; Duhon-Sells, Peoples, Moore, & Page, 1996). However, this trend is being reversed as college graduates and people from nontraditional fields have begun to consider teaching as a possible career choice in response to innovative strategies and incentives to recruit teachers. Since the teaching field is primarily Euro-American, female, middle class and English-speaking (Boyer & Baptiste, 1996) efforts have been made to recruit teachers of color. For example, African Americans were strongly represented as teachers in the segregated schools of the South before the Brown decision (Duhon-Sells, Peoples, Moore, & Page, 1996). According to a report from the National Center for Education Statistics (NCES) in urban school districts, 49% of the K-12 school population is comprised of racial minorities, yet persons of color comprised less than 14% of the teaching force (NCES, 1996). In contrast to teachers, the pool of prospective site-level administrators has dwindled, exasperating superintendents as they seek to fill vacancies (Olson, 2000b; Malone & Caddell, 2000). Persons of color and women are underrepresented in this pool that traditionally has been comprised predominately of Euro-American males (Shakeshaft, 1999; McAdams, 1998; Banks, 1995). On the whole, these selections are made from the teaching pool; however, many teachers no longer aspire to become principals. From their classrooms, they are daunted by the responsibilities thrust upon principals who are required to work longer hours and weeks and whose increased responsibilities and diminution of authority are often rewarded with minimal financial compensation (McAdams, 1998; Cooley & Shen, 1999; Educational Research Service, 2000, Malone & Caddell, 2000).

More responsibilities include responding to stakeholders' demands to improve achievement, often with little time and money to provide staff development to assist their teachers. In some instances, principals must work to improve the level of academic achievement in schools plagued with high rates of poverty, disproportionate levels of students receiving some form of special education, little community support, increased incidents of school violence, racial conflict, and limited financial resources. While learning to operate in the current system of standards-based education, principals have had to assume new roles as facilitators to create a school climate and culture supportive of these changes. Media has often been unsympathetic to the challenges educators encounter and their difficult roles serving and working with youth. Generally, public criticism of schools has been unrelenting.

Public schools have entered the millennium in a state of fragility, their history marred by underachievement. Unlike other public institutions, schools have many responsibilities thrust upon their doorsteps: they have had to respond to overwhelming demands to make changes in the curricula in order to be responsive to the changing demographics; issues of health; a global economy; the infusion of media and technology; environmental issues; and international competition. Schools have struggled to raise the levels of achievement on standardized tests of basic skills, which have shown an increase since the 1970s (Resnick and Nolan, 1995). However, when compared to the national average, poor students and students of color who have been traditionally underserved in the public education system, continue to score far below the standard. The 1998 test results from the Third International Mathematics and Science Study (TIMSS) reveal some disparaging results. Of the participating countries, twelfth graders' academic performance was found to be among the lowest in physics, mathematics, science, general knowledge, and advanced mathematics (NCES, 1998). Furthermore, all too frequently, particularly in urban communities, schools continue to harbor many of the same elements of "risk" so aptly identified in A Nation at Risk (National Commission on Excellence in Education, 1983). In keeping with current practice, some schools have implemented research-based comprehensive reform models to improve the quality of education. Nevertheless, far too many schools continue to be characterized either as mediocre or low achieving. Generally, the curriculum, which consists of academic, general and vocational tracks, does not provide the information and experiences all students need to engage effectively either in postsecondary education or work experiences in a global society (Goodlad, 1984; Forsyth & Tallerico, 1993). Those placed at the greatest disadvantage—who are most affected by the chronic level of mediocrity—are students historically failed by public schools: African American, Hispanic American, and Native American students, and some immigrants.

Twenty-first-century educational challenges call for the training of strong and effective leaders to work in public schools in urban communities. Professors and practitioners in the field of educational administration, those who have the responsibility for preparing school leaders, must ensure that they are providing the highest quality of knowledge and training possible to help aspiring leaders make the difficult transition from teacher to administrator. Governmental policymakers, corporations and foundations have begun to focus national attention on reshaping the preparation and training of principals (Olson, 2000a). The focus of this chapter is to seek answers to the following questions: What are some key historical and legal policies that inform the preparation of educational leaders for urban schools? Do issues of race and diversity pose specific challenges which must be addressed in the preparation of educational leaders to enable them to become effective and responsive leaders in complex organizations such as schools? What curricula must be included in administrator preparation programs of the twenty-first century to best prepare prospective leaders to be strong and effective?

THE CHALLENGE OF DIVERSITY:
A HISTORICAL AND SOCIAL CONTEXT

As a society we are still wallowing in cesspools filled with unresolved issues of racism and intolerance for diversity. These issues, like tentacles of an octopus's body, are deeply rooted in the historical and social contexts of American history and touch the very depths of our total humanity. Rather than making an exuberant appearance with the glow of the rising sun breaking forth from the darkness of night at the beginning of a new day, the millennium's dawning has been dimmed by the pressing need for society to create solutions for its multitudinous issues of diversity.

Paradoxical though it may be, American culture is multicultural. But while the individual benefits which accrue from living in a diverse or multicultural society are infinite, the enjoyment of these benefits has not been entirely possible for many racial or ethnic groups who seek to experience a peaceful coexistence in America. Notwithstanding the inability of schools to teach true democracy, the nation has nowhere else to turn; the nation must entrust its educational leaders to create schools which can serve as incubators which nurture and support the development of innovative programs or ideas aimed at the eradication of problems of racism and intolerance for diversity. This responsibility admonishes those who train educational leaders to make a moral and conscious decision to integrate and include courses and topics in the curricula that impel the prospective leader to examine the historical and social contexts of race and diversity in the American experience, as a critical element in the development of strong and effective leaders. A review of American history is beyond the scope of this discussion; however, an attempt has been made to provide a kaleidoscope of specific examples of the growth of ethnic and cultural diversity in the twentieth century and the turbulence associated with this growth. Many of the challenges facing our schools are rooted in issues of race and diversity.

In his essay "Of the Dawn of Freedom," written in 1903, W.E.B. Du Bois issued a prophetic declamation about the state of racial and social relations: "The problem of the twentieth century is the problem of the color-line,—the relation of the darker to the lighter races of men in Asia and Africa, in America and the islands of the sea" (p.13). Reflecting upon Du Bois' poignant statement, written shortly after the turn of the century, one is astounded by his wise and accurate identification of race as the quintessential problem that faced the twentieth century. One is astounded even more that despite the prophetic warning, among the most reprehensible and continuing themes in the history of the United States of America has been the inability of the majority of national leaders, policymakers, and the legal system to engage issues of diversity equitably and wisely.

Problems with the "color-line" are central to the daily lives of all people of color, many of whom have been victimized through turbulent human interactions, attitudes of intolerance, and acts of violence which they continue to endure in their struggles to make the system more responsive to their needs. And especially clear in our culture is the persistent tension in the interactions between Euro-Americans and African Americans, a tension that has been superimposed on issues which some consider, unrelated to race, e.g. gender, age, sexual orientation, religious affiliation, and physical or mental disability. Typically, those who have experienced ostracism for these reasons, tend to view these issues under the guise of diversity as "color-line" experiences (Banks,

1994b; Grant & Sleeter, 1986). As communities have become more diverse, problems of economics and social class have assumed center stage, obscuring discussions of race. Recent acts of violence that have occurred on school campuses have focused attention on the need to create inclusive climates in schools to create a sense of belonging for all students. Educational leaders have implemented programs to train students in "bully proofing" strategies which they can use to protect themselves from harassment or unwarranted onslaughts due to their uniqueness (Vail, 1999). These strategies are also designed to help students to become more tolerant of others, teaching them to proactively accept, rather than to violently and aggressively reject those who are different.

Though the millennium marks the dawning of a new age, clearly the year 2000 will not be free from the problems of race and social relations that garnered attention, both nationally and globally, during the twentieth century. That this was indeed a turbulent time in history is attested to by records of countless deaths of innocent persons, African Americans and Euro-Americans, whose lives were ended prematurely, either through intentional or random acts of violence, orchestrated by those determined to maintain the status quo. This was certainly true in the case of Martin Luther King, Jr., minister, Civil Rights leader, and winner of the Nobel Peace Prize in 1964. Ironically, King was assassinated in 1968 by James Earl Ray, an illiterate, poor, Euro-American from a segment of the population King was trying to help. On television, people around the world had watched—as King led thousands of people, using tactics of nonviolence to dismantle systematic segregation, particularly in Southern cities where there were strongholds opposed to legislation providing access to equal education, housing, and employment to Blacks—and hearing his speeches for equality, they had taken notice. King's successful "March on Washington" in 1963, at which he delivered his "I Have A Dream" speech, mobilized thousands across the nation from different races and social strata and drew attention to the need for employment and education for the poor (Young, 1996). Although King's dream has yet to be fully achieved, his humanitarian efforts are remembered across the nation as people of all races and social persuasions seek to honor his life and work on the national King holiday.

The United States was peopled by waves of immigrants during the twentieth century, thus contributing to the turbulence of diversity. Three major waves of immigration occurred at various intervals throughout the twentieth century (Noel, 2000). In the early nineteenth century, first wave immigrants came from Protestant European countries, England, Holland, and Germany. During the second wave, from 1900 to the 1920s, immigrants came from Russia, the Balkans, Asia, Austria-Hungary and from Italy and were viewed with suspicion largely because of their language, customs and religious backgrounds which included Eastern Orthodox, Jewish, Catholic, and Asian religious. Mexicans were drawn to the United States in the 1930s mainly because of the development of the Southwest region and the desire to escape the ravages of the revolution that was underway in Mexico.

In the 1960s, a third wave of immigrants came from Mexico, Latin American countries and Southeast Asian countries. Whether they came from Eastern or Western Europe, Asia, Mexico, or Latin America, and regardless of the reasons these immigrants gave for their emigration to the United States, as the newcomers attempted to understand and define for themselves the meaning of being an "American," policies were developed against them in response to perceived societal imbalances caused by the often violent clashing of the newcomer's values and lifestyles with those of the established American majority who embraced "core American" values and culture that either disregarded newcomer differences or gave little appreciation to their uniqueness. Some immigrants became victims of mass hysteria caused by racial intolerance and feelings of nationalism; the result was the enactment of laws requiring their containment. As involuntary immigrants much earlier, African Americans had been enslaved, as were the land's first inhabitants, Native Americans. Their removal from the east to the west of the Mississippi had been authorized in 1830 when Congress passed the Indian Removal Act. The "Trail of Tears" is a permanent reminder of the forceful removal of the Cherokee from Georgia westward to Indian Territory in Oklahoma (Harvey, Harjo, & Jackson, 1990).

From 1910 to 1940 Chinese immigrants seeking entrance into the United States were quarantined in North Garrison on Angel Island in the San Francisco Bay as investigations regarding the legitimacy of their papers were conducted (Cao & Novas, · 1996). Executive Order 9066 signed by President Franklin Delano Roosevelt in 1942 authorized the relocation and internment of Japanese Americans, the majority of whom were citizens. Under Proclamation No. 1 all Japanese were evacuated from the West Coast of the United States and parts of Arizona to places in the interior such as Montana, Idaho, Colorado, Utah, and Nevada (Cao & Novas, 1996).

Multicultural education is an outgrowth of protests from the civil rights movement and urban rebellion waged by disenfranchised racial and ethnic groups who agitated in the late 1960s for changes in curriculum to provide students with a true and balanced interpretation of American History, including the contributions of non-European Americans. With the support of Euro-American college and high school students, ethnic minority groups made demands for the development of ethnic history departments and courses in their history, culture, and literature; their demands also included bilingual education programs (La Belle & Ward, 1994; Cordeiro, Reagan, Martinez, 1994; Novak, 1971). Viewed as the institution responsible for helping diverse ethnic groups assimilate mainstream culture and ideas into the "melting pot," public schools played a major role. This concept of the "melting pot" was popular during the 1960s and 1970s; however, as many ethnic minorities sought to value their racial and cultural heritages, they no longer desired to assimilate but viewed themselves more pluralistically as parts of a mosaic or a tossed salad (Cordeiro, Reagan & Martinez, 1994; Levine & Havighurst, 1996; Novak, 1971). Opposition from conservatives and essentialists centered on their beliefs that all students be exposed to the "core knowledge" found in the canon of western civilization. Since many Euro-American educators and others had not read some of the suggested works of non-European authors to ascertain how they would contribute to the approved canon, they perceived the addition of these works as watering down the curriculum (Banks, 1994a).

School violence has emerged as a national health issue (Prothrow-Stith, 1991; Earls, 1994; Kneidek, 1994), and the perception of American public schools as dangerous places has become commonplace. Kneidek (1994) asserts that the final decade of the twentieth century has been replete with a plethora of violence including "race-related fights, gang warfare, tagger turf battles, threatened teachers, and guns in school" (p. 5). Recent shootings and killing of innocent students and adults on public school campuses, however, have been committed primarily by Euro-American males living in rural communities (Capozzoli & McVey, 2000). Media images and feelings associated with the April 20, 1999, Columbine High School massacre in Littleton, Colorado, are still vivid in the minds of many. In a high school whose student population is almost completely homogeneous, two angry middle-class Euro-American male students, considered isolates, used semiautomatic weapons and shotguns to wage a violent attack on the school. Killed in the carnage were a teacher and fourteen students; twenty-nine students were injured in the melee of bullets and were left with severe physical injuries (Capozzoli & McVey, 2000). Although it will never be known for sure, allegedly the killers took the lives of students whom they perceived as jocks, leaders, Christians, and, in the case of the African American male, "for being a stupid nigger." The massacre ended violently when the killers turned the guns on themselves, ending their own lives. This incident represents one of the most extreme acts of school violence in America (Capozzoli & McVey, 2000). In other instances, acts of violence on school campuses were perpetrated by youth who, for whatever reason, had trouble handling their anger and aggression. In several of the cases, violence symbolized disdain toward peers or even adults whom the killers felt contributed in some way to their feelings of alienation, humiliation, or rejection from their peers.

All of these examples whether motivated by a desire for peace or for violence epitomize the egregious nature of intolerance for diversity in our nation and are urgent warnings that school leaders must understand the historical and social contexts (i.e., the foundation) in the lives and communities of the students they encounter.

SCHOOL REFORM: LAWS AND POLICIES

During the second half of the twentieth century internal and external factors forced the nation to focus on reforming its schools. An internal factor, the *Brown v. Board of Education* decision declaring separate educational facilities "inherently unequal," reversed the 1896 *Plessy v. Ferguson* decision which sanctioned segregated railroad car facilities for black and white patrons, and subsequently was used to sanction separate educational facilities. In Brown II, issued one year later, the Court instructed federal courts to "enforce remedies" with "all deliberate speed" (Lunenburg & Ornstein, 1996, p. 398). This landmark decision altered the structure of education and provided the legal framework to desegregate public schools. Many school districts were forced to bus students to schools outside of their neighborhoods to achieve integration. Violence and acts of intolerance often met students of color who attended schools whose population was predominantly Euro-American. Forced bussing ended in September 1999 in Charlotte, North Carolina, a city that was in the forefront in bussing for desegregation more than thirty years ago (Yellin & Firestone, 1999). Almost forty-five years have passed since the *Brown* decision and many question whether significant gains, educational and social, impacted the lives of African Americans and other persons of color. The current texture of urban schools without bussing contains student populations that are segregated and isolated by neighborhoods, race, social class, and economics.

In 1957, Russia's launching of Sputnik caused great concern that the United States was losing its supremacy as a world leader, increasing fears that the security and defense of the nation was at stake. These concerns reverberated to the schools where criticism was aimed at "fixing the damages" inflicted by progressives. According to Williams (1999), in the 1950s the federal government had viewed the schools as playing a vital role in eradicating racial, economic and social injustices (p. 78). Schools were reformed using funds from the National Science Foundation to support curriculum development and teacher training in the areas of math, science and social studies.

The Civil Rights Act of 1964 approved by Congress under the leadership of President Lyndon B. Johnson, was designed to "eliminate segregation and discrimination" in areas such as education, employment, voting rights and public facilities (Katz, 1971, p. 487). The Twenty-fourth Amendment to the Constitution, ratified in 1964, eliminated the poll tax in federal elections and The Civil Rights Act of 1965 made illegal such contingencies as passage of literacy tests to keep African Americans from exercising their voting rights.

The 1965 Elementary and Secondary Education Act (ESEA) granted funds to schools to improve the curriculum especially in English, reading, mathematics and science. These funds also supported programs fostering inter-group relations. Responding to growing numbers of non-English-speaking students, the Bilingual Education Act or Title VII of ESEA was enacted in 1968 to promote bilingual education programs in public schools. The Bilingual Reform Act approved in 1973 updated the 1968 law mandating not only language instruction but instruction in history and culture in programs of second-language instruction. In the 1974 *Lau v. Nichols* case the Supreme Court found that the San Francisco School District's failure to provide non-English-speaking students a program consistent with their language needs to be in violation of Title VI of the Civil Rights Act of 1964. The Court upheld the right of non-English-speaking Chinese students to equal access and equal education opportunity. Congress approved Public Law 94–142 (PL

94–142), the Education for All Handicapped Children Act, in 1975. Under PL94–142 handicapped children receive free and appropriate public education; the law also requires states receiving funds to adhere to specific guidelines specified in the provision of the act. Also referenced widely in schools to protect the rights of students, educators, and parents are due process of law and equal protection under the law guaranteed to all citizens in the Fourteenth Amendment.

Affirmative Action policies and programs originated from a need to eliminate employment discrimination for minorities and nonminority women by actively recruiting to fill job vacancies. Though the glass ceiling still remains in some jobs traditionally held by males, women continue to experience small gains. Title IX has helped to promote gender equity in hiring, education, participation in athletics, instructional practices and many other areas.

Educational reform continues to be a prime focus in our nation and schools. Legislation has helped to provide equal opportunity and access to education for all students. Knowledge of the historical and social context of these policies can help educational leaders to more effectively respond to issues of diversity. Commenting on diversity Kouzes and Posner (1993) state that it "makes work situations less predictable and principals and teachers' jobs less routine, and more stressful" (cited in Seyfarth, 1999, p. 86).

THE CHALLENGE OF LEADERSHIP IN URBAN SCHOOLS

Schools are complex organizations, social systems whose interactions with their environments are categorized by three different phases: input, conversion, and output. In the form of input, public schools enroll students from different ethnic and racial backgrounds and socioeconomic strata, with a myriad of intellectual talents and learning styles. Through the process of schooling, the raw materials students possess at the outset of their education are converted into useable output, or human capital, which must be expended to sustain the society, fulfilling its infinite need for new workers. As microcosms, schools mirror the racial, social and economic inequities of the larger society both in the composition of students and in the structure of the curriculum. Whether viewed independently or collectively, these inequities place enormous stress on principals, school staffs, and the formal and informal subsystems of the school. Nowhere in the public school system is this more apparent than in urban schools. Some urban schools in low-income neighborhoods cater to students whose daily life experiences present unimaginable circumstances that appear insurmountable. These conditions might include living in toxic, life-endangering, environmentally challenged neighborhoods riddled with crime, including heavy drug trafficking activities, infested with gang warfare, and replete with health crises to which many, being poor, fall prey because they lack the health insurance necessary to access medical services.

The training and preparation of urban school leaders received little attention during the twentieth century but has emerged at the beginning of the millennium as a major challenge and a national educational priority. Experiences with issues of diversity are critical and must be included as an integral component in the training of administrators. But administrative preparation program instructors question whether it is possible to prepare urban school leaders to be strong and effective leaders in twenty-first-century urban schools. They also question how this leadership is best defined in the urban school setting. The concept of leadership has many meanings and varies depending upon the theoretical model referenced. According to Leithwood & Duke (1999, p. 45), during the past century within the field of school leadership, no agreement had been reached on a definition of leadership. Relying on Yukl's definitional analysis, they defined leadership generically as "an influence process concerning the choice of goals and the development and implementation of the means for their achievement" (p. 67). Through a review of articles on leadership in schools, published in four major journals from 1985–1995, Leithwood and Duke found six different models or approaches to leadership (p. 46). Though the six models—instructional, transformational, moral, participative, managerial, and contingent—are distinct, the researchers posit that they are not pure (p. 55). Knowledge of these conceptual models of school leadership provides a theoretical framework which educational leaders should find useful in the practice of leadership in urban schools. As leaders and individuals, school administrators might find one model to be more consistent with their philosophical orientation and their school's environmental needs and concerns.

The challenges which face principals and teachers in urban public schools as they seek to educate youth from diverse backgrounds, many of whom have numerous factors that place them "at risk" in public schools, are confounded by social, economic, and educational disparities. In a chapter titled "Social Class and Educational Equality" Caroline Hodges Persell (1989, pp. 72–74) describes the differences between suburban schools attended mainly by upper- and upper-middle-class students, private parochial schools attended by middle-class and working-class students, and urban schools whose population is comprised mainly of lower-class or poor students. Some of the differences included the appearance of the campuses, the scope of the facilities, access to technology, the quality of the curriculum, teacher quality, class size, school size, discipline policies, academic advisement availability, and the presence of an academic school culture which is known and valued by students. Unlike students who attend suburban schools whose enrollments reflect socioeconomic and ethnic homogeneity, students who attend urban schools are more likely to attend large schools with heterogeneous populations. They will experience large classes, poorly trained teachers, limited access to technology, tracking, and limited availability of economic and political resources (Persell, 1989, p. 74; Krei, 1998, p. 71). Many of the students will not have mastered the basic skills at a level necessary for even minimal academic participation. And often in urban school districts, there is a discrepancy in the quality of education based on social class. Kantor and Brenzel (1992) view the manipulation of these discrepancies that result in "islands of quality" within the purview of the school districts. Low-income students who have poor academic skills are simply warehoused in lower quality schools until they reach the legally required age at which they can be dropped.

Inequitable teacher allocation also poses a serious challenge for urban school principals who have access to a pool of lower qualified teachers from which to fill staffing needs. Their attempts to hire qualified teachers are exacerbated by faulty district-level decisions and lack of equity regarding teacher allocations (Krei, 1998, p. 71). Consequently, these schools become victims of problems of teacher allocation which result not only in assigning a number of inadequately prepared teachers to teach in urban classrooms, but also illegally assigning larger numbers of teachers to teach courses for which they hold no state license or certification. Krei (1998) cites evidence that the practices and policies of teacher allocation in urban districts results in the assignment of inexperienced, poorly qualified teachers to teach in schools with large numbers of low-income students (p. 85; Oakes, 1990; Darling-Hammond, 1995). Villegas and Clewell (1998) report that during the 1993–1994 school year, 10 percent of the teachers hired to teach had failed to obtain either emergency or state certification in the subjects in which they were assigned (p. 41). This practice was found to be more prevalent in school districts located in urban areas in the West and in the South (NCES, 1998 cited in Villegas and Clewell, 1998). Within these schools, it is not uncommon to find that the better teachers are assigned to teach students who have stronger cognitive skills or those who might be considered academically talented, leaving teachers whose skills are questionable to teach the more "academically challenged" students who have excessive educational needs. In her research on teacher allocation in low-income urban schools, Krei (1998) found evidence that misappropriations of teachers, contributed to serious harm to students in the quality of instruction they received (p. 71). Sanders and Horn's (1998) research from the Tennessee Value-Added Assessment System (TVAAS) found poor teaching to have a negative effect on students for as many as five years after they have had the teacher. They also found poor teachers assigned disproportionately to work in low-income schools.

Creating culturally responsive schools in which every student feels connected requires strong instructional leadership from principals and leaders in the school who are responsible for supporting teachers, experts in curriculum and teaching. Often a teacher's preferred teaching style is incongruent with the student's learning style and has little cultural relevance to the student (Gay, 2000; Noel, 2000; Delpit, 1995; Ladson-Billings, 1994; Ramirez & Castaneda, 1974). This mismatch might serve as a contributory factor in low academic achievement and feelings of intellectual inadequacy. Clearly then, knowledge of the cultural background and practices of the students are absolutely essential for educational leaders. With rapidly changing demographics, principals find they must scrounge to find qualified bilingual educators who not only speak the language, but also understand the cultural dynamics of the students. This knowledge should extend beyond the classroom and school into the community where vital linkages can be established to connect the parents of immigrant children to the school.

Consistent with understanding the culture and language of immigrant children would be the structuring of classroom management and school discipline practices and policies. Currently these practices are based on mainstream or middle-class values that have little connection to students served in low-income urban schools (Noguera, 1995; Delpit, 1995; Lightfoot, 1978). These policies have been applied inconsistently to higher percentages of students of color, in particular African American males, and in some instances, Latino students—resulting in inordinately higher rates of suspension for these students when compared to their Euro-American counterparts. Noguera's (1995) research on school violence cites startling statistics from a national study conducted by the U.S. Office of Civil Rights: "Black students are 74 to 86 percent more likely than White students to receive corporal punishment; 54 to 88 percent more like to be suspended; and 3 to 8 times as likely to be expelled" (p. 211). Therefore, the educational leader is challenged to plan staff development opportunities to educate the staff regarding diversity, to create an understanding of family and cultural expectations toward discipline and the relationship to the school discipline policies and expectations, to the goal of helping parents to become partners in the educational process.

The nationwide increase in the number of students raised by single parents with little income significantly impacts the schools. Many of these students are latchkey children with limited supervision from adults. Moreover, the number of students living in homes in which the primary caregiver is a grandparent, is on the increase in low-income communities. Raising a second generation of children, these grandparents encounter a school system whose curriculum and academic requirements are quite different from their earlier experiences. The high rate of teenage pregnancy in low-income communities has contributed to a phenomenon of young grandparents between the ages of 29 and 34, who are the primary caregivers for their unmarried teenager daughters and their grandchildren (Camblin & White, 2000). Community and parent support for education and schools can be directly correlated to the level of education attained by the parents. Some principals must garner support for their schools from a parent population in which a significant number have not completed high school. These schools have higher dropout rates, especially among youth of color.

MILLENNIAL CHALLENGES FOR EDUCATIONAL LEADERS

The current focus of school reform is on implementing President Clinton's Goals 2000, approved by Congress in 1994; these goals extend the focus of America 2000, the Bush administration's educational goals which hinted at the idea of national standards. National education goals were developed in 1989, at the first National Education Summit (The Charlottesville Summit) hosted by former President George Bush, to which state governors were invited. The standards movement was birthed during the Summit. Developed with bipartisan efforts, the national education goals specifically targeted standards and performance accountability (Kolb, 1998, p.10), aimed at state-level implementation of "world class" standards. Standard-based education has raised the level of accountability for principals and teachers forcing them to focus on outcomes. As clients and stakeholders, students and parents have become more accountable for the quality of education provided by their schools. This focus has moved schools beyond the "gotcha game" to implementing content standards which clearly state what students are to know and be able to do and the assessments that will be used to measure their mastery of the content. The standards specify what teachers are to teach and what students need to know and, how they will demonstrate what they have learned. Most states have developed content standards for students and some have connected student performance on high stakes tests to the evaluation of teachers and principals. But, some critics question the feasibility of the standards movement to really "raise the bar" for students and teachers, viewing standards-based education as a barrier for students in low-income schools riddled by underachievement. When students fail to achieve the required level of proficiency on grade-level tests, school districts often provide various interventions, for example, retention, mandatory summer school attendance, tutorials and assignment to remedial classes during the regular school year to assist these students to improve their achievement in areas of academic deficiency. Frequently, academic failure negatively impacts these students' self-esteem and diminishes their interest in school. Although standards-based education might be welcomed by some parents whose children are having difficulty achieving in schools, it is viewed differently by some upper- and middle-class parents whose students are academically gifted and college bound (Kohn, 1998). While one of the goals of standards-based education is to equalize education for all students, students tend to be segregated according to their curriculum tracks, socioeconomic level, "privileged parents," and future aspirations (Kohn, 1998).

Standards-based education challenges school leaders to conceptualize their schools in significantly different ways that hold some promise for building learning organizations that support and solicit participation from students, teachers, administrators, parents, and the stakeholders in the community. Consequently, new forms of leadership will be needed to transform and to build the capacity within these organizations to support change. With the intention of developing strong and effective leaders for urban schools, some researchers and policymakers have called for a redefinition of the principalship (Olson, 2000a; Olson, 2000c). Relying on research from Campbell, Cunningham, Mystrand, and Usdan (1990), Malone and Caddell (2000) provide a brief history of five different evolutionary stages the principalship has undergone

moving from one teacher, head teacher, teaching principal, school principal and supervising principal (p. 163). In their view, the principalship has moved to a sixth
stage—"the principal as a change agent" (p. 163). This conceptualization is supported
by a set of model standards developed by the Interstate School Leaders Licensure
Consortium (ISLLC), a program of the Council of Chief State School Officers
(CCSSO), which has become the basis for administrator licensure in 25 states
(Mayeski, Gaddy & Goodwin, 2000). If principals are to become change agents they
must adopt a stewardship approach to leadership (Sergiovanni, 1996). Sergiovanni,
defines stewardship "as a way to use power to serve through the practice of partnership and empowerment" (p. 63). He adds that our organizations need to be redefined
so that service is at the center "and ownership and responsibility are strongly felt by
those close to doing the work and contacting customers" (p. 63). Stewardship also requires that leaders transform their ways of thinking. Transformational leadership, conceptualized by Leithwood (1994), includes seven dimensions of leadership:

> building school vision, establishing school goals, providing intellectual stimulation, of-
> fering individualized support, modeling best practices and important organizational val-
> ues, demonstrating high performance expectations, creating a productive school culture,
> and developing structures to foster participation in decisions.
>
> (Leithwood & Duke, 1999, p. 49)

Transforming the system requires change that is fundamental, involving new ways
of thinking rather than incremental change which occurs on an ongoing basis in organizations and does not require a dramatic shift in thinking (Nadler & Tushman,
1995). According to Heifetz & Laurie (1997) fundamental change creates adaptive
challenges for organizations which require the organization to change the way it op-
erates in order to survive. The implementation of standards-based education is an example of fundamental change. Schools have found that they must change past practices in order to thrive in a new environment.

In The Fifth Discipline, Senge (1990) identifies five "basic disciplines" (p. 7) or tools
useful to schools in their transformation from traditional organizations to learning organizations. Senge describes the "fifth discipline," systems thinking, as a conceptual framework comprised of knowledge and tools helpful to identifying underlying patterns in organizations that serve as roadblocks to change. The four remaining disciplines include
personal mastery, mental models, shared vision, and team learning. Each discipline requires individuals to seek personal growth and development in preparation for creating a
learning organization. Thus, systems thinking propels leaders to multiple levels of exploration to enable them to understand the underlying interrelationships and patterns of
diverse problems. School leaders must empower persons in their organizations to become
lifelong learners and innovators who feel confident in taking the necessary risks to create
personal changes that increase their abilities ultimately to create organizational changes.
In the early stages of change Heifetz and Laurie (1997) call for the leader to create a

"holding environment" or temporary place where diverse groups can interact with one another regarding their perceived challenges (p. 127).

Amid the complexities of providing leadership in schools within a standards-driven system, one of the principal's main tasks will be to transform the schools into learning organizations. To do so the leader must function as a catalyst, orchestrating critical systemic changes which impel teachers to relinquish traditional thought patterns incongruent with the shared vision. Change always includes both losses and gains. But, these changes must occur in schools, within the teaching ranks, to ensure students equity and equal access to educational opportunities.

Learning organizations hold the most promise for providing the infrastructure principals and teachers needed in urban schools to build greater accountability for education and shared responsibility for the academic achievement of all students. Typically, if students feel good about their academic accomplishments, they are better equipped to negotiate the social challenges presented in their schools. Students of color are least prepared socially to enact successful academic negotiations, and most often, are grossly underserved by those whom they must depend upon to provide education in their schools. Having limited interactions with role models from their ethnic or cultural backgrounds might work as a serious handicap and give the perception that career goals are not attainable.

Challenges of diversity require principals and teachers to engage in intense introspection before seeking to develop and implement solutions to effect changes beneficial to all students. Some of this introspection must help educators to connect with their deepest feelings regarding concepts such as race, "white privilege," equal access and poverty. Learning is to leadership, what software is to a computer. In this analogy, one condition is inextricably linked to the other. Without strong leadership, a school's staff would lack direction and have difficulty accomplishing its vision. Similarly, in order for the computer to function effectively as a tool, it must be programmed with the necessary software. People who work in schools must be challenged continually to grow and to discover new skills they can use for personal development as well as to help the organization and its people learn.

Urban school principals must provide the leadership to assist teachers to dislodge deeply held beliefs that imprison their thinking, and perpetuate lower academic expectations for students who are either poor or from diverse backgrounds. They must guard against the tendency to let their assessments of the devastating and depressing conditions in the neighborhoods from which their students come serve as the sole determinant of the quality of education that they should be provided. Standards-based education seeks to equalize education for all students. Principals in urban schools must help teachers to support students to move beyond the conditions within their control, that place them at risk, to complete their educational goals. How often do we see only the thorns that grace the branches of the bougainvillea bushes and miss the beautiful, colorful blossoms that adorn the branches?

The transformation of a school into a learning organization begins with an examination of those beliefs or mental models held by principals, teachers, and support staff around key areas of concern to the school. For example, one area where views differ is on the structure of education in a given middle school. If teachers view this structure along the lines of a traditional junior high school, solely limited to a six-period day with 50-minute teaching blocks, different types of teaching arrangements such as interdisciplinary teams found in middle schools would not be feasible. When this mental model is questioned, it provides the opportunity to discuss beliefs about how adolescents learn, in what structural arrangements, and the significance of integrating learning across various disciplines. Interdisciplinary teams require teachers to work together to share leadership roles and planning responsibilities. Mental models might need to be addressed to clarify meanings of leadership which serve as a hindrance to the team's questioning the value of traditional models to new structures for the delivery of instruction. These discussions engage people in communicating about their values and beliefs in ways that foster the collaboration essential to helping staffs to engage in team learning and understanding.

When selecting models of leadership receptive to the needs of diverse populations, school leaders often miss the mark. To provide meaningful leadership consistent with the needs of schools in the twenty-first century, leaders will need to think systemically to examine their values, ethics and feelings toward persons from races, cultures and social orientations different from their own. If this conceptualization deems each human being as equally worthy regardless of race and socioeconomic status, then each leader would be required to undergo a significant personal transformation in thinking, to build the connections between the mind and spirit to support this view. A leader must be willing to deal with chaos, treading unfamiliar waters to experience new models of thinking that enrich her leadership.

RECOMMENDATIONS AND CONCLUSIONS

Educational leaders have a limited understanding of the complexities of the environment and systems in which they must operate, in order to implement policies and programs to diminish racial and socioeconomic inequities and intolerance to diversity. In a summary of research on leadership preparation programs, McCarthy (1999) found that the core curricula of administrator preparation programs has remained the same since the 1970s. Most programs offer courses in "educational organization and administration, curriculum, supervision, finance, school law, research, educational psychology, history and philosophy of education, school plant, and personnel" (p. 75). Missing from the core curricula are courses that prepare prospective administrators to engage issues of diversity knowledgeably and effectively. McCarthy's (1999) summary indicates that in 1989, the National Policy Board for Educational Administration

(NPBEA) recommended a change in the focus of curriculum and leadership programs to include:

> social and cultural influences on schooling; teaching and learning processes and school improvement; organizational theory; methodologies of organizational studies and policy analysis; leadership and management processes and functions; policy studies and politics of education; and the moral and ethical dimensions of schooling (p. 75).

Among the seven courses that appeared to be included most frequently in administrator preparation programs, none addressed the social and cultural aspects of education. State licensure requirements heavily influence curriculum content in administrator preparation programs. However, even though state standards might include standards that address diversity, universities must make the decision to include these courses in the curriculum. Very often the courses are offered based upon the expertise and interests of the professors. Issues of diversity address difficult topics that might make students uncomfortable, and this discomfort is acknowledged in the lower rating received by professors who teach these courses. Administrator preparation programs must work to train more faculty in teaching courses in diversity, to ensure that the responsibility does not fall solely on one professor. And as much as possible, these courses should engage practitioners from the field in interactions with prospective leaders, to help them become more knowledgeable about the historical framework and scope of some of the issues of diversity they will encounter.

The major paradigm for administrator preparation programs, prior to the 1990s, was on the leader as a manager. This conceptualization is inconsistent with the current focus on standards-based education. To effectively lead in the standards environment requires that principals be trained as instructional leaders who serve as facilitators, coaches, mentors (McCarthy, 1999). Leadership must be broad-based and shared in a manner that helps administrators to build capacity utilizing the talents of teachers, students, parents, and other stakeholders to improve schools (Lambert, 1998). Toward this end, McCarthy suggests the inclusion of courses that emphasize these new roles such as shared governance, team leadership, school-based councils, "the centrality of teaching and learning, the social context of education, school culture, and ethical concerns" (p. 76). Lambert (1998) asserts that the concept of leadership must change from "individual people, role, and "a discrete set of individual behaviors" (p. 6) to capacity building for shared leadership. Training needs to move away from the university into the schools to enable prospective principals to make immediate connections between theory and practice.

To meet the educational, social and cultural challenges of diversity in this new millennium, particularly in urban schools, administrator training programs must seek new and different relationships in the environment to ensure viability and responsiveness to these life-shaping issues of diversity. These programs must also prepare leaders to address the adaptive challenges (Heifetz and Laurie, 1997) which threaten the survival of public schools. The crisis in leadership must be fully addressed to attract prospective leaders who have completed their coursework to apply for administrative positions. Since leadership is developmental and constantly evolving, it should begin as one is inducted into the teaching ranks. New strategies for preparing leaders must cross discipline-specific boundaries to involve both teacher preparation and administrator preparation candidates in shared classroom and internship learning opportunities to foster leadership, problem solving, capacity building, and lifelong learning.

In A Simpler Way (1999) Wheatley and Kellner-Rogers describe how in difficult times, various species learned to adapt in order to remain together. To do so, these species had to place less importance on their differences to learn how to coexist, or specialize in order to remain together (p. 43). The current crisis in leadership requires that administrator preparation programs develop innovative partnerships with teacher training programs, focusing on their similarities, and begin to explore new ways of working together either through joint courses and intensive internships in schools, to prepare leaders and teachers for positions in urban public schools.

REFERENCES

Banks, C. M. (1995). Gender and race as factors in educational leadership and administration. In J. A. Banks & C.M Banks (Eds.), Handbook of research on multicultural education (pp. 65–80). New York: Macmillan.

Banks, J. A. (1994a). An introduction to multicultural education. Boston: Allyn and Bacon.

Banks, J. A. (1994b). Multicultural education: Theory and practice (3rd Edition). Boston: Allyn and Bacon.

Boyer, J. B. & Baptiste, H. P. (1996). The crisis in teacher education in America: Issues of recruitment and retention of culturally different (minority) teachers. In J. Sikula, T. Buttery, & E. Guyton (Eds.), Handbook of research on teacher education (pp. 779–794). New York: Macmillan.

Camblin L. D. & White, P. H. (2000). Teen mothers and young grandmothers. In M. A. Pitman & D. Zorn (Eds.). Caring as tenacity: Stories of urban school survival. (pp.15–26). Cresskill, New Jersey: Hampton Press, Inc.

Cao, L. & Novas, H. (1996). Everything you need to know about Asian American history. New York: Penguin Books.

Capozzoli, T. K. & McVey, R. S. (2000). Kids killing kids: Managing violence and gangs in schools. Boca Raton, Florida: St. Lucie Press.

Cooley, V. & Shen, J. (1999, April). Who will lead? The top 10 factors that influence teachers moving into administration. NASSP, 83(606), 75–80.

Cordeiro, P. A., Reagan, T. G. & Martinez, L. P. (1994). Multiculturalism and TQE: Addressing cultural diversity in schools, Vol. 7. Thousand Oaks, California: Corwin Press, Inc.

Darling-Hammond, L. (1995). Inequality and access to knowledge. In J. A. Banks & C.A. Banks (Eds.), The handbook of research on multicultural education (pp. 465–483). New York: Macmillan.

Delpit, L. (1995). Other peoples' children: Cultural conflict in the classroom. New York: The New Press.

DuBois, W. E. B. (1903). The souls of Black folk. New York: Bantam Books.

Duhon-Sells, R. M., Peoples, V. A., Moore, W.E. & Page, A.T. (1996). Teacher preparation programs at historically Black colleges and universities. In J. Sikula, T. Buttery, & E. Guyton (Eds.), Handbook of research on teacher education (pp. 795–801). New York: Macmillan.

Earls, F. J. (1994, Winter). Violence and today's youth. In The Future of Children: Critical Issues for Children and Youth, 4(3), 4–23. Center for the Future of Children, The David and Lucile Packard Foundation.

Educational Research Service. (2000). The principal, keystone of a high-achieving school: Attracting and keeping the leaders we need. Arlington, VA: Educational Research Service.

Forsyth, P. B. & Tallerico, M. (Eds.) (1993). City schools: Leading the way. Newbury Park, CA: Corwin Press, Inc.

Gay, G. (2000). Culturally responsive teaching: Theory, research, and practice. New York: Teachers College Press.

Goodlad, J. I. (1984). A place called school: Prospects for the future. New York: McGraw-Hill.

Grant, C. A. & Sleeter, C. E. (1986). Race, class, and gender in education research: An argument for integrative analysis. Review of Educational Research (56), 195–211.

Harvey, K. D., Harjo, L. D. & Jackson, J. K. (1990). Teaching about Native Americans (Bulletin No. 84). Washington, DC: National Council for the Social Studies.

Heifetz, R. A., & Laurie, D. L. (1997). The work of leadership. Harvard Business Review, 75(1), 124–134.

Kantor, H. & Brenzel, B. (1992). Urban education and the "truly disadvantaged": The historical roots of the contemporary crisis, 1945–1990. Teachers College Record, (94), 278–314.

Katz, W. L. (1971). Eyewitness: The Negro in American History. New York: Pittman Publishing Corporation.

Kneidek, T. (1994, March). Saving the kids: It's time to work together. Western Center News, 7 (2), 5.

Kohn, A. (1998). Only for my kid: How privileged parents undermine school reform. Phi Delta Kappan, 79(8), 569–577.

Kolb, C. (1998). The importance of NAEP to American education reform. In Standards count: How can the National Assessment of Educational Progress make a difference in the next ten years? (pp. 8–11). Washington, DC: The National Assessment Governing Board and the Institute for Educational Leadership.

Krei, M. S. (1998). Intensifying the barriers: The problem of inequitable teacher allocation in low-income urban schools. Urban Education, 33(1), 71–94.

La Belle, T. J. & Ward, C. R. (1994). Multiculturalism and education: Diversity and its impact on schools and society. Albany, New York: State University of New York Press.

Ladson-Billings, G. (1994). Dreamkeepers: Successful teachers of African American children. San Francisco: Jossey-Bass.

Lambert, L. (1998). Building leadership capacity in schools. Alexandria, VA: Association for Supervision and Curriculum Development.

Leithwood, K. & Duke, D. L. (1999). A century's quest to understand school leadership. In Murphy, J. & Louis, K. S. (Eds.), Handbook of research on educational administration: A project of the American Educational Research Association (pp. 45–72). San Francisco: Jossey-Bass Publishers.

Levine, D. U. & Havighurst, A. J. (1996). Society and education (9th edition). Boston: Allyn and Bacon.

Lightfoot, S. L. (1978). Worlds apart: Relationships between families and schools. New York: Basic Books.

Lunenburg, F. C. & Ornstein, A. C. (1996). Educational administration: Concepts and practices, 2nd edition. Belmont, California: Wadsworth Publishing Company.

Malone, B. G. & Caddell, T. A. (2000, January/February). A crisis in leadership: Where are tomorrow's principals? The Clearing House, 73(3), 162–164.

Mayeski, F., Gaddy, B. B., & Goodwin, B. (2000, March). Leadership for school improvement. Aurora, CO: Mid-continent Research for Education and Learning.

McAdams, R. P. (1998, August). Who'll run the schools? The coming administrator shortage. The American School Board Journal, 185(8), 37–39.

McCarthy, M. M. (1999, Winter). How are school leaders prepared: Trends and future directions. Educational Horizons, 74–81.

Nadler, D. A. & Tushman, M. L. (1995). Types of organizational change: From incremental improvement to discontinuous transformation. In D. A. Nadler, R. B. Shaw, A.E. Walton, & Associates. Discontinuous change: Leading organizational transformation (pp. 15–34). San Francisco: Jossey-Bass.

National Center for Education Statistics. (1996). Urban schools: The challenge of location and poverty (NCES 90–184). Washington, DC: Author.

National Center for Education Statistics. (1998). A study of twelfth-grade mathematics and science achievement in international context. Washington, DC: Author.

National Commission on Excellence in Education. (1983). A nation at risk: The imperative for school reform. Washington, DC: U.S. Government Printing Office. (Author).

National Commission on Teaching and America's Future. (1996). What matters most: Teaching for America's future. New York: Author.

Noel, J. (2000). Developing multicultural educators. New York: Longman.

Noguera, P. A. (1995, Summer). Preventing and producing violence: A critical analysis of responses to school violence. The Harvard Educational Review, 65(2), 189–212.

Novak, M. (1971). Rise of unmeltable ethnics. In M. Friedman (Ed.). Overcoming middleclass rage. Philadelphia: Westminster Press.

Oakes, J. (1990). Multiplying inequalities: The effects of race, social class, and tracking on opportunities to learn mathematics and science. Santa Monica, CA: RAND.

Olson, L. (2000a, January 12). Policy focus converges on leadership: Several major new efforts under way. Education Week, pp. 1, 16.

Olson, L. (2000b, January 12). Principals wanted: Apply just about anywhere. Education Week, p. 16.

Olson, L. (2000c, January 19). New thinking on what makes a leader. Education Week, pp. 1,14.

Olson, L. (2000d, January 19). New demands, new pressures alter administrator' roles. Education Week, p. 14.

Persell, C. H. (1989). Social class and educational equality. In J. A. Banks and C. A. M. Banks (Eds.), Multicultural education: Issues and perspectives, 2ed. (pp. 71–89). Boston: Allyn and Bacon.

Prothrow-Stith, D. (1991). Deadly consequences: How violence is destroying our teenage population and a plan to begin solving the problem. New York: HarperCollins.

Ramirez, M. & Castaneda, A. (1974). Cultural democracy: bicognitive development and education. New York: Academic Press.

Resnick, L. B. & Nolan, K. J. (1995). Standards for education. In D. Ravitch, (Ed.), Debating the future of American education: Do we need national standards and assessments? (pp. 94–119). Washington, DC: The Brookings Institution.

Sanders, W. L. & Horn, S. P. (1998). Research findings from the Tennessee Value-Added Assessment system (TVAAS) database: Implications for educational evaluation and research. Journal of Personnel Evaluation in Education 12 (3), 247–256.

Senge, P. M. (1990). The fifth discipline: The art & practice of the learning organization. New York: Currency Doubleday.

Sergiovanni, T. J. (1996). Leadership for the schoolhouse: How it is different? Why it is important? San Francisco: Jossey-Bass.

Seyfarth, J. T. (1999). The principal: New leadership for new challenges. Upper Saddle River, New Jersey: Merrill.

Shakeshaft, C. (1999). The struggle to create a more gender-inclusive profession. In Murphy, J. & Louis, K. S. (Eds.), Handbook of research on educational administration: A project of the American Educational Research Association (pp. 99–118).

The California Commission on the Teaching Profession. (1985, November). Who will teach our children: A strategy for improving California's schools. San Francisco, CA: Josey-Bass.

The Council of State Governments. (1997, Winter). Quality counts: A report card on the condition of public education in the 50 states. Spectrum, 16–21.

Tyack, D. & Cuban, L. (1995). Tinkering toward Utopia. Cambridge, MA: Harvard University Press.

Vail, K. (1999, September). Words that wound. American School Board Journal, 186 (9), 37–40.

Villegas, A. M. & Clewell, B. C. (1998). Increasing the number of teachers of color for urban schools: Lessons from the Pathways National Evaluation. Education and Urban Society, 31(1), 42–61.

Wheatley, M. & Kellner-Rogers, M. (1999). <u>A simpler way</u>. San Francisco: Berrett-Koehler Publishers.

Williams, R. C. (1999). K-12 educational change: Building responsive schools. In K. A. Sirotnik & R. Soder (Eds.), <u>The beat of a different drummer: Essays on educational renewal in honor of John I. Goodlad</u> (pp. 75–93). New York: Peter Lang.

Yellin, E. & Firestone, D. (1999, September 11). Busing set to end where it began. <u>The Denver Post</u>, pp. 2A, 16A.

Young, A. (1996). <u>An easy burden: The civil rights movement and the transformation of America</u>. New York: HarperCollins.

Preparing Female Superintendents: Curriculum Considerations

GENEVIEVE BROWN and BEVERLY J. IRBY

Traditional university programs have been criticized by politicians, corporations, professional organizations, practicing superintendents, and professors of educational administration. Weaknesses in preparation programs, cited in a report by the National Policy Board for Educational Administration (1989) included the underrepresentation of women and minorities, easy entry standards, weak faculties, curriculum that was too theoretical, and insufficient attention to relationships with school boards. Unchallenging curriculum, lack of usefulness to practitioners, fragmented coursework, lack of connection to practice (Murphy, 1992), failure to infuse into the curriculum information about gender and ethnicity differences (McKay & Grady, 1994), lack of attention to school finance training (Glass, 1992), and too much time on the written and spoken word, with too little time spent on preparing aspiring administrators to work in school systems (Lortie, 1998) have also been identified as weaknesses.

Female superintendents have pointed out several deficiencies in their university preparation programs, including the lack of attention to: superintendent/school board interactions, feminist inquiry, career planning, political influences, working with the media, visibility and vulnerability of the superintendent, and school facilities (Grogan, 1996; Pavan, 1999; Scherr, 1995; Tallerico, Burstyn, & Poole, 1993).

This chapter is based on 20 years of research related to females in educational leadership positions. Even though the past 20 years has provided our field with research on female superintendents' characteristics, career patterns, and experiences (Tallerico, 1999), there continues to be a paucity of information directly related to graduate preparation issues for women aspiring to the superintendency.

In this chapter we share preparation program concerns, particularly related to women, and curriculum considerations for superintendency preparation programs that take into account research on female administrators' leadership needs over the past

Genevieve Brown, Sam Houston State University
Beverly J. Irby, Sam Houston State University

two decades. As reform efforts in educational leadership programs are considered, the female voice must be integral to this process.

METHODOLOGY

When we conducted the initial thematic analysis of literature (Cooper, 1989) to determine specific topics relevant to preparation of women leaders, we discovered that the literature was scarce (Brown & Irby, 1996). Thus, we expanded the existing literature base by gathering data from 90 women who were then enrolled in our leadership preparation program, 25 women principals and superintendents throughout Texas, and 10 women professors of educational administration from other state and national universities. These data included women's perceptions regarding preparation needs for their successful job performance and for removing barriers to obtaining leadership positions (Brown & Irby, 1996). Over the past three years, using multiple channels, we have validated the original findings and further expanded our thematic literature review. We conducted computer searches for abstracts of the management, psychological, and educational literature databases, books in print, and dissertation and theses abstracts. Next, we followed up on references cited in journal articles on the topic, as well as those appearing in bibliographies and papers presented at annual meetings of the American Educational Research Association. Further, we spent time browsing in bookstores and libraries, discussing women's leadership preparation needs with experts on the topic, and attending professional meetings in which related topics were discussed.

CURRICULUM CONSIDERATIONS

Our formal and informal thematic analysis of the literature revealed 24 specific topics in five broad areas that are particularly important for addressing women's preparation needs for the superintendency: Leadership and Management, Socialization to the Profession, Communications and Community Relations, Career Advancement, and Theory and Scholarship. See Figure 1 for these five areas and specific topics. While it is possible that these 24 topics may also be relevant for men, practicing female superintendents have identified them as particularly relevant.

Leadership and Management

Personnel

Hoyle, English, and Steffy (1998) emphasized that superintendents should acquire knowledge and skills in personnel administration. Female superintendents reported

JOB-SPECIFIC EXPERIENCES THROUGH A FIELD-BASED APPROACH

LEADERSHIP & MANAGEMENT • Personnel • Decision making • School Plant • Ethics • Board Relations • Finance • Legal Issues • Political Issues • Collaboration	
SOCIALIZATION TO THE PROFESSION • Leadership Identity • Gender Issues • Time Management • Stress Management • Networking • Role Models/Mentors • Reflective Practice	COMMUNICATIONS AND COMMUNITY RELATIONS • Working with the Media • Conflict Resolution • Ethnic Issues
CAREER ADVANCEMENT • Career Planning • Résumé • Development • Interviewing Practice	THEORY AND SCHOLARSHIP • Inclusive Feminine • Leadership Theory • Feminist Methodology

FIGURE 1. Curriculum Considerations for University Superintendent Preparation Programs Based on Research Related to Concerns of Female Administrators

that personnel issues were extremely relevant to their job performance; however, they perceived this topic received insufficient emphasis in their programs.

Decision Making

According to Sharp and Walter (1997), the superintendent should learn skills and options needed in making decisions themselves and in promoting sound decision making in the district. Females perceived the skill of decision making as highly relevant to their job performance; however, their preparation programs did not emphasize this topic sufficiently (Iselt, 1999). Relevant programs should offer opportunities for students to learn how to utilize good judgment and to solve problems effectively by collecting, analyzing, and using data.

School Plant

Pavan (1999) discovered that female superintendents felt that school facilities and building construction were areas in which they lacked expertise. Female superintendents felt their preparation programs were inadequate in this area (Iselt,1999). According to Lowe (1998), curriculum for aspiring superintendents should include a course in which students formally evaluate existing school facilities, plan new facilities, and interview architects and/or school administrators regarding designing and building new schools.

Ethics

Female superintendents indicated that their superintendent preparation programs did not stress ethics; however, they regarded ethics as critical to their success on the job (Iselt, 1999). Witmer (1995) suggested that female superintendents use a set of principles to apply moral rules to specific situations and recommended that superintendent preparation programs should address this issue. The inclusion of ethics in the superintendent preparation program has been recommended by Hoyle, English, and Steffy (1998), and Heslep (1997). While Hoyle, English, and Steffy (1998) stated that ethics should be included in the preparation of all school administrators, Heslep (1997) suggested that ethics should be infused in every course and every learning activity.

Board Relations

Although school board interactions are problematic for both men and women superintendents (English, 1992; Glass, 1992; Lindle, Miller, & Lagana, 1992; Kowalski, 1995), they are particularly a problem for women. In a study of 20 women who had exited the superintendency, Tallerico, Burstyn, and Poole (1993) found that proportionately more than men, women were vulnerable to significant school board conflict. In fact, 13 of the 20 women left their posts due to school board dysfunction. Pavan (1999) found that women superintendents identified board relations as being important for any woman superintendent.

Preparation programs should emphasize the importance of written and unwritten district policies and practices regarding the role and expectations of the board, as well as school board training and the superintendent's communication with the board (Hoyle, English, & Steffy, 1998). It is also important for preparation programs to make students aware of the informal, unwritten practices related to school board operations.

Finance

The female superintendents in Pavan's (1999) and Grady and Gosmire's (1995) studies indicated that they lacked financial expertise; while practicing female superintendents in Iselt's (1999) study perceived finance and managing organizational budgets as having a greater relevance to job success than the emphasis it was given in university preparation coursework.

Women's preparation programs should emphasize management of organizational budgets, including: (1) budget development, (2) school district financial audit reports, (3) tax rates, and (4) school bond elections (Brown & Irby, 1996).

Legal Issues

A need for better understanding of legal issues has been indicated by female administrators (Grady & Gosmire, 1995). According to Iselt, Brown, and Irby (in press), female superintendents rated legal issues as highly relevant to their successful job performance; however, they indicated that their preparation programs gave this topic only moderate emphasis. Hoyle, English, and Steffy (1998) posited that superintendents, in general, must have skills in legal concepts, regulations, and codes for school operations; Brown and Irby (1996) suggested that programs include legal issues deemed relevant for women.

Political Issues

Women should "expect to deal with political issues and be aware of all stakeholder groups" (Pavan, 1999, p. 119). Reese and Czaja (1998) pointed out that women find the superintendency to be more about politics than education; however, according to Gupton and Slick, (1996), women appear to be more dedicated to education than to politics. Iselt (1999) found that female superintendents perceived that the topic of working within the cultural and political system was highly relevant to their job performance, yet they reported only slight emphasis on this topic in their preparation programs. Brown and Irby (1996) suggested that understanding and working in a cultural and political system should be a component of preparation programs. Aspiring superintendents should be able to define and apply the characteristics of the internal and external political systems and to identify the political context of the community environment.

Collaboration

Several studies reported that women had a more participatory style of leadership and that, among women, collaboration took precedence over rigid control-oriented management (Grady & Wesson, 1994; Reese, 1993; Shakeshaft, 1989; Walker, 1995). Female superintendents in Iselt's study rated collaboration as highly relevant to their success in the job. They noted, however, that preparation programs only moderately emphasized the learning of collaborative skills. Hoyle, English, and Steffy (1998) and Brown and Irby (1996) recommended that collaboration be a basic skill in preparation programs.

Culture/Climate

Culture and climate emerged as a needed topic in women's training programs (Grady & Gosmire, 1995); females indicated that this topic held high relevance for their success as superintendents (Iselt, 1999). Iselt (1999), however, found that this topic was only slightly emphasized in university programs. Brown and Irby (1996), and Hoyle, English, and Steffy (1998) recognized that culture and climate were important components in the preparation of superintendents.

Socialization to the Profession

Leadership Identity

Understanding the administrative culture, the way individuals in leadership roles think, act, and interact, and the expectations of behavior within the administrative ranks is critical in socialization to the profession. Because women express a lack of comfort in imaging themselves as leaders (Walker, 1995), the development of a leadership identity as a part of this socialization is essential for women. In Iselt's (1999) study, female superintendents stated that confidence building was crucial to job performance. A critical objective in the development of leadership identity, the enhancement of professional image can be fostered through curriculum that places high priority on developing strong communication skills, situational leadership style, ability to observe and assess the behavior of others, and awareness of the perceptions of others (Brown & Irby, 1996). Brown and Irby (1995) reported that experiences in these areas can be valuable in building confidence and in assisting women in imaging themselves in top leadership roles.

Time Management

Time management is a needed training topic for women (Grady & Gosmire, 1995; Iselt, 1999) because of their need to balance family and career (Pavan, 1999; Walker, 1995; Watkins, Herrin, & MacDonald, 1993; Wilmore, 1998). Brown and Irby (1996) suggested that preparation program curriculum should include how to manage time more efficiently due to the many demands of balancing family and career responsibilities.

Stress Management

Related to time management needs of women leaders is stress management. Funk (1998) found that heavy workloads, constant demands on their time, and balancing homelife with career were stressors for women. Female superintendents in Scherr's (1995) study reported that their stress came from the long hours and high visibility of the position. Proportionately more than men, women reported stress in the superintendency (Tallerico & Burstyn, 1996). The need for stress management training has been advocated by Brown and Irby (1996), while Czaja (1998) suggested several specific strategies for dealing with stress that might be included in the superintendency curriculum.

Networking

A major problem for women leaders is the lack of adequate networks and/or the lack of understanding of the importance of networks (Brown & Irby, 1995; Gupton & Slick, 1996). Female superintendents indicated that their programs did not adequately address networking or how to network (Iselt, 1999). An emphasis related to creating and maintaining networks and joining professional organizations and support groups would benefit females in superintendency programs (Irby & Brown, 1998).

Role Models

Studies found that women leaders in a male-dominated profession need role models (Beekley, 1999; Brown & Merchant, 1993; Grady & Wesson, 1994; Lyman, 1993; Reese, 1993; Slick & Gupton, 1993). The most successful female administrators, according to Gupton and Slick (1995), had important role models. Women superintendents in Iselt's study (1999) believed role models to be relevant to their jobs, but indicated that the use of role models was hardly addressed in their preparation program. Irby and Brown (1998) advocated the inclusion of successful female superintendents as role models.

Mentors

The importance of mentoring to socialization was stressed by Hill and Ragland (1995): "From the mentor in one's work setting, the novice learns political realities, secrets of moving a project through the chain of command, techniques for dealing with the bureaucracy, ways to creatively budget, contacts throughout the narrow and broader community, and other survival techniques not written in any employee handbook" (pp. 73–74). Traditionally, there has been a lack of mentoring and sponsorship for females (Brown & Merchant, 1993). Although the use of mentors was rated by female superintendents as highly relevant to their success; superintendency preparation programs gave this topic only slight emphasis (Iselt, Brown, & Irby, in press). It is important for superintendency preparation programs to teach aspiring superintendents how to select mentors and how to establish rewarding relationships with mentors.

Reflective Practice

Women indicated that they needed a better understanding of the importance of the relationship of reflection to improved practice (Walker, 1995; Scherr, 1995) and that reflection was relevant to their job performance (Iselt, 1999). Brown, Irby, Buckner, and Lammel (1997) advocated that leaders who engage in reflection are more likely to grow professionally and to have greater positive impact on staff and students. Encouraging students in preparation programs to self-analyze, to think critically about their work and to reflect on their beliefs and practices will assist in leadership development and growth and enhance program relevance.

Career Advancement

Career Planning

Career planning is the "the personal process of planning an individual's career path," (Lunenburg & Ornstein, 1996, p. 542). Numerous studies have pointed out female leaders' failure to develop career plans (Brown & Irby, 1996; Hill & Ragland, 1995; Lyman, 1993; Witmer, 1995). Further, Iselt (1999) reported that female superintendents cited career planning as relevant. Gupton and Slick (1996) reported that women leaders emphasized the importance of women planning their careers and their career strategies.

Female superintendents in Iselt's study (1999) perceived résumé development and interviewing practice to be relevant to their careers. Brown and Irby (1995) found that among women the lack of information regarding résumé development and interview skills was a concern, while a need for women to practice interviewing skills was documented by Shepard (1999) and Witmer (1995). Career planning, including résumé development and interview practice, should be included in leadership preparation program curricula (Grady, 1995) and Irby and Brown (1995).

Gender Issues

Several studies have determined there is bias against women compared to men for school administrative positions (Ortiz and Marshall, 1988; Grogan, 1997; Funk, 1993; and Shakeshaft, 1986). This finding is possibly related to Lynch's notion that the myth still remains that the ideal manager conforms to a masculine stereotype (p. 2.) "Women aspirants to the superintendency are seen as women first and administrators second. Despite being recognized as professional educators skilled at the administrative functions of their work, most of the women expressed a tension arising from other colleagues' gender perceptions" (Grogan, 1996, p. 107). Based on her research, Pavan (1999) advised women superintendents to expect differential treatment, as they may note feelings of being "unaccepted" and unsupported among male superintendents and some board members. Shepard (1997, 1999) indicated that women were often perceived as not having the self-confidence to be in a leadership position, and that they were often viewed as timid and too emotional. Gender issues were reported as important but as not addressed in superintendent preparation programs in several studies (Gupton & Slick, 1995; Iselt, 1999; McKay & Grady, 1994; Scherr, 1995). According to Grady, LaCost, Wendel, and Krumm (1998), institutions of higher education should assure that their programs include dimensions that dispel myths, stereotypes, and gender bias.

Communications and Community Relations

Communications Skills

Communication skills are critical to success in the superintendency, particularly for women. Research has indicated that women have more difficulty than men in demonstrating their authority, speaking so that others will listen, and gaining respect for their ideas (Belenky, Clinchy, Goldberger, & Tarule, 1986; Regan & Brooks, 1995). Female superintendents gave communications skills heavy relevance to their job success; however, they indicated that in their preparation programs this topic was given only moderate emphasis (Iselt, 1999). Grady and Gosmire (1995) also noted that female leaders expressed a need for communications skills training. Curriculum in preparation programs should provide experiences for aspiring superintendents that emphasize that importance of communications and that enhance communications skills.

Working with the Media

Women administrators, according to Scherr (1995), perceived that the media was a source of job-related stress. The importance of superintendents being able to articulate priorities to the media was stressed by Hoyle, English, and Steffy (1998). Iselt (1999) determined that female superintendents perceived that working with the media had a higher relevance to their job than the emphasis it received in their preparation programs. Including curriculum content and experiences related to working with the media in the superintendency preparation program should be beneficial to women.

Conflict Resolution

Women leaders in Grady and Gosmire's (1995) study identified dealing with conflict as their most critical training need. While female superintendents in Iselt's research (1999) rated conflict resolution as having high relevance to job success, they perceived this topic having been only slightly emphasized in their programs. School leaders, according to Hoyle, English, and Steffy (1998), should be adept in conflict resolution and consensus-building. Preparation programs should address conflict-handling styles, strategies for conflict resolution, chaos theory, and information about how women have handled challenging situations (Brown & Irby, 1996).

Ethnic Issues

Females perceived an understanding of ethnic issues as having great relevance to success in the superintendency (Iselt, 1999). However, Scherr (1995) found that administrative preparation programs did not focus on ethnic issues, and McKay and Grady (1994) observed that professors of educational administration did not infuse information about ethnic issues in the coursework. Inclusion of multicultural ethnic understanding and related behaviors in preparation programs will not only enhance program relevancy, but will also assist superintendents in addressing the needs of a diverse population and in interacting more effectively with all constituencies.

Theory and Feminist Scholarship

Theory

Leadership theory has been criticized as failing to include the female perspective (Bell & Chase, 1995; Shakeshaft & Newell, 1984; Grogan, 1996; Irby & Brown, 1995; Irby, Brown, & Trautman, 1999). Related to these criticisms is the research by Iselt (1999) which indicated that female superintendents found that theory was heavily emphasized in their superintendency preparation programs, but had little relevance for them on the job. Preparation programs need to ensure that as theory is taught, students are clear as to the relationship to practice and that attention is given to the biased nature of leadership theory (Irby, Brown, & Trautman, 1999).

Feminist Scholarship

Alston (1999) stated that "often in research on women in administration, there is an absence of feminist scholarship. This absence and silence of women in leadership is perpetuated by the contention that women are trying to be leaders inside of hierarchical organizations that promote gender stratification by roles and maintain values and beliefs based on men's experiences" (p. 83). Feminist scholarship, according to Grogan (1996), propels change which leads to more "gender equitable distribution of influential positions like the superintendency so that nontraditional and alternative strategies for educational leadership can be identified and examined critically." (p. 22). Hoyle, English, and Steffy (1998) stated, "By using naturalistic methodologies, researchers can observe many realities that interact and effect the entire organization" (p. 144). Superintendency preparation programs should encourage feminist perspective research by including and supporting qualitative research methodology in research courses within the program.

RECOMMENDATIONS

In addition to the specific recommendations made throughout the preceding discussion related to the 24 topics of particular concern to women in superintendency preparation programs, we offer two overarching program recommendations: (a) that a curriculum audit be conducted and (b) that a specific course focusing on women in leadership be included in the curriculum.

Curriculum Audit Targeted to Women's Preparation Needs

A targeted curriculum audit on all administrative coursework leading to superintendent certification should be conducted. In this audit each course is analyzed for the inclusion of the 24 topics we have identified as women's preparation needs. The following format for the audit facilitates open discourse about curriculum revisions related to these topics. It is suggested that (a) the audit be conducted in a retreat format with all professors who teach the courses in attendance, (b) multiple copies of all syllabi be made available for each faculty member's use in the audit, (c) teams or pairs of faculty members select or be assigned topics found in Figure 1 and systematically analyze each syllabi for inclusion of the topics, and (d) professors teaching a particular course be interviewed during the retreat by the audit team if it is unclear whether a topic is included or sufficiently addressed.

A Specific Course Targeted to Women's Preparation Needs

Our second broad recommendation is to include a specific course targeted to meet leadership preparation needs of women in superintendency programs. A model for such a course, titled Women in Educational Leadership, is described in detail in the 1996 Yearbook of the National Council of Professors of Educational Administration (Brown & Irby, 1996). Thematic presentations by university and public school personnel revolve around the 24 identified topics. Participants, both male and female, have positively evaluated this course.

CONCLUSIONS

Research clearly indicates that women aspiring to and serving in the superintendency have particular needs and concerns related to their successful job performance. The curriculum revisions suggested above are based on this research and on the assumption that addressing these needs and concerns in university preparation programs will enhance the relevancy of these programs for women and will assist women in attaining and achieving success in superintendency positions.

REFERENCES

American Association of School Administrators. (1993). Professional standards for the superintendency. Arlington, VA. (ERIC Document Reproduction Service No. ED 368 045).

Beekley, C. (1999). Dancing in red shoes: Why women leave the superintendency. In C. C. Brunner (Ed.), Sacred dreams: Women and the superintendency (pp. 161–176). Albany, NY: State University of New York Press.

Belenky, M. F., Clinchy, B. M., Goldberger, N. R. & Tarule, J. M. (1986). Women's way of knowing. New York: Basic Books, Inc.

Bell, C. S., & Chase, S. E. (1995, April). Gender in the theory and practice at educational leadership. Journal for Education, 1(2), 200–223.

Brown, G., & Irby, B. J. (1995). The development of a feminist-inclusive leadership theory. In P. V. Bredeson, J. P. Scribner, & J. L. Burdin (Eds.), The professoriate: Challenges and promises (pp. 41–44). Lancaster, PA: Technomic.

Brown, G., & Irby, B. J. (1996). Women in educational leadership: A research-based model for course design. In J. L. Burdin, J. S. Yoon, R. Morris, P. V. Bredeson, & J. P. Scribner (Eds.), Prioritizing instruction (pp. 131–138). Lancaster, PA: Technomic.

Brown, G., & Merchant, J. (1993). Women in leadership: A support system for success. In G. Brown & B. J. Irby (Eds.), Women as school executives: A powerful paradigm (pp. 87–92). Huntsville, TX: Sam Houston Press.

Brown, G., Irby, B. J., Buckner, K., & Lammel, J. (1997). The administrator appraisal system: Professional development and assessment programs. Reston, VA: National Association of Secondary School Principals.

Cooper, H. (1989). Integrating research: A guide for literature review. Newbury Park, CA: Sage.

Czaja, M. (1998). The CEO and dealing with stress. In G. Brown & B. J. Irby (Eds.), Women and leadership: Creating balance in life. Commack, NY: Nova Science Publishers Inc.

English, F. W. (1992). Deciding what to teach and test. Newbury, CA: Corwin Press.

Funk, C. (1993). Leadership in school administration: The female advantage. In B. J. Irby & G. Brown (Eds.), Women as school executives: Voices and visions (pp. 64–70). Huntsville, TX: Sam Houston Press.

Funk, C. (1995). Women as school executives: The winter and the warm. In G. Brown & B. J. Irby (Eds.), Women as school executives: Voices and visions. Huntsville, TX: Sam Houston Press.

Glass, T. (1992). The 1992 study of the American school superintendency. Arlington, VA: The American Association of School Administrators.

Grady, M., & Gosmire, D. (1995). Topics of interest to women in educational administration. Educational Considerations, 22, 18–20.

Grady, M. L., La Cost, B.Y, Wendel, F. C., & Krumm, B. L. (1998). A pernicious problem: The absence of women from administrative roles. In C. Funk, A. Pankake, & M. Reese (Eds.), Realizing the vision. Commerce, TX: Texas A&M University – Commerce Press.

Grady, M. L., & Wesson, L. H. (1994, April). Two national studies of women superintendents. Paper presented at the annual meeting of the American Educational Research Association, New Orleans, LA. (ERIC Document Reproduction Service No. ED 372 474).

Grogan, M. (1996). Voices of women aspiring to the superintendency. Albany, NY: State University of New York Press.

Gupton, S. L., & Slick, G. A. (1995). Women leaders: Who are they and how do they compare. In B. J. Irby & G. Brown (Eds.), Women as school executives: Voices and visions (pp. 6–14). Huntsville, TX: Sam Houston Press.

Gupton, S. L., & Slick, G. A. (1996). Highly successful women administrators: The inside story of how they got there. Thousand Oaks, CA: Corwin Press, Inc.

Haller, E. J., Brent, B. O., & McNamara, J. H. (1997, November). Does graduate training in educational administration improve America's schools? Phi Delta Kappa, 79(3), 222–227.

Heslep, R. (1997, August). Ethics in educational leadership. Paper presented at the annual meeting of the National Council of Professors of Educational Administration, Vail, CO.

Hill, M. S., & Ragland, J. C. (1995). Women as educational leaders: Opening windows pushing ceilings. Thousand Oaks, CA: Corwin Press.

Hoyle, J. R., English, F., & Steffy, B. (1998). Skills for successful 21st century school leaders: Standards for peak performers. Arlington, VA: American Association of School Administrators.

Irby, B. J., & Brown, G. (1995, April). Constructing a feminist-inclusive theory of leadership. Paper presented at the annual meeting of the American Educational Research Association, San Francisco, CA. (ERIC Document Reproduction Service No. ED 384 103).

Irby, B. J., & Brown, G. (1998, Winter). Exploratory study regarding the status of women in educational administrative support organizations. [28 paragraphs]. Advancing Women in Leadership [On-line journal], 1(2). Available FTP: Hostname: www.advancingwomen.com.

Irby, B. J., Brown, G., & Trautman, D. (1999). Analysis of thirteen leadership theories for an androcentric bias. Paper presented at the National Council of Professors of Educational Administration, August, 1999. Jackson Hole, Wyoming.

Iselt, C. (1999). Texas superintendents' perceptions of their superintendent preparation programs: In general and by gender. Doctoral dissertation, Sam Houston State University, Huntsville, TX: Sam Houston Press.

Iselt, C., Brown, G., & Irby, B.J. (in press). Gender differences in superintendents' perceptions of superintendency preparation programs. In C. C. Brunner & L. G. Bjork (Eds.), Advances in research and theories of school management and educational policy: The new superintendency. JAI Press.

Kowalski, T. J. (1995). Keepers of the flame: Contemporary urban superintendents. Thousand Oaks, CA: Corwin Press.

Lindle, J. C., Miller, L. D, & Lagana, J. F. (1992). Coping in the superintendency: Gender-related perspectives. In F. C. Wendel, (Ed.), Issues of professional preparation and practice (pp. 33–55). University Park, PA: University Council for Educational Administration.

Lortie, D. C. (1998, Summer). Teaching educational administration: Reflections on our craft. The Journal of Cases in Educational Leadership [Online] (1), 1–9. Hostname: www. ucea org/cases/V 1 -Iss 1 /Lortie 1. html.

Lunenburg, F. C., & Ornsteim, A. C. (1996). Educational administration: Concepts and practices (2nd ed.). Belmont, CA: Wadsworth.

Lyman, L. L. (1993, April). Connected knowing: Evaluating a woman and leadership seminar. Paper presented at the annual meeting of the American Educational Research Association, Atlanta, GA. (ERIC Document Reproduction Service No. ED 395 873).

McKay, J., & Grady, M. (1994). Turnover at the top. Executive Education,16, 37–38.

Murphy, J. (1992). The landscape of leadership preparation: Reframing the education of school administrators. Newbury Park, CA: Corwin Press.

National Policy Board for Educational Administration. (1989). Improving the preparation of school administrators. Tempe, AR: University Council for Educational Administration.

Ortiz, F. I. (1982). Career patterns in education: Women, men and minorities in educational administration. New York: Praeger.

Ortiz, F. & Marshall, C. (1988). Women in educational administration. In N. Boyan (Ed.), Handbook of research on educational administration. NY: Longman.

Pavan, B. N. (1999). The first years: What should a female superintendent know beforehand? In C. C. Brunner (Ed.), Sacred dreams: Women and the superintendency (pp. 105–124). Albany, NY: State University of New York Press.

Reese, M. A. (1993). Rethinking the paradigm: The potential effect on aspiring women administrators. In G. Brown and B. J. Irby (Eds.), Women as school executives: A powerful paradigm (pp. 29–33). Huntsville, TX: Sam Houston Press.

Reese, M. A. & Czaja, M. (1998). Women's perspectives on power structures and politics. In B. J. Irby and G. Brown (Eds.), Women leaders: Structuring success. Dubuque, Iowa: Kendall-Hunt Publishers.

Regan, H. B., & Brooks, G. H. (1992, November). Out of women's experience: School leadership for women and men. Paper presented at the meeting of the American Educational Research Association's Special Interest Group: Research on Women in Education, University Park, PA. (ERIC Document Reproduction Service No. ED 354 593).

Scherr, M. W. (1995). The glass ceiling reconsidered: Views from below. In D. M. Dunlap & P. A. Schmuck (Eds.), Women leading in education (pp. 313–323). Albany: State University of New York Press.

Shakeshaft, C. (1986). A gender at risk. Phi Delta Kappan, 76(7), 499–503.

Shakeshaft, C. (1989). Women in educational administration. Newbury Park, CA. Corwin Press.

Shakeshaft, C., & Nowell, I. (1984). Research on theories, concepts, and models of organizational behavior: The influence of gender. Issues in Education, 2 (3), 186–200.

Sharp, W. L., & Walter, J. K. (1997). The school superintendent: The profession and the person. Lancaster, PA: Technomic Publishing Company.

Shepard, I. S. (1999). Superintendents: Who will fill their shoes? AASA Online [Online], (13) 1–3. Hostname: www. aasa. org/Issues/Women/shepard 1–13–99. html.

Tallerico, M. (1999). Women and the superintendency: What do we really know? In C. C. Brunner (Ed.), Sacred dreams: Women and the superintendency (pp. 29–48). Albany, NY: State University of New York Press.

Tallerico, M., & Burstyn, J. N. (1996). Retaining women in the superintendency: The location matters. Educational Administration Quarterly, 32.

Tallerico, M., Burstyn, J. N., & Poole, W. (1993). Gender and politics at work: Why women exit the superintendency. Fairfax, VA: National Policy Board for Educational Administration.

Walker, D. (1995). Patterns in women's emerging leadership. Educational Considerations, 22, 15–17.

Watkins, R. M., Herrin, M., & MacDonald, L. R. (1993). The juxtaposition of career and family: A dilemma for professional women. In G. Brown & B. J. Irby (Eds.) <u>Women as school executives: A powerful paradigm</u>. Huntsville, TX: Sam Houston Press.

Wilmore, E. L. (1998). Creating balance and success in the male world. In G. Brown & B. J. Irby (Eds.), <u>Women and leadership: Creating balance in life</u>. Commack, NY: Nova Science Publishers Inc,

Witmer, J. T. (1995*).* <u>Moving up</u>! Lancaster, PA: Technomic Publishing Company.

Leadership in Latino Schools: Challenges for the New Millennium

LANCE D. FUSARELLI

It is widely recognized, if little understood, that educational leadership is facing increasing complexity generated by numerous changes in society—social, political, and economic—whose impact is most felt in our nation's schools. The demographic composition of the U.S. population is in a period of great flux. As Reyes and Valencia (1993) observe, "The U.S. population is not only becoming older, poorer, more linguistically diverse, but it is also [becoming] less White" (p. 260). No ethnic group is having (or will continue to exert) a greater impact than Latinos. As Latino students move from minority to majority status in public schools, many schools "are still struggling with the challenges of serving these linguistically and culturally different students" (Gonzalez, Huerta-Macias, and Tinajero, 1998, p. xv).

This chapter analyzes trends in population growth, poverty, (un)equal access to educational opportunities, and Latino student achievement, and discusses what school leaders need to do to manage these trends. If educators fail to meet this growing challenge, we risk losing an entire generation of children—particularly in our urban areas—with the attendant consequences of that loss to society (National Research Council, 1993).

TRENDS IN LATINO STUDENT POPULATION

Schools throughout the nation are becoming increasingly diverse—experiencing a massive influx of Latino students in recent years. The percentage of Latino students in schools has increased dramatically in the past two decades, from 8 percent in 1980 to 13 percent in 1994 (NCES, 1996). Mexican American students, representing ninety percent of all Latino students, are increasing in numbers at a rate nearly ten times greater than the overall population (U.S. Bureau of the Census, 1992). From 1982 to 2020, the number of Latino youth is expected to nearly triple, rising from 9 percent in

Lance D. Fusarelli, Fordham University

1982 to 25.3 percent in 2020 (Pallas, Natriello, and McDill, 1989). The proportion of Latino youth is predicted to change from one in ten in 1982 to one in four in 2020 (Pallas, Natriello, and McDill, 1989).

In 1990, Latino and other minority K-12 students constituted over 50 percent of public school enrollment in California and Texas (Valencia, 1991). In New York City, nearly 40 percent of public school students are Latino—making Latinos the single largest ethnic group in the school system. According to Pallas, Natriello, and McDill (1989), these trends constitute a "remarkable transformation of the American youth population" (p. 19). The key issue is what effect this changing student population will have on the public school system in the United States. Analysis of trends in poverty and access to preprimary education suggests that this impact will be significant.

TRENDS IN POVERTY AND (UN)EQUAL ACCESS TO EDUCATIONAL OPPORTUNITIES

Between 1970 and 1980, the Latino population in the United States grew 61 percent; from 1980 to 1990, it increased another 53 percent (U.S. Bureau of the Census, 1993). Since 1980, the Latino population "has increased at a rate five times that of non-Hispanic whites, African Americans, and Asians *combined*" (emphasis added) (Howe, 1994, p. 42). Nearly three of every four Latinos in the United States live in California, Texas, New York, or Florida, with much of this growth concentrated in urban areas (U.S. Bureau of the Census, 1993). In 1990, nearly 90 percent of Latino children were enrolled in urban, predominately minority schools (Pallas, 1991, cited in Sosa, 1998), a situation largely attributable to the structure of the labor market, racial discrimination, and federal housing policies.[1] For the past two decades, nearly 40 percent of Latino children were living below the poverty line, however, poverty is not evenly distributed within the Latino population. For example, in 1990, 57 percent of Puerto Rican children were living in poverty (ASPIRA, 1993).

A related issue to high poverty rates and urbanicity is the increasingly unequal access of Latinos to preprimary education. Significant differences exist in the rate of participation (enrollment) by family income and ethnicity. According to data from the National Center for Education Statistics, in 1973 an enrollment difference of 20 percent existed between low income and high income families; two decades later, the gap had widened to 28 percent (NCES, 1995c). In 1973, enrollment rates by ethnicity were relatively similar, with Latino children enrolled at nearly the same rates as Anglos and African Americans (the difference was less than 5 percent). However, by 1993, the gap in enrollment rates between Anglo and Latino children had widened to 22 percent (NCES, 1995c).

[1] The argument that residential (and educational) segregation is largely the product of individual choice and preferences is facetious, particularly when the "choice" is between living in central cities and homelessness.

Significant differences in enrollment rates were found even within the Latino community. Latino children from families earning less than $20,000 were only one-third as likely to attend nursery school as Latino children from wealthier families (ASPIRA, 1993). These trends led Reyes, Wagstaff and Fusarelli (1999) to suggest, "Given the importance of such programs for preparing children for formal schooling, the widening gap along class and ethnic lines may result in growing numbers of students who are ill-prepared to function at the expectation levels of public schools" (p. 192).

TRENDS IN LATINO STUDENT ACHIEVEMENT

Given high rates of poverty and limited access to preprimary education—particularly when compared with other ethnic groups in schools—it is not surprising that Latino student achievement would be adversely affected. As Howe (1994) observes, "Compared to blacks or whites, Hispanics enter school later, leave school earlier, and are less likely to complete high school and enter or complete college" (p. 42). Latino student achievement consistently lags behind that of Anglo students. A report by the National Center for Education Statistics concluded, "Despite a narrowing in the white-minority gap in achievement during the 1980s, recent data raise the possibility that the gap is no longer closing" (1995c, p. v).

In fact, a comparison of Anglo/Latino student performance on the National Assessment of Educational Progress (NAEP) indicates that the gap is widening. In 1973, the gap between 13-year-old Latinos and Anglos in mathematics was 35 points. By 1986, it had narrowed to 19 points. Less than a decade later, however, the gap had widened to 25 points (Reyes, Wagstaff, and Fusarelli, 1999). Similar performance gaps have been found in other subjects as well, including reading (Council for the Great City Schools, 1997). According to Howe (1994), "At every grade level, a higher percentage of Hispanic children lags behind their modal grade than either non-Hispanic whites or blacks" (p. 42).

A comparison of high school dropout and completion rates reveals significant differences by ethnicity. Latinos comprise "the largest group of high-school dropouts, as well as the group most affected by poverty" (Gonzalez, Huerta-Macias, and Tinajero, 1998, p. xv). According to data collected by the National Center for Education Statistics (1995a), the completion rate for Latinos was only 63 percent, which is 21 percent lower than for African American students and 26 percent lower than that of Anglo students. A comparison of dropout rates suggests that Latino students are not closing the gap relative to Anglos and are losing ground relative to other minority groups, including African Americans. Between 1970 and 1994, the dropout rate for Anglos and Latinos declined only 5 percent for each group, while the dropout rate for African Americans decreased 15 percent during the same period (NCES, 1995b). These trends in achievement and dropout/completion rates are particularly disturbing given the correlation between these variables and other indices, such as access to postsecondary opportunities and lifetime career earnings.

THE LEADERSHIP CHALLENGE

The trends discussed in this chapter present significant challenges to educational leaders in the new millennium. Although a great deal of research has been conducted on the critical role of the principal in creating effective schools, little research "has focused on the role of the principal in the education of Latino students" (Gonzalez, 1998, p. 3; Howe, 1994). Educators traditionally assume students are homogeneous, which often creates barriers in comprehending and managing Latino student diversity (Reyes and Valencia, 1993). It is not an accident that our conceptions of effective leadership are so narrow and limited as well.

In a study of the education of Latino students in Massachusetts, Frau-Ramos and Nieto (1993) emphasized the crucial role of administrative leadership in fostering Latino student achievement and growth. The researchers argued, "Perhaps even more important than what can be accomplished at the classroom level is what can happen through the leadership of administrators," particularly in the areas of curriculum reform and parent outreach (p. 166). Many studies call for administrators to reduce or eliminate Latino overplacement in low-track curriculum (Lucas, Henze, and Donato, 1990; Romo and Falbo, 1996). Howe (1994) pointed out, "Hispanics are consistently less likely to be placed in programs for the gifted than any other ethnic group" (p. 42).

An implicit and seriously damaging assumption of this systematic, low-track curriculum placement is that Latino students are somehow deficient compared to other ethnic groups in schools. Criticizing the low expectations of school personnel, Nieto (1993) reminds administrators of their responsibility to educate Latino students, noting, "It has been standard practice for educators and policymakers to look outside the schools for the causes of Latino students' failure" (p. 244). Echoing the findings of earlier reports, Frau-Ramos and Nieto (1993) urged school administrators to engage in curriculum reforms to remove Latino students from low-level courses. Research indicates that effective principals reject the deficit model of schooling so often associated with educating Latino students and instead build upon the strengths of the students (Gonzalez, 1998; Valencia, 1997).

While there are several explanations for the widespread acceptance among educators of deficit models of schooling (See Valencia, 1997), one major factor is the inability of many educators to identify with Latino students and their culture(s). Although the student population is becoming ever-more diverse, teachers and administrators in the public schools are not. For example, in 1993, only 3 percent of public school teachers were Latino (ASPIRA, 1993), which makes this group the most severely underrepresented ethnic group in the K–12 teaching profession (Valencia and Aburto, 1991). Similarly, only 4 percent of principals are Latino (NCES, 1999). In New York, a state where 44 percent of students are from ethnic minority backgrounds, Latinos received only 6 percent of all administrator certificates issued in 1994–95 (Bernhardt, Kress, and Garam, 2000). As Reyes and Valencia (1993) point out, "the picture that emerges is quite clear: The great majority of the school personnel are

White, monolingual English-speaking, with a professional training that considered little or nothing about the emergent demographic patterns and today's cultural diversity" (p. 261).

Little effort has been made on the part of schools, universities, or professional associations to create a more diverse professional educator profession. At Harvard, a informal survey of district efforts to address the critical shortage of principals found that 35 percent of districts have no strategy in use to address this growing need (available at www.gse.harvard.edu). The "Nothing" categorical response was number one in the survey; only 11 percent of districts reported trying to form partnerships with local universities to meet this shortage. Similar findings have been documented in several recent studies (Keller, 1998; New Visions, 1999).

A growing body of research suggests that establishing an effective linkage between the culture of the school and the student's own culture is crucial to student success. In a seminal study of Latino students in six high schools in California and Arizona, Lucas, Henze, and Donato (1990) identified eight features that promote the success of language-minority students, including: (1) valuing and respecting students' languages and cultures, (2) high expectations, (3) making the education of Latino students a priority, (4) strong emphasis on staff development, (5) variety of courses and programs (beyond the low-level track), (6) well-developed counseling programs (including information about post-secondary educational opportunities), (7) welcoming and encouraging parental involvement, and (8) strong staff commitment to student empowerment through education. However, for a school to incorporate successfully these features into a coherent educational program, effective leadership at the campus and district level is essential.

Recent studies of effective principal behavior in Latino schools have reached similar conclusions. In her study of three effective elementary school principals in the border Southwest, Gonzalez (1998) cited the following as key elements of success: (1) shared decision making, including school-based budgeting practices, (2) collaborative school culture emphasizing communication among diverse constituents, (3) focus on professional development, (4) use of vertical teaming strategies, (5) self-study and reflective practice, (6) empowerment of all stakeholders, (7) respect for teacher professionalism and autonomy, (8) modeling behavior, (9) cultural competence and respect for students' backgrounds, and (10) an ethic of care.

In a related study, Gonzalez and Huerta-Macias (1998) found that effective principals: (1) implement block scheduling and vertical teaming, (2) respect teacher professionalism, (3) create a collegial atmosphere through shared decision making, (4) lead by example, (5) engage staff in extensive professional development, and (6) have high expectations and are committed to helping their students succeed.

A recent study by Wagstaff and Fusarelli (1999) of the leadership and governance styles of principals in high performing Latino schools along the Texas-Mexico border found that effective leaders: (1) are collaborative and foster open communication among school personnel, students, and the community,[2] (2) possess a clear, coherent vision and mission, (3) view leadership as facilitative rather than dictatorial,[3] (4) treat teachers as professionals, (5) practice humanistic leadership through modeling behavior, (6) create opportunities for empowerment, inclusion, and trust, (7) emphasize continued professional development, (8) exhibit an ethic of care and believe in success for all students, (9) accept accountability for student achievement, and (10) foster a culture of innovation that rewards success.

Montero-Sieburth (1993) stresses the need for administrators to empower teachers, support staff, and parents to effectively educate Latino students. Before we can begin to empower others, however, we must first create a more welcoming school climate. To do this, school leaders need to provide more opportunities for greater bonding between students and staff, particularly teachers. Most schools, particularly comprehensive high schools in urban areas, as Amitai Etzioni (1993) has noted, are "organized as if a powerful sociological engineer were intent on minimizing the bonds between students and teachers" (p. 107). According to Reyes, Wagstaff and Fusarelli (1999), "Although these conditions are most commonly found in high schools, increasingly middle and even some elementary schools have become depersonalized" (p. 195). It is not uncommon for elementary schools to enroll over 1000 students; in many urban and suburban areas, high schools are two to five times larger.

In his analysis of forces affecting minority educational advancement, Miller (1995) argued, "If the school is to have a chance of becoming a learning community for disadvantaged children and youth, it must have a small student enrollment" (p. 348). Sergiovanni (1995, 1996) noted that creating learning communities was much easier in smaller schools. The preponderance of evidence suggested that smaller schools provided a higher quality and more equitable education for students than did large schools (Lee, Bryk, and Smith, 1993). The ever-increasing size of schools, particularly in urban areas, has led many reformers (and parents) to support charter schools, arguing that they offer a way to improve the education of students "by creating smaller schools that promote the development of community and foster the close interpersonal relationships among administrators, teachers, parents, and students necessary for success" (Fusarelli, 1999, p. 217).[4]

---

[2] One major finding in the Wagstaff and Fusarelli study was that, although all the principals in highly successful schools practiced some form of shared decision making or school-based management, it was the process of collaboration and the communication itself, through the school leadership teams, that created an environment of caring, sharing, and trust found in these schools. This was found to be much more significant in facilitating Latino school success than formal differences in the structure, power, and authority of the school leadership teams themselves—suggesting that much of the academic hair-splitting over differences in types and scope of school-based management plans may miss the point.

[3] A typical comment from a principal was "How can we [administrators] help you [teachers] serve this child?" (Wagstaff and Fusarelli, 1999, p. 21).

[4] Early data on minority student achievement in charter schools suggests that the success of this reform may not be forthcoming or may be less than proponents claim.

In large, impersonal schools, peer bonding tends to center on student interests, rather than classroom or educational concerns. School leaders need to develop creative ways for bonding between teachers and students—such as the re-organization of schools into houses or "schools within schools" in which groups of teachers follow students throughout their high school career (Miller, 1995).[5] These arrangements give teachers time to get to know their students and their parents. Such arrangements are commonly found in high-performing schools with large Latino populations (Reyes, Scribner, and Scribner, 1999; Romo and Falbo, 1996).

Too often, administrators working in schools with large numbers of Latino children become disconnected from the "school lives" of their students. This observation follows from Romo and Falbo (1996) who argued that many administrators do everything but participate "in the learning of students" (p. 219). Effective leadership in schools with large numbers of Latino students requires administrators who are culturally sensitive to the needs of their students and who create space for "institutionalized caring," which Valenzuela (1999) identifies as a critical component often missing in the education of Latino children (p. 101).

NEXT STEPS: WHAT MUST BE DONE TO MEET THE CHALLENGE

Schools

- Create smaller schools. We will not see substantial school improvement until we undertake this most basic reform. Building construction is seldom a high priority in the reform game, but few initiatives are more important to student success, creating the structural and organizational conditions necessary to establish true communities of learners in schools. Such conditions are critical to counter the rising alienation and disconnectivity common in large schools.
- Emphasize humanistic, caring leadership in schools. Although this is a common mantra in education, it is seldom practiced in schools. Yet, numerous studies of high-performing schools with large Latino student populations repeatedly demonstrate the effectiveness of this leadership style.
- Practice culturally sensitive leadership in schools. Effective leadership in Latino schools must also be connected to the culture of the students, their families, and the surrounding community. Culturally sensitive leadership explicitly rejects the deficit model of schooling so often associated with educating Latino students and embraces the cul-

---

[5] Miller (1995) notes that while educators have little control over students' horizontal mobility (students moving from school to school), they have a great deal of control over students' vertical mobility (changing teachers each year within the same school). Miller asserts that, "Low vertical and horizontal mobility rates are crucial in the creation of an effective learning community for disadvantaged minority children" (p. 349).

ture, using it to strengthen the mission of the school (Banks, 1999). Practices such as tracking and grade retention are much less common where such leadership is institutionalized throughout the school. As our students become increasingly diverse, our leadership styles must be similarly adaptive. Delpit (1995) noted that good teaching is not thought of in the same way in different communities. It makes little sense for school leadership not to be similarly diverse.

Universities

- Aggressively recruit exemplary Latino teachers for administrator preparation programs. Do not assume that potential administrators will come to you—go out and get them, including developing partnership agreements with school districts and professional associations, and offering discounted tuition (with the cost shared by the student, district, and university) for highly qualified candidates.[6] This is particularly critical in large, urban areas. Utilizing the talents of local Latino school administrators, create an advisory committee to recommend strategies to recruit potential minority candidates.
- Develop administrator preparation programs (such as Harvard's Urban Superintendents Program) specially designed to prepare administrators to work in urban schools. Offer diverse program scheduling options, including weekend classes, off-site locations, and intensive institute-style modules.
- Develop an alumni recruitment program that utilizes successful Latino graduates to identify and contact potential applicants. All too often, universities fail to utilize what should be their greatest asset—successful minority alumni. These alumni can serve as role models and mentors for aspiring administrators.

CONCLUSION

Given the trends discussed in this chapter, it is imperative that school leaders in the new millennium take the steps necessary to adequately address the needs of Latino students, creating places of realized potential in our schools (DePree, 1997). As our schools become increasingly diverse and increasingly poor, school leaders must be prepared to adapt to these changes. If educators fail to meet this growing challenge, we risk losing an entire generation of children—particularly in our urban areas. Our nation can ill-afford such a loss. Our future depends on the decisions we make today as school leaders confront these challenges.

---

[6] This model is being used in a growing number of administrator preparation programs as a way to recruit minority candidates into school administration (see Fusarelli and Smith, 1999).

REFERENCES

ASPIRA Institute for Policy Research. (1993). Facing the facts: The state of Hispanic education 1993. Washington, DC: Author.

Banks, J. A. (1999). An introduction to multicultural education. 2d ed. Needham Heights, MA: Allyn & Bacon.

Bernhardt, R. G., Kress, J. E., & Garam, B. K. (2000). A commitment to diversity: A plan for results. New York: Fordham University.

Council for the Great City Schools. (Jan./Feb. 1997). Urban educator. Washington, DC: Author.

Delpit, L. (1995). Other people's children: Cultural conflict in the classroom. New York: The New Press.

DePree, M. (1997). Leading without power. San Francisco: Jossey-Bass.

Etzioni, A. (1993). The spirit of community: The reinvention of American society. New York: Simon & Schuster.

Frau-Ramos, M., & Nieto, S. (1993). I was an outsider: An exploratory study of dropping out among Puerto Rican youths in Holyoke, Massachusetts. In R. Rivera & S. Nieto (Ed.), The education of Latino students in Massachusetts: Issues, research, and policy implications (pp. 147–169). Boston: Mauricio Gaston Institute.

Fusarelli, L. D. (1999). Reinventing urban education in Texas: Charter schools, smaller schools, and the new institutionalism. Education and Urban Society, 31(2): 214–224.

Fusarelli, L. D., & Smith, L. (1999). Improving urban schools VIA leadership: Preparing administrators for the new millennium. Journal of School Leadership, 9(6): 534–551.

Gonzalez, M. L. (1998). Successfully educating Latinos: The pivotal role of the principal. In M. L. Gonzalez, A. Huerta-Macias, & J. V. Tinajero (Eds.), Educating Latino students: A guide to successful practice (pp. 3–28). Lancaster, PA: Technomic.

Gonzalez, M. L., & Huerta-Macias, A. (1998). Profile of leadership at the middle-high-school levels: Successful schools and their principals. In M. L. Gonzalez, A. Huerta-Macias, & J. V. Tinajero (Eds.), Educating Latino students: A guide to successful practice (pp. 213–236). Lancaster, PA: Technomic.

Gonzalez, M. L., Huerta-Macias, A., & Tinajero, J. V. (Eds.). (1998). Educating Latino students: A guide to successful practice. Lancaster, PA: Technomic.

Howe, C. K. (1994). Improving the achievement of Hispanic students. Educational Leadership, 51(8): 42–44.

Keller, B. (1998). Principals' shoes are hard to fill, study finds. Education Week, 17(27): 3.

Lee, V. E., Bryk, A. S., & Smith, J. B. (1993). The organization of effective high schools. In L. Darling-Hammond (Ed.), Review of Research in Education, 19 (pp. 171–267). Washington, DC: American Educational Research Association.

Lucas, T., Henze, R., & Donato, R. (1990). Promoting the success of Latino language-minority students: An exploratory study of six high schools. Harvard Educational Review, 60(3): 315–340.

Miller, L. S. (1995). An American imperative: Accelerating minority educational advancement. New Haven: Yale University Press.

Montero-Sieburth, M. (1993). The effects of schooling processes and practices on potential at-risk Latino high school students. In R. Rivera & S. Nieto (Ed.), The education of Latino students in Massachusetts: Issues, research, and policy implications (pp. 217–239). Boston: Mauricio Gaston Institute.

National Center for Education Statistics. (1995a). Dropout rates in the United States, 1994. U.S. Department of Education. Washington, DC: U.S. Government Printing Office.

National Center for Education Statistics. (1995b). Mini-digest of education statistics 1995. U.S. Department of Education. Washington, DC: U.S. Government Printing Office.

National Center for Education Statistics. (1995c). The condition of education 1995. U.S. Department of Education. Washington, DC: U.S. Government Printing Office.

National Center for Education Statistics. (1999). Digest of education statistics 1998. U.S. Department of Education. Washington, DC: U.S. Government Printing Office.

National Research Council. (1993). Losing generations: Adolescents in high-risk settings. Washington, DC: National Academy Press.

New Visions for Public Schools. (1999). Crisis in leadership: Finding and keeping educational leaders for New York City's public schools. New York: Author.

Nieto, S. (1993). Creating possibilities: Educating Latino students in Massachusetts. In R. Rivera & S. Nieto (Ed.), The education of Latino students in Massachusetts: Issues, research, and policy implications (pp. 243–261). Boston: Mauricio Gaston Institute.

Pallas, A. M., Natriello, G., & McDill, E. L. (1989). The changing nature of the disadvantaged population: Current dimensions and future trends. Educational Researcher, 18(5): 16–22.

Reyes, P., Scribner, J. D., & Scribner, A. P. (Eds.). (1999). Lessons from high-performing Hispanic schools: Creating learning communities. New York: Teachers College Press.

Reyes, P., & Valencia, R. R. (1993). Educational policy and the growing Latino student population: Problems and prospects. Hispanic Journal of Behavioral Sciences, 15(2): 258–283.

Reyes, P., Wagstaff, L. H., & Fusarelli, L. D. (1999). Delta forces: The changing fabric of American society and education. In J. Murphy & K. Seashore Louis (Eds.), Handbook of research on educational administration, 2nd ed. (pp. 183–201). San Francisco: Jossey-Bass.

Romo, H. D., & Falbo, T. (1996). Latino high school graduation: Defying the odds. Austin: University of Texas Press.

Sergiovanni, T. J. (1995). Small schools, great expectations. Educational Leadership 53(3): 48–53.

Sergiovanni, T. J. (1996). Leadership for the schoolhouse. San Francisco: Jossey-Bass.

Sosa, A. S. (1998). Latinos in the United States: A tapestry of diversity. In M. L. Gonzalez, A. Huerta-Macias, & J. V. Tinajero (Eds.), Educating Latino students: A guide to successful practice (pp. 197–212). Lancaster, PA: Technomic.

U.S. Bureau of the Census. (1992). Census of population and housing (CD90–3A-54). Washington, DC: U.S. Government Printing Office.

U.S. Bureau of the Census. (1993). We are the American Hispanics. Washington, DC: Author.

Valencia, R. R. (1991). The plight of Chicano students: An overview of schooling conditions and outcomes. In R. R. Valencia (Ed.), Chicano school failure and success: Research and policy agendas for the 1990s (pp. 3–26). London: Falmer Press.

Valencia, R. R. (Ed.). (1997). The evolution of deficit thinking: Educational thought and practice. Austin: University of Texas Press.

Valencia, R. R., & Aburto, S. (1991) Competency testing and Latino student access to the teaching profession: An overview of issues. In G. D. Keller, J. Deneen, & R. Magallan (Eds.), Assessment and access: Hispanics in higher education (pp. 169–196). Albany: State University of New York Press.

Valenzuela, A. (1999). Subtractive schooling: U.S.-Mexican youth and the politics of caring. Albany: State University of New York Press.

Wagstaff, L. H., & Fusarelli, L. D. (1999). Establishing collaborative governance and leadership. In P. Reyes, J. D. Scribner & A. P. Scribner (Eds.), Lessons from high-performing Hispanic schools: Creating learning communities (pp. 19–35). New York: Teachers College Press.

ISSUES OF PERFORMANCE AND QUALITY IN LEADERSHIP PRACTICE

Superintendent Performance Evaluation:
Its Relationship to Standards, Policy, and Quality

CLARK EALY, DAWN HOGAN, LINDA SKRLA, and JOHN HOYLE

As we usher in the new millennium, the focus for public education is on accountability. Based on the belief that achieving goals for academic success is imperative for the economic security of our nation, educational stakeholders want proof that educational goals are being met for all children. Not unlike big business, the ultimate responsibility for the achievement of goals lies with the chief executive officer. Public school superintendents are considered the chief executive officer for the school district in which they serve. Like most major corporations, school districts continue to be structured as traditionally hierarchical systems, providing the superintendent with a considerable amount of power, influence and responsibility. Accompanying such impressive amounts of power, influence, and responsibility is the accountability for results. For the public school superintendent, the most crucial form of accountability is tied to the academic success of the students in his or her district. That is, along with the increasing political and economic focus on public education, greater public demand for accountability for student performance has arisen in the past decade.

One result of this accountability movement has been legislative policy mandates to develop personnel evaluation systems for public educators including teachers, counselors, principals, and financial officers. Ironically, however, systematic evaluation processes for the most powerful position in public schools, the superintendent, have been among the last accountability measures to appear in state legislation. Likewise, evaluation models currently in place for public school leaders nationwide vary widely in quality and consistency (Hoyle & Skrla, 1999).

Recently, the state of Texas began the process of addressing superintendent evaluations. In 1995, as a part of a sweeping rewrite of the Texas Education Code (TEC), the 74th Texas legislature issued academic and fiscal performance mandates of school

Clark Ealy, Texas A&M University
Dawn Hogan, Texas A&M University
Linda Skrla, Texas A&M University
John Hoyle, Texas A&M University

districts to be used by school boards in the evaluation of superintendents (TEC 39.054). The mechanism for accomplishing this mandate was linking superintendent performance evaluation to the Academic Excellence Indicator System (AEIS), the accountability system that reports both fiscal and academic performance for public school districts in Texas. In an attempt to give teeth to this policy mandate, the Texas legislature also specified that state funds could not be used to pay any administrator who had not been evaluated within the previous 15 months.

Thus, Texas is among the states implementing public policies that explicitly tie the performance (both fiscal and academic) of public schools to the evaluation of their superintendents. Texas, then, is a site that offers significant opportunity for research on the evaluation of school superintendents. The study on which this paper was based was designed to take advantage of this research opportunity by surveying superintendents and board presidents about their views on the superintendent evaluation process.

Specifically, this study analyzed the effectiveness of the superintendent evaluation process in Texas as perceived by current superintendents and school board presidents. This chapter discusses the study in three sections. The first section on the study background includes a review of the relevant literature on the superintendency and superintendent evaluation. The second section describes research procedures used to collect and analyze the data from the superintendents and school board presidents about the performance evaluation process. In the third section, the authors present the study findings and conclusions as well as implications for future research toward improving the superintendent evaluation process.

STUDY BACKGROUND

Leading textbooks on the superintendency devote relatively little attention to the process of performance evaluation and even less on the results of such evaluations (Hoyle & Skrla, 1999). Most information written about the superintendent evaluation process comes in the form "best practice" processes to be used as a resource or focus on the inconsistencies found in evaluation instruments and procedures being used. For example, Konnert and Augestein (1995) presented a brief overview of the superintendent/board leadership team evaluation model. They concluded, "In the final analysis, student accomplishments that have been achieved in an ethical, legal, and caring manner provide the ultimate evaluation for the superintendent/board leadership team" (p. 163). Carter and Cunningham (1997) mentioned the AASA Professional Standards for the Superintendency as a means for assessing the performance of superintendents along with ten criteria that school boards could use for superintendent evaluation. In addition, Goodman, Fulbright, and Zimmerman (1997) supported the AASA standards as a base for the job description of the superintendent. They also provided extensive information on school board-superintendent collaboration, but offered very little on the actual evaluation process of the superintendent.

While these works on the superintendency contain limited discussion of the super-intendent evaluation, they all stressed the importance of teamwork and trust among board members and the superintendent if the district is to be successful. A well-de-signed and positive approach to superintendent evaluation is characteristic of a board and superintendent who "work together to establish a vision that drives the district to-ward excellence," according to Rosenberger (1997, p.75). In other words, the evalua-tion of the superintendent is a critical event that can either strengthen the teamwork and trust between the board and the superintendent or one that can bring about con-troversy and conflict (O'Hara, 1994).

In fact, conflict and controversy are inherent in the position of superintendent; it has long been thought of as a position that encounters contention on a regular basis (see, for example, Blumberg, 1985; Cuban, 1985; Knezevich, 1975). In addition, conflict must be recognized as a natural state in the superintendency and in school governance, and su-perintendents must learn to manage it as part of their jobs. Central to understanding and managing conflict is the ability of the superintendent to communicate effectively with his or her board members. In fact, "poor communication" has become the code for explain-ing a wide range of negative factors in board-superintendent relations. Communication skills are imperative for being successful in a highly political environment.

As the United States becomes a more diverse society, both conflict and politics have become more intense in public education (Kowalski, 1998). Educators, however, tend to have a negative reaction to the idea of education being a political venture. Per-haps the most significant reason for this reaction is the belief that education is for chil-dren and, as such, is too important and sacred to be mixed up in politics (Blumberg, 1985; Johnson, 1996). Despite our desires for schooling to be apolitical, the reality is that "schools are miniature political systems, nested in multi-level governmental structures, charged with salient public service responsibilities, and dependent on di-verse constituencies" (Malen, 1995, p. 148).

This idea of schools as mini political systems and the terminology of micropolitics of education have emerged in clearly articulated form in the research literature within the past 30 years (Marshall & Scribner, 1991). Micropolitics has been defined in terms of power and how individuals use power to protect themselves, get what they want out of the organization, and cooperate with whom they choose (Malen, 1995; Blase, 1991). In addition, Scribner, Reyes, and Fusarelli (1995) stated that micropolitics is about "who plays the game, why and how it is played, and who wins and loses" (p. 207).

Framed by this highly political perspective, the relationship between the superin-tendent and his or her board of trustees is often the focal point for the district's polit-ical dynamics. This political relationship is characterized by the "perennial disequi-librium between lay control and the power of professional expertise" (Tallerico, 1989, p. 216). Hence, the process of superintendent evaluation plays an essential role in the political dynamics of the board-superintendent relationship.

As noted earlier, the performance evaluation of the public school superintendent has been a recent phenomenon. While the literature is shallow with regard to superintendent evaluation during the first 50 years of the twentieth century, more recent literature addressed this concept by advocating desired evaluation models without exploring effectiveness or usefulness for today's educational system. Suggested models included models common to business and industry such as R. E. Callahan's cult of efficiency, in which corporate leaders were evaluated on their ability to increase profits and expand markets. In addition, there have been goal driven models or management by objective (MBO) models as seen in the works of George Redfern (1980) and D. L. Bolton (1980) who stressed job targets.

More recently, adaptations of the MBO model included Leadership by Objectives and Results (LBO/R) and the Administrator Evaluation for Continuous Improvement Model (AECI) (Hoyle, English, & Steffy, 1998). The AECI model is closely tied with district goals and objectives; in fact, the process is based on the vision and strategic plan for the district and requires that the superintendent design his or her evaluation plan in collaboration with board members, central office staff, principals and assistant principals, teachers, counselors, and site-based committee representatives from the community. The AECI model also includes the 360-degree Feedback Model that "includes feedback from principals, peers, parents, and students as well as a self-reflection piece and the inclusion of student achievement data" (Manatt, 1997, p. 9). This model is perceived to be an essential ingredient for improving the evaluation of superintendents and other administrators.

Likewise, proponents for a more comprehensive model of evaluation see portfolios as a needed ingredient for improving the superintendent evaluation process. Portfolios are a collection of "artifacts" that represent the superintendent's achievements, productivity, and growth as an administrator. Portfolios can be used as a hiring tool or to strengthen the evaluation process for the board and the superintendent as well as other administrators (Brown & Irby, 1997; Stufflebeam, Candoli, & Nichols, 1995). While portfolios provide a richer picture of the superintendent and his or her job performance, other evaluation considerations, such as the use of the AASA standards as an evaluation guideline, provide tools for structuring the evaluation process and shaping the professional development of the superintendent (Horler, 1996; Candoli, Cullen, & Stufflebeam, 1997).

Thus, the quest for finding an efficient process of evaluating superintendents is ongoing. The rising pressure for accountability in public education adds another critical dimension to this task. Considering that 49 states now test their students, 36 publish annual report cards on individual schools, 19 publicly identify low-performing schools, 19 require students to pass state tests to graduate from high school, and 14 provide monetary rewards for individual schools based on performance ("Demanding Results," 1999, p. 5), it is likely that state accountability policies will play an increasingly important role in shaping how superintendents are evaluated. This accountability thrust, especially when paired with the political environment within which the superintendent functions, makes ever more crucial the need for an effective instrument and process by which to measure the performance of the top-ranking official in a school district.

Research on the evaluation of superintendents remains in the initial stages of identifying such processes and criteria that will promote a collaborative effort between the boards of education and superintendents. Research is still needed to investigate this crucial question: Will a sound research-based superintendent evaluation model improve the performance of the superintendents? With few consistent or widely used models for superintendent evaluation available, research must be conducted to determine the effectiveness of some of the alternative models currently in use. Thus, the Texas Legislature's mandate for superintendent evaluation, as well as required inclusion of financial and academic performance domains as part of the procedure, provides a significant opportunity for research on the effects of state accountability policy on the superintendent evaluation process.

STUDY DESIGN

Purpose of the Study

The purpose of this study was threefold: 1) to develop a profile of the evaluation models in use in Texas in relation to those advocated in the research literature; 2) to compare perceptions of the superintendent evaluation process from the perspectives of superintendents and board presidents; and 3) to compare superintendent perceptions of the current models with their perceptions of an ideal superintendent evaluation model.

Research Questions

The following specific research questions were addressed:

1) How closely do current superintendent evaluation models in Texas align with models proposed in the literature?
2) Is there a difference between how superintendents and school board presidents in Texas view the evaluation process?
3) How does the current evaluation system differ from an ideal evaluation process as perceived by superintendents?

Methods

The study design included both quantitative and qualitative components and used questionnaires that were completed by superintendents and school board presidents in participating districts.

Population and sample

The populations of interest in this study were superintendents and school board presidents in Texas. To ensure equal representation of small, medium, and large districts, a stratified random sample for district enrollment was employed. Questionnaires were mailed to superintendents and board presidents from 50 small, 50 medium, and 50 large school districts. These districts were randomly selected from three roughly equivalent groups of Texas school districts that were grouped according to the following student enrollments: 19 – 700 students, 701 – 2,500 students, and 2,501 – 210,000 students. Due to small numbers of women superintendents in Texas (fewer than 10% of districts have a female superintendent), an additional 35 districts were randomly selected from the districts with female superintendents in an attempt to get sufficient representation in the sample for women superintendents.

The stratified random sample of districts yielded a large enough sample to ensure that it was representative of all districts in Texas, thus making the conclusions of the study generalizable to most districts in the state. However, the study findings are not generalizable to school districts in other states. Our findings may, though, provide direction for further research into superintendent evaluation procedures in other U.S. states.

Instrumentation

Data were gathered from participants using questionnaires. One questionnaire was mailed to the superintendent and one to the board president in each randomly selected district. The questionnaires included eleven, five-point Likert items, with numerical scales representing responses ranging from strongly disagree to strongly agree, and six open-ended questions. The Likert items were arranged in pairs; one scale to measure how closely current superintendents evaluation procedures related to procedures addressed in the literature and one to measure how superintendents and board presidents feel evaluations need to be structured. The six open-ended questions allowed the researchers to gather additional qualitative data from both superintendents and board presidents on their perceptions of the current superintendent evaluation process and the political implications of superintendent evaluation. Both the quantitative items and the qualitative questions were developed by a committee of university professors, practicing school administrators, and superintendents in Texas and drew from the existing knowledge base in the areas of personnel evaluation and school district accountability.

Procedure

The 1,061 public school districts in Texas were divided into three groups by enrollment: small, medium and large, and the researchers randomly selected 50 districts from each group. Questionnaires were mailed to the superintendents and their school board presidents in late June 1999. Most of the questionnaires were returned during the first two weeks of July. Unfortunately, most of the questionnaires that were initially received came from the superintendents, and very few were returned by the school board presidents. Since board presidents typically receive their mail once a week, and since many families vacation in June and July, the researchers felt that some of the board presidents did not have enough time to respond. The researchers followed up with a second letter to the school board presidents to try to increase their response rate. A second round of follow-up letters was mailed to both superintendent and board president nonrespondents in September.

To maintain confidentiality, a pre-encoded number was printed on each questionnaire. The researchers use these pre-encoded numbers to determine which participants had responded and who needed to be contacted again. The researchers did not have access to the names of the superintendents or board presidents, but used the encoded numbers to identify the data.

Quantitative Analysis

Eleven survey questions described various aspects of evaluation models proposed in the literature and were rated by participants on Likert scales. Descriptive statistical analysis on superintendent responses to the eleven Likert items produced means and frequency tables. Paired samples t-tests were performed to determine which of the 11 survey items had significant differences between current and ideal states in the views of superintendents and which items differed for the current state between superintendents and board presidents. Additional comparative analyses measured the effect of the various independent variables (i.e., district size, gender of superintendent, superintendent vs. board president respondent) on the 11 mutually exclusive Likert items, which served as the dependent variables in the study.

Qualitative Analysis

Qualitative data was collected for this study by including six open-ended questions on the survey. The six survey questions were as follows:

1. What do you feel are the strengths of the current superintendent evaluation process being used in your district?
2. What are the weaknesses of the current superintendent evaluation process being used in your district?
3. What aspects of the current superintendent evaluation process directly correlate with the superintendent's job description?

4. What would you add to the process to improve the effectiveness of the superintendent evaluation? Is there anything that you feel should be eliminated from the current process?
5. Do you feel the current superintendent evaluation process aides in achieving the district goals?
6. How is the superintendent evaluation process used by your district aligned with TEA evaluation requirements?

These questions were developed specifically to ascertain how the superintendent and board president felt about the evaluation process currently being used in their district in terms of the strengths and weaknesses of the evaluation process, how the evaluation related, if at all, to the superintendent's job description, how it could be improved, and if it was aligned with the Texas Education's Agency evaluation requirements. Once the questionnaires were returned, the authors began arranging the data for analysis. Glesne (1999) described this process:

> Data analysis involves organizing what you have seen heard and read so that you can make sense of what you have learned. Working with the data, you describe, create explanations, pose hypotheses and develop theories . . . To do so, you must categorize, synthesize, search for patterns, and interpret the data you have collected. (p.130)

Similarly, according to Lincoln and Guba (1985), "Data analysis involves taking constructions gathered from the context and reconstructing them into meaningful wholes" (p. 333).

Constant comparative analysis was used for coding and thematizing the data. The constant comparative method for analyzing research data begins with unitizing the data. "Unitizing data may be defined as disaggregating data into the smallest pieces of information that may stand alone as independent thought." (Erlandson, Harris, Skipper, & Allen, 1993, p. 117). After the data was unitized, it was then coded and categorized. Categorizing data refers to the process of sorting units of data by emergent categories, that is, "categories that emerge intuitively as the researcher's own background and latent theory interact with these data" (Erlandson et al., 1993, p. 118). Once the data were categorized, the categories served as the framework for the qualitative findings presented in this chapter.

FINDINGS

Quantitative Results

The 103 superintendent respondents (53% return rate) indicated on the 11 Likert items how closely several aspects of their evaluation process matched with superintendent and personnel evaluation procedures advocated in the literature. The superintendents responded using a five-point Likert scale (1 = strongly disagree to 5 = strongly agree). The questionnaire results are summarized in Table 1.

The first two questions examined the familiarity of superintendents and school boards with the evaluation process before the actual evaluation. Over 70% of participating superintendents agreed or strongly agreed that they clearly understood the evaluation process. According to these superintendents, board familiarity with the process was mixed with more board members understanding the process than not. Nearly 36% of superintendents agreed that school boards clearly understood the process before implementation, while 26.2% disagreed.

The next six questions examined superintendent perceptions of how closely their evaluations followed evaluation procedures advocated in the research literature. A majority of superintendents (66.1%) agreed or strongly agreed that their superintendent evaluation process is closely tied to their job description. However, these superintendents came to no consensus on whether their evaluations were closely tied to district strategic plans or superintendent administrative models. Of the participating superintendents, 22.3% disagreed, 27.2% agreed, and 29.1% neither agreed nor disagreed that their evaluations were closely tied to their district strategic plans. In 1998, both the Texas Association of School Administrators (TASA) and the Texas Association of School Boards (TASB) published guides to help school boards evaluate their superintendents. When superintendents were asked if their evaluation process followed one of these or similar evaluation models, 22.3% disagreed 26.2% agreed, and 34.0% neither agreed nor disagreed. The high percentage of scores in the neither agree or disagree range could signal that these superintendents are unsure of the standards advocated by the two groups.

Portions of the superintendent evaluation procedures in Texas are to include measures of student performance. In March of 1999, Texas Commissioner of Education Mike Moses released his recommended student performance domain. Question six of the survey sought to examine how closely each superintendent's evaluation was tied to this recommended student performance domain. A majority of respondents, 33.0% agreed and 32.0% strongly agreed, felt that their evaluation was closely tied to the student performance domain.

The use of authentic assessment measures to evaluate both students and teachers has increased over the last ten years. According to the sample of Texas superintendents, this trend did not extend to their evaluation process. A majority (66.0%) of superintendents reported that their evaluations were not closely tied to an assessment of a portfolio of their work. Finally, 37.9% of respondents agreed and 16.9% strongly agreed that their superintendent evaluation process was tied to the Academic Excellence Indicator System (AEIS), the public school accountability system in Texas.

The final three questions of the survey examined political dimensions of superintendent and school board relations. Question nine asked how closely the superintendent evaluation process was tied to interpersonal relationships with the board members. Superintendents overwhelmingly agreed (67.4% agreed or strongly agreed) that their

TABLE I. Mean and percent of responses about the closeness of current superintendent evaluation models with models advocated in the literature.

Current Superintendent Perceptions	N	Strongly Disagree 1	2	%Responding 3	4	Strongly Agree 5	Mean
1. Expectations for superintendent evaluation procedures are clearly understood by superintendent prior to evaluation.	103	1.9	17.5	9.7	39.8	31.1	3.8
2. Expectations for superintendent evaluation procedures are clearly understood by school board prior to evaluation.	103	5.8	26.2	18.4	35.9	13.6	3.2
3. The superintendent evaluation process is closely tied to job description.	103	1.0	15.5	17.5	44.7	21.4	3.7
4. The superintendent evaluation process is closely tied to district strategic plan.	103	5.8	22.3	29.1	27.2	15.5	3.2
5. The superintendent evaluation process is closely tied to a superintendent administrative model (e.g., AASA/TASA Professional Standards for the Superintendency).	103	8.7	22.3	34.0	26.2	8.7	3.0
6. The student performance component of the evaluation process is closely tied to the Commissioner-Recommended Student Performance Domain.	103	1.0	14.6	19.4	33.0	32.0	3.8
7. The superintendent evaluation process utilizes portfolios of superintendent work.	103	30.1	35.9	21.4	8.7	3.9	2.2
8. The superintendent evaluation process is closely tied to student performance goals (i.e., AEIS Indicators).	103	1.9	17.5	24.3	37.9	18.4	3.5
9. Superintendent performance rating is closely tied to interpersonal relationships with board members.	103	6.8	13.6	12.6	42.7	24.3	3.6
10. The school board acts primarily as a policy-making body.	103	5.8	13.6	15.5	42.7	22.3	3.6
11. The school board engages in administration of policy.	103	20.4	36.9	15.5	19.4	7.8	2.6

evaluations were tied to interpersonal relationships with their board members. The last two questions sought to gauge the degree to which a school board acted primarily as a policy-making body or the board actively engaged in the day-to-day administration of policy. A majority of respondents (42.7% agreed, and 22.3% strongly agreed) felt that their boards acted primarily as a policy-making body. Similarly, 57.3% of the superintendent respondents either disagreed or strongly disagreed that their boards engaged in administration of policy.

Superintendent vs. School Board Perceptions of Current Evaluation Practices

Of the 185 randomly sampled districts, only 28 districts had both the superintendent and school board president return their questionnaires. Due to the small sample size, only 1 of the 11 paired samples t-tests achieved a $p < .05$ level of significance. Question 10 was one of the questions added to the survey to examine the politics of superintendent evaluation. In the 28 districts where both the superintendent and board president responded, there was a difference in how each group perceived the role of the school board. Board presidents had a mean just over .39 greater than the superintendents. Thus, according to this sample, board presidents feel more strongly than the superintendents that the boards act primarily as a policy-making unit. Paired-samples t-test results are summarized in Table 2.

Superintendent Perceptions of Current Evaluation Models and Ideal Evaluation Models

The superintendents who responded to this survey had different ideas about how future evaluations should differ from their current evaluation systems (see Table 3).

Paired-samples t-tests that compared current evaluation systems with future evaluation systems were significantly different for all 11 questions included in the questionnaire. Results of these t-tests are summarized in Table 4.

First, participating superintendents feel that future evaluation situations should be characterized by greater awareness of the evaluation process for both superintendents and school board members prior to the actual appraisal. The mean for future evaluations outdistanced the current model by 1.02 for superintendent understanding and an even greater 1.54 for school board members. According to these superintendents, the mean response for how closely board members understand the current process was only 3.26, compared to where the superintendents believed it should be, 4.80.

Second, the respondents believed that future evaluations should be tied more to evaluation procedures advocated in the literature than the current systems in place.

TABLE II. Paired-samples T-tests for differences of means between superintendent and board president perceptions.

	Paired Differences				
	Mean Difference	Standard Error of Mean	t	df	Significance (2-tailed)
1	-.0714	.2053	-.348	27	.731
2	.2857	.2512	1.137	27	.265
3	.0000	.2300	.000	27	1.000
4	.3571	.2793	.128	27	.899
5	-.1429	.2986	-.478	27	.636
6	.1429	.2851	.501	27	.620
7	-.2500	.2846	-.878	27	.388
8	.3214	.2470	1.302	27	.204
9	.3571	.2919	1.223	27	.232
10	-.3929	.1732	-2.268	27	.032
11	.1071	.1879	.570	27	.573

Superintendents believed that their evaluations should be tied more closely to their job description, district strategic plan, superintendent administrative model, the Commissioner's Recommended student performance domain, AEIS indicators, and portfolios. The greatest increase was seen in tying the evaluations to district strategic plan and the use of portfolios. The means for future evaluations were 1.15 points higher for district strategic plan and 1.18 points higher for the use of portfolios.

Finally, the superintendents believed that future evaluation systems should be less political and less reliant on interpersonal relationships. These superintendents wanted their future evaluations characterized by less emphasis on interpersonal relationships (.79), and for their school boards to deal more in policy making (-1.07) and less in administration of policy (.81).

Qualitative Results

For the purpose of this study, survey results for the six open-ended questions were gathered and recorded in document form with a bulleted list of the responses under each question. This system allowed the authors to group like units from which categories emerged. By unitizing the data in conjunction with the coordinating research question, the authors were able to analyze the results and delineate the categories representing the greatest number of like responses for each question. The categories follow the sequence of the research questions and will be presented in the following section in that manner. The categories emerged from a combination of both the superintendents' and board presidents' responses to our survey instrument.

TABLE III. Mean and percent of responses about perceptions of more ideal superintendent evaluation models.

Superintendent Perceptions of Future Models	N	%Responding					Mean
		Strongly Disagree 1	2	3	4	Strongly Agree 5	
1. Expectations for superintendent evaluation procedures are clearly understood by superintendent prior to evaluation.	101	0	1.0	2.0	10.9	86.1	4.8
2. Expectations for superintendent evaluation procedures are clearly understood by school board prior to evaluation.	101	0	1.0	1.0	17.8	80.2	4.8
3. The superintendent evaluation process is closely tied to job description.	101	0	1.0	3.0	20.8	75.2	4.7
4. The superintendent evaluation process is closely tied to district strategic plan.	101	0	3.0	9.9	32.7	54.5	4.4
5. The superintendent evaluation process is closely tied to a superintendent administrative model (e.g. AASA/TASA Professional Standards for the Superintendency.	101	1.0	4.0	31.7	33.7	29.7	3.9
6. The student performance component of the evaluation process is closely tied to the Commissioner-Recommended Student Performance Domain.	101	0	1.0	7.9	42.6	48.5	4.4
7. The superintendent evaluation process utilizes portfolios of superintendent work.	101	5.9	12.9	34.7	28.7	17.8	3.4
8. The superintendent evaluation process is closely tied to student performance goals (i.e. AEIS Indicators).	101	1.0	1.0	8.9	48.5	40.6	4.3
9. Superintendent performance rating is closely tied to interpersonal relationships with board members.	101	16.8	24.8	20.8	30.7	6.9	2.9
10. The school board acts primarily as a policy-making body.	101	0	1.0	3.0	21.8	74.3	4.7
11. The school board engages in administration of policy.	103	62.4	20.8	3.0	5.0	8.9	1.8

TABLE IV. Paired-samples T-tests for differences of means between superintendent perceptions of current and ideal evaluation models.

| | Paired Differences | | | | |
	Mean Difference	Standard Error of Mean	t	df	Significance (2-tailed)
1	-1.0202	.1148	-8.883	98	.000
2	-1.5354	.1238	-12.405	98	.000
3	-.9798	.1015	-9.653	98	.000
4	-1.1515	.1178	-9.772	98	.000
5	-.8384	.1109	-7.557	98	.000
6	-.6162	.1072	-5.750	98	.000
7	-1.1818	.1319	-8.962	98	.000
8	-7475	.1115	-6.702	98	.000
9	.7879	.1262	6.243	98	.000
10	-1.0707	.1212	-8.835	98	.000
11	.8081	.1455	5.554	98	.000

Initial Themes Grouped by Survey Question

The categories that emerged from the first question concerning the strengths of the current evaluation model ranged from the evaluation being tied to the performance domains to having no reportable strengths. In direct contrast to the strengths of the evaluation model, question two required insight as to the weaknesses of the current evaluation model. Categories relating to the weaknesses were strongly tied to the idea of school board members as lay people evaluating professionals as well as the entire process being highly subjective. The third question, designed to discover what aspects of the current evaluation process correlate with the superintendent's job description, generated responses that ranged from the statement that 100% of the process is tied to the superintendent's job description to actual descriptions of specific aspects that are included in the evaluation process. For question four, a request for perceptions of improvement, board training and more objective practices were by far the largest categories.

Question five asked about the contribution of the process to the attainment of district goals, over half reported that it played a large part, contrasted by one-third of the responses that reported the process contributed little to no part in the achievement of goals. The sixth and last question, asking how current evaluation processes are aligned with the TEA evaluation requirements, revealed one-half of the responses reporting not as much as it should be and one-third reporting that the evaluation process for their district did not align with the TEA model.

Themes Related to Research Questions

Once the aforementioned categories emerged from the unitized data, it became apparent that all the categories could then be absorbed into the three research questions to use as preliminary framework for the qualitative findings of this study. The three overarching categories framed by the research questions dealt with the relationship between the school board and the superintendent, the different models currently in place throughout the state of Texas, and the difference between the current models and an ideal evaluation model.

While the state of Texas has mandated that superintendents must be evaluated on their job performance, how they are evaluated has yet to be prescribed by the legislature. As a result, our findings support the idea that models of evaluation are not consistent throughout the state. However, a majority of districts uses some type of guideline by which to measure the superintendent performance. The basis for Texas superintendent evaluations most commonly referenced in the responses were the superintendent's job description and the goals for the district. A majority of superintendents reported having their evaluation tied to district goals. One superintendent stated, "Our evaluation process is directly tied to district goals and expectations." A school board president added, "We established what performance means. For us, it (performance) is goals agreed upon by the superintendent and school board."

In addition, the second most common framework for the evaluation process was the superintendent job description, as stated by one superintendent: "Our evaluation model is based 100% on my job description. My first year on the job, the personnel department revised the job descriptions and evaluation forms were directly linked to those descriptions." Furthermore, other comments brought to light limitations to be considered when using the superintendent's job description as a guideline for evaluation. A board president put it this way: "All parts of our evaluation system relate to the job description of our superintendent; however, there are numerous aspects of the job not reflected in the evaluation." Another board president mentioned that "We've never seen the job description for our superintendent."

Proponents of evaluation models based on job description or district plan support this process by acknowledging the potential for communication and collaboration between the school board and superintendent. One board member explained: "We sit down with the superintendent in September to plan district goals and line out the evaluation process at the same time." Other comments included "It (job description) is a communication tool for the board and superintendent," and "District goals are a good place to begin the process of evaluating the superintendent." Overall, a large number of respondents claimed to use either the superintendent's job description or the district goals as a guideline for evaluating the top office in the district. Other methods included checklists, instruments designed by individual districts based on chosen criteria, and a rare mention of the portfolio.

Using instruments already tied to the superintendent position allows for an established, district approved document to guide the process for evaluating the superintendent. Attempting to evaluate without some sort of a performance guideline invites the opportunity for personalities to influence the process and, thereby, create a highly subjective outcome. As stated in the research literature, the relationship between the board and superintendent is politically charged at best, and subjectivity is anything but productive in this type of environment. While acknowledging the political nature of the relationship between the school board and the superintendent is imperative, succumbing to the natural tendencies of personal feelings and perceptions as well as personal agendas is extremely dangerous. Personal feelings and agendas become especially dangerous in a public school district where the decisions affect the lives of many children.

One response that resonated throughout a majority of responses from both school board members and superintendents was the frustration felt by subjective influences on both the relationship of the board and superintendent with the evaluation process. Numerous statements reflected the negative impacts of subjectivity and evaluation outcomes based on feelings and perceptions of school board members. The following statements exemplified the magnitude of this impact: "It does not matter how objective you try to make the evaluation process, the board will still evaluate based mostly on subjective feelings," "The board ignores the guidelines and evaluates based on who called and complained," "It is based on the personal biases of the individual board members," and "Board members rely too much on personal opinion instead of facts. What happened yesterday versus what the overall picture is from the previous evaluation period. They also remember and bring up items from the first day you walked into the district."

In addition, while subjectivity is a relatively common problem, another common issue is the lack of training for board members, which may very well be a factor in lack of objectivity experienced in school board/superintendent relationships. Moreover, the lack of training undoubtedly affects the evaluation process. As one respondent stated: "We are evaluated by lay persons who are elected (called your school board) and it takes a lot of time and energy to educate them as to their responsibilities when evaluating the superintendent." Other similar statements included: "The board is not knowledgeable enough to effectively evaluate this position," "Board members are not professional," and an overwhelming number of respondents who simply stated that board members need on-going training. The frankness with which the respondents wrote about the lack of training and the overall subjective nature of the board-superintendent relationship spoke volumes about the lack of effectiveness not only in the evaluation process but within general interactions as well.

The awareness of what superintendents and school boards experience during the evaluation process, how it comes about, and what it measures provides researchers, policymakers, and other administrators knowledge with which to work toward a more efficient process for superintendent evaluations and overall relationships with school boards. By and large, respondents felt a strategically planned evaluation process would improve relationships between the board and the superintendent. If indeed the process were improved, the evaluation process could serve its purpose of helping the school district meet district goals and improve student performance. When asked for suggestions of improvement, responses ranged from "more extensive board training" to "expanding the use of portfolios" as well as adding a "component of praise or reward for achievement of goals." One respondent suggested a mutual evaluation process where superintendents evaluate the board simultaneously with his or her evaluation. Again, the thoughtful responses in reference to improving the evaluation process were indicative of a system in need of attention. While it is evident that evaluation of the superintendent is taking place, the effectiveness of the process is in question for many Texas school districts.

DISCUSSION AND CONCLUSION

Superintendent evaluation in U.S. public school districts has had an unsettled history. After decades during which the literature was virtually silent on the issue, a small but growing body of research within the past 20 years described emerging evaluation practices that were based largely on models borrowed from business and industry and recommended best practices for schools that were tied to various sets of national standards. The advent of state accountability systems has pushed the process of superintendent evaluation into a new phase. Texas, with one of the most highly developed accountability systems in the nation, one that has been described as "com[ing] the closest to having all the components of a complete accountability system" (Demanding Results, 1999, p. 5), is an ideal site to research the effects of state accountability policy on superintendent evaluation processes.

The research described in this paper was designed to gather perceptions from superintendents and school board presidents in a representative sample of Texas districts about the relationship between current evaluation practices and standards and procedures mandated by state law and recommended by the research literature. Perceptions were also gathered as to the ideal state of affairs for these same issues.

The majority of superintendents and board presidents responding to the survey reported that their current evaluation practices were linked to the superintendent's job description, the district strategic plan, and student performance data, though significant percentages of both groups (close to 30% on the question dealing with the strategic plan) said evaluations were not closely linked to these items. This finding departs from what Stufflebeam (1995) described as typical of the national picture — that only 50% of superintendent evaluations were tied to the job description (pp. 309–310).

Further, when asked to describe the ideal state for superintendent evaluation processes, the superintendents in our survey overwhelmingly recommended even stronger links between their evaluations and their job descriptions, the district strategic plan, and student performance. In a state in which 55% of school children are children of color (38% Hispanic, 14% African American, 3% "Other," including Native American and Asian American), 49% of children come from economically disadvantaged homes, and the accountability system disaggregates student performance and holds schools, districts, and superintendents accountable for the success of all groups, this is a strongly important finding. In short, the superintendents who responded to our survey seemed clearly willing to accept responsibility for the academic success of all their students and to be evaluated on that basis.

What these superintendents seemed less willing to accept was the persistent dilemma of their evaluation being tied to political, subjective, and interpersonal relations with individual school board members. In both the qualitative and quantitative findings, superintendents called for clearer understanding among board members about the evaluation process, less subjectivity in the process, and improved training for board members on what the superintendent's job is all about and how to judge the success of it. While this is a familiar theme from the superintendency literature, what is new is the strong call by the superintendents to link their evaluation to job descriptions, plans, and performance and include these links in the training provided for board members.

Findings related to links between professional standards (such as AASA) and evaluations and use of portfolios as evaluative tools showed lower mean scores than questions related to linking superintendent evaluation to job descriptions, strategic plans, and student performance, both for the current and ideal view of the superintendent evaluation process. However, over 63% of superintendents agreed or strongly agreed that their evaluations ideally should be linked to professional standards. Also, while only 11% of superintendents agreed or strongly agreed that portfolios were currently in use, 52% agreed or strongly agreed that portfolios of superintendent work would ideally be used in the evaluation process.

These findings raise interesting and provocative possibilities for future research. First of all, our survey was brief and exploratory in nature; a more extensive quantitative survey of superintendents and board presidents would provide deeper understandings of the issues raised in our study. Also, given our findings about superintendents' desires to link their evaluations to state accountability measures, the question arises as to whether this same finding would appear in other states with highly developed accountability systems, such as Kentucky, North Carolina, Tennessee, and New York. Finally, the strong call by the superintendents in our survey for extensive board training on the superintendent evaluation process highlights the need for exploration into the context and content of such training, whether such is currently available, and what superintendents believe it should look like.

Mandated superintendent evaluation in Texas forced school districts and their superintendents to take accountability seriously. Including the top position in the evaluation process represents an additional step in the transformation of the superintendent's position from a political post to a position of academic leadership. This has powerful implications for the school success of all children.

REFERENCES

Blase, J. (1991). The micropolitical perspective. In J. Blase (Ed.), The politics of life in schools: Power, conflict, and cooperation (pp. 1–18). Newbury Park, CA: Sage.

Blumberg, A. (1985). The school superintendent: Living with conflict. New York: Teachers College Press.

Bolton, D. (1980). Evaluating administrative personnel in school systems. New York: Teachers College Press.

Brown, G., & Irby, B. (1997, August). Administrative appraisal system. Paper presented at the annual meeting of the National Council of Professors of Educational Administration, Vail, CO.

Candoli, C. I., Cullen, K., & Stufflebeam, D. L. (1997). Superintendent performance evaluation: Current practice and directions for improvement. Boston, MA: Kluwer.

Carter, G. R., & Cunningham, W. G. (1997). The American school superintendent: Leading in an age of pressure. San Francisco: Jossey-Bass.

Cuban, L. (1985). Conflict and leadership in the superintendency. Phi Delta Kappan, 67(1), 28–30.

"Demanding results." (1999). Education Week, XVII(17), 5.

Erlandson, D.A, Harris, E.L., Skipper, B.L., & Allen, S. D. (1993). Doing naturalistic inquiry: A guide to methods. Thousand Oaks, CA: Sage.

Glesne, C. (1999). Becoming qualitative researchers: An introduction. Reading, MA: Addison Wesley Longman.

Goodman, R. H., Fulbright, L., & Zimmerman, W. G. (1997). Getting there from here: School board-superintendent collaboration: Creating a school governance team capable of raising student achievement. Arlington, VA: Education Research Service.

Horler, B. (1996). A comparison of criteria used in evaluation of the superintendency in Illinois as perceived by school board presidents and public school superintendents. Unpublished doctoral dissertation, Northern Illinois University, DeKalb.

Hoyle, J. R., English, F. W., & Steffy, B. E. (1998). Skills for successful 21st century school leaders: Standards for peak performers. Arlington, VA: The American Association of School Administrators.

Hoyle, J. R., & Oates, A. (1994). New professional standards for the superintendency: Will they close the governance gap?. In J. Burdin (Ed.), Leadership and diversity in education: The second yearbook of the National Council of Professors of Educational Administration (pp. 213–227). Lancaster, PA: Technomic.

Hoyle, J. R., & Skrla, L. (1999). The politics of superintendent evaluation. Journal of Personnel Evaluation in Education, 13(4), 405–419.

Johnson, S. M. (1996). Leading to change: The challenge of the new superintendency. San Francisco: Jossey-Bass.

Knezevich, S. (1975). Administration of public education. New York: Harper & Row.

Konnert, M. W., & Augenstein, J. J. (1995). The school superintendency: Leading education into the 21st century. Lancaster, PA: Technomic.

Kowalski, T. J. (1998). Critiquing the CEO: Tie superintendent to school improvement. The American School Board Journal, 185(2), 13–14.

Lincoln, Y., & Guba, E. (1985). Naturalistic inquiry. Thousand Oaks, CA: Sage.

Malen, B. (1995). The micropolitics of education. In J. D. Scribner & D. H. Layton (Eds.), The study of educational politics (pp. 147–168). Washington, DC: Falmer.

Manatt, R. (1997). Feedback from 360 degrees: Client-driven evaluation of school personnel. The School Administrator, 3(54), 8–13.

Marshall, C., & Scribner, J. D. (1991). It's all political: Inquiry into the micropolitics of education. Education and Urban Society, 23(4), 347–355.

O'Hara, D. G. (1994). The superintendent's first contract. The School Administrator, 51(7), 19–27.

Redfern, G. B. (1980). Evaluating teachers and administrators: A performance objective approach. Boulder, CO: Westview Press.

Rosenberger, M. K. (1997). Team leadership: School boards at work. Lancaster, PA: Technomic.

Scribner, J. D., Reyes, P., & Fusarelli, L. D. (1995). Educational politics and policy: And the game goes on. In J. D. Scribner & D. H. Layton (Eds.), The study of educational politics (pp. 201–212). Washington, DC: Falmer.

Stufflebeam, D. (1995). Improving superintendent performance. Journal of Personnel Evaluation in Education, 9, 305–316.

Stufflebeam, D., Candoli, C., & Nichols, C. (1995). A portfolio for evaluation of school superintendents. Kalamazoo, MI: Center for Research on Educational Accountability and Teacher Evaluation, The Evaluation Center, Western Michigan University.

Tallerico, M. (1989). The dynamics of superintendent-school board relationships: A continuing challenge. Urban Education, 24(2), 215–231.

Restructuring Administrator Pay to Support Twenty-First Century Schools

JUDITH A. ADKISON and JENNY D. THOMAS

INTRODUCTION

Throughout the twentieth century, reformers have targeted professional salaries in public school systems. These salaries are a major public cost; professional salaries make up at least 80% of the operating budget of most school systems. When salary categories are examined on a per employee basis, administrator salaries are the single most costly expenditure (Young, 1988, p. 11). A district's salary policy contributes to its ability to attract, retain, and motivate employees.

The Progressive movement brought the fixed salary schedule into widespread use. This system supposedly removed salary decisions from the political arena and made salaries equitable within districts. Based on experience and formal education, fixed salary schedules motivated educators to remain in education and to continue their formal schooling. During the "second wave" of educational reform of the 1980s, many states and school districts responded to criticisms of the fixed salary schedule by implementing merit pay and career ladder approaches designed to reward effective teachers. By 1991, at least 22 states were piloting, implementing, or developing an alternative teacher compensation system (Odden & Conley, 1992). The 1980s saw similar attention to the salaries of school administrators as districts abandoned the fixed salary schedule for other types of schedules or systems. In designing their salary schedules, salary administrators emphasized the goals of internal consistency and external competitiveness.

As a new century begins, school systems are challenged to develop new compensation systems, not only for teachers but for administrators. According to Hajnal and Dibski (1993), "Public organizations should be required to set the example of pay for performance and productivity for the rest of the country, which is opposite of how the

Judith A. Adkison, University of North Texas
Jenny D. Thomas, Leesburg, Virginia

public sector is currently viewed" (p. 310). Economic and social changes have promoted reengineering and restructuring in many organizations. As hierarchies flatten and decisions move to the building level, traditional assumptions about compensation no longer hold. Recent calls for the reform of traditional salary policies in both the private sector and in public education recommend tying compensation to individual performance, organizational productivity, and the organization's principles and values (Lawler, 1990; Odden & Conley, 1992). Lawler proposed that firms develop salary systems that support the organization's strategic direction. Similarly, Odden and Conley have suggested ways to restructure teacher compensation to foster teacher collegiality and the development of the professional expertise needed to accomplish national educational goals.

A school district's salary structure can contribute to school effectiveness in several ways. Salaries affect a profession's attractiveness in general, and administrator salaries should be an incentive to persuade prospective school leaders to accept the "heavy responsibility of managing today's schools" (Hess, 1988, p. 44). An individual district's salary structure affects its ability to attract and retain high-quality administrators as it competes with other districts and other organizations. A pay system can do more to improve effectiveness than minimizing dissatisfaction and maintaining a competitive position with similar organizations (Lawler, 1990). A salary plan can motivate employees to perform more effectively, create a culture in which people care about the organization and its success, attract and retain the kind of talent needed to be successful, encourage people to develop abilities in areas that will benefit the organization, and contribute to creating a realistic cost structure (Lawler, 1990).

This chapter describes traditional approaches to administrator salaries and reviews research on what factors are rewarded. It then discusses Lawler's (1990) proposals for reform of corporate salary structures and suggests how using them in school systems might contribute to efforts to restructure schools for the twenty-first century.

TRADITIONAL APPROACHES TO SETTING ADMINISTRATOR SALARIES

The first widely used compensation system in education was the fixed salary schedule. Fixed schedules establish a two-dimensional grid based on years of experience and level of education and thus reward experience and advanced training. This has been the most common approach to paying teachers. It was used in 94% of school districts as late as 1990–1991 (U.S. Department of Education, 1993). Until the 1960s, most districts based administrator salaries on the fixed schedule for teachers, with added money for the increased responsibility of the administrative position (Dejnozka & Kapel, 1991). As late as 1969–1970, 72% of school districts set administrator pay in this way.

Formal salary schedules maintain internal consistency, are relatively easy to administer, and provide for fairness and due process. In 1982 an influential text on school personnel administration argued that most districts had no formal or systematic way to determine administrator salaries (Castetter, 1982). Within a decade this was no longer true as school districts moved to implement administrator salary systems. By 1991 only 11% of districts used a fixed salary schedule to set administrator salaries (Educational Research Service [ERS], 1991). They implemented a variety of schedules.

Ratio or index schedules set administrator salaries as a proportion of the salary of another position such as that of teacher or superintendent. Dollar differential schedules base administrator pay on the schedule for another position, such as that of teacher, then designate an across-the-board dollar increase relative to that schedule. Independent schedules set a subjective amount unrelated to the teacher salary schedule, then increase pay in steps from that beginning amount. Minimum/maximum schedules establish a range of salaries for each position; some districts set the beginning administrator's salary through negotiations then build a schedule on this "base" pay (Herman, 1994, p. 71). Other approaches base annual individual salary increases on (a) the previous year's salary, (b) comparisons to the teacher salary increase in the district, or, (c) comparisons to increases in the cost of living in the area (Caldwell, 1986). The personnel administration literature recommends that compensation systems reward the individual's skills, knowledge, and experience as well as the demands of the job. McGee and Gibson (1985) identified managerial level, span of control, level of work, and school size as salary criteria for school administrators. The Educational Research Service identified the following factors for use in designing administrator salary schedules:

Instructional level of the school; scope of responsibility indicators such as number of students, staff, or certified staff; number of contract days; academic preparation required; experience as a principal or teacher; experience within the district; and total experience in the position or in a similar position. (ERS, 1991, p. 1)

If these criteria are used to structure salary schedules, individuals should believe that their relative contributions to the organization are rewarded and their salaries are similar to comparable positions within the district.

SALARY DETERMINANTS

Relatively little research has been done on what criteria school districts actually reward. Studies addressing equity in administrator salaries suggest that districts reward gender and race. Gender bias affects not only who enters administration (Whitaker & Hein, 1981) but how much women in administration are paid (Edson, 1988). Pigford (1993, p. 6) reported that, although women in administration were more educated and had more teaching experience than men, they received only

65% of men's salaries. McKenzie (1989) found that women holding positions as assistant superintendents, elementary principals, and elementary assistant principals in Texas suburban school districts received lower salaries than men with comparable education and experience.

Many sources report that minorities earn less than Whites in all areas of the economy (e.g., Belcher & Atchison, 1987, p. 67). School administrator salaries reflect this pattern. In McKenzie's sample (1989, p. 88), Black elementary principals and senior high assistant principals received lower salaries than Whites. Thomas (1998, p. 91) reported that Black administrators in New Jersey were paid less than whites.

Researchers have identified factors that have the most effect on administrator pay. Not surprisingly, given the linkage between administrator and teacher salary schedules in many systems, experience is recognized and rewarded (McKenzie, 1989; Pounder, 1988; Thomas, 1998; Sheehan, 1987). In Thomas's sample of New Jersey administrators, experience explained 7% of the total salary variance among all administrators. Administrator salaries also tend to increase with years of education or advanced degrees (Polachek & Seibert, 1993; Thomas, 1998). McKenzie found that, although education was positively associated with salary at the building level, the link was inconsistent among central office positions.

Research on how districts reward the demands of the position shows no consistently rewarded factors. School size is a measure of scope of responsibility. The U.S. Department of Education (1993, p. 70) reported that principals' salaries tend to be positively related to school size. This finding might be related to level, because secondary schools tend to be larger than middle and elementary schools. McKenzie (1989) found that, while personnel directors reported that their districts pay more for supervision of larger student populations, there was no relationship between enrollment and salaries for most building-level positions. Thomas (1998) also found no relationship between school size and elementary or middle school principals' salaries; however, size had a negative effect on high school principals' salaries.

Lawler (1990) indicated that the bureaucratic model typically shapes compensation in the private sector. The same pattern is found in educational systems as salaries increase with level in the hierarchy (National Association of Secondary School Principals, 1993; Thomas, 1998, pp. 97–98). The instructional level of the school also affects salary, because high school principals earn higher salaries than junior high principals, and junior high school principals earn more than elementary principals (ERS, 1991). Thomas (1998) reported that high school principals earned more than elementary or junior high school principals, but level did not differentiate elementary and junior high administrators.

School system conditions unrelated to the individual administrator's skill and knowledge or to the demands of the job also impact administrator pay. The socioeconomic status of a district's community affects salaries. King (1979) found that a community's socioeconomic status was the strongest predictor of teacher salaries in New York State. Similarly, Thomas (1998) reported that per pupil income in the district (total personal income divided by number of students) had a strong positive effect on the salaries of New Jersey administrators. McGee and Gibson (1985) reported a positive relationship between family income in the community and property tax value and salaries. Socioeconomic conditions affect community ability and willingness to support education.

Collective bargaining for administrators also has an impact. Cooper (1988) reported that, in a 15-year period beginning in the mid-1970s, collective bargaining raised administrator salaries and benefits as much as 21% above the salaries of nonunionized administrators. Thomas (1998) also found that collective bargaining had a positive impact on New Jersey administrator salaries.

When all contributing variables in the salary studies are examined, they explain significant, but not all, salary variance. Thomas's (1998) New Jersey study reported data on all positions in a statewide sample of districts. The 14 organizational and personal variables in her analysis explained 46.27% of the salary variance for all administrators and from 61% (for elementary school assistant principals) to 39% (for middle school principals) of the salary variance for individual positions. The 7 variables in McKenzie's (1989) earlier study explained from 23% (for senior high school assistant principals) to 48.9% (for deputy superintendents) of salary variance. It is possible that variables such as years of experience in administration or in the current position, which were not included in these studies, would reduce the unexplained variance. However, much of the unexplained variance probably results from differences among individuals in negotiating ability, objective and subjective merit judgments, and factors unique to individual situations.

Traditional administrator salary policies have drawbacks. They do not prevent the influence of racial or gender bias. A reward system based on experience and degrees earned does not assure that school systems reward effective administrators who promote district goals. Lawler (1990) indicated that traditional compensation systems "tend to produce hierarchical, rigid cultures with low levels of teamwork and cooperation" in the private sector (p. 5). This criticism is equally appropriate for administrator compensation systems in education.

NEW DIRECTIONS IN ADMINISTRATOR SALARY SYSTEMS

As the twentieth century ended, many private and public sector organizations had restructured to flatten hierarchies, empower employees, and respond flexibly to individual needs and environmental changes. Restructuring efforts promoted teamwork and collaboration, and management theory recognized the importance of building effective organizational cultures.

Restructured organizations require restructured reward systems. McKenzie and Lee (1998) have argued that, "in firms with growing production sophistication and flattened organizational structures, constant direct supervision of workers is no longer possible" (p. ix). Thus, incentive systems become more influential in motivating people to work toward organizational goals. McKenzie and Lee showed that compensation plans or reward systems can be structured to reinforce values desired in an organization's culture.

Lawler (1990) also argued that social and economic changes have created a need for new approaches to management, including pay systems that motivate effective behavior, unify the organization, and attract the best people. Pay systems can motivate employees to perform more effectively, create a culture in which people care about the organization and its success, attract and retain the kind of talent the organization needs to be effective, and encourage people to develop their abilities in areas that benefit the organization. To accomplish this, the organization must align its pay system with its strategic direction. It must identify the individual and organizational behaviors needed for success.

Over 30 years of research on motivation and pay indicate that pay can affect behavior (Lawler, 1971; Vroom, 1964). Lawler (1990) cited research showing that an effective pay system can increase motivation by as much as 40%. To develop such a pay system, an organization first must be able to identify and measure the performance it wants to motivate and identify the rewards that people value. Then leaders must be able to communicate the link between an individual's performance and the reward. Where individual performance goals are set, people must believe that their goals are achievable, and when group or organizational goals are set, individuals must see that they can influence organizational performance. To motivate skill development, valued rewards must be tied in a credible way to the skills needed in the organization (Lawler, 1990). The rewarded behaviors must reflect the organization's core principles—such as teamwork, internal equity, or entrepreneurship—and values, such as minimizing hierarchical differences. These core principles and values, and how the compensation system reflects them, must be communicated to all employees for the pay system to be effective.

To develop an administrator pay system that supports the school system's strategic direction, a district must answer several questions: What school goals define productivity? What are the skills, knowledge, behaviors, goals, principles, and values to be rewarded? How can they be identified, measured, and communicated throughout the district?

A widely used measure of school productivity or effectiveness is student performance on standardized tests. Other productivity indicators might be student attendance, graduation rates, employment, or post-secondary school enrollment of graduates. Productivity also might be defined as the achievement of specific organizational goals. In addition, the school or school district may wish to support principles such as collaboration among teachers, school community partnerships, collegiality, and broader participation in decision making. The system may value innovation, building community, and creating a culture of civility, ethical behavior, and social responsibility among its students and staff.

Pay for Performance

Pay-for-performance approaches include merit pay, individual bonuses, group bonuses, and pay for organizational performance. Gainsharing, a relatively new approach in the public sector, combines group incentives with participative management.

Merit Pay

Merit pay rewards individual achievement, and in public schools this system has tied teacher salaries to their performance evaluations. It is widely supported in concept but difficult to implement successfully. The perceived advantage is that of attracting and retaining high performers without having to pay all employees above the prevailing market wage (Lawler, 1990). In the 1980s many states tried versions of merit pay for teachers, but the approaches did not succeed. They proved difficult and costly to administer, were not accepted by teachers, and promoted a "bureaucratic and legalistic culture in schools when what is needed are more organic and flexible modes of management" (Odden & Conley, 1992, p. 73).

To relate pay to individual performance, organizations must develop credible, comprehensive performance measures. Lawler (1990) cited evidence that most organizations do not do performance appraisal well and they lack good measures of individual performance. In the absence of objective measures, organizations rely on subjective measures, which employees often consider invalid, unfair, and discriminatory (Lawler, 1990). Because most organizations add merit pay into an employee's base pay, they end up paying for past performance as long as an individual remains in the organization. Merit increases in any given year often are so small that they fail to motivate. If a school district has a minimum-maximum pay schedule, high performers may "top out," and pay no longer can be a motivator. Lawler also noted that average and poor performers rarely quit because of how they are treated by merit pay systems (1990).

Although merit systems can be implemented successfully, designing and implementing an effective system is not easy. In addition, merit pay systems may work against efforts to promote cultures of teamwork, collaboration, knowledge sharing, and community. Thus, this approach would not support most school reform strategies being recommended for twenty-first-century schools.

Individual Bonuses

Annual bonuses based on performance avoid the organizational costs of adding performance-based rewards into the permanent salary base. Although he considered this form of compensation inappropriate for lower level employees, Lawler has recommended it for top management (Miller, 1977). To attract high performers, he argued that a salary structure should provide a below-market guaranteed salary but offer large bonuses for achievement. Such a compensation plan would not attract mediocre executives but would attract confident, motivated, and competent executives. The annual bonuses would have to be substantial. To motivate, Lawler recommended executive bonuses ranging from 0 for the poor performer to 50% for the outstanding performer. He suggested that, for motivation alone, a spread of 0 - 30% would work, but argued that few managers are willing to give no bonus, so the real level is likely to be between 15% and 30%. He believed that this smaller range would not be motivating. Such large bonuses would bring the performance-based annual pay for the effective executive well above the market.

The same problems of identifying and measuring performance goals that work against merit pay systems would apply to this approach for paying school administrators. In public sector organizations that do not produce dollar profits, it would be hard to justify such bonuses to others in the organization and to the larger community.

Gainsharing

Lawler (1990) identified many benefits in private sector organizations of basing rewards on organizational performance. Gainsharing is a public sector version of profit sharing. Applied to education, annual bonuses for teachers and administrators based on school productivity could improve motivation and promote a culture in which members are committed to school goals and care about the entire organization's effectiveness. Profit sharing, which bases bonuses on the organization's profitability, is widely used in the private sector, but is not applicable to nonprofit schools. However, gainsharing, a reward approach that combines a bonus plan with participative approaches to management and bases bonuses on units of output and cost reduction rather than profits, is increasingly popular and could be applied to nonprofit organizations (Lawler, 1990). In designing a gainsharing plan, a district would set a base period of performance as a basis for determining whether or not gains have occurred in the future. When performance improves, a bonus pool is funded, and all employees receive the same percentage of their base pay in the bonus. Lawler emphasized that motivation results not only from the bonus but from employee participation in decisions that led to increased productivity.

For gainsharing to succeed, people must see a relationship between what they do and the reward. Good and simple performance measures must be available. Employees must want to participate, and they must understand and trust the system. Administrators must support participatory management, have the skills to work with empowered employees, and communicate effectively (Lawler, 1990).

Lawler's (1990) research has shown that gainsharing enhances coordination, teamwork, and sharing of knowledge at lower levels of the organization; recognizes social needs; and promotes acceptance of change. Including gainsharing as part of an educational organization's compensation system is attractive, because this system reflects principles associated with recent educational reforms, such as site-based management, teacher professionalism, and teacher empowerment. Gainsharing could reinforce efforts to build community in schools and establish a performance-oriented culture. By linking the compensation of teachers and administrators, it could reduce the effects of hierarchy. Because bonuses are not added to the base pay, gain sharing can be used in combination with the district's existing salary schedule. Gainsharing reinforces continuous improvement.

However, the complexity of education and the multiple goals of schools make gainsharing difficult to implement. Simple gains, such as student scores on standardized tests, are easy to measure, communicate, and understand. A focus on simple gains can have the unintended consequence of focusing employees attention and efforts on the measured outcomes to the neglect of unmeasured areas. Complex educational gains are difficult to define and measure in a way that all stakeholders accept. Thus, before implementing gainsharing, a school system must have developed and communicated a clear mission and strategy.

Rewarding Professional Growth

Pay systems also can reward individuals who develop skills and talents that contribute to the organization's effectiveness. To use these rewards effectively, a school district must be able to identify the skills and knowledge needed to improve effectiveness, determine how to measure them, and be able to communicate them throughout the organizations. The organization also must determine what the increases in different skills or knowledge areas are worth.

Where schools are seen as learning organizations or learning communities, this reward system would reinforce key values. Even where schools do not define themselves as learning communities, the changing and increasing demands on administrators require that they continually acquire new skills and knowledge to be effective. As with bonuses or gainsharing, these rewards can be added to an existing salary system.

A CAUTIONARY NOTE

Compensation systems should be included in the discussions of how to restructure public schools. Shortages of qualified teachers, principals, and superintendents suggest that current salary structures do not even attract and retain, much less motivate, enough high-quality educators to meet demand. Reformers have made a convincing argument that traditional compensation systems do not support the best practices recommended for twenty-first-century schools.

However, compensation systems that reward performance and growth are difficult to implement successfully. As the history of merit pay for public school teachers shows, a poorly designed or poorly implemented compensation policy may create more problems than it solves. These implementation difficulties may indicate an underlying flaw in the belief that linking rewards to performance will increase organizational effectiveness. Kohn (1993) argued that any approach that offers a reward for improved performance is destined to be ineffective, and he cited many cases of failed incentive plans.

Recommendations for strategic pay assume an economic model of rational decision making. Miller (1977) stated the case succinctly: "Psychological research has provided an unequivocal answer to the question of how to make compensation programs effective motivators: make rewards clearly and closely dependent on performance" (p. 4). Kohn (1993) argued that this assumption is wrong, because behavior is shaped by intrinsic motivation as people seek to do what is satisfying.

When considering how to restructure their compensation systems, school districts must recognize that motivation is complex and that considerations other than money attract people to careers as teachers and administrators and retain and motivate them in their positions. However, pay and the way it is determined are among those considerations. Open discussions of the relationship between salary policies and the overall mission, goals, and values of the school system, combined with stakeholder input into decisions on what factors to reward, should help decision makers develop compensation policies that teachers, administrators, and the community consider legitimate.

As school systems and other organizations link their salary policies to organizational strategy and culture, they will create many opportunities for conducting research that adds to our understanding of the effects of different approaches. Research can help educational policy makers determine whether rewarding individual, group, or schoolwide performance promotes or subverts long-term school improvement.

REFERENCES

Belcher, D.W., & Atchison, T.J. (1987). Compensation administration. Englewood Cliffs, NJ: Prentice-Hall.

Bianchi, S., & Rytina, N. (1986). The decline in occupational sex segregation during the 1970s: Census and CPS comparison. Demography, 23, 79–85.

Caldwell, W. E. (1986). Equity in principal salaries–a model. NASSP Bulletin, 70, 67–71.

Castetter, W. (1982). The personnel function in educational administration. New York: Macmillan.

Cooper, B. S. (1988). Administrator unions. In R. A. Gorton, G. T. Schneider, & J. C. Fischer, (Eds.), Encyclopedia of school administration and supervision. Phoenix, AZ: Oryx Press.

Dejnozka, E. L., & Kapel, D.E. (1991). American educators' encyclopedia. Westport, CT: Greenwood Press.

Edson, S. K. (1988). Pushing the limits, the female administrative aspirant. New York: State University of New York.

Educational Research Service. (1991). Methods of scheduling salaries for principals. Arlington, VA: Educational Research Services.

Forsyth, J., & Brown, J. H. (1995). Principals' salaries and benefits, 1994–1995. Principal, 74, 49–55.

Hajnal, V. J., & Dibski, D. J. (1993). Compensation management: Coherence between organization directions and teacher needs. Journal of Educational Administration, 31, 53–69.

Herman, J. J. (1994). Designing your own career. Thousand Oaks, CA: Corwin Press.

Hess, F. (1988). When our veteran superintendents retire, who'll step in their shoes? American School Board Journal, 175, 43–44.

King, R. A. (1979). Toward a theory of wage determination for teachers: Factors which determine variation in salaries among districts. Journal of Education Finance, 4, 358–369.

Kohn, A. (1993). Punished by rewards. Boston: Houghton Mifflin.

Lawler, E. E., III (1971). Pay and organizational effectiveness: A psychological view. New York: McGraw-Hill.

Lawler, E. E., III (1990). Strategic pay: Aligning organizational strategies and pay systems. San Francisco: Jossey-Bass.

McAdams, J. L. (1996). The reward plan advantage: A manager's guide to improving business performance through people. San Francisco: Jossey-Bass.

McGee, W. L., & Gibson, R. O. (1985, March 31–April 4). The work for pay exchange in public school administration. Paper presented at the Annual Meeting of the American Educational Research Association. Chicago. (ERIC Document Reproduction Services No. ED 253 943).

McKenzie, C. M. (1989). A study of the relationship of selected wage criteria to administrative salaries in suburban school districts in Texas. Unpublished doctoral dissertation, University of North Texas, Denton.

McKenzie, R.B., & Lee, D. R. (1998). Managing through incentives. New York: Oxford University Press.

Miller, E. C. (Ed.) (1977). Motivating with money: Edward E. Lawler, III's views. New York: AMACOM.

National Association of Secondary School Principals. (1970). The principalship: Job specifications and salary considerations for the 70's. Washington, DC: Author.

National Association of Secondary School Principals. (1993). Salaries paid principals and assistant principals 1992–1993. Reston, VA: Author.

National Education Association Research Division (1970). Salary schedules for principals (Report 1970–R5). Washington, DC: Author.

Odden, A. R., & Conley, S. (1992). Restructuring teacher compensation systems. In A. R. Odden (Ed.), Rethinking school finance: An agenda for the 1990s (pp. 41–96). San Francisco: Jossey-Bass.

Picus, L. O. (1992). Using incentives to promote school improvement. In A. R. Odden (Ed.), Rethinking school finance: An agenda for the 1990s (pp. 166–200). San Francisco: Jossey-Bass

Pigford, A. B. (1993). Women in school leadership: Survival and advancement guidebook. Lancaster, PA: Technonic Publishing, Co.

Polachek, S. W., & Siebert, W. S. (1993). The economics of earnings. Cambridge: Cambridge University Press.

Pounder, D. (1988). The male/female salary differential for school administrators: Implications for career patterns and placement of women. Educational Administration Quarterly, 24, 5–19.

Robinson, G. E., & Brown, M. H. (1990). School salaries 1989–90. Principal, 69, 59–63.

Thomas, J. D. (1998). The relationship of selected wage criteria to administrative salaries in the public schools of New Jersey. Unpublished doctoral dissertation, University of North Texas, Denton.

Tracy, S., & Sheehan, R. (1987). Factors accounting for salary differentials. Paper presented at the Annual Meeting of the American Educational Research Association.

U.S. Department of Education (1993). School and staffing in the U.S.: A statistical profile, 1990–91 (NCE 593–146) Washington, DC: Office of Educational Research and Improvement.

Vroom, V. H. (1964). Work and motivation. New York: Wiley.

Whitaker, K. S., & Hein, A. (1981). Principals' perceptions of female capabilities in school administration. Journal of Research and Development in Education, 25, 40–50.

Young, I. P. (1988). Administrator salaries. In R. A. Gorton, G. T. Schneider, & J. C. Fischer, (Eds.), Encyclopedia of school administration and supervision. Phoenix, AZ: Oryx Press.

The Identification of Correlates Impacting Effective Curriculum Revision and Educators' Perceptions of the Pursuant Project Effectiveness

JUDY A. JOHNSON

INTRODUCTION

School districts across the nation have begun revising instructional programs in an effort to meet society's demands for a twenty-first-century workforce. Amidst the call for "educational reform," major issues of contention and concern are centering around the need for review and revision of the educational curriculum offered by many school districts across the nation. Determining what these needs are, how to address them, and how to revise instructional programming sits in the laps of many building principals. Often these building principals find themselves at the center of a controversy they did not want, do not deserve, and cannot fix. Yet, they are charged with full responsibility for this "revision of the curriculum." Many times these same educational leaders have not had adequate preparation for, nor do they have a full understanding of, what is expected with regard to this specific educational reform effort called for by "curriculum revision" projects. This demand for change to meet the needs of a twenty-first-century educational program is challenging even the best educational leaders.

SUMMARY OF LITERATURE REVIEW

Within the literature review, three major premises were presented. First, society perpetuates itself with educational programming, i.e., the content and methodology of instruction referenced as educational curriculum. Second, the society and culture served by an educational community dictate the needs, obligations, and responsibilities expected of the educational program. Third, systemic change, as in the form of transitioning educational curriculum, is difficult at best and controversial at worst. Cognizant of this premise, therefore, the view that involvement of all stakeholders, es-

Judy A. Johnson, Murray State University

pecially the individuals who will be directly involved with the instruction of students, is an especially vital piece in the move toward successful curriculum revision for the next century. These three elements combine to offer a strong foundational base from which educators at all levels can begin to address what is taught in all grade levels, the needs of a respondent society, and the changing roles of classroom practitioners.

Borrowman (1989) stated that education is the process by which individuals gain knowledge, skills, values, habits, and attitudes. Societal mores, cultural norms, and practical needs compel the incorporation of various components of learning and information. Hence, the educational curriculum is vitally important to societal success and may become extremely controversial when conflicting views emerge.

A traditionally accepted view of educational curriculum states that it is the information that should be taught with the underlying purpose of "standardizing" the behaviors of the society through educating the young in the traditions and rituals of that culture (Beyer & Liston, 1996; Borrowman, 1989; Glatthorn, 1987; Gwynn & Chase, 1969; Tanner & Tanner, 1995). Likewise, Glatthorn (1987) offered that beliefs and behaviors of each ethnic group or geographical area were developed in order to foster and teach children specific skills necessary for the transition from childhood to adulthood, thereby sustaining or advancing the convictions of that culture. In the same vein, but addressing the need for change, Purpel (1989) proposed that the primary responsibility for children's learning was determined by parents, but as society became more complex, the need for specialized learning grew, necessitating more formal training. It is obvious, therefore, that the curriculum, or what educational institutions mandate as topics of learning, must meet the needs and current demands of the culture, the society, and the expectations of the population being served. To this end, the educational reform process, in this study focusing on the educational curriculum, is still undergoing review, revision, and constant change.

James B. MacDonald's (1975) work (as cited in Beyer & Liston, 1996) suggested that in "many ways, all curriculum design and development is political in nature." And continuing in that line of reasoning, Olson and Rothman (1993) offered that while the "last decade has been one of the richest and most exciting in American education, (with regard to changes in educational programming and instructional methodology) the . . . fragmented, isolationist manner in which many of the reform movements were implemented brought about no lasting change." Substantiating further the view that change was and must continue to occur despite overt resistance, various authors (Henderson & Hawthorne, 1995; Jelinek, 1978; Kallen, 1996; Patterson, 1997; Toch & Daniel, 1996; Wagner, 1998) presented strong arguments that outdated strategies had to be discarded and ineffectual methodology eliminated. Concurring with these views that change was not only necessary but imminent Scott (1994) declared that curriculum revision projects of the past twenty years had in reality been dismal failures with a high cost to taxpayers, students, and educators.

Monson and Monson (1993) presented the need for collaborative, sanctioned revision by all stakeholders with an emphasis on the performance of teacher leaders. Brandt (1995) concurred with this view as he stated that the educational community must include those not usually considered to be at the leading edge of school reform initiatives. Hargreaves (1995) and Kyriakides (1997) both emphasized the importance of creating coordinated efforts which supported a modification of teachers' roles in the policy revision as it related to curriculum review and revision. Despite the fact that the emergent view of teachers' roles is often in conflict with the traditional view of teachers' performance (Monson & Monson, 1993; Hargreaves, 1994; Scott, 1994), the leadership roles of teachers are becoming more prevalent, more dominant, and more demanding. The queries facing the educational community, therefore, revolve around what reforms will be implemented, what process will be used, and how to make the revisions effective and sustaining. The review of literature substantiated the concern that until the parameters of curriculum revision (as an educational reform effort) are defined and understood, the process will suffer from failure and confusion for decades to come.

BACKGROUND OF THE STUDY

As in many states during the 1990s, educational reform efforts in Missouri addressed educational curriculum revision which had become closely tied to school district's accreditation process, assessment procedures, and staff evaluations. Pleasing the constituencies, parents, business, and communities, while simultaneously addressing test scores, community values, and student needs, found principals and teachers torn between understanding what to present, how to teach, and when to test. The overall expectation, however, was to "jump in" and revise the instructional curriculum, thereby addressing the outcry for school reform to improve our schools. Excellent materials were available; good resources were developed; professional development was heavily emphasized. Why then were so many curriculum revision projects considered a "bust" when evaluated by the administrative teams or community steering committees? Test scores did not indicate strong improvement; in fact, in many cases they were considered inadequate or even worse, disastrous. Teacher morale was down. Communities were in an uproar about "changing what their kids were taught." While some districts were experiencing tremendous success in the curriculum revision projects and the subsequent assessment procedures, others were experiencing total lack of improvement. There did not appear to be a correlation between amount of money spent and success of the curriculum revision projects, nor did there appear to be a relationship to the geographic or economic status of the districts experiencing success. The reasons for the lack of improvement were as varied as the school districts or community members with whom one spoke. What was the difference?

Based upon the anecdotal review of Missouri's curriculum reform initiative and the review of literature accentuating the purpose of the educational curriculum, questions began to arise. While several primary research questions were developed, an overview of noteworthy areas included ten primary research questions, two primary hypotheses, and four sub-hypotheses.

RESEARCH QUESTIONS AND GUIDING HYPOTHESES

The purpose of the study was to identify correlates which affect successful curriculum revision in schools located within the Southeastern Quadrant of Missouri. The goal was to identify factors common in schools which have implemented (or were currently undergoing) curriculum revision projects.

Research questions that guided the investigation and the ensuing development of the research tool are listed below.

1. What determined the "success" of curriculum revision projects?
2. What determines the effect of specific characteristics/correlates have on a curriculum revision project?
3. Can these identified correlates be integrated/introduced into all school programs?
4. What are the major factors impacting curriculum revision?
5. What is the purpose of the curriculum revision process?
6. Do teacher attitudes/backgrounds have an impact on the curriculum revision process?
7. Do the procedures used to implement curricular revision have an impact on the success of the implementation?
8. To what extent does the "pre-service" training have an effect on the success or failure of the curricular revision?
9. Why is curricular revision necessary?
10. What is the purpose underlying the Missouri standards for curriculum revision.

The dependent variable addressed in this study was the effective implementation curriculum revision processes within school districts. The ten research topics were representative of the independent variables used within the study.

Hypotheses

From these initial research questions, two primary hypotheses were formulated as the controlling premises of the study. Sub-hypotheses were also developed to gain further clarification.

Primary Hypotheses

1. There will be no identifiable, specified factors which are common in districts effectively implementing successful curriculum revision projects.
2. There will not be correlates which are consistently noted affecting successful curriculum revision as derived from data collection of respondents who are active educational practitioners.

Sub-hypotheses

1. There will be no significant difference in responses from participants with regard to subject area and/or grade level teaching assignments.
2. There will be no significant difference in responses from participants with respect to gender of respondent.
3. There will be no significant difference in responses from participants with regard to professional tenure.
4. There will be no significant difference in responses from participants in relation to the level of educational attainment.

GENERAL OVERVIEW OF THE STUDY

Based on this initial examination of the topic, the research study was developed. The purpose of the study was to determine what, if any, key elements would affect successful curriculum revision projects. The goal of the study was to determine correlates of successful programs which would enable teachers and administrators to progress through the revision process and culminate the project with a strong instructional program and a useable curriculum. The study was conducted in a two-year doctoral research project concluding in the spring of 1999. The findings offered significant opportunity for further study, knowledge for practicing administrators and teachers, and information for teacher and principal preparation programs. Conclusions offer methods and means of improving the effectiveness of curriculum revision programs. Since it is obvious that education will continue to change and curriculum will perpetually alter, this information is of vital importance regarding principles of effective curriculum revision to address the demands for school reform across the nation.

Limitations of the Study

While addressing a concern of nationwide significance, this study had specific limitations that affected the generalization of findings. Qualifying factors which impacted the study included the following: 1) The research encompasses a relatively small geographical area, 2) The number of participants and the number/size of schools participating in the study were limited and located solely within the State of Missouri, 3) The demographic factors structured the style and focus of the entire study, 4) The selection of respondents was specified in the methodology of the survey coordinator; however, the actual request for participants was in the control of the building administrator or district representative, and 5) While educational change is occurring throughout the country, this study specifically focused on the Missouri Standards and the effects of those provisos.

These limitations will impact the generalization of the study. The information elicited, however, from practitioners in the field yields substantive data that lends itself to further investigative efforts.

Procedure

The research design focused on perspectives of practitioners. The study design was a quantitative analysis using a Likert scale response checklist. Analyses of 28 response options were combined with 6 constructed response opportunities blending a quantitative analyses with a qualitative review. To further substantiate the data, 4 focus groups were interviewed with general patterns and themes evaluated. The focus group participants were selected from school districts not participating in the print survey instrument.

Instrumentation

Instrumentation used for data collection was a differential sliding scale checklist. Developed by the investigator, the survey was constructed from a practitioners' viewpoint responding to current practices within schools and from speakers/presenters' topics on curriculum revision. Areas addressed in the survey were noted throughout the review of literature as having direct influence on educational programs and were identified as having direct impact on curriculum reform projects.

A total of 28 items were included in the research instrument. The survey addressed 4 areas of study including school district/respondent demographics, in-service components of the curriculum revision process, district involvement/personal involvement in the curriculum revision process, and baseline knowledge levels of the respondents. The research tool addressed the following 10 general areas: 1) The size of school district, 2) Tenure of administration/faculty, 3) In-service opportunities, 4) Teacher involvement (personal involvement), 5) Design structure of the curriculum revision process, 6) Baseline knowledge of the participants, 7) Baseline curriculum status, 8) Demographics of the professional staff, 9) Demographics of the community, and 10) Professional assignment. Each section then became more specific. The demographic section sought information relative to professional assignment, educational experience, and training. The composite data were disaggregated by gender. In-service components included questions regarding amount of in-service provided, method of dissemination, time and travel allotments, and overall perspective/attitude regarding the in-service training procedures. The survey solicited details with respect to involvement of district/building level personnel and the respondents' personal level of knowledge regarding the curriculum revision process. The research document concluded with an open-ended response option for additional comments. Focus groups were conducted at 4 school districts identified in the initial selection process. These districts represented the 4 size (student population) ranges contained within the study. The primary research questions prompting the study were used as discussion coordinates. Demographic information and specific questions noted on within the written survey were also included in the focus group discussion guides. Participants' responses were noted by the interviewer and transcribed into general patterns and themes of generalization.

The triangulation process among the 3 sets of data, numerical statistics from the survey, constructed responses from the survey, and focus group responses from the non-surveyed districts, were analyzed for emergent patterns and themes.

Population Sample

The study sample consisted of educational practitioners employed by public school districts within the Southeastern Quadrant of Missouri. The Southeastern Quadrant of Missouri was described in the Definitions section of the study corresponding to the area identified by the Missouri State Department of Education The sample population was determined by listing the counties located within the pre-determined geographical area and identifying school districts located within these counties. A total of 147 districts were included in the initial research sample. Districts were listed alphabetically, grouped according to size of student population, and chosen for participation by a random numerical designation. A total of 49 school districts were specified representing 33.3% of the total school districts located within the designated geographical area.

Data Collection

Initial information letters were sent to superintendents of selected school districts with a request for participation. Upon receipt of participation approval, surveys were sent to building principals for their response and dissemination to staff members. The breakdown of instructional staff was comprised of one building level administrator, one secondary educator from the areas of English/social studies, math/science, and physical education/fine arts/practical arts. The upper elementary grades or middle grades, 5 through 8 were represented as were the lower elementary grades 1 through 4 with one teacher from each division. This selection of the 49 school districts identified to participate provided a possible total of 294 practicing educators for initial response to the survey.

Administrators, or district representatives, were asked to distribute the surveys on a random basis. Distribution was accomplished by submitting the survey to teachers on the third preparation period/block of the day, or as close as possible to that preparation time. Of the 49 school districts identified and requested to participate, a total of 41 superintendents responded in the affirmative. This represented an 84% participation rate. Based upon this agreement for participation, a total of 246 surveys were submitted to practitioners. Of the initial mailing, the total return was 190 respondents, a 77% return rate. Twenty-seven of the respondents were central office, building level, or district level administrators. The remaining 163 respondents were classroom teachers.

Data Collection Strategies

Subjects were asked to complete a confidential survey directed toward information about curriculum revision (research instrument). Respondents were identified only by numerical assignment. The investigator provided a letter to each participant providing explanation, permission notation, and instructions for completion of the research tool (a confidential survey instrument). Each respondent was asked to return a sealed envelope to the coordinator, and all results were returned in a self-addressed, stamped envelope.

Data Analysis

The data analysis was a statistical assessment using a frequency tabulation of all the items. This was carried out using percents of frequencies. Each item having to do with perception of the effectiveness of the curriculum revision component was treated as an interval level variable. A series of one-way analyses of variance (ANOVA) was carried out to determine how the various demographics and in-service histories of the in-service related to the perception of the program. All tests were carried out to the .05 level.

All comparison of qualitative data with quantitative data was comprised of reviewing information. Generalization of patterns, themes, and recurrent perceptions were noted.

RESULTS OF STUDY

This research study focused on 10 basic research questions developed in response to the Missouri curriculum revision mandates. These questions addressed broad areas of purpose, process, correlational factors, and practitioners' perceptions. Current literature was reviewed for perspectives relating to these questions, and primary hypotheses were subsequently developed to guide the research project. Areas for inquiry addressed characteristics of curriculum revision, practitioners' perceptions of the process, factors impacting revision procedures, and the successful implementation of the overall procedure. Based on this information, a review of current literature elicited four primary areas of interest: practitioner demographics, in-service components, district level or personal (individual) involvement in the curriculum revision process, and perception of overall effectiveness. The research was then conducted to determine if the null hypotheses developed for study direction could be validated or disproved. Areas of significance were duly noted. The following sections present the results.

Demographic Components

Hypotheses guiding the demographic section of the study proposed that there would be no significant difference in perceptions of educators with regard to professional assignment, gender, professional training level, or educational tenure. The resulting data supported this hypothesis that there was no significant difference between educators in relation to their perceptions of curriculum revision effectiveness with regard to professional teaching assignment such as grade/age level, subject area taught, or combination of those two components. Similarly, with respect to the gender of the study participants, there was no significant difference in the responses or perceptions.

Continuing in the vein of demographic data, the domain of professional training levels comparing baccalaureate, master's, and above a master's degree recipients did not elicit a significant difference in the practitioner's perceptions of effective curriculum revision.

The final area submitted for review in the demographic portion of the research study was educational tenure, time spent in the field of teaching and/or administration. Again, this area did not demonstrate a significant occurrence of differing perceptions with regard to the process of curriculum revision.

In-service Components

Areas of study within the in-service segment of the investigation cited seven broad areas. These encompassed: 1) provision of training, 2) type of expertise used for training, 3) consistency of review, 4) type of review throughout the revision process, 5) type of information for curriculum models, 6) type of training implemented, and 7) length of time provided for training. Statistical analysis yielded areas of significance in this piece of the study.

In-service training appeared to be prevalent throughout the districts surveyed. Seventy-seven percent of the respondents indicated that in-service training was provided.

The statistical test result of .05 further supported the perspective that this provision of training (in-service) was a significant component in the respondents' perceptions of effective revision processes. Furthermore, 3 additional areas of study were also determined to have rankings at the level of statistical significance with regard to the perceptions of educators and curriculum revision. Respondents confirmed at the .02 level of significance that *out-of-district* expertise was provided in the in-service format. In-service training using *in-district* expertise established a .002 range in comparison with *in-district assistance* and *consistent review* ranges at the .005 levels. This information appears to strongly corroborate the initial inference that in-service training did have a significant impact on the respondents' perceptions of effectiveness in the curriculum revision process.

In contrast, *style* of in-service training or *informational structure* was not determined to be of significance. Out-of-district visits, outside curriculum models, printed research materials, or video and interactive presentations were not determined to be at the level of significance. Out-of-district visits and curriculum models were at the .91 range. Printed research materials, video and interactive presentations ranged from .91 to .93 indicating no strong consequence. A point of note, however. The video and interactive presentations did occur at the .08 level indicating this area might be in need for further study or review.

Concluding the in-service section, the elements of time frames and length of time provided for the in-service training offered information for further examination. The time frame suggesting hourly ranges of 1 to over 20 hours affirmed a level of significance at the .004 level. This was in direct contrast to the time frame of hours, weeks, and days that resulted in a .86 statistical range. Respondents offered the view that shorter durations of time (hours) provided a more effective training scenario than longer time frames (days) with less frequent reviews/discussions. The participants' reports suggested that increased effectiveness occurs when the training procedures are in shorter lengths of time with consistent, periodic reviews in-district.

District Level/Personal (Individual) Involvement

The final portion of the print survey focused on district and personal (individual) involvement by the practitioners in the curriculum revision process. Within the review of literature, areas of note suggested that there were categorical areas, which strongly impacted the success of a curriculum revision process (Scott, 1994; Brandt, 1995; Thompson, 1994). Changing roles of teachers, isolationism of teaching and curricular development, lack of collaboration between stakeholders, and a minimum of understanding regarding curriculum revision as a whole were the key components which may create a negative response toward curriculum revision projects (Scott, 1994; Brandt, 1995; Thompson, 1994). The results of the research in this area offered pertinent data related to these views.

Areas determined to offer no significant differences included personnel (people involved) primarily involved in the development and/or implementation of the initial procedure and/or culminating process. Nor did the initiation of procedural format impact the individual perceptions of the respondents with regard to the overall effectiveness of the revision process. Results did indicate strong statistical significance, however, in areas concerning personal (individual) understanding and personal (individual) involvement with the in-service training and the active revision process. Respondents affirmed that there was a considerable difference in their reactions prior to and following in-service training opportunities. Requesting information about proficiency of curriculum revision processes *before* and *after* in-service training derived a .001 statistical result. The overall outcome of in-service training offered a 30% increase in participants' responses with relation to their personal (individual) proficiency level in curriculum revision. This would indicate that providing in-service training for curriculum revision is vitally important to the successful implementation of the curriculum revision project.

This increase in effectiveness, is supported by the level of direct involvement with the final curriculum revision procedures. Participants were asked to identify their perceptions regarding personal knowledge (of curriculum revision processes) and level of involvement with respect to the district's curriculum revision process. Again, a strong indication of statistical significance was presented with a .001 range in the familiarity address and a .005 level in the direct involvement segment was established. These areas offer support to the view that direct involvement and ownership of the curriculum revision process will increase overall effectiveness of the project.

Overall Effectiveness of Curriculum Revision Process

Results substantiate that there was no statistical significance demonstrated by the curriculum revision process as it relates to direct classroom instruction. One hundred four survey respondents indicated that they had made modification in classroom instruction. Sixty-four stated that they had not made changes in direct classroom instruction. The statistical result of this area was at the .55 level (significance noted at the .05 level). This area may need further review to determine if the curriculum revision process is having the desired effect for direct instruction.

Qualitative Results

To establish validity of the quantitative results, a qualitative component was added to the investigation. These results corroborated the survey results. Research questions were used as discussion guides with practitioners' responses catalogued into the four general areas of the written survey.

The focus group analyses echoed the confidential survey results. First, an overwhelming majority of focus group participants suggested that hourly training sessions with consistent review by a committee or coordinator offered the most effective type of revision process. Additionally, significant improvement in personal knowledge increased after participation through in-service training. The respondents also emphasized ownership, involvement, and understanding of the need for curriculum revision. Finally, the focus groups responses' confirmed the quantitative results addressing the issues that direct class instruction and educational methodology did not appear to be significantly altered via the curriculum revision procedures.

CONCLUSIONS OF THE STUDY

Based upon the data gathered from this research study, the following conclusions have been defined addressing the primary and sub-hypotheses.

1. There are identifiable, specified factors which are common in districts implementing successful curriculum revision projects.
2. There are correlates that are consistently noted affecting successful curriculum revision as derived from data collection of respondents who are active educational practitioners.

   With regard to areas specified by the sub-hypotheses areas, the following results were found:
3. There were no significant differences in responses from participants with regard to subject area and/or grade level teaching assignments.
4. There were no significant differences in responses from participants with respect to gender of respondent.
5. There were no significant differences in responses from participants with regard to professional tenure.
6. There were no significant differences in responses from participants in relation to the level of educational attainment.

Specific areas indicating statistical significance included components of the in-service/training procedures, personal level of understanding (on an individual basis), and familiarity/involvement with the process and procedures of the revision project. In-service components specified the following:

1. In-service was vital.
2. Out-of-district expertise combined with in-district expertise was valuable.
3. In-district expertise and consistent review of the curriculum revision process strongly enhanced the overall project.
4. The importance of shorter periods of time for in-service training was considered to be significantly more effective than longer time frames.

Personal knowledge and involvement of the revision process was strongly noted. Practitioners' views on personal involvement with the project, and familiarity with the project prior to and during the actual curriculum rewriting, was directly related to the perceptions of the project's effectiveness. When the respondents clearly understood the revision process, procedures, and project outcomes, their perception of the project effectiveness was significantly higher than those respondents who did not indicate strong levels of knowledge or outcome expectations.

A point of significance to the researcher was in the area of classroom instruction. While 104 of the respondents confirmed that they had made some adjustment in direct classroom instruction, 64 of the respondents indicated that they had made no change in their instructional program. This area should receive further review, if indeed, the purpose of curricular revision is to improve direct instruction to students and achieve increased student performance.

RECOMMENDATIONS

On the basis of this research and investigation and the conclusions developed from prescribed data of the study, the following subsequent recommendations were developed. The study determined that there are identifiable, specific factors that are common to all school districts, which are effectively implementing successful curriculum revision. It was further noted that there are specific correlates related to effective curriculum revision which are consistently noted in responds obtained from practicing Missouri educators. It is recommended that practicing administrators and/or curriculum directors note the areas of significance as indicated by the participants of the study. In-service training should be provided and adjusted to the time frame suggestions as noted in the results section. Concurrently, the changing roles of teacher leaders and their professional need to know and understand the full picture of curriculum revision should be acknowledged. Teacher involvement, as individuals as well as in committees, should be integrated throughout the change process. Furthermore, consistent review of the process, an on-going discussion of needs, issues, and progress should be maintained throughout the project. Acceptance of the responsibility and leadership of the classroom practitioner is a must.

While this research confirmed basic areas in which the curriculum revision process can be improved, one area of concern remains. There does not appear to be long lasting, substantive change in relation to curriculum revision projects. It appears however, that the purpose of curriculum revision needs to be more clearly established. Then, supporting the classroom practitioner as the driving force behind the needed changes, the curriculum revision process might have a stronger, more significant impact on changing classroom instruction. These areas need further study to determine exactly what and how to utilize educational curriculum revision projects to better enhance student performance in the classroom.

REFERENCES

Beyer, L.E. & Liston, D.P. (1996). Curriculum in conflict: Social visions, educational agenda, and progressive school reforms. New York: Teachers College Press Columbia University.

Borrowman, M.L. (1989). Curriculum. The world book encyclopedia. (Vol. 6). (pp. 85–106). Chicago, IL: World Book, Inc.

Glatthorn, A. (1987). Curriculum renewal. Alexandria, VA: Association for Supervision and Curriculum Development.

Hargreaves, A. (1994). Changing teachers, changing times: Teacher's work and culture in the postmodern age. New York: Teacher College Press.

Hargreaves, A. (1995). Renewal in the age of paradox. Educational Leadership, 52(7), 1-9.

Henderson, J. & Hawthorne, R (1995). Transformative curriculum leadership. Englewood Cliffs, NJ: Merrill Publishing Company.

Jelinek, J. (Ed.) (1978). Improving the human condition: A curricular response to critical responses. Washington, D.C.: Association of Supervision and Curriculum Development.

Kallen, D. (1996). Curriculum reform in secondary education: Planning, development, and implementation. European Journal of Education, 31(1), 43–56.

Kyriakides, L. (1997). Influences on primary teachers' practice: some problems for curriculum changes theory. British Educational Research Journal, 23(1), 1-8.

MacDonald, J.B. (1975). Curriculum and human interests. In W. Pinar (Ed.), Curriculum theorizing: The reconceptualist (pp. 283–294). Berkeley, CA: McCutchan.

Monson, M.P. & Monson, R.J. (1993). Who creates the curriculum: New roles for teachers. Educational Leadership, 2, 19–21.

Olson, L. (1997). Quality counts: A report card on the condition of public education in the 50 states. Spectrum: The Journal of State Government, 70(1), 16–21.

Olson, L., & Rothman, R. (1993). Roadmap to reform. Education Week, 12(30), ss13–ss17.

Patterson, J. (1997). Coming clean about organizational change: Leadership in the real world. Arlington, VA: American Association of School Administrators.

Purpel, D. (1972). Curriculum and the cultural revolution: A book of essays and readings. Berkley, CA: McCutcheon Publishing Corporation.

Scott, F.B. (1994). Integrating curriculum implementation and staff development. ERIC Clearinghouse on Educational Management, 67(3), 157–161.

Tanner, D. & Tanner, L. (1995). Curriculum development: Theory into practice. (3rd ed.). Columbus, OH: Prentice Hall Publishers.

Toch, T. & Daniel, M. (1996). Schools that work. U.S. News and World Report, 121 (4) 58–65.

Wagner, T. (1998). From compliance to collaboration. Education Week, 7(32), 40–45.

CREATING LEARNING COMMUNITIES AND CULTURES OF CHANGE

How Leadership Is Shared and Visions Emerge in the Creation of Learning Communities

KRISTINE A. HIPP and JANE B. HUFFMAN

"The most promising strategy for sustained, substantive school improvement is developing the ability of school personnel to function as professional learning communities" (DuFour & Eaker, 1998, p. xi). Although simple in concept, this latest call for hope is nonexistent in most schools. Following a five-year study of Coalition of Essential Schools, Muncey & McQuillan (1993) argued that,

> It is all the rage for people to say that the latest wave of reform will be the reform that's going to make the difference . . . our evidence suggests that even when there seems to be consensus that change is needed and even when dedicated and well-intentioned people are trying to bring it about, issues and problems—often unanticipated—arise that threaten and impede the change process almost from its inception . . . many lessons still need to be learned about achieving the ambitious aims of current reform efforts. (p. 489)

Fullan (1995, 2000) added that most school reform efforts have created overload and fragmentation, thereby resulting in a lack of coherence and meaning which continues to divert us from issues of greatest importance—teaching and learning. For instance, many governance structures have been designed to empower a greater number of staff in decision making, yet students fail to benefit. Efforts are often unrelated to curriculum and instructional issues, and systems are not aligned to focus on the process it takes to move students to higher levels of achievement (Fullan, 1995; Guskey & Peterson, 1993; Lindle, 1995/1996; Newmann & Wehlage, 1995). In the guise of teacher empowerment, "Traditional opportunities for teacher decision making have done little to advance the professionalism of teachers, or to involve them in critical educational concerns" (Brown, 1995, p. 337).

A more recent trend suggests that "change will require a radical reculturing of the school as an institution, and the basic redesign of the teaching profession" (Fullan, 1995). Reculturing is said to occur by developing work cultures that affect the core of

Kristine A. Hipp, Cardinal Stritch University
Jane B. Huffman, University of North Texas

the culture of schools, which will drive structural change. In an interview conducted by Dennis Sparks (1999), Ann Lieberman defined these cultures as professional learning communities, or "places in which teachers pursue clear, shared purposes for student learning, engage in collaborative activities to achieve their purposes, and take collective responsibility for students learning" (p. 53). To institutionalize this concept, she proposes the need to develop capacity through a community of leaders, which necessitates increased responsibility, greater decision making, and more accountability for results among all staff.

Beyond dispute, the preparation of school administrators is key. Educational administration programs need to prepare potential school leaders to move beyond issues of management and provide practical experiences that focus on people, particularly how to facilitate change centered on teaching and learning. Principals can make a difference indirectly in student learning by influencing internal school processes, engaging teachers to fully participate in decision-making, and developing a shared sense of responsibility on the part of all staff members to improve the conditions for learning in schools (Davis, 1998). The principal's most significant effect on student learning comes through his/her efforts to establish a vision of the school and goals related to the accomplishment of the vision (Hallinger & Heck, 1996 in Davis). Sharing leadership and aligning people to a vision is crucial and leads to a "leadership-centered culture . . . the ultimate act of leadership" (Kotter, 1990, p. 11).

Organizations learn only through individuals who learn (Senge, 1990, p. 139). Therefore, school leaders establish conditions that encourage new ways of thinking and interacting to build capacity and schoolwide commitment to a shared vision. Learning evolves and must engage and nurture interdependent thinking in an environment where all people are valued. "The organizations that will truly excel in the future will be the organizations that discover how to tap people's commitment and capacity to learn at all levels in an organization" (Senge, 1990, p. 4). Leaderships preparation programs must guide potential leaders in setting direction, aligning the energies of diverse groups of people, supporting the interdependency of its individuals, and empowering collaborative decision-making to actualize a shared vision. Further, school administrators need to change their paradigms of leadership. As Lambert (1998) stated in her book, <u>Building Leadership Capacity in Schools</u>,

> School leadership needs to be a broad concept that is separated from person, role, and a discrete set of individual behaviors. It needs to be embedded in the school community as a whole. Such a broadening of the concept of leadership suggests shared responsibility for a shared purpose of community. (p. 5)

The literature is replete with information defining professional learning communities and their characteristics (DuFour & Eaker, 1998; Hord, 1997; Louis & Kruse, 1995). Nonetheless, little is known as to how to create, much less sustain these communities of learning (Hord, 1997; Zempke, 1999). Zempke's interview with Peter Senge revealed the task to be more formidable than expected—"a slippery concept to put into practice" (p. 41). The challenge for educational leadership programs in the next millennium is to prepare students to move their school communities from concept to capability—a capability that is self-sustaining.

PURPOSE

In the initial stages of a five-year project, *Creating Communities of Continuous Inquiry and Improvement*, sponsored by the Southwest Educational Development Laboratory (SEDL), Hord (1997) engaged in an extensive review of the literature and found that schools operating as professional learning communities shared five common dimensions: shared and supportive leadership, shared vision and values, collective learning and application, supportive conditions, and shared practice. The purpose of this chapter is threefold: a) to present a theoretical framework that defines the concept of a professional learning community, b) to further describe the above-mentioned project and efforts underway to create professional learning communities, and c) to report the findings related to the interdependency of two dimensions (shared and supportive leadership and shared vision and values) and their effects on readiness for creating professional learning communities. This study was guided by the following questions:

1. In what ways do principals in high readiness schools share leadership, empower decision making, and inspire responsibility for a shared vision?
   a) Do these practices distinguish themselves from those exhibited by principals in low readiness schools?
2. Are practices in shared leadership, shared decision making, and visioning more inclusive among staff in high rather than low readiness schools?

The findings reported in this chapter reveal important data and direction for the preparation of school administrators about initiating the process of creating communities of learners.

THEORETICAL FRAMEWORK

In this study the theoretical framework is based on the work of Hord (1997). Among the many related definitions of professional learning communities, she focused on what Astuto and her colleagues (1993) labeled as *professional communities of learners*, "in which teachers in a school and its administrators seek and share learning and then act on what they learn" (p. 1). Five defining dimensions emerged from her extensive review of the literature, which include:

1. *Shared and supportive leadership:* School administrators participate democratically with teachers sharing power, authority and decision making.

2. *Shared vision and values:* Staff share visions for school improvement that have an undeviating focus on student learning, and are consistently referenced for the staff's work.
3. *Collective learning and application:* Staff's collective learning and application of the learnings (taking action) create high intellectual learning tasks and solutions to address student needs.
4. *Supportive conditions:* School conditions and capacities support the staff's arrangement as a professional learning organization.
5. *Shared personal practice:* Peers review and give feedback on teacher instructional practice in order to increase individual and organizational capacity.

This chapter focuses specifically on the dimensions of shared and supportive leadership and shared vision and values in the context of high and low readiness schools. Schools that distinguished themselves as high or low readiness appear on a continuum as measured by Hord's School Professional Staff as Learning Community questionnaire (1997). Table 1 illustrates the range of practice in these district schools from highest to lowest ratings.

Hord's theory reflects the work of several researchers (Kleine-Kracht, 1993; Leithwood, Leonard, & Sharratt, 1997; Louis & Kruse, 1995; Sergiovanni, 1994; Snyder, Acker-Hocevar & Snyder, 1996;). New conceptions of leadership are defined that eliminate hierarchies, and promote expanded roles and responsibilities among staff,

TABLE I. Range of Practice in School Districts.

Shared and Supportive Leadership	School administrators consistently involve the staff in discussing and making decisions about most school issues.	Administrators never share information with the staff nor provide opportunities to be involved in decision making.
	Administrators involve the whole staff.	Administrators do not involve any staff.
Shared Visions and Values	Visions for improvement are discussed by the entire staff such that consensus and a shared vision results.	Visions for improvement held by the staff are widely divergent.
	Visions for improvement are always focused on students, and learning and teaching.	Visions for improvement do not target students and teaching and learning.
	Visions for improvement target high quality learning experiences for all students.	Visions for improvement do not include concerns about the quality of learning experiences.

empower decision making, and attend to the human side of the organization. These images reflect a principal's belief in the capacity of teachers to respond to the needs of students by establishing conditions that support continuous learning among its professionals. Further, the conception of a learning community embraces shared values and visions that "lead to binding norms of behavior that the staff supports" (Hord, 1997, p. 3) in a climate made possible by trust and respect.

METHODOLOGY

Overview of Project

This study is part of an extensive five-year exploration into the development of professional learning communities, which began in 1995. The study is being funded by the Department of Education through the Southwest Educational Development Laboratory (SEDL), one of 10 research and development laboratories located across the United States from 1995 to 1997, Shirley Hord, SEDL program director, and her staff (1997) reviewed the literature and identified five interactive dimensions of a professional learning community: shared and supportive leadership, shared vision and values, collective learning and application, supportive conditions, and shared personal practice. Next, the researchers investigated schools and identified one school in each of the five-state region, which qualified under these dimensions. Interviews with teachers, administrators and others working with the schools uncovered only part of the story as to how these learning communities emerged.

In August of 1997, Hord invited 30 Co-developers, who were selected for their interest and expertise as change agents, to participate in this project. They represented school districts, state departments of education, regional laboratories and higher education in nine states from the Midwest, southeast, northwest, and predominantly Texas, Louisiana, Oklahoma, New Mexico, and Arkansas. During the 1997–1998 school year, this diverse group of educators met three times in Austin developing trust, pooling knowledge and talents, developing facilitation tools, engaging in a series of group processes, and experiencing the challenges and excitement of coming to "be" a communities of learners. By September of 1998, each Co-developer selected a school whose staff was interested in becoming a professional learning community. These K–12 schools represented rural, suburban, and urban settings and ranged in their perceived level of readiness toward becoming professional learning communities.

In September of 1998, the fourth year began with a joint meeting involving SEDL staff, 20 returning Co-developers, and a principal and teacher representative from each study site. The Co-developers and SEDL staff continue to meet approximately three times a year, whereas, principals and teachers return on an annual basis.

Data Collection/Analysis

Phase 1

Once school sites were selected, principals and teacher representatives from 19 schools were interviewed by telephone using a semi-structured interview protocol designed around Hord's five-dimensional framework of a professional learning community (Bogdan & Biklen, 1992). One school was eliminated from the study due to a move on the part of the Co-developer leaving 19 schools in total. The 38 interviews were audiotaped, transcribed, and analyzed by a six-member research team (five Co-developers and one SEDL staff member) using a series of inter-rater reliability techniques in a systematic process to achieve trustworthiness (Leedy, 1997). The five Co-developers each selected one of Hord's five dimensions and coded all 38 transcripts for recurring themes (Miles & Huberman, 1984). The analyses were then reviewed and validated by a second researcher for agreement and refinement. Next, the researchers met to share their analysis of each dimension, to work in pairs to study the transcriptions, and to place the schools in an initial sort of high, mid, and low readiness. Secondly, each pair developed distinguishing descriptors for high and low readiness schools. The research team compared paired sorts and engaged in "round the clock" dialogue to ultimately place schools within two clusters—High Readiness Level (high and mid-high level schools) and Low Readiness Level (mid, mid-low and low level schools). The analysis was based on a wholistic interpretation of the dimensions of a professional learning community.

Phase 2

In June of 1999, teachers and principals returned to SEDL and were interviewed for evidence of the five dimensions existing within their schools. The 38 interviews were analyzed by the research team; however, during the second phase, the team analyzed the data per assigned dimensions and again, generated emerging themes. They reconvened and discussed distinguishing characteristics across schools and found the previous placement of remained intact. Phase 1 and 2 data sets were used for this study which included 76 interviews. The evidence in this study illuminated a contrast between schools exhibiting characteristics of a high-level of readiness following the first year of involvement, and those schools that were less ready in developing a learning community. Although most schools were not at a high level of readiness in this early stage of the study, seven schools demonstrated characteristics of high-level readiness with regard to shared and supportive leadership, shared vision and values, and inclusiveness of staff. The primary purpose of this preliminary investigation was to capture the stories of these learning communities as they emerge.

FINDINGS: DISTINGUISHING EVIDENCE BETWEEN HIGH AND LOW READINESS SCHOOLS

The discussion of findings distinguishes the evidence between high and low readiness schools for creating professional learning communities. Specifically, it addresses the following questions. In what ways do principals in high readiness schools share leadership, empower decision making, and inspire responsibility for a shared vision? Do these practices distinguish themselves from those exhibited by principals in low readiness schools? Are practices in shared leadership, shared decision making, and visioning more inclusive of all staff in high versus low readiness schools? Applying direction from Hord's (1997) model, this section is organized around the following sections: shared leadership, inspired responsibility for a shared vision, and empowered decision-making.

Shared Leadership

An analysis of staff efforts in developing a professional learning community around shared leadership revealed the following interactive themes: capacity building, creating conditions for participation, and empowered decision making. Evidence related to empowered decision making will follow the shared vision section to reflect the natural sequence of developing communities of learners and leaders emerging from the data. High and low readiness schools varied significantly in shared leadership.

High Readiness Schools

In *high readiness schools*, principals mirrored new conceptions of leadership. They were proactive; chameleon-like it seemed—intuitively sensing where support was needed, when to stand back and when to take the lead, revealing the interactive nature between leadership and followership. Principals built on the strengths of their teachers. They had high expectations that focused on student learning and were purposeful in building capacity. One principal commented, "The job is simply too big for just one principal. We as a school do better at problem solving and meeting the needs of kids when enhanced by a meeting of the minds." At another school, a teacher revealed specifics,

> The principal models what she expects teachers to do—read, study, discuss common goals, share, attend professional development, and grow professionally. The support is there . . . and choices. She is building a team of experts full of confidence in their abilities . . . validated as professionals.

Teachers who asserted leadership were growing in knowledge, skill and number. As one teacher emphasized, "Some leaders are designed by position, others have stepped forward to take on leadership roles. One teacher used the metaphor of having an "anchor at each grade level that can really make a difference." On a broader scale another teacher a described her perceptions at a deeper level of shared leadership,

> I would almost say that we are a community of leaders. What I see in the function of the community spirit to be is to identify strengths and divide responsibilities up amongst different members of the faculty . . . and defer to each other for those areas where we might have expertise. So, it is not unusual, for example, for her [the principal] to turn right around and come to me for questions in my area of expertise. And I see that happening all over the staff.

High readiness schools were characterized by schools that were reculturing as reflected in the literature (Fullan, 1995, 2000). Roles and responsibilities are being embraced more deeply throughout the organization. Structures were established that enhanced the values, beliefs, and goals of the organization with a clear focus on student learning. The growing pains of change were revealed through one principal,

> The faculty has more power than ever before. At first the teachers were overwhelmed with their new roles, but now they enjoy taking responsibility. I keep emphasizing, 'It's your school.' I want them to feel empowered and engaged in all aspects of the school.

Teachers did not view principals as abdicating their power, but recognized the emerging nature of changing roles,

> It's envisioning leadership so that you realize that this person is still a strong leader even though they are not the one making all the decisions and directing everything, because it requires strength of leadership to stand behind you and your decisions. I consider a strength of leadership to say, 'You are the expert. You make the decisions and I will support you.'

Principals in high readiness schools took the risk of "letting go" and appeared to believe in the capability of their teachers. Leaders were apparent in multiple structures in these schools—working systematically to establish greater teamwork at a whole school level. Beyond leadership teams, which were present in every school in the study, others included: grade level and subject area teams, team leaders, special projects coordinators, curriculum specialists, teacher facilitators, trainer of trainers, committee chairs, team leaders. Structures were organic and relate to the unique context of each school. There was a common perception that leadership is emerging and lies deep within the school, both formally and informally. There is also the perception that the principal was key in establishing the conditions that make it successful.

Principals were proactive and innovative. They "planted seeds," encouraged teachers to initiate change, and provided resources to make things happen. They had creative ways of getting around the rules instead of just saying 'no' or vetoing suggestions. Teachers were apt to embrace leadership responsibility as compared to those in low readiness schools because conditions were established for trust and respect. One teacher described this with confidence,

> The steps that I've taken as a teacher leader in the unit and as a perceived teacher leader on staff will model activities that are necessary to build trust within the staff. The great part of that is that my principal understands and accepts my role.

Teachers were made to feel like professionals. Principals depended on teachers for their input, guidance and ideas. They were keenly aware of what teachers were addressing with students and how they were working on campus goals. Teachers weren't granted authority; they had it—in a "power to" rather than "power over" sense. Team building was a part of the school culture, as teachers noted,

> We are doing a number of things to create team building to enhance the level of trust within staff members, and that willingness to discuss areas and issues head-on, as opposed to engaging in parking lot conversations. Trust is the first level at getting to a professional learning community.
>
> Leadership teams facilitate strategic planning processes. . . . They trained facilitators from all grade levels and disciplines to use consensus.

Low Readiness Schools

In *low readiness schools*, teachers viewed shared leadership more suspiciously than their counterparts in high readiness schools. It was reported that teachers were content to exhibit leadership in their classrooms, but wary of accepting responsibility at the building level. One teacher expressed, "We have opportunities for leadership and you go because she asks you and you hate not to go." Others indicated that shared leadership existed in their schools, but were unable to offer examples in practice. Most examples for shared leadership were evidenced in a position, a person who was second in command, or more limited in single structures such as the school's leadership team. Evidence suggested that teachers were empowered to deal with managerial and classroom tasks, but were minimally involved in teaching and learning at the school level or with organizational issues in general. One teacher finally expressed that "minute responsibilities by certain individuals were allowed," after some real probing.

The style of principals in low readiness schools were expressed through teachers as varied, ranging from directive to laissez faire to focusing on managing rather than leading. One teacher hesitantly spoke to the varying level of commitment to shared leadership in her school,

> I think we are still very much . . . uh . . . we are . . . that our leadership is still very much dominated by the principal. I feel that a lot of our older staff members have a difficult time blurring that line. They are not proactive. They are reactive. I feel that younger staff members are taking it upon themselves to share the leadership and broaden the scope.

Another teacher discussed that assertive teachers in his school asserted power, while others did not. Various socialization processes were tried unsuccessfully, attempting to regain a level of support and trust that once existed. Other comments related to principal autonomy and mixed messages,

> Our principal listens to suggestions but has the final word . . . He works a step ahead, not side-by-side.
>
> Our principal has the final word, but teachers pretty much have a voice in what goes on.

A more laissez faire style was also evident in some schools in terms of commitment or in the pretense of purposeful leadership. For instance, one teacher revealed the lack of principal enthusiasm for the SEDL project and the need for the Co-Developer and teachers to urge participation. "Commitment and trust are improving, but generally a climate of apathy regarding shared leadership exists. It is perceived as more responsibility and work." Another teacher reiterated the words of his principal: "Y'all decide how you want to do it. You know, however you want to do it is fine with me." Another school revealed different styles between building administrators—one focusing on leadership, and the other on management, "Our assistant principal is not as open to new ideas [as the principal]. I think he is more worried about procedure rather than results." A principal in another school concurred,

> I see management as the key component in shared leadership. Once persons under your charge understand philosophically, as well as theoretically, where you are, you tend to get more out of an ongoing process that will eventually be recognized in results and products.

Finally, some low readiness schools are highly committed and becoming more reflective of high readiness schools as a result of their involvement with SEDL. Trust is developing in some schools as more extensive shared leadership structures are being established and goals are established. Moreover, some schools had greater obstacles to overcome in the beginning. One principal argued,

> I feel shared leadership must precede visioning. Trust is critical and building slowly with shared leadership. Our situation is that we had to overcome a lot of obstacles and this is very new to us. Just to get to the point where we could trust and talk freely to each other about issues related to education has been an obstacle to overcome. There are not enough of us to take us where we want to go. As long as teachers aren't doing anything to prevent us from achieving the goals for our school, then there won't be a problem.

The next section relatedly focuses on inspiring responsibility for shared visions, as a precursor to empowered decision making.

Inspired Responsibility for a Shared Vision

An analysis of staff efforts in developing a professional learning community around inspired responsibility for a shared vision revealed the following interactive themes: purposeful visioning, embedded values, systematic structures, and monitoring processes. In terms of inspiring responsibility for a shared vision, high and low readiness schools differed, but to a lesser degree than was evident in shared leadership.

High Readiness Schools

The concept of a shared vision in many schools is often misunderstood and confused with the mission and goals. *High readiness schools* in this study lacked these distinctions as well. Only one school engaged in a formal visioning process, conducted five years before the project began using a variety of group processes. They perceived this vision as evolving "as faculty change to include everyone's input. Through total group participation there is a focus on the student and academic and personal success." The faculty visited their vision three times a year—fall, mid-year, and year-end, collecting and analyzing data and updating as needed. Participation in this vision separated this school from the rest, through its history, it systematic process, and its involvement of the whole school, parents, and community.

This community continues to ask, "What would be the documentation that we have become a model school?" They are intentional. They measured their progress, and celebrated their progress through the following philosophy, "Show not Tell." The principal expressed that, "We will celebrate because what you have to do with change is create an event and an event will create change and if you don't have one you create one." This principal maintained that,

> Developing a shared vision requires collaboration, broad input, ongoing feedback and readjustment by design. A vision needs to be knowledge-based, realistic, workable and based on achievable goals . . . more strategies with coaching, portfolios, rubrics, exhibitions, action research, and focus on student achievement. A successful vision is built on a shared orientation and a common vocabulary. We have a plan for everything; nothing happens by accident anymore. Visioning should be proactive and responsive to changing trends and needs within the school and community.

The teacher representative from this distinguished, high readiness school added,

> Even the recalcitrant teachers have softened—informal get-togethers show that it's on people's minds. It's always at the forefront. There is a strong informal culture related to vision based around curriculum, instruction and students. Internal communication structures exist to operationalize the vision.

Even at this level, the teacher indicated that they were beginning to falter and that the SEDL project refocused their efforts, and created a deeper trust among teachers.

In all other schools, except one, the vision was expressed in multiple sentences, describing, rather than stating it concisely. One pair of interviews indicated that, " a district vision exists, but the school goals are what drive decisions." This was more typical in smaller schools that used their district visions. Another teacher stated that staff used the following statement for direction,

> Is it good for kids? Vision is the litmus test for decision-making. We have a staff that is highly committed to student academic success. Our vision is to improve student learning and knock down barriers that prevent student learning.

Others defined their vision as the current change topic, i.e., Alternative Education project, Alliance, Standards and Benchmarks, Technology, etc. Schools with lower student performance saw the vision as "trying not to be a targeted school"—improving test scores. The test was the touchstone. In contrast, schools with higher student performance saw the vision as moving beyond the tests to the next level.

Visioning is a process and it appears to be emerging in these schools with a focus on student learning. Multiple structures are in place in these schools that function systematically—usually an off shoot of some type of strategic planning that focuses on the vision or a needs assessment. Before the project began, principals often talked about school activities, but did not focus on the school's vision. According to one principal, at the beginning of the SEDL project,

> The vision or mission varied from teacher to teacher. Teachers now feel excited about what the children are learning. They are beginning to express concerns such as, 'What will happen to our children after they leave here?' They are asking how to make change happen so that good things will continue to happen for our children.

Others spoke of changing norms, "We were isolated but now we have come together." These schools value continuous improvement, collaboration and student learning and structure activities to support these values. A teacher expressed, "Our vision, the bottom-line, is all students will be successful. We will do what it takes and you can't find that because it's different for every kid. Whatever it takes." Staff meetings, for the most part, focused on curriculum and instruction issues. For instance, one teacher noted, "We align our curriculum in those staff meetings." Other teachers noted that staff meetings focused on standards and benchmarks, and assessment of progress toward accomplishing school goals.

The vision of the school was usually seen as "shared" in the sense that virtually everyone supported the school vision, but in some cases the explanations by teachers and principals seemed to lead toward a vision that was created by the principal and then shared "with" the staff to endorse. In response to how the vision was developed, one teacher expressed, "I believe that it came from the principal." However, another teacher stated it like this,

> Our principal is the visionary. She has a vision for the school of what she wants it to be, but expects us, and we expect it of ourselves, to come up with the innovations that are going to help us meet that vision of a school where kids respect each other, respect their facilitators [teachers] and become empowered learners.

Most visions that were cited generally linked to the school improvement plans.

Visions were monitored where they existed and were seen as ongoing. However, one principal expressed the challenge of maintaining momentum,

> We feel that the mission of the school is an ongoing task. Because our teachers are inexperienced, they have a tendency to get discouraged. That's where the collaboration, the team building has been so vital for us. We have come together, talking out difficulties. The vision has been shared, embraced and is articulated by me every opportunity that we have . . . constantly keeping that in the forefront and constantly trying to support, and give them resources that will support implementation.

Another principal suggested that, "[you must] always look at what you are doing . . . what is working . . . abandoning it if it doesn't work, coming back to it, redefining — constant continual improvement." In a different school, a teacher maintained, "We're always in continuous improvement, everyday in every way." Others expressed frustration with competing efforts, a lack of resources and fragmentation, "We have several areas that we're trying to work on, probably too many at one time." Still others revealed distracters, such as limited resources and construction of new building facilities.

Low Readiness Schools

In low readiness schools, shared visions did not exist and the desire to create them was mixed on the part of teachers. In most schools, principals and teachers denied having a shared vision. Most respondents talked about student learning, but collaboration and commitment to the vision were not shared or valued by their faculty as a whole. One principal indicated that,

> We want what's best for kids, but don't know how to get to that point. We aren't on the same page. It's more of an individualized thing. Teachers see themselves as autonomous units not working together. I don't see progress. People are aware but they aren't doing anything about it.

Another principal described pockets of interest, but not enough to make a difference. "Not all of the team has a complete commitment to the task. We are drawing on others to bring them into the fold by meeting regularly with team members and using their suggestions." Some respondents believed that they had a shared vision, but could not articulate what it was or how it was manifested in day-to-day behavior.

Many obstacles were raised in the interviews including: a lack of parent involvement, external pressures, a lack of trust and unwillingness to change. One principal from a low-income school lamented the apathy of parents toward their children's learning. Her vision was limited, "Our vision is to love the children and take care of them." A series of factors emerged from another principal,

> high turnover, low pay, a break in continuity. . . . It's difficult to get a sense of family. Some fit and some don't. The shared vision belongs to the people who return. Many others are not certified and can't stay — nothing to do with the vision.

One teacher shared his frustration related to his colleagues' resistance to change and improvement,

> The older faculty don't see the need to change. They have no desire to be introspective and look at themselves and what they can do to improve their teaching methods and improve the school. They aren't willing to look at the broader picture and see we aren't doing the job we need to be doing. They think it's everyone's fault but ours.

This attitude was fueled by a lack of trust and openness, not uncommon across schools. Comments from principals and teachers in low readiness schools suggested they were just beginning to break through some of these barriers. One teacher indicated,

> Just to get to the point where we could trust and talk freely to each other about issues related to education has been an obstacle to overcome. We had to lay the groundwork to get to shared vision. We see it as something that comes on the heels of shared leadership.

Another teacher bemoaned the slow pace of change, "On a continuum we are at the very beginning, but I believe we've made progress. Teachers are beginning to open up, to an extent, not as much as we'd hoped." Others stated that they felt their teachers perceived commitment to student learning as lip service, and that the status of and expectations for teachers needed to be reexamined, before teachers would be motivated to comply.

In some cases the vision was perceived as belonging to the principal, therefore it lacked meaning and ownership among staff. One principal illustrated this attitude in the following statements,

> don't see the school where it needs to be in terms of shared vision. I see the vision as some buying into what needs to be done, some straddling the fence, and some not sure what direction they want to go. I take that as a challenge as well as a charge . . . to get them to see the vision needs to be about collaboration and addressing the assessed needs that were identified as it relates to the total educational process in the school.

Principals and teachers interviewed were consistent in their commitment to student learning, thus mirroring their counterparts in the high readiness schools. However, in contrast, most schools focused on improving test scores in lieu of creating a shared vision. Frustration and anxiety were evident in these comments made by teachers and principals who wanted more for their students:

> We need to reach the 30% on the Iowa Tests in order not to be under state remediation.

> Focus on student learning . . . test taking. We're worried about having them do well on the test rather than having them actually learn deep knowledge.

> We need to focus on test scores and bring our children up to standards or where we want them to be. You know, to raise our test scores, I think that is going to be our priority right now—to see our strengths and continue with those and also look at our weaknesses and see what we can do to improve them.

> Our vision is to pass the state test. Let us get out of there so we don't get put into remediation. But I think there's more. We want these kids to really grab more than, hey, come

on, let's just pass the test. I mean we want to really put inside of them some things that, hey, the world can be different than the world they know.

Some schools are taking action as one principal noted whose staff is collaborating around a common issue, meeting regularly, and discussing students' grades, concerns and problems:

> We need to be in the same boat rowing in the same direction. Our vision is student learn-ing. Everyone works together to help students improve test scores by accommodating skills learned in one class to another. Tests are made in the standardized form in order to give the students the opportunity to become familiar with the test form. The lines of sub-ject areas have been erased, and teachers are collaborating to discuss content outside the realm of their particular subject areas.

Empowered Decision Making

An analysis of staff efforts in developing a professional learning community around empowered decision making revealed the following interactive themes: deep and fo-cused governance structures, systematic processes, and embedded decision making. In terms of empowered decision making, high and low readiness schools varied sig-nificantly.

High Readiness Schools

In *high readiness schools*, principals focused on building trust and involving all staff at various stages in the decision-making process. Multi-interrelated structures ex-isted that were characterized by active, focused and productive involvement of staff. Generally, these structures focused on teaching and learning and appeared in the form of: leadership teams, grade level and subject area teams, vertical teams, advisory councils, special committees, special activities, parent groups, task forces, and hiring committees. Teachers worked collaboratively across grade levels and shared respon-sibility for decisions regarding student learning. Principals monitored these processes and created pathways for success.

In these schools, decisions were made in groups of people who were closest to the issue. One principal reported "rotating responsibilities . . . and building a sup-port system across staff. She expressed that "teachers want to make decisions re-garding the curriculum being used and are having a choice in the adoption of new texts." The principal asserted that empowerment was critical as she often reminds her staff, "I'll be gone, but you'll still be here. You need to decide how you want the school to be." She may have assumed that the staff would outlive her tenure at this particular school.

Most teachers want a voice in issues that touch the heart of the school and have a direct effect on students—issues related to teaching and learning. Several principals acknowledged working on their listening skills to gain respect and establish trust. One principal revealed, "The teachers respect each other and most respect me. I am building supportive conditions by letting them make decisions that most affect them." The teacher in this school viewed the principal as an advocate for teachers and students, encouraging site-based decision-making in the truest sense. In restructuring this school according to the school's vision, "teachers abandoned an out-dated computer lab, and hired an additional paraprofessional . . . abandoned a gifted and talented pull-out program, and implemented an inclusion model." In another school, teachers felt fortunate to have an administration that valued their opinions and was willing to listen. The teacher contended that,

> the whole school is involved in exchange and sharing. There is a high degree of trust and shared decision-making, mutual respect between teachers and administrators. Administrators trust that teachers know what's best for students. New teachers are surprised. They are not used to being listened to at the top. Often they come from more of a dictatorship.

In this school, the leadership team trained facilitators from all grade levels and disciplines. As one principal stated, "It is important to take the time, not just to bring in new things, but to talk about how do we, organizationally, support each other in this learning process and in making decisions."

Moreover, in some schools teachers were given the budget and asked to plan staff development at the school level in lieu of having it dictated at the district level. One principal emphasized,

> It's up to the teachers. They know what they need. I'm not going to make the decision for them. I know that by giving them the budget they are more in control of the money. It's being spent on what they need.

One school had cadres that "divides up the problems and works toward solutions. We meet and present the solutions until the school comes to a consensus." Collectively, teachers and principals revealed that before the SEDL project, input was most often afforded a select group of teachers, whereas now input is requested throughout the organization. People were learning how to talk with one another, reach consensus, and determine appropriate decision-making patterns.

In high readiness schools, teachers were beginning to gain a sense of the "big picture" and, in some cases, decisions were data-driven, monitored, and evaluated. One principal described the process of empowered decision-making in detail. She felt that by analyzing the data, she could easily make some decisions herself, but chose to share information and elicit opinions from various levels of the organization until consensus was reached. She gained consensus by saying, "Nobody is going to walk out of this room and say, 'They made us do this.' It doesn't matter how great we think things are going to be because if they don't like it or do it, it is just not going to work."

In another school, one principal described how the entire staff had input into the first banked day since the project began. Banked days were full days devoted to professional development planned by the staff. They were earned as a result of adding five minutes to the school day to support the SEDL project.

> They [the teachers] were real instrumental in the use of our first banked day in terms of talking about ideas as to how the day would work, taking those ideas back to their teams, finding out what people wanted through surveys, and helping to organize information to determine our agenda. I'm very pleased at getting across the idea that I'm not the only person capable of making decisions or having good ideas.

Decisions in high readiness schools are most often tied to school goals. As one teacher noted, "The planning for the next year starts with our goals and then is translated into the budget and decisions that we make when we sit down to write the goals." Again, teachers and principals noted that although structures and processes were in place, the SEDL project helped them "fine tune" and relate them more directly to the vision and goals of their schools. As one teacher maintained,

> When everybody is involved in a decision-making process, that results in discussions which lead to understanding what the common vision is, where we ought to be. If our Campus Improvement Plan is used properly, we meet with the faculty to discuss it and produce a plan that really articulates the faculty as a whole.

Each person's personal knowledge and insight adds to the whole, enriches the quality of the vision, and ensures ownership across levels.

While recognizing the value of shared leadership or responding to the local mandate to organize in this way, all the schools built structures for shared decision-making. The contrasts between high and low readiness schools were not so much in procedural decisions as they were in their actual operation. In the high readiness schools, the principals and teachers described a fluid, ever-changing arrangement that responded to the immediate needs of the school.

Low Readiness Schools

Decisions in *low readiness schools* were usually made by leadership teams, or other small "autonomous units," thus excluding a significant number of the total staff. The structures were described as more formal and less developed than the informal, yet systematic structures evident in high readiness schools. Several school structures were relatively new and they were evolving through typical group process changes. For instance, in one school the leadership council, with representation from each subject area was established to work to achieve common goals and make decisions that affected school policy. In a somewhat autonomous fashion, a teacher described a typical process, "The committee will listen to a teacher's proposal and then decide if it is good for the welfare of the school."

The staff in low readiness schools was more reactive to problems rather than proactive and creative. Nonetheless, teachers were becoming more open, and decision-making structures were expanding and becoming more focused. As one teacher stated, "There is broadening membership on committees. Members are appointed by their peers who are beginning to focus on curricular issues. Experts are stepping forward. Teachers are facilitating faculty meetings."

A lack of trust was evident when principals invited input, yet also reserved veto power and merely granted the appearance of empowerment. One teacher revealed that the principal "is willing to hear our opinions, take advice, and admits to not having all the answers, but she makes the decisions." The illusion of empowered decision-making was also depicted rather poignantly by one teacher who expressed that teacher were

> very disempowered systematically within the [larger structure], where they feel like they are empowering us, but they come back and second-guess us on the decisions we make. It's not true empowerment. True empowerment is giving someone, in my opinion, the trust.

In other schools, principals took on a more passive role and promoted a freedom of choice resulting in fragmentation and lack of focus. Decisions were at times made by consensus, but were often unrelated to student learning.

SUMMARY

DuFour and Eaker (1998) asserted that the best hope for reform lies in the creation of schools as professional learning communities. However, Fullan (2000) sheds doubt on, what may be considered, "distant dreams" without radical reculturing. Not only does this pertain to single efforts, but whole school reform and an infrastructure to institutionalize it. School reform will require connectedness (Fullan, 2000; Bivins-Smith, 1996), driven by values and vision, and a passionate effort by all members of school community to achieve a level of excellence that does not currently exist. In order for reform efforts to achieve intended results, schools cannot get by with just doing enough.

Administrative preparation programs need to relinquish traditional methods and requirements. They need to engage students in group processes, self-reflection, and continuous practica experiences in "real" settings with "real" people that build over time. This will require faculty to design integrated programs that mirror the realities of schools and address the time it takes change to occur. If professional learning communities are possible to create, they must first be created in classrooms and then tried in schools. Theory without immersion in practice and an exchange of experiences will not prepare future leaders to build communities that allow leadership to permeate traditional boundaries within the school and visions to emerge from the interactions which reflect the shared values, beliefs, and commitments of the whole organization. New conceptions of leadership must guide their actions, such as the definition that Rost (1993) proposed, "an influence relationship among leaders and followers who intend real changes that reflects their mutual purposes" (p. 102).

This chapter provides a snapshot into 19 diverse school settings that have committed to whole school reform to make a meaningful difference in the lives of their students. The journey of these schools illuminates the challenge for leadership preparation, as the schools in this study reflect schools across our nation and represent various levels of readiness. Earlier findings in these schools indicated that "although schools are attending to many things, many of them are not attending to matters that make a difference in the way schools operate and in the outcomes for students" (Olivier, Cowen & Pankake, 2000). Preparation programs need to help students establish priorities, co-create visions and empower their people to focus on the needs of students.

In light of these findings, Hord's (1997) five-dimensional model offers a comprehensive design to achieve these results. The key factor in our findings was the leadership of the principal. The evidence indicated that leadership practices in high readiness schools were more effective than those in low readiness schools in all areas under study: shared leadership, inspiring responsibility for a shared vision, empowered decision-making, and inclusivity of staff.

Principals in high readiness schools were not coercive or controlling; they shared leadership, imaging it in the likeness of new conceptions of leadership (Ellis & Joslin, 1990; Lambert, 1998; Rost, 1993). This has required a shift in perspective; all leaders can be followers and all followers can be leaders. Evidence indicated that the focus on capacity building was purposeful and reinforced, as staff members increasingly became open to changing roles and responsibilities. The principal's belief in the capabilities of teachers and the trust level reported by respondents was evident in broad participation through both formal and informal structures. The principals in these schools let go of power and nurtured the human side and expertise of their people. Thus, they gained collective commitment to continuous improvement and student learning.

Principals in high readiness schools were selective in their focus on a shared vision. Some elicited the dreams of others, while some shared their own visions and sought to mobilize efforts accordingly. Some were more successful than others. Those who co-created or presented an agreed upon vision seemed to have buy-in; those who imposed their visions looked for more. The success that was apparent in the single school that engaged in a comprehensive visioning process with all stakeholders offers lessons for others. Their vision was purposeful. It required broad participation, it had ownership from all involved in the teaching and learning process, and it was linked to school improvement. Clearly the focus in these schools differed from low readiness schools, particularly in that visions moved beyond test scores. Multiple structures were in place that embraced and built upon espoused values centered on student learning and continuous learning.

The principals in high readiness schools empowered decision making through deep and focused governance structures and systematic processes that were embedded in the school as a whole. However, data-driven decision-making processes were limited in the details of respondents. In professional learning communities, teachers and administrators gather information, make decisions, and implement those decisions (Hord, 1999). We also found the greater the sense of direction and information communicated; the greater the alignment. Alignment led to empowerment in these schools through the principal's trust, support, openness to input, and unsolicited perspectives. Unlike traditional implementation of site-based decision-making, responsibilities were dispersed and staff had significant voice in decisions related to teaching and learning. Collectives and individuals with expertise or a stake in the outcome made the decisions. Empowered decision-making was more than appearance.

A decade ago, in Restructuring America's Schools, Lewis (1989) asserted that, "If schools are, as some charge, 'dismal places to work and learn,' it is because people have created them as such" (p. 220). Preparation programs must address this issue and bring life to the apathy and mistrust that currently exists. The intent of this chapter was not to disclose the successes of existing professional learning communities, for these answers elude even the most experienced researchers. Instead, our purpose was to report preliminary findings from the *Creating Continuous Communities of Inquiry and Improvement* project, in its attempt to examine the readiness levels of schools attempting to create inclusive, vibrant, and enduring places of learning. We have tried to capture the details of schools in the midst of purposeful change to provide insights into their successes and struggles. In turn, if success is achieved, the details of their journey will not be lost. The map each school will follow will differ because of their unique contexts, issues, and people. This study is ongoing and data is currently being collected schoolwide through interviews, surveys, and field notes. Once analyzed within and across schools, new findings will provide us with further direction.

REFERENCES

Astuto, T. A., Clark, D. L., Read, A. M., McGee, K., & Fernandez, L. (1993). Challenges to dominant assumptions controlling educational reform. Andover, MA: Regional Laboratory for the Educational Improvement of the Northeast and Islands.

Bivins-Smith, D. M. (1996). Connectedness: A path to the learning organization. Adult Learning, 7(4), 21–22, 25.

Bogdan, R. C., & Biklen, S. K. (1992). Qualitative research in education: An introduction to theory and methods. Boston, MS: Allyn and Bacon.

Brown, D. F. (1995). Experiencing shared leadership: Teachers' reflections. Journal of School Leadership, 5(4), 334–355.

Davis, S. H. (1998). Taking aim at effective leadership. Thrust for Educational Leadership, 28(2), 6–9.

DuFour, R., & Eaker, R. (1998). Professional learning communities at work. Bloomington, IN: National Education Service.

Ellis, N. E., & Joslin, A. W. (1990). Shared governance and responsibility: The keys to leadership, commitment and vision in school reform. (ERIC Document Reproduction Service No. ED 328985).

Fullan, M. (1995). The school as a learning organization: Distant dreams. Theory Into Practice, 34(4), 230–235.

Fullan, M. (2000, April). The three stories of education reform. Phi Delta Kappan, 581–584.

Guskey, T. R., & Peterson, K. D. (1993). The road to classroom change. Educational Leadership, 53(4), 10–14.

Hord, S. (1997). Professional learning communities: What are they and why are they important? Issues About Change, 6(1), Austin, TX: Southwestern Educational Development Laboratory, 1–8.

Hord, S. (1999). Principals and teachers: Continuous learners. Issues About Change, 7(2), Austin, TX: Southwestern Educational Development Laboratory, 1–8.

Hord, S. M. (1997). School professional staff as learning community questionnaire. Austin, TX: Southwestern Educational Development Laboratory.

Johnson, S. M. (1996). Leading to change. San Francisco, CA: Jossey Bass.

Kleine-Kracht, P. A. (1993, July). The principal in a community of learners. Journal of School Leadership, 3(4), 391–399.

Kotter, J. P. (1990, May–June) What leaders really do. Harvard Business Review, 3–11.

Lambert, L. (1998). Building leadership capacity in schools. Alexandria, VA: Association for Supervision and Curriculum Development.

Leedy, P. D. (1997). Practical research: Planning and design. Upper Saddle River, NJ: Prentice-Hall.

Leithwood, K., Leonard, L., & Sharratt, L. (1997). Conditions fostering organizational learning in schools. Paper presented at the annual meeting of the International Congress on School Effectiveness and Improvement, Memphis, Tennessee.

Lewis, A. (1989). Restructuring America's schools. Arlington, VA: American Association of School Administrators.

Lindle, J. C. (1995/1996). Lessons from Kentucky about school-based decision making. Educational Leadership, 53(4), 20–23.

Louis, K. S., & Kruse, S. (1995). Professionalism and community: Perspectives on reforming urban schools. Thousand Oaks, CA: Corwin Press.

Miles, M. B., & Huberman, M. (1994). Qualitative data analysis: An expanded sourcebook. Thousand Oaks, CA: Sage Publications.

Muncey, D. E., & McQuillan, P. J. (1993). Preliminary findings from a five-year study of the Coalition of Essential Schools. Phi Delta Kappan, 74(6), 486–489.

Newmann, F., & Wehlage, G. (1995). Successful School Restructuring. (Madison: Center on Organization and Restructuring of Schools, University of Wisconsin.

Olivier, D. F., Cowen, D., & Pankake, A. (2000). Professional learning communities: Cultural characteristics. Paper presented at the annual meting of the Southwest Educational Research Association, Dallas, TX.

Rost, J. C. (1993). Leadership for the twenty-first century. Westport, CT: Praeger Publishers.

Senge, P. M. (1990). The fifth discipline: The art and practice of the learning organization. New York: Doubleday.

Sergiovanni, T. J. (1994, May). Organizations or communities? Changing the metaphor changes the theory. Educational Administration Quarterly, 30(2), 214–226.

Snyder, K. J., Acker-Hocevar, M., & Snyder, K. M. (1996, Winter). Principals speak out on changing school work cultures. Journal of Staff Development, 17(1), 14–19.

Sparks, D. (1999). Real-life view: Here's what a true learning community looks like. Journal of Staff Development, 20(4), 53–57.

Zempke, R. (1999, September). Why organizations still aren't learning. Training, 40–49.

A School/University Partnership to Implement a Parent Involvement Program

JAMES E. BERRY, MARVIN PASCH
and LAURA CHEW

Every school district leader claims to value parent involvement, but not every school district has a system in place to incorporate parents fully as a valued part of the school system. Epstein (1995) argued that there were many reasons to develop school, family, and community partnerships. "They can improve school programs and school climate, provide family services and support, increase parents' skills and leadership, connect families with others in the school and in the community, and help teachers with their work" (p. 701). Some school districts may not know how best to engage parents and community, but there are few that dismiss the importance and support of parents.

On a practical level, the need to engage parents and families in the schooling of children is a transparent problem for school systems. It is easier to describe a shared value than it is actually to organize a school district into the kind of caring educational environment that every community desires. School districts have every intention to connect parent involvement to children through school. However, parent involvement isn't just a program to determine what to do; it is to know how to do it. Implementing a successful parent involvement program faces the same barriers to change as any other program reform. For administrators there is the leadership challenge to understand what works for a school district and how best to implement a sustainable program that makes a difference for parents and children. As soon as administrators confront issues related to implementation they soon discover that, "Lots of research exists on parent involvement, but frankly very little on the specifics of how to do it" (Cooper, 1999, p. 7). Parent involvement efforts have to be oriented around shaping the school district organization as way to address its own culture. Building an infrastructure to support parent involvement is an altogether different project than inviting parents to raise money for a school trip.

James E. Berry, Eastern Michigan University
Marvin Pasch, Eastern Michigan University
Laura Chew, Willow Run Community Schools

Parent involvement should be viewed as a systemwide commitment by the entire school district to accomplish a goal established by the board of education. Knowing what is needed to engage parents in schooling and doing what is needed to engage parents in the schooling of their children create different approaches to program implementation. Educational change literature is filled with knowing what is needed. This project focused upon doing program reform at a systems level to improve student achievement.

PARENT INVOLVEMENT: AN AVENUE FOR REFORM

The authors believe that a well-developed parent involvement model is an opportunity to reform the K–12 system through a comprehensive effort to have parents become partners in schooling. However, parent involvement cannot simply be devolved to individual schools to plan, implement, and evaluate. District-level support is necessary, as building level activities do not often produce sustainable outcomes. This chapter reports on a study of a school and university partnership in Southeastern Michigan that focused on parental involvement. Key in this partnership was a multidistrict approach to capacity building, and a well-focused and coordinated initiative.

Southeastern Michigan Consortium: A Multidistrict Approach to Capacity Building

Capacity building to sustain programs and people became a cornerstone in the national conversation about systemic reform during the 1990s. Floden, Goertz, and O'Day (1995) wrote that "capacity building often focused upon teachers' professional development" (p. 19). Capacity building in schools, however, has a much broader context. It also means that school district leaders must organize people, plan expenditures, deliver services, and build school district infrastructure to support teachers in the delivery of instruction so that achievement outcomes are improved for all students. Systemic change literature consistently describes how multiple layers of organizations must operate as interrelated units because change touches every aspect of the educational institution (see Fuhrman & Massel, 1992; Fullan, 1996; O'Day & Smith, 1992; Sashkin & Egermeier, 1993; Senge, 1990; Wheatley, 1993). Systemic in this project meant that school buildings were connected to each other, each district's central office, and to a regional consortium. What was required for one building was required for all of the buildings.

The measure of success for K–12 school districts, one that attracts recognition and indicates district achievement, is consistently to produce high learning outcomes for students. If educators can't show progress for improving student achievement to what degree is the school district responsible? Districtwide K–12 model programs like parent involvement grow in importance if they can go to scale as system initiatives to improve student achievement. Thorkildsen and Stein (1998) indicated in a review of literature that parent involvement had a "small to moderate but educationally significant effect size" on student achievement (p. 20). The project reported in this chapter, and its subsequent evaluation, reinforced this finding and indicated parent involvement at the district-level can be implemented with success as a systemwide initiative if focused and well-coordinated.

Southeastern Michigan Consortium and Its Goals

Three school districts and the Educational Leadership Program at Eastern Michigan University (EMU) formed an educational consortium to provide a broader base for ensuring improvement of student outcomes in the greater geographic area. The three school districts represented approximately 11,900 children in 26 buildings sharing the same urban community. The key strategy of the consortium effort was to develop a structure within which all agents could complement the work of coterminous partners to strengthen the partnership. Utilizing a systems approach, representatives of the three school districts worked with EMU personnel to frame parent involvement as a component of each district's school improvement effort. Following is an outline of the approach.

A capacity-building framework was used to implement the Southeastern Michigan Consortium parent involvement model. Members of the consortium joined Epstein's (1995) Partnership 2000 effort as buildings and as districts. Within this framework, each district actively organized parent involvement initiatives that involved parents in the effort to improve student achievement. The mission statement of the consortium was: "Working better together to serve our shared community." The Southeastern Michigan Consortium was structured to achieve four primary goals:

1. Develop and enhance the existing school improvement process at the building level through action teams.
2. Promote school/family/community partnerships within the three school districts.
3. Implement district level organizational support to improve student learning.
4. Implement strategies to assist parents from under served populations.

Consortium Activities

The Southeastern Michigan Consortium members agreed that each district and each participating school would develop activities and organizational structures to affirm and achieve the four goals. This agreement became a foundation for working together in a multi-institutional partnership and set minimal expectations for participation and organizational support. All of the partnership school districts agreed to work within a broad framework to build capacity so a high level of parent involvement could be maintained once grant support ended. The consortium partners put in place a plan to:

1. Establish a consortium board that represented EMU and the three school districts.
2. Develop a strategic plan.

3. Add a parent involvement goal to building Action Plans for each building in the consortium.
4. Initiate Partnership 2000 (Epstein's parent involvement program and six types of involvement) across the school districts.
5. Identify district level strategies to enhance organizational support for improving student achievement.
6. Evaluate the progress of the consortium in meeting the above goals.

RESULTS AFTER THREE YEARS: EXPECTATIONS FULFILLED AND UNFULFILLED

To enhance the school improvement process in each district and participating school, mini-grants were given to schools that integrated parental involvement into their action plans for school improvement. All schools made proposals for doing so and modest sums of money were allocated to each school. At the conclusion of three years, external evaluators collected action plans and conducted face-to-face interviews with a member of each school improvement team to compare what had been submitted as activities to enhance parental involvement and what actually transpired. Each interview was recorded and a transcript prepared. From these transcripts the evaluators created charts of the parental involvement activities organized by the six standards for guiding parental involvement programs as determined by the National PTA. The standards were based upon Epstein's six types of involvement and adapted by the National PTA (National PTA, 1997).

Epstein (1995) described the six types of involvement as overlapping spheres of influence between schools, families, and communities, with the student at the center of program activity. Students become engaged, motivated, and energized "to produce their own successes" through well-designed school, family, and community programs (p. 702). The six National PTA/Epstein standards frame practices of partnership between the three spheres. The standards are as follows:

Standard I: Communicating

Standard II: Parenting

Standard III: Student Learning

Standard IV: Volunteering

Standard V: School Decision-Making and Advocacy

Standard VI: Collaborating with Community

From an examination of charts describing dozens of parental involvement activities implemented in the consortium schools, the evaluators identified a few exemplary activities that they believed had special merit in implementing parental involvement, or strengthening its impact. In regard to those activities judged as exemplary, the evaluators selected two activities within each of the six standards. The decision as to which activities were chosen as exemplary was based upon the twin criteria of depth and breadth. Depth of parental involvement was the likelihood that the activity would strengthen parental involvement in that school and persist over time. Breadth of parental involvement was the extent to which the activity impacted many parents and teachers. These exemplary activities are contained in Table 1.

The interview responses from action team members demonstrated that the projects chosen by each school to enhance parental involvement led to many positive and sustainable activities. The charts of parental activities provide evidence of a varied and rich array of initiatives that would not have been possible without external consortium financial support. Thus, the goal of working through building-level action teams was successfully achieved and demonstrated that this component was critical. It insured both local control and stakeholder ownership. In this parent involvement program a plan without an action team was the same as no plan.

TABLE I. Exemplary Involvement Activities Within Each of the Six Parent Involvement Standards.

Activity	National PTA/Epstein Standards					
	I	II	III	IV	V	VI
Newsletter mailed to homes and focused on parenting, helping child to succeed with activities in school	X					
Parent Action Committee met once/month with the principal	X					
Parent/teacher contracts that focused on achievement		X				
Megaskills workshops on responsibility, confidence, employability skills (Rich, 1992)		X				
Monthly family science night w/hands-on activities that can be done at home			X			
Parent night to explain MEAP student packets (state achievement tests). Parents assist and monitor student work, and sign off when completed			X			
A building parent data base for volunteers numbering 300				X		
Volunteer luncheon with presents and "Thank you" cards				X		
Parents on interview and school improvement teams					X	
Funded half-time parent coordinators at buildings					X	
High school students earn awards/rewards (redeemed at local businesses) for behavior and achievement						X
Workshop with Chamber of Commerce						X

School/Family/Community Partnerships Within the Three School Districts

Epstein's model of parent involvement framed the activities of the consortium. The knowledge and insights generated from Epstein's Partnership 2000 network provided conceptual structure and shared vocabulary to organize and plan parental involvement activity. The participation of the Michigan Education Association's (MEA) Center for the Revitalization of Urban Education (see Gary, Hansen, Marburger, & Witherspoon, 1996) and the National PTA standards extended and enhanced partnership support of the project. The participation of the MEA proved to be another element necessary for success. Districts with a strong union presence identified and invited this stakeholder group to become an active partner. Consortium-level decisions that were supported by the teachers' union had a better chance of successful implementation.

Representatives from the three school districts and the leadership program at EMU worked together through monthly meetings. Consortium meetings were held in member districts. This was a small step, but important in building the relationships that created a working trust. The relationships among the three contiguous districts, together with EMU, and later a local Intermediate School District (ISD), were increased and strengthened. The group continued activities when external funding for the project ended.

District-Level Organizational Support to Improve Student Learning

Although relationships among the participating organizations were enhanced during the life of external funding, it is also true that there were substantial differences in the way each district viewed parental involvement and their allocation of resources to its development. Each district had a responsibility to define "what" would be done and "how" it would be done consistent with district goals. Within the common structure, districts were reminded of the need for individual expression of the consortium goals. This flexibility led to many innovative school activities.

However, flexibility also mitigated against district-to-district and school-to-school collaboration. Thus, the expectation that the districts and EMU would work in concert, one to others, was only partially realized. The activities and energy focused on parental involvement were more in evidence at the school level, with district involvement, less so, and consortium level, a distant third.

One interviewee expressed it thus, "I feel that it would help to get more support from the administration, things like coming to our meetings, calling us, attending some events . . . maybe we need to coordinate with other schools and see what they do." "We need absolute board support and administrative support and a district coordinator." There is "support verbally but there hasn't been the commitment to implement it in schools across the district." There was a widely believed conclusion that school faculties were expected to develop their own strategies to enhance parental involvement. In some schools teachers were expected to implement strategies in their own classrooms without any concerned supervision/coordination/support from the principal.

Student Achievement Outcomes

A focus upon student achievement was the reason for the project. Enhancement of parental involvement in participating districts was predicted to be a significant factor in increasing student achievement. The external evaluators examined three-year standardized testing results in Mathematics, Reading, Science and Writing in the State of Michigan Educational Assessment Program (MEAP). They concluded that achievement rose significantly in the three consortium districts in the area of Reading. There were only modest increases in Math and Science and none in Writing in the 4th and 7th grades. The evaluation of the consortium documented a focused effort to increase parental involvement with a hoped-for increase in student achievement. An increase in reading achievement occurred during the time this project was in effect and, therefore, may have had some link to increased parent involvement. This is consistent with results on the overall impact of parent involvement in a review of literature by Thorkildsen and Scott Stein (1998). However, the authors do not claim that the reported increases in student academic achievement were caused only by the enhanced level of parental involvement.

There is mounting evidence that parent involvement facilitates children's academic achievement (Lee & Croninger, 1994; Snow et al., 1991; Tocci & Engelhard, 1991). It is also true that parental involvement research suffers from a lack of scientific rigor. The major problem is that nonexperimental designs are too weak to determine if effects can be attributed to parental involvement as opposed to other program elements. Studies have often concluded that parental involvement was the critical intervention strategy when, in fact, overall success could be attributed to a variety of concurrent activities. An improved educational curriculum developed through parent involvement interaction with the school or enhanced social services for the family, although they may be related to a parent involvement initiative, have an independent effect (Baker & Soden, 1998). Increases in achievement may be attributable to something other than increased parental involvement.

Enhanced parental involvement was identified by the consortium as a K–12 goal for all three school districts. However, parental involvement was most apparent in the elementary schools. All elementary schools submitted their action plans and arranged interviews with school improvement team members. Only one of four middle schools and three of four high schools participated in the structured interview process. Furthermore, the quantity and quality of the activities diminished as the focus moved from the elementary schools to the middle and high schools. A number of elementary schools made substantial progress in developing and implementing buildingwide parental involvement activities. The same could not be said for the middle or high schools.

Making A Wider Circle for Connection to Parents

Parents have few forums in which to be heard. Few attend board meetings on a regular basis and only a handful serve on advisory committees. A Parent Summit was held twice during the three years of consortium activity. The summit brought together school personnel, representatives from community organizations, political leaders and activists in the three school communities. Activities at the summit included a menu of workshops and a town meeting. This forum will continue and has the potential to become a powerful vehicle to encourage parent input. An invitation only format, which restricted attendance to a select group of key parents and staff could be altered to invite interested parents across all three school districts.

Another method to reach parents in new ways was developed by the consortium. A Southeastern Michigan Consortium home page (http://isd.wash.k12.mi.us/~fscc/) linking home pages from the three school districts, EMU, the ISD, and Johns Hopkins University was added to the Internet. The consortium web page provided the technological infrastructure and framework for two-way communication links with parents, school personnel, and the community at large. Through the "Some Useful Links" button on the Southeastern Michigan Consortium Web site users had direct linkage to the National Parent Information Network (NPIN), the National Association of Elementary School Principals (NAESP) Family Involvement, and other useful parent and student links. The links offered information to families on ways technology is changing how we learn, work, and live.

An external evaluator interviewed the regional district technology technician responsible for finalizing the development of the consortium website. He made a number of suggestions to extend the work that had been completed. Specifically, consortium partners should:

1. Continue to collaborate in the design and implementation of a plan that would deliver a systematic process of logging users and linking them with each participating district/school's home page.
2. Create a web e-mail form that applies the common gateway interface origin as a means of establishing a family-school-community resource directory.
3. Identify a facilitator from each district or one facilitator who would represent the three districts and would receive e-mail summaries and be responsible for follow-up within the district(s).
4. Develop a consortium calendar and consider a link with the regional school district calendar.
5. Develop a data collection process that provides names of users who electronically visit a school.

The potential of electronic communication linkages with external audiences in the consortium is unlimited. With infrastructure in place, the site has the capacity for regular contact with parents and the community. This contact can include school district goals, building news, curriculum offerings, homework hints, calendar of events, successful parenting practices and tips, and a parent involvement resource directory.

CONCLUSION

Parent involvement programs need to be integrated into a school district's organizational reform strategy. Systems change and parent involvement, integrated as one overall approach, can achieve organizational renewal. The long-term result is lasting change and higher levels of parent satisfaction with a school district.

The Southeastern Michigan Consortium had as its overall goal to facilitate the creation of a parent involvement program as a critical K–12 organizational structure to help in the systematic and systemic improvement of student achievement. After three years of activity, the evidence suggests that student achievement has shown an increase in reading, modest increases in math and science and none in writing as measured by the Michigan Educational Assessment Program tests. Because of the many variables related to building-level and school-district change it is difficult to posit a cause-and-effect relationship between increasing parental involvement and student achievement.

Examination of school action plans and interviews with action team members reveal the implementation of dozens of initiatives involving all six of Epstein's types and the National PTA standards for parent involvement. The evaluators identified some activities as especially meritorious in either strengthening or extending the impact of parent involvement.

The evidence of partnership activity supports a conclusion that relationships among the three districts in the consortium have been enhanced, one to another and with EMU, and to a fifth member that joined the partnership to lend support for the work of the group. In 1998–99 the Intermediate School District (ISD) added its energy and participation to the consortium. The linking of districts, a university, and an ISD is an organizational success that brought resources to bear on parent involvement as a school district priority. Regardless of the involvement of school districts, an ISD, and a university, the positive impact of parent involvement is greatest at the school rather than at the district level, and weakest in terms of consortium initiatives.

Finally, the Southeastern Michigan Consortium partners continue their quest to create a support mechanism to sustain district-level programs that improve student achievement. There is indication that the cooperative linking of educational agencies at the macro level can meaningfully shape school district outcomes. "Working better together to serve our shared community" was a mission statement and an opportunity for these educational agencies to link together as a more focused learning system.

REFERENCES

Baker, A. J., & Soden, L. M. (1998). The challenges of parent involvement research. (ERIC/CUE Digest Number 134). New York: Institute for Urban Minority Education Clearinghouse on Urban Education (ERIC Document Reproduction Service No. ED 419030).

Cooper, C, (1999). Beyond the bake sale: How parent involvement makes a difference. North Central Regional Educational Laboratory's Learning Point 1(3), 4–8.

Epstein, J. L. (1995). School/Family/Community partnerships. Phi Delta Kappan 76(9), 701–712.

Floden, R. E., Goertz, M. E., & O'Day, J. (1995, September). Capacity building in systemic reform. Phi Delta Kappan 77(1), 19–21.

Fuhrman, S. H., & Massell, D. (1992). Issues and strategies in systemic reform. Consortium for Policy Research in Education. New Brunswick, NJ: Eagleton Institute of Politics, Rutgers.

Fullan, M. G. (1996). Turning systemic thinking on its head. Phi Delta Kappan 77(6), 420–423.

Gary, W., Hansen, B., Marburger, C., & Witherspoon, R. (1996). Family, school, community partnerships. National Education Association Center for the Revitalization of Urban Education. Washington, DC.

Lee, V. E., & Croninger, R. G. (1994). The relative importance of home and school in the development of literacy skills for middle-grad students. American Journal of Education, 102(3), 286–329.

National Parent Teacher Association. (1997). National Standards for Parent/Family Involvement Programs. Chicago, IL: Author

O'Day J. A., & Smith, M. S. (1992). Systemic reform and educational opportunity. In S.H. Fuhrman (Ed.), Designing coherent education policy (pp. 250–312). San Francisco: Jossey-Bass Publishers.

Rich, D. (1992). Megaskills. Boston: Houghton Mifflin Co.

Sashkin, M., & Egermeier, J. (1993). School change models and processes. U.S. Department of Educational Research and Improvement Program for the Improvement of Practice, Washington, DC: US Government Printing Office.

Senge, P. J. (1990). The fifth discipline. New York, NY: Bantam Doubleday.

Smith M. S., & O'Day, J. A. (1991). Putting the pieces together: Systemic school reform. Consortium for Policy Research in Education. New Brunswick, NJ: Eagleton Institute of Politics, Rutgers.

Snow, C., Barnes, W. Chandler, J., Goodman, I., & Hemphill, L. (1991). Unfulfilled expectations: Home and school influences on literacy. Cambridge, MA: Harvard University Press. (ERIC Document Reproduction Service No. ED 356 303)

Southeastern Michigan Family-School-Community Consortium Home Page. (2000). Available: http://isd.wash.k12.mi.us/~fscc/

Thorkildsen, R., & Scott Stein, M. R. (1998). Is parent involvement related to student achievement? Exploring the evidence. (Center for Evaluation, Development, and Research, Research Bulletin No. 22). Bloomington, IN: Phi Delta Kappa.

Tocci, C. M., & Englehard, G. (1991, May–June). Achievement, parental support, and gender differences in attitudes toward mathematics. Journal of Educational Research, 84(5), 280–286. (EJ 430 606)

Wheatley, M. J. (1991). Leadership and the new science. San Francisco, CA: Berrett-Koehler Publishers, Inc.

Wheatley, M. (1993). Leadership and the new science: Learning about organization from an orderly universe. San Francisco, CA: Berrett-Kochler Publishers.

Creating a Culture for Educational Change: Contexts of Collaboration, Authentic Participation and Interactive Professionalism

School change is difficult work, and sustaining that change, oftentimes, is more difficult than creating the change itself. There are several factors within the educational institution that inhibit innovation and reform, and which makes it even more improbable for intended changes to take hold and be elaborated upon. Among these and the most important to consider, is one which has been consistently ignored, the structure of schooling itself. Both the roles and responsibilities of teachers and administrators, have been constituted by, within, and for a school system based on a bureaucratic model of schooling, designed by specified policies and practices that results in the development of a standard product, student outcome. Change efforts have been consistently based on a continued reliance on rationalistic organizational behavior, a trust in the power of institutional rules and roles to (re)direct human behavior, and a dependency on experts who are the dominant source of legitimate research and knowledge production regarding the achievement of expected outcomes.

School reform efforts have invariably remained at the skin level, since they have been based on traditional assumptions regarding change. The predominant view suggests: educational change is made by changing the way work is done in schools. Thus, instead of redesigning the purposes, structures, and functions of schools, and education in general, what has simply occurred is a continuous stream of top-down management and production directives to be implemented by school functionaries. As a hierarchical procedure, administrators manage and oversee the implementation of these directives by teachers, who are simply responsible for the technical delivery of these mandates. The underlying premise of this procedure perpetuates the limitations of reform efforts by presuming that teachers cannot be trusted to make sound decisions about school design, curriculum, pedagogy, assessment, ed-

Elizabeth R. Saavedra, The University of New Mexico

ucational goals and purposes on their own accord (Sarason, 1990; Fullan & Hargreaves, 1991; Wasley, 1991).

In the last twenty years, important and convincing research has demonstrated that teachers, too long silent and isolated in classrooms, must take more leadership in the restructuring of public education (Hargreaves, 1994; Lieberman & Miller, 1992, 1999; Miller, 1990; Lester & Onore, 1990; Connelly & Clandinin, 1999). Though much has been written about how teachers must assume leadership in the redesign of schools, mentor their colleagues, redefine the profession, engage in problem solving at the school level, and provide professional growth opportunities for themselves, and their colleagues, little has been done to create the working conditions and contexts in which this can be achieved (Fullan & Hargreaves, 1992; Little & McLaughlin, 1993; Grimmett & Neufeld, 1994, Saavedra, 1995). Schools continue to be organized as fundamental bureaucracies with hierarchical decision-making structures in place and continue to focus on striving for efficiency and productivity.

Educational institutions have failed to capitalize on the strengths that both teachers and administrators can provide if they worked more collaboratively and forged an "interactional relationship" (Fullan & Hargreaves, 1991) within and across schools. As Fullan and Hargreaves explain, " The challenge for schools, teachers, and their leaders, as we approach a new century, is the challenge of developing what we call interactive professionalism in our schools. The challenge of interactive professionalism is the challenge of continuous school improvement. It is a process that leads in turn to gains in student achievement" (p. xi).

Reforming schools will remain at a surface unless visions, purposes, and goals of education are forged through the actualization of interactive professionalism and authentic democracy, whereby the transformation of roles and responsibilities of those within the school system occurs, and educators are engaged in what Anderson (1998) calls, "authentic participation." He describes authentic participation as shared control, participatory, inclusive of issues of equity; and an analysis of how power is exercised in educational systems. Education contexts built upon the notion of authentic participation are sites which produce informed citizens and institutions with greater moral authority. Ultimately, Anderson emphasizes that authentic participation is "important for the development of the individual, important for the creation of democratic institutions, and important as a means to increase learning outcomes" (p. 595).

As Fullan and Hargreaves (1991) claim, it is difficult for administrators and teachers to engage in interactive professionalism and shared leadership, since they lack the tradition of working together in open, proactive, and collaborative ways within the system. Interactive professionalism relies on the development of collaborative cultures and the engagement and equal control of those who participate in them. Basically, this turns the predominant view of reform on its head, instead of teachers and administrators responding to mandates, they respond to reform through building their own localized goals and actions derived from contexts based on concepts of interactive professionalism and authentic participation. Ultimately, teachers and administrators work together to make their own schools.[1] This approach requires that teachers and administrators define their roles, their work, and their relationships differently. Unfortunately, they rarely have had, if ever, the opportunity to learn how to do this.

Through my own experiences, I have found that study groups can serve as a vehicle for principals and teachers to learn how to work together, to create a learning and collaborative culture, provide a context where they can redefine their roles and relationships, and collectively strive for interactive professionalism and shared or parallel leadership for the purpose of restructuring or constituting their own schools (Anderson & Saavedra, 1995; Saavedra, 1995, 1996).

STUDY GROUPS: A VEHICLE FOR CREATING A COLLABORATIVE CULTURE

The basic purpose of a study group is to provide a context in which teachers and administrators can engage in activities and actions that will lead to the transformation of their practices and beliefs, their roles and their purposes as educators, and the ways they work with each other and their students. In essence, to have an opportunity to engage in a process of developing collaborative cultures in which they can learn how to cultivate interactive professionalism and authentic participation. A culture of collaboration, inclusive of administrators and teachers will strengthen a sense of common purpose and enable them to interact assertively with external pressures for change—adopting changes that they value, selectively incorporating aspects of them that fit their agreed upon vision and goals, and rejecting those changes that are seen as educationally unsound or irrelevant. New visions for schools, and new structures to support these visions must be developed. The responsibility for vision-building is a collective, not an individual one. Interactive professionalism should mean creating the vision together, not complying with an administrative view. All stakeholders should be involved in authoring and establishing the mission and purposes of the school. Thus, the study group context can provide a space for such an endeavor.

Within a sustained study group context, participants construct personal and professional relationships, redefine beliefs, knowledge, and actions, and reshape their roles by challenging themselves in sustained problem posing and problem solving.

The basic premise underlying the formation of study groups is that anyone (a teacher, a group of teachers, a principal, a content area specialist, etc.) interested in gathering a group of educators together for the purpose of collaborative learning can do so at a negotiable time and place for a mutually agreed upon purpose. Participation in the study group is voluntary, it is never required or mandated. Those interested and

---

[1] It is imperative that teachers and administrators provide a space for authentic participation and parallel leadership that is inclusive of students, parents, and community members in their collaborations toward constructing a collective vision and action for schooling.

willing to attend the study group begin the process, all the while, informing nonattending peers, faculty and staff, about the activities and accomplishments of the study group, and regularly inviting them to join. Eventually, if the study group is mutually constructed as an authentic site for professional development, those who have been leery of it may be encouraged to join.

The study group serves as a source for participants to develop intellectually and professionally. Participants, through this encounter, can take a step back away from their practice and in a supportive environment, critique their practice and beliefs, and reconstruct their beliefs and practice using knowledge gained through their readings, reflection, and discussions. It is a space of time that is purposefully created, set aside, and well-guarded by its creators.

Participants are able to create a community of learners/researchers and recreate and develop their professional knowledge to discover how they can transform their beliefs and practice. It provides time for educators to work together in collaboration, providing a time to think, analyze, critique, reflect, and create new goals and changes in classrooms and schools. The study group provides a social context for critical dialogue; presents members with opportunities to learn about current theories and practices; permits collaboration and planning with peers; provides a supportive context to experiment with ideas and innovative practices and to share these experiences with each other; and it allows each member to become actively responsible for their own learning and change. As participants take ownership and responsibility for their learning, they become involved in a process that enables them to express, define, address, and resolve problems by creating appropriate changes.

To develop a culture of collaboration and authentic participation, I recommend that interested individuals should work toward the following measures:

1. Create a Space for Transformative Learning and Collaboration

Since it is always very difficult to meet with peers during the standard teaching day, it is essential to create a time and space for dialogue, collaboration, and learning. Participants construct personal and professional relationships, beliefs, knowledge and actions that reshape their roles by challenging themselves in sustained problem posing and problem solving in the study group.

Create a Time and Place to Meet.

Study groups can be held before or after school, or during established preparation or professional development time. For example, at the elementary level many school districts have an early release day and teachers have an afternoon once a week for planning or professional development. At the high school level, coordinated course prep time can be used. Study groups can be advertised district wide to attract a broader group of educators and provide university credit, or be specifically designed for individuals such as professional development specialists, classroom teachers, or administrators who are interested in learning how to become facilitators and conduct study groups.

Organize study group goals and activities.

Once this space is created, participants must concern themselves with what occurs during study group sessions. There is a tendency to only take care of immediate business and to share what is occurring in day-to-day events. Study group participants are challenged to develop different ways to spend their time together utilizing the time to inquire about issues and interests; to learn more about the topics and issues chosen; to pose questions and articulate problems; to collaborate with each other and find activities that would challenge and expound each others thinking and knowledge. This is achieved by engaging consciously in the process of inquiry which is vital to transformative learning. *However, it is critical that goals and activities are not assigned, predetermined, or controlled by the principal, the facilitator, or any other person. The study group must be a jointly negotiated and constructed context by all participants.*

2. Engage in Inquiry

Through the process of inquiry participants are able to explore the complexity of their roles as principal, teachers and learners. They are able to ask questions, as individuals and as a collective, which are of interest and of importance to them. Having this purpose and the space enables them to explore, shift, change, and develop themselves, their group, and their actions within the study group, classroom and school contexts.

Participants can learn about various topics and issues and venture far beyond the typical learning of methodology and practice that they are accustomed to. They are able to learn about the content taught, the contexts they work in, and the reasoning and beliefs which ground both the content and contexts they are responsible for. They are able learn about themselves and each other. They are able to learn about the experiences that have shaped their thinking and actions, about the knowledge and expertise they have, and the ways these experiences and interactions have shaped the ways they act out their institutional and professional roles.

Inquiry is built upon the exploration and utilization of various activities and strategies that keep participants engaged in critical reflective learning. Their questions should be continuously explored through dialogue, reading, reflective writing.

There are four major progressions in the study group cycle:

A. Establishing a Learning Topic and Direction
B. Establishing Uses of Information, Resources and Strategies
C. Establishing a Collaborative Learning Context
D. Establishing New Knowledge, New Directions, New Questions

Though this inquiry cycle progresses successively in one dimension, the entire cycle also occurs within each given progression at another dimension, and continually is evolving. In other words, throughout the study group cycle aspects of the entire cycle are occurring simultaneously within any given study group session. Within these progressions are various elements that lead study group participants through their investigations and facilitate their transformations. At this time, I would like to briefly elaborate on each of the progressions in order to describe the events that may occur through the study group process.

Establishing a Learning Topic and Direction

The inquiry cycle of a new study group begins by negotiating and choosing topics, questions, issues, and problems for study. Study group participants discuss their interests, expectations, and needs, then decide on specific questions and activities that can be pursued. Usually once a topic has been chosen, participants discuss various issues and questions they have about the topic. From these questions, the entire group can decide on one or two that they will focus on. Simultaneously, each participant chooses questions that will be studied individually. Usually, two or three study groups sessions are needed in order to reach a level of comfort and collaboration for generating and negotiating the topic and question choices.

Establishing Uses of Information, Resources and Strategies

Once each individual, and the group as a whole, has established the questions for study, the next step is to collaboratively plan the investigative directions, activities and strategies. Individual and group goals and plans are created. Participants choose materials, resources, readings, and expertise, both outside of and within the group. Plans involve what articles and books are going to be read, when will they be read, and by whom; what kinds of activities will be undertaken (reflective journals, demonstrations, classroom observations, data collection such as students' reading or writing samples); and how study group sessions will be conducted to reach the goals. A couple of sessions are needed to develop these goals before participants can precede with their activities. These plans are open ended since many new ideas and discoveries of materials and resources are made while conducting the activities themselves. At each study group session more precise plans and agendas are developed for the following session.

Establishing a Collaborative Learning Context

Study group participants proceed by accomplishing their goals and plans. They research, read, dialogue, write, demonstrate, mediate, and share, while striving to integrate their experiences from their classrooms and other contexts with their investigations in order to enrich their learning in the study group sessions. What is of utmost importance in establishing a learning context is not solely forming new knowledge, but also in developing challenging, collaborative, cooperative, respectful, and nurturing interactions while engaging in study.

Establishing New Knowledge, New Directions, New Questions

Though what has been discovered through study group inquiry is informally shared during each study group session, it is important to plan a formal presentation of what was learned in order to culminate the investigation. Sharing and assessing what has been accomplished is essential toward integrating what has been learned, and developing what new directions and questions remain for study. Taking stock of what has been achieved does not only uncover new challenges, but is also very rewarding. From this point, study group participants reenter the study group cycle of inquiry, and determine new questions, plans and directions that will be taken. Interestingly enough, each accomplished cycle leads participants to greater proficiency and depths of study that promulgates transformations.

Structuring the Student Activities

Inquiry is built upon the exploration and utilization of various activities and strategies that keep participants engaged in critical transformative learning. Participants are able to analyze the experiences that have shaped their thinking and actions, the knowledge and expertise they have, and the ways their interactions with students, colleagues and community members shape their roles and rituals.

To reiterate the inquiry process, the following steps are taken:

- Brainstorm questions, issues and topics of interest.
- Rank order, and determine which topic and questions will be studied as a group, and which questions will be studied by each individual.
- Decide what activities will be used to investigate chosen questions, such as articles and books to be read, data to be gathered and demonstration lessons to be conducted.
- Share what is being learned during each study group session.
- Make formal presentations of what has been learned are planned and presented to all study group members, the entire school staff, and for various groups such as other schools, and larger district meetings.
- Develop new questions and directions for reentry into the study group inquiry cycle.

The following diagram demonstrates the cycle of inquiry within a study group context (See Figure 1).

Through inquiry, both individual and collective, participants can develop as individuals and can develop from individuals to a collaborative and reflective collective. This is a major transformative potential, to learn how to learn together and to work to-

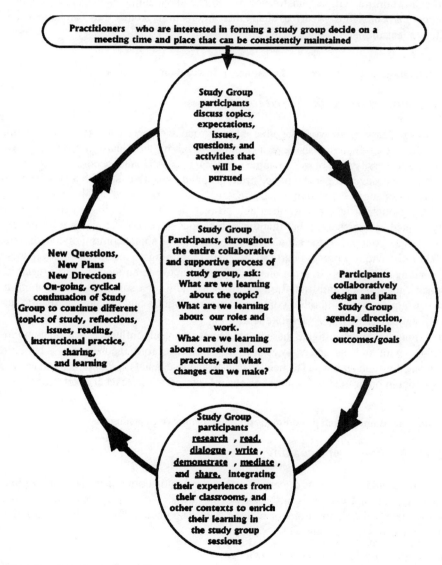

FIGURE 1. The Study Group Process

gether. This is not done quickly, smoothly, and easily. Participants will experience dissonance, frustration, and even conflict. However, the work is to struggle to understand what they are learning and sharing with and from each other, and how to utilize what is learned to transform themselves and their roles. As members of the study group learn to rely on each other and other resources for their learning, the dissonance, frustration and conflict will be transformed into trust and encouragement. As a result, each member can consciously learn to shape their interactions so that they can support and cultivate learning and growth together.

3. Understand and Act upon the Dynamics of Interactions

Learn how to work and learn together

Through learning to work together, study group members learn to recognize that there are certain dynamics that either facilitate or inhibit their learning, such as power struggles, diversity, and biases to name a few. Once participants become conscious of this, they can develop perspectives, strategies, and conscious actions that would encourage or change certain dynamics effecting their interactions.

Study group participants are then able to recognize that certain dynamics are not only created by themselves, but that these dynamics have roots in, and are influenced by the larger contexts of the school, the district, and the social community. Within the collaborative inquiry process participants need to investigate the social forces that are influencing their beliefs and actions, and find ways to remain conscious of these influences, manipulate and transform them, resist them, and survive or avoid them in study group sessions and other contexts. This recognition and change can lead to authentic empowerment and facilitate learning.

Learning how to investigate these social forces ultimately influences teaching and interactions with students, and exposes how these influences form much of what is believed about teaching and learning. The need to transform these beliefs, assumptions and actions is essential in order to transform the various roles of principal, teacher and learner.

4. Understand and Develop the Forms of Transformative Learning

Utilize All Forms of Learning

A conscious development of certain interactions and actions facilitate explorations of learning beyond acquiring information and ideas. These intentioned interactions can facilitate learning and transformations. Learning occurs through the construction of combinations of learning which ranges from:

• Elaborating on currently held knowledge;
• Learning new knowledge;

- Forming or reforming theories; and
- Forming or reforming beliefs and actions.

Through the process of sharing experiences of sustained inquiry and interactive professionalism within a study group context, participants are able to discover and learn in ways that encourage forms of transformative learning that are not available to them in traditional professional development activities. The majority of professional learning occurs through inservice and staff development activities that provide little more than new ideas for accomplishing what is already known and acted upon in schools, thus maintaining the status quo. Through the process of shared experiences within a study group context, participants will come to the realization that very few events within their professional lives lead them to question or challenge their knowledge and beliefs, much less to transform currently held knowledge and beliefs which underlie their practices. The study group provides an opportunity for each participant to actively engage in changing this by seeking to uncover answers to their own questions; by exploring, observing, gathering information and reflecting on what they are discovering; and by understanding the interrelationship between their roles as learners and their roles as principal or teacher in day to day contexts.

A conscious development of certain interactions and actions facilitate explorations of learning beyond acquiring information and ideas. These intentioned interactions can facilitate learning and transformations. Learning occurs through the construction of combinations of learning which ranges from the gaining of new information to challenging and changing currently held knowledge and beliefs.

5. Know, Value and Utilize Resources

Overcome Isolation and Individualism

One of the largest obstacles that practitioners have to overcome is the isolation from other teachers, administrators, other schools, and community members. This isolation is built into the structure of the practitioners working day; in the scheduling; in the description of roles, duties, and responsibilities; in the divisions of programs, content, and students; and in the physical design of the school. It is essential for study group participants to discover ways to work within and away from their normal setting to overcome these obstacles by learning what resources are available to them. Participants can learn how to value the knowledge and expertise they have available to them; in each other, in other peers, and in the immediate community they serve. Learning how to tap into this expertise and discover ways to share it is important in order to encourage learning and change for each other. Practitioners must learn how to reach out beyond the school, and tap into the resources available to them through their students, their students' parents, university professionals, and community members and activists.

6. Generate and Share Knowledge

Share What is Being Learned With Each Other Through Mediation and Demonstrations

The knowledge that study group participants construct, results from study, reflection, empirical investigation, and substantiated by theory and research. Therefore, this knowledge should be considered valuable and legitimate. These learning endeavors are part of, and further develop the theories and research study group members rely on. Practitioners need to develop faith in the knowledge they construct and to act upon it.

Throughout study group activities, as members discover insights into their interests and questions, they must also learn how to value this knowledge and help themselves and others see it as legitimate. Sharing what is learned with others is crucial. First it is shared within the study group, where feedback and further reflection can further develop the work. Then it is shared with peers who may not be attending the study group or with colleagues in other schools. It is important to realize that there are others who are interested in these explorations and discoveries.

GUIDELINES FOR STUDY GROUPS

Based on the perspective that the study group is a socially constructed collaboration by participants for the purpose of facilitating interactive professionalism and insuring that ownership of learning and work is consistently maintained by participants, there are certain guidelines that underlie this approach to the study group. The following guidelines reflect these beliefs.

- Participants need to be active members in the joint development of the study group and all its activities.
- Participants share and develop their collective knowledge on the selected topic(s), issues, and questions.
- Questions or learning issues upon which learning experiences are based are collaboratively generated by participants.
- Activities include authentic participation in learning experiences that focus on posing and exploring issues and questions.
- Sessions provide opportunities for participants to challenge each other and share ongoing developments, reflections, and questions.
- The study group environment is a safe social context for critical dialogue, reflection and interactions without fear of criticism, retaliation, or marginalization.
- Resources and experts are sought by the participants and included to enhance study group endeavors, not control them.
- Evaluation of the study group is conducted in terms of how successful participants transformed and actualized their own theoretical position, knowledge, and reflections into learning and action.

The study group alone does not provide all the solutions for its participants. It is a resource available to practitioners and should facilitate the recognition and use of other resources such as the classroom, district programs, and personnel; university classes, programs, and experts; and community members, parents, and students. Study group participants learn to use these resources to further their professional growth, define school purposes, and co-construct localized educational visions.

It is important for the study group to be grounded in an understanding of particular theoretical conditions if it is to be considered a method that offers practitioners a difference in terms of professional development. Practitioners forming study groups without informing themselves of the necessary conditions in which they can construct and negotiate contexts for their professional development are offered little more than an interesting communicative opportunity.

Transformations occur within contexts through consciously constructed conditions. Practitioners occupy many contexts and are challenged daily with making sense of and acting upon events within these contexts. Their reactions to these daily exposures and events provoke and create changes. These changes constitute transformations when conscious reflection, action, and generation of strategies are constructed as intentional responses and actions to these daily events. It is through consciousness and concerted construction of transformative conditions within these events that transformations are facilitated. The study group process, though important, does not guarantee transformation unless practitioners come together with a conscious understanding of the theoretical and pedagogical conditions that underlie the intended conceptualization of the study group.

Transformations for practitioners do not occur solely in the study group, but can also occur in all other contexts that they find themselves in, such as their classrooms, the school, and other outside community and personal contexts. However, through the study group, practitioners can consciously interrogate and change these contexts, thus working towards their own transformations as well as the transformation of these contexts.

DEVELOPING TRANSFORMATIVE CONDITIONS IN THE STUDY GROUP CONTEXT

At this point I would like to discuss the development of transformative conditions through study group interactions. The transformative conditions are in essence ideological conceptualizations or perspectives that underlie action or direction to be undertaken through study group development and participation. The tendencies of transformative conditions are toward facilitating transformative learning. This means that the study group is a place where participants can engage in transformative learning promulgated by conditions built upon a critical social constructivist view of teaching and learning.

The transformative conditions are socially and intellectually created as a means to develop an awareness or consciousness of the dynamics within social interactions. The creation of these conditions is intentional and takes shape through the effort of the participants. As practitioners work at not replicating social and power structures, ideological stances, and other aspects of the institutional status quo through critique and reflection, the conditions are developed. It is through the individual and collective struggle to construct the study group as an alternative and empowering context that the transformative conditions emerge. In the one sense, the transformative conditions are consciously constructed through study group interactions, and in another sense they emerge as a result of the development of professional and intellectual strength, knowledge and ability by the participants for dealing with expected roles in educational and school establishments.

CONDITIONS FOR TRANSFORMATIVE LEARNING

The transformative conditions to be discussed in this section have resulted from a combination of my history of experience in past study groups, through my research on teacher transformation in study group contexts, and through investigative study toward understanding the dynamics of transformative learning (Saavedra, 1995). I believe that these conditions augment the conceptual foundation of the transformative process. Based on my experiences in study groups, I have developed what I believe to be some of the transformative conditions that maximize those situations and settings that are not only occupied by practitioners, but also those intentionally created by them to facilitate their own transformative learning and growth. These conditions are not necessarily provided by an outside force, but are constructed and developed within social contexts by involved participants in order to promote transformative learning (Saavedra, 1990, 1992).

The transformative conditions that sustains the transformation process as it occurs in the study group context are: dialogic context; identity and voice; ownership of goals of the group and direct access to sources of knowledge; agency; recreating practice; dissonance and conflict; mediational events; demonstrations; reflection and action; generation; and self-assessment and evaluation. At this point I will provide a very brief description of each condition.

Dialogic Context

Quality social transactions occur when each individual enters a setting, and brings and shares his/her own social, political, and cultural history of experiences and knowledge with others. Therefore, there must be an intentional effort to create a democratic setting in which all participants' voices are heard and valued.

Identity and Voice

Although one brings a voice to the group, one's voice/identity is also constructed within the group through dialogue. The study group must provide a location in which participants can become consciously active in the (re)construction of their identities and voices.

Ownership of Goals of the Group and Direct Access to Sources of Knowledge

Current in-service and restructuring models convene practitioners groupings to discuss agendas determined elsewhere and present knowledge about practice to practitioners that is mediated and predigested by others. In transformative groups, practitioners must be able to negotiate their own goals and be in control of deciding what knowledge about their practice they wish to access and how, that is, library searches, action research, reflective journaling, and so forth.

Agency

As practitioners transform, develop new beliefs, practices, and relationships with their own contexts, they construct a critical awareness of social processes and practices in such a way that what is made clear is not simply how the forces of social control work but also how they can be overcome and changed individually and collectively.

Recreating Practice

Participants' work to become creators of knowledge, through endeavors such as the inquiry with the study group context. This can widen the practice of teaching and administration to include research, professional reading and writing, and the development and use of tools that challenge and broaden the currently held conceptualization of their roles. Through critical analysis of their work, participants can move beyond defining these roles from a rote-like application of goals and responsibilities, to recreating roles that reflects a socioculturally situated construct of educator engaged in interactive professionalism and parallel leadership, teaching, and learning.

Dissonance and Conflict

An inevitable and necessary condition of transformative learning is dissonance and conflict. Usually, when practitioners begin critiquing their beliefs and practices, they are faced with clashes between conflicting paradigms, ideological commitments, and personal histories. These conflicts occur cognitively in each individual practitioner, within the study group, and in the relationship between the individuals and their institutions. Embracing the dissonance and conflict as learning opportunities is essential for transformative learning.

Mediational Events

A mediational event occurs as individuals translate their understandings, interpretations, and practices to their peers, offering differing perspectives and strategies to each other in ways that will assist in reciprocal transformation. This process involves utilizing one's own capabilities and knowledge, and working collaboratively with another to accomplish what one cannot do alone. Vygotsky (1978) believed that learners internalize and transform the help they receive from others and eventually use these same means of guidance to direct their subsequent problem-solving events.

Demonstrations

Demonstrations provide practitioners occasions in which they can actively interact in actual authentic activity, in essence observing interpretations and acts of learning. Demonstrations can vary from presentations during study-group sessions to sharing of research activities, journal entries, and reflections and responses to experience. Demonstrations are more than planned activities; they are events in which a particular individual invites others to view and experience past or current events collaboratively.

Reflection and Action

Reflection is a necessary professional responsibility for practitioners. As Freire states, "reflection renders our action more effective . . . in throwing light on an accomplished action, or one that is being accomplished, authentic reflection clarifies future action, which in its given time will have to be open to renewed reflection" (1985, p. 156). Practitioners need to reflect upon situations and events that occur in the various classroom and school contexts in order to (re)construct knowledge and action.

Generation

Generation is a result of reflective action that leads to shifts in knowledge, belief and future action. The generation of new knowledge can take place during mediated events through demonstrations or through reflection on actions within practice settings themselves.

Self-Assessment and Evaluation

Through critique and reflection practitioners establish distance from the work they do. In the study group context, participants, together with their peers, learn to assess and evaluate collectively and individually, their experiences and actions. This condition is one that should be consciously and consistently pursued throughout the study group process, since it leads to shifts and generation of new knowledge.

CONCLUSION

The study group is a socially constructed context negotiated by all participants involved. This is not done instantaneously or automatically but is developed over time through intentioned practice. In establishing future study groups, it is important to follow the basic tenets set forth in this chapter, but every study group will be as unique as it's participants and as distinctive as the setting in which it is developed.

Interactive professionalism, shared leadership and promoting inclusive professional development for the purposes of developing a collaborative culture among teachers and administrators, is deeper and more complex than is often assumed. Interactive professionalism isn't "contrived collegiality" (Hargreaves, 1994), nor is it an alternative and innovative way to engage practitioners in maintaining the mundane and common experiences they are already involved in. Shared leadership is not just involvement in a school decision-making committee, nor is it having all practitioners participate in every decision. Inclusive professional development is not simply a matter of encouraging teachers and administrators to become involved in a variety of status quo inservice activities together. Instead, interactive professionalism, shared leadership, and inclusive professional development are possibilities for engaging teachers, administrators, and other stakeholders in learning together in contexts which strive for authentic participation, in growing into a collective and collaborative culture, and in working toward reforming schools in relevant, authentic, and localized ways.

REFERENCES

Anderson, G. (1998). Toward authentic participation: Deconstructing the discourses of participatory reforms in education. American Educational Research Journal, Vol. 35, No. 4, Winter: 571–603.

Anderson, G., & Saavedra, E. (1995). 'Insider' Narratives of Transformative Learning: Implications for Educational Reform. Anthropology and Education Quarterly. June.

Connelly, F. M., & Clandinin, D. J. (Eds.) (1999). Shaping a professional identity: Stories of educational practice. New York, NY: Teachers College Press.

Freire, P. (1985). The politics of education: Culture, power, and liberation. South Hadley, MA.: Bergin & Garvey.

Fullan, M. & Hargreaves, A. (1991). What's worth fighting for in your school. New York, NY: Teachers College Press.

Fullan, M., & Hargreaves, A. (1992). Understanding Teacher Development. New York, NY: Teachers College Press.

Grimmett, P., & Neufeld J. (Eds.) (1994). Teacher Development and the struggle for authenticity. New York, NY: Teachers College Press.

Hargreaves, A. (1994). Changing teachers, changing times: Teachers' work and culture in the postmodern age. New York, NY: Teachers College Press.

Lester, N., & Onore, C. (1990). Learning change: One school district meets language across the curriculum. Portsmouth, NH: Heinemann.

Lieberman, A., & Miller, L. (1992). Teachers their world and their work: Implications for school improvement. New York: NY: Teachers College Press.

Lieberman, A., & Miller, L. (1999). Teachers—Transforming their world and their work. New York, NY: Teachers College Press.

Little J. W., & McLaughlin, M. W. (1993). Teachers' work: Individuals, colleagues, and contexts. New York, NY: Teachers College Press.

Miller, J. (1990). Creating spaces and finding voices: Teachers collaborating for empowerment. Albany, NY: State University of New York Press.

Nias, J., Southworth, G., & Yeomans, R. (1989). Staff Relations in the Primary School. London: Casell.

Saavedra, E. (1990). Teacher Transformation: The Study Group as an Innovative Approach to Teacher Change. Presented in the Innovative Approaches Research Project Symposium, Collaboration in Teaching and Learning: Assuring the Academic Success of Language Minority Students. Sponsored by OBEMLA, Washington, D.C.

Saavedra, E. (1992). Examining the Transformation Process and Conditions for Change. Paper presented at the Annual Meeting of the American Education Research Association, San Francisco, CA.

Saavedra, E. (1995). Teacher transformation: Creating texts and contexts in study groups. Unpublished doctoral dissertation, University of Arizona, Tucson.

Saavedra, E. (1996) Teacher study groups: Contexts for transformative learning and action. Theory Into Practice, Vol. 35, No.4, Autumn.

Sarason, S. (1990). The predictable failure of educational reform: Can we change course before it's too late? San Francisco, CA: Jossey -Bass Publishers.

Vygotsky, L. S. (1978). Mind in society: The development of higher psychological processes. Cambridge, MA: Harvard University Press.

Wasley, P. (1991). Teachers who lead: The rhetoric of reform and the realities of practice. New York, NY: Teachers College Press.

Author Index

Subject Index